Theorizing Medieval Race
Saracen Representations in Old French Literature

LEGENDA

LEGENDA is the Modern Humanities Research Association's book imprint for new research in the Humanities. Founded in 1995 by Malcolm Bowie and others within the University of Oxford, Legenda has always been a collaborative publishing enterprise, directly governed by scholars. The Modern Humanities Research Association (MHRA) joined this collaboration in 1998, became half-owner in 2004, in partnership with Maney Publishing and then Routledge, and has since 2016 been sole owner. Titles range from medieval texts to contemporary cinema and form a widely comparative view of the modern humanities, including works on Arabic, Catalan, English, French, German, Greek, Italian, Portuguese, Russian, Spanish, and Yiddish literature. Editorial boards and committees of more than 60 leading academic specialists work in collaboration with bodies such as the Society for French Studies, the British Comparative Literature Association and the Association of Hispanists of Great Britain & Ireland.

The MHRA encourages and promotes advanced study and research in the field of the modern humanities, especially modern European languages and literature, including English, and also cinema. It aims to break down the barriers between scholars working in different disciplines and to maintain the unity of humanistic scholarship. The Association fulfils this purpose through the publication of journals, bibliographies, monographs, critical editions, and the MHRA Style Guide, and by making grants in support of research. Membership is open to all who work in the Humanities, whether independent or in a University post, and the participation of younger colleagues entering the field is especially welcomed.

ALSO PUBLISHED BY THE ASSOCIATION

Critical Texts
Tudor and Stuart Translations • *New Translations* • *European Translations*
MHRA Library of Medieval Welsh Literature

MHRA Bibliographies
Publications of the Modern Humanities Research Association

The Annual Bibliography of English Language & Literature
Austrian Studies
Modern Language Review
Portuguese Studies
The Slavonic and East European Review
Working Papers in the Humanities
The Yearbook of English Studies

www.mhra.org.uk
www.legendabooks.com

RESEARCH MONOGRAPHS IN FRENCH STUDIES

The *Research Monographs in French Studies* (RMFS) form a separate series within the Legenda programme and are published in association with the Society for French Studies. Individual members of the Society are entitled to purchase all RMFS titles at a discount.

The series seeks to publish the best new work in all areas of the literature, thought, theory, culture, film and language of the French-speaking world. Its distinctiveness lies in the relative brevity of its publications (50,000–60,000 words). As innovation is a priority of the series, volumes should predominantly consist of new material, although, subject to appropriate modification, previously published research may form up to one third of the whole. Proposals may include critical editions as well as critical studies. They should be sent with one or two sample chapters for consideration to Professor Diana Knight, Department of French and Francophone Studies, University of Nottingham, University Park, Nottingham NG7 2RD.

Editorial Committee
Diana Knight, University of Nottingham (General Editor)
Robert Blackwood, University of Liverpool
Jane Gilbert, University College London
Shirley Jordan, Newcastle University
Neil Kenny, All Souls College, Oxford
Max Silverman, University of Leeds

Advisory Committee
Wendy Ayres-Bennett, Murray Edwards College, Cambridge
Celia Britton, University College London
Ann Jefferson, New College, Oxford
Sarah Kay, New York University
Michael Moriarty, University of Cambridge
Keith Reader, University of Glasgow

PUBLISHED IN THIS SERIES

20. *Selfless Cinema? Ethics and French Documentary* by Sarah Cooper
21. *Poisoned Words: Slander and Satire in Early Modern France* by Emily Butterworth
22. *France/China: Intercultural Imaginings* by Alex Hughes
23. *Biography in Early Modern France 1540–1630* by Katherine MacDonald
24. *Balzac and the Model of Painting* by Diana Knight
25. *Exotic Subversions in Nineteenth-Century French Literature* by Jennifer Yee
26. *The Syllables of Time: Proust and the History of Reading* by Teresa Whitington
27. *Personal Effects: Reading the 'Journal' of Marie Bashkirtseff* by Sonia Wilson
28. *The Choreography of Modernism in France* by Julie Townsend
29. *Voices and Veils* by Anna Kemp
30. *Syntactic Borrowing in Contemporary French,* by Mairi McLaughlin
31. *Dreams of Lovers and Lies of Poets: Poetry, Knowledge, and Desire in the 'Roman de la Rose'* by Sylvia Huot
32. *Maryse Condé and the Space of Literature* by Eva Sansavior
33. *The Livres-Souvenirs of Colette: Genre and the Telling of Time* by Anne Freadman
34. *Furetière's* Roman bourgeois *and the Problem of Exchange* by Craig Moyes
35. *The Subversive Poetics of Alfred Jarry,* by Marieke Dubbelboer
36. *Echo's Voice: The Theatres of Sarraute, Duras, Cixous and Renaude,* by Mary Noonan
37. *Stendhal's Less-Loved Heroines: Fiction, Freedom, and the Female,* by Maria C. Scott
38. *Marie NDiaye: Inhospitable Fictions,* by Shirley Jordan
39. *Dada as Text, Thought and Theory,* by Stephen Forcer
40. *Variation and Change in French Morphosyntax,* by Anna Tristram
41. *Postcolonial Criticism and Representations of African Dictatorship,* by Cécile Bishop
42. *Regarding Manneken Pis: Culture, Celebration and Conflict in Brussels,* by Catherine Emerson
43. *The French Art Novel 1900-1930,* by Katherine Shingler
44. *Accent, Rhythm and Meaning in French Verse,* by Roger Pensom
45. *Baudelaire and Photography: Finding the Painter of Modern Life,* by Timothy Raser
46. *Broken Glass, Broken World: Glass in French Culture in the Aftermath of 1870,* by Hannah Scott
47. *Southern Regional French,* by Damien Mooney
48. *Pascal Quignard: Towards the Vanishing Point,* by Léa Vuong
49. *France, Algeria and the Moving Image,* by Maria Flood
50. *Genet's Genres of Politics,* by Mairéad Hanrahan
51. *Jean-François Vilar: Theatres Of Crime,* by Margaret Atack
52. *Balzac's Love Letters: Correspondence and the Literary Imagination,* by Ewa Szypula
53. *Saints and Monsters in Medieval French and Occitan Literature,* by Huw Grange
54. *Laforgue, Philosophy, and Ideas of Otherness,* by Sam Bootle
55. *Theorizing Medieval Race: Saracen Representations in Old French Literature,* by Victoria Turner

www.rmfs.mhra.org.uk

Theorizing Medieval Race

Saracen Representations in Old French Literature

❖

Victoria Turner

LEGENDA
Research Monographs in French Studies 55
Modern Humanities Research Association
2019

Published by Legenda
an imprint of the Modern Humanities Research Association
Salisbury House, Station Road, Cambridge CB1 2LA

ISBN 978-1-78188-667-0 (HB)
ISBN 978-1-78188-668-7 (PB)

First published 2019
Paperback edition 2021

All rights reserved. No part of this publication may be reproduced or disseminated or transmitted in any form or by any means, electronic, mechanical, photocopying, recording or otherwise, or stored in any retrieval system, or otherwise used in any manner whatsoever without written permission of the copyright owner, except in accordance with the provisions of the Copyright, Designs and Patents Act 1988, or under the terms of a licence permitting restricted copying issued in the UK by the Copyright Licensing Agency Ltd, Saffron House, 6–10 Kirby Street, London EC1N 8TS, England, or in the USA by the Copyright Clearance Center, 222 Rosewood Drive, Danvers MA 01923. Application for the written permission of the copyright owner to reproduce any part of this publication must be made by email to legenda@mhra.org.uk.

Disclaimer: Statements of fact and opinion contained in this book are those of the author and not of the editors or the Modern Humanities Research Association. The publisher makes no representation, express or implied, in respect of the accuracy of the material in this book and cannot accept any legal responsibility or liability for any errors or omissions that may be made.

Trademark notice: Product or corporate names may be trademarks or registered trademarks, and are used only for identification and explanation without intent to infringe.

© Modern Humanities Research Association 2019

Copy-Editor: Priscilla Sheringham

CONTENTS

	Acknowledgements	ix
	Abbreviations	xi
	Note on Translations	xii
	List of Illustrations	xiii
	Introduction	1
1	Race and Gender: Cross-dressing and Performative Identity in the Nanteuil Cycle	27
2	Race and Time: Genealogy and Logical Race in the *Estoire del Saint Graal*	53
3	Race and Religion: Spectrality and Conversion in Gautier de Coinci's *Miracles de Nostre Dame*	84
4	Race and Community: Knowledge, Faith, and the Prophet in the *Roman de Mahomet*	135
	Conclusion	167
	Bibliography	193
	Index	206

For Mum, Dad, and Beth

ACKNOWLEDGEMENTS

This book began life as my doctoral thesis, 'Representing the Saracen: Identity, Race and Religion in Medieval French and Occitan Literature', and could not have been completed without the help of so many wonderful people. For this particular project, the biggest thanks must undoubtedly be reserved for my two supervisors: Emma Campbell and Linda Paterson. Their comments continue to encourage me to strive for clarity, elegance, and rigour, while the tireless intellectual guidance I have received from both is a constant source of inspiration: it is essentially through and thanks to them that this book is in being.

For the metamorphosis of this project from PhD thesis to book manuscript I also owe a debt to my examiners, Bill Burgwinkle and Simon Gaunt, who provided such helpful and detailed readings of my work. Special thanks here are additionally due to Bill for setting me on the academic path of a medievalist. Funding for the original PhD project came from a Departmental Studentship at the University of Warwick, and I am very grateful to have been given this opportunity. Subsequently, my colleagues at the University of Leeds and now at the University of St Andrews have had a significant impact upon the form and focus of this book. For her comments on revisions, and for being so generous with her time and professional experience, I particularly wish to thank Rosalind Brown-Grant. For their input into my thinking and drafting processes, as well as for their excellent company and friendship, thanks go to Katie Garner, Emma Herdman, and Katie Jones. The members of St Andrews Institute of Mediaeval Studies have been a regular source of intellectual stimulation and support throughout the revision process; I am especially indebted to Bettina Bildhauer for continually reminding me of the value and excitement of literary theory. In the broader medieval French community, I also wish to thank Marianne Ailes for being an extraordinarily kind and insightful interlocutor on all matters Saracen-related and Miranda Griffin for enthusiastically helping me to navigate the gulf between PhD and book.

On a personal level, I wish to thank first and foremost my parents, Alan and Judy, and my sister Beth for always listening despite the obscurity of first medieval literature then literary theory. Alongside my family, many friends have given me invaluable encouragement, including at times long-distance cheer and inspiration and I particularly thank: Sarah Arens, Eleanor and Tom Crookes, Jonathan Durham, Merryn Everitt, Hannah Grayson, Sara Leasure, Charlotte Lee, David and Jess Lees, Tony and Chris Penson, Virginie Sauzon, and Megan and Paul Welton-Morrow.

Staff at the following libraries have given vital assistance with images and permissions at various stages of this project: the Bibliothèque municipale, Besançon; Bibliothèque nationale, Paris; Bibliothèque Royale Albert Ier, Brussels; Koninklijke

Bibliotheek, The Hague. Finally, I wish to thank the editorial team at Legenda for supporting me through the publication process with such understanding and guidance. In particular, I thank Graham Nelson one further time for being so patient and for always seeming to know just what to say with the very best of humour to help the writing process along at the most crucial of moments.

v.t., St Andrews, April 2019

ABBREVIATIONS

B. Ars.	Paris, Bibliothèque de l'Arsenal
BM	Bibliothèque municipale
BnF	Paris, Bibliothèque nationale de France
f. fr.	fonds français
n. a. fr.	nouvelle acquisition française
BR	Brussels, Bibliothèque Royale Albert Ier
ESG	*L'Estoire del Saint Graal*, ed. by Jean-Paul Ponceau, Les Classiques français du Moyen Âge, 120–21, 2 vols (Paris: Champion, 1997)
JMEMS	*Journal of Medieval and Early Modern Studies*
KB	The Hague, Koninklijke Bibliotheek, National Library
MLN	*Modern Language Notes*
PMLA	*Publications of the Modern Language Association of America*
Q	*La Quête du Saint-Graal: Roman en prose du XIIIe siècle*, ed. by Fanni Bogdanow, trans. by. Anne Berrie, Lettres gothiques, 4571 (Paris: Librairie Générale Française, 2006)
Roman	Alexandre du Pont, *Le Roman de Mahomet de Alexandre du Pont (1258) avec le texte des "Otia de Machomete" de Gautier de Compiègne (XIIe siècle), établi par R. B. C. Huygens*, ed. by Yvan G. Lepage, Bibliothèque française et romane, Series B, 16 (Paris: Klincksieck, 1977)

NOTE ON TRANSLATIONS

Translations of passages from the Vulgate Cycle are taken from Carol J. Chase's translation of the *Estoire del Saint Graal* and E. Jane Burns's translation of the *Quête du Saint-Graal* which are respectively volumes 2 and 6 of *Lancelot-Grail: The Old French Arthurian Vulgate and Post-Vulgate in Translation*, Norris J. Lacy, General Editor, 5 vols (New York: Garland, 1993–96).

For translations from the *Roman de Mahomet* I have used *The Prophet of Islam in Old French: The Romance of Muhammad (1258) and The Book of Muhammad's Ladder (1264)*, trans. by Reginald Hyatte, Brill's Studies in Intellectual History, 75 (Leiden: Brill, 1997).

Translations from all other primary texts are my own, unless otherwise stated.

LIST OF ILLUSTRATIONS

FIG. 3.1. Paris, BnF, MS f. fr. 22928, fol. 113^v
FIG. 3.2. Paris, BnF, MS f. fr. 25532, fol. 68^r
FIG. 3.3. Brussels, BR, MS 10747, fol. 67^v
FIG. 3.4. Paris, B. Ars., MS 5204, fol. 58^v
FIG. 3.5. Brussels, BR, 9229–30, fol. 32^v
FIG. 3.6. The Hague, KB, MS 71.A.24, fol. 31^r
FIG. 3.7. Paris, BnF, MS n. a. fr. 24541, fol. 67^v
FIG. 3.8. Besançon, BM, MS 551, fol. 58^r (1)
FIG. 3.9. Besançon, BM, MS 551, fol. 58^v
FIG. 3.10. Besançon, BM, MS 551, fol. 58^r (2)
FIG. 3.11. Paris, BnF, MS n. a. fr. 24541, fol. 154^v
FIG. 3.12. Paris, BnF, MS n. a. fr. 24541, fol. 149^v
FIG. 3.13. Paris, BnF, MS f. fr. 22928, fol. 200^r
FIG. 3.14. Paris, BnF, MS f. fr. 22928, fol. 255^r
FIG. 3.15. Paris, BnF, MS f. fr. 25532, fol. 194^v
FIG. 4.1. Paris, BnF, MS f. fr. 1553, fol. 367^v
FIG. C.1. Paris, BnF, MS f. fr. 12572, fol. 155^v

INTRODUCTION

> If race was invented as a way of ordering humanity, a technique for making difference and distinction, then race is, in some sense, *about* what it does; it is how similarities and differences are enacted by being assumed.
>
> SARA AHMED, 'Race as Sedimented History'.[1]

The *Sarrasin*: Everywhere and Nowhere

Type the term 'Saracens' into an internet search engine and you are more likely to find information about rugby than about the Middle Ages. Based in London, the Saracens football club is a professional rugby union team founded in 1876, whose early local rival was, unsurprisingly, the 'Crusaders'. Nonetheless, the explanation and origins of the club's name have been a longstanding matter of debate.[2] While no further details appear on the professional club's official website, bloggers and journalists have been quick to comment elsewhere that the name makes reference to the reputed endurance, skill, and bravery of Saladin's twelfth-century warriors.[3] Historically speaking, the club's emblem, the star and crescent, was not associated with Saladin's forces, and throughout its complex history was not only used by some Christian crusaders of the Middle Ages but also, and most recognizably, by the later Ottoman Empire; likewise, the fez often worn by supporters does not conventionally appear in medieval portrayals of Saracens, who tend to be shown wearing turbans or headbands known as *tortils*.[4] In this respect, the club is a perfect example of the fact that, while references to Saracens have generally been associated with a Middle Ages of crusading and conflict, the meaning of this word is actually far from clear; in the public consciousness it acts as a repository for numerous periods, geographies, and identities.

In many ways, the first challenge of studying the medieval Saracen is then to define a figure that does not really exist, or one that exists by virtue of its very inexistence. A similar conundrum is highlighted by historian Anthony Cutler's assessment that, in scholarship on the medieval Crusader States, Muslims are both 'everywhere and nowhere'.[5] Even in Norman Daniel's succinct summary of this problematic term in his focused study of Saracens in medieval French *chansons de geste*, he comments that 'Saracen' can mean both 'Arab' and 'Muslim' 'according to context'.[6] The details of such contexts, however, have long been overlooked, as has the contextual layering of identities encompassed within one single word — whether these might be racial, religious, regional, linguistic, or cultural, for example. This is the spirit of the present book, which problematizes the meaning of 'Saracen' as a way to explore medieval concepts and representations of racial identities, focusing on medieval literary and modern theoretical sources. It is not, therefore, a study of Saracens and medievalism, or of the often-nefarious appropriations of these medieval figures by modern organizations. Seeking both to recognize the range of possible representational factors associated with Saracens and to eschew reductive generalizations as far as possible, I offer a snapshot of medieval French representations in a way that prioritizes scope as well as depth of analysis. The second aspect of my analysis — medieval concepts of race — similarly concentrates on questions of context and use rather than historical development. My overall purpose is threefold: to discuss the ways in which literary texts may construct and exploit the racial identities of Saracens for the particular narratives at hand; to examine how race as a concept in this period was not solely (or even predominantly) dependent upon and defined by skin colour or physiognomy, taking inspiration from modern theoretical discourses on race; and above all to consider how and where representations of race in these works intersect with other aspects of identity such as gender, religion, and genealogy.

In Daniel's definition above, even the attribute 'Muslim' is potentially inaccurate in the context of the elusive literary Saracen of the Middle Ages, whose religious beliefs and practices often appear only as obscure and distorted melting pots of those proper to extant faiths. John Tolan in his historical survey of medieval Christian views of Islam underlines the contingency of religious identities, since

> Christian writers referred to Muslims by using ethnic terms: Arabs, Turks, Moors, Saracens. Often they call them "Ishmaelites," descendants of the biblical Ishmael, or Hagarenes (from Hagar, Ishmael's mother). Their religion is referred to as the "law of Muhammad" or the "law of the Saracens".[7]

In this respect, the meaning of the term 'Saracen', the genealogy of the Saracens as a people, and concepts of race or ethnicity cannot be dissociated from the origins of their religion and vice versa. The first such account giving details of Muhammad's ancestors from Abraham appears in the *Chronica Prophetica* (dated to 883):

> Sarraceni perverse se putant esse ex Sarra: Verius Agareni ab Agar, et Ismaelitae ab Ismael. Origo autem eorum ita est: Abraham genuit Ismael ex Agar [...] Abdallah genuit Mahomat, qui putatur a suis Prophetam esse.[8]
>
> [The Saracens perversely think themselves to be descended from Sarah. In truth, they are Agarenes from Hagar and Ishmaelites from Ishmael. This is their origin: Abraham bore Ishmael [...] Abd Allah bore Muhammad who is thought by them to be a prophet.][9]

Yet while the *Chronica* seems to posit a linear, apparently biblical genealogy, the ancestry of the Saracen people (in the plural) is fundamentally linked to that of Muhammad (as Prophet). Muhammad's own familial descent is equated here with that of the Saracens as a people, which rather suggests that genealogy, in this sense, may be different from biological bloodline. In truth, this genealogy makes blood descent subservient to religion: the Saracens are descended from Hagar and Ishmael because Muhammad is descended from Hagar and Ishmael.

Given this complex relationship between religion and genealogy, bodies and beliefs, it is understandable that the term 'Saracen' is not consistently attached to the same somatic features in the Middle Ages; corporeal and associated physiognomic representations of Saracens are legion in the vast panorama of medieval literature. Saracens may be white-skinned, black-skinned, monstrous, noble, chivalrous, or even pious, with the result that they are too diverse to be easily defined yet not always familiar enough to be assimilated by their probable western, Christian, writers. The term for 'Saracen' in Old French — *Sarrasin* — is particularly ambiguous, as writers not only use it when referring to a range of foreign figures of Arab or North African provenance but also to those of Danish, Spanish, or Hungarian origin. Moreover, they use it to denote different racial and/or religious attributes in different texts and in different periods.[10] It can refer just as easily to Turks, Armenians, and Kurds as well as Prussians, Lithuanians, and Canary Islanders. In its most general form it is often synonymous with 'pagan', even referring to the pagans of antiquity, whether heroes such as Alexander the Great, tormentors of martyrs, or early Frankish kings.[11] A broad-brush definition might be that it appears to connote those with both non-Christian beliefs and origins that lie beyond, or on the fringes of, medieval Christendom. There is even a lack of consensus about the term's origins among modern etymologists.[12] In the confines of the present book, I will focus primarily on characters who are described both as being Arab, Eastern, or Middle Eastern in some way and as non-Christian by their authors. Nonetheless, it is important to stress from the outset that there is no one-size-fits-all definition of this figure in medieval sources. Just as likely to be associated with acts of disguise and desecration as with desire or devotion, the medieval Saracen is simultaneously familiar and unknowable: a fundamentally nebulous being that resists any attempt at a fixed definition.

Examples of just how difficult it can be to precise the parameters of what makes a Saracen begin to appear as soon as one scratches the surface. Some Saracens are clearly depicted as idolaters: the Saracen nobles in the thirteenth-century drama *Le Jeu de Saint Nicolas* by Jean Bodel worship golden statues of their gods, while those in the *chanson de geste* of *Simon de Pouille* go as far as to animate their idols by climbing inside. Other Saracens are depicted as worthy chivalric opponents whose bravery shows both their own value and reflects back that of their Christian adversary. Perhaps the most famous of this kind of 'chivalrous Saracen' is Fierabras of the eponymous *chanson de geste*, whose vast literary tradition is testament to the popularity of such representations.[13] While his military defeat by his Christian counterpart, Oliver, is central to the narrative, the layering of traditions, conventions, and messages complicates our reading of this Saracen's identity: he may have stolen holy relics from Rome and ransacked the city, but he carries a sword called 'Baptesme' and is able to be healed by the holy ointment he wrongfully took. He also possesses standard attributes of warriors: he is physically stocky and formidable (v. 610) and displays chivalric values recognizable to a Christian, noble readership, such as when he offers to fight on foot after Oliver loses his horse during their confrontation (v. 1185).[14] Still further examples show how the idea of 'Saracenness' can also overlap with class: the beautiful Nicolette of the thirteenth-century *chantefable Aucassin et Nicolette* is rejected by her beloved's family because they object to her status as both a (former) Saracen and a slave. Yet Saracens may equally appear as the ancestors and relatives of illustrious literary and historical personages such as Charlemagne, Saint Thomas Becket, and Galahad, supplementing rather than diminishing their worth.[15]

While such variety frustrates an attempt to summarize Saracen representations and provide a concise and consistent definition of the term, it is also this very nebulousness that makes literary representations of Saracens ideal for exploring the question of medieval race, a contentious concept itself plagued by a plurality of meanings in any historical or indeed contemporary context. The period that is often called the long thirteenth century saw a flourishing of literary works involving Saracens, as well as legislative and military actions designed to control, conquer, and convert the peoples that inspired such representations.[16] It included, for instance, the continued rise of Saladin after the Battle of Hattin in 1187, Innocent III's decree in Canon 68 of the Fourth Lateran Council of 1215, and Franciscan missions to Muslim realms (e.g. the preaching of Saint Francis to the Sultan of Egypt al-Kâmil c.1219). Far from marking the beginning of contact between Christians and Saracens, this is a time where previous writings on Islam and Muslims come into dialogue with increased crusading propaganda, growing first-hand experiences of territories beyond Christendom, and new opportunities for interaction and engagement through the translation of Arabic materials, including the Koran.[17]

Literary depictions of relations between Christians and Saracens in western European texts have been said to evince a lack of curiosity;[18] an indulgence in fantasies of difference;[19] an aesthetic of chaos;[20] or forms of opposition associated with a nascent French nationalism.[21] Yet the issue of how depictions of the Saracen may be affected by literary factors has featured only tangentially in discussions of the socio-historical realities of cross-cultural contact, where rhetorical technique and material presentation is subordinated to historical context. Questions of boundaries and binaries have dominated scholarship on the relationship between self and other in the Middle Ages and continue to encourage us both to reassess assumptions about medieval social divisions and self-definition and to rethink the construction of discourses regarding, for instance, nation or gender. This book contributes to this broader focus on the construction of discourses and their reciprocal power to create identities by considering the ideological construction of the Saracen primarily in relation to literary conventions. Adopting a theoretical approach shows how concepts of performativity in particular may provide a means of reassessing how literary texts engage with racial and religious difference. Such a methodology not only brings contemporary theoretical discussions of identity to bear in a medieval literary context but also combines scholarship on identity with that of race. While not losing sight of questions of nation and geography, features such as language, behaviour, and dress situate the Saracen in relation to other aspects of racial and religious identity and offer a broader interpretation of just what race may have meant in the context of this figure.

Ever present in scholarship on the medieval other, the Saracens of literary texts are frequently assumed to be a kind of constant point of reference against which western, Christian identity may be defined. As a result, there all too often remains a resistance to accepting the ambiguity of Saracen identity, so that it is inevitably distilled into a narrow definition predicated upon race or religion: a definition usually supported by reference to epic representations and, more often than not, to that most well-known of *chansons de geste*, *La Chanson de Roland*. For too long the Oxford *Roland* has functioned as a yardstick against which all other manifestations of the Saracen must be measured, with the hero's infamous comment that 'paien unt tort e crestïens unt dreit' [pagans are wrong and Christians are right] seen as representative of social attitudes and used as a base and pervading ideology for studies of other works.[22] This tendency is problematic for two main reasons. Firstly, it overlooks the fact that Roland's comment is actually troubled throughout the text as a whole: the Christians are not univocal in their attitude towards the cross-cultural negotiations and ensuing warfare that occur, while depictions of Saracens are notably diverse rather than reductive, from the beautiful and chivalrous Margariz of Seville and fierce warrior Balaguer, to the monstrous hoards comprising the Emir Baligant's army.[23] Secondly, this prioritization risks preserving the reverence with which nineteenth-century scholars treated the *Roland* rather than recognizing the exceptional nature of this work, particularly as it appears in the Oxford version.[24]

Alongside this focus on the *Roland* as representative of Saracens more broadly, scholars have also mainly isolated single elements of Saracen identity for study or single text types; physical appearance, for instance, is prioritized in Jacqueline de Weever's study on depictions of blackness in relation to gender and epic.[25] Most recently, Suzanne Conklin Akbari has examined the question of religious difference and medieval Islam through theories of theology, geography, and physiology.[26] In order to recognize the instability of both Saracen representations and concepts of race, the present book deliberately ranges across different genres and less well-known representations, from epic and romance to a life of the Prophet Muhammad and miracle tales, the latter being largely neglected in analyses of the Saracen. Genre is, in itself, a thorny issue within literary studies and the purpose of sampling various text types is not to suggest a stability of form or categorization but rather the opposite: that Saracen representations cannot so easily be classified as those of 'romance' or 'epic', 'secular' or 'learned', especially when works that themselves trouble such divisions are brought into the discussion. Nor is this to propose my corpus as a new benchmark, but rather to widen our field of vision with regard to Saracens in literature and medieval racial thinking. For this reason, discussion of the manuscript contexts and material presentation of the works in question features alongside literary analysis where possible and practicable. While a comprehensive study of visual representations of Saracens has been done elsewhere by art historians,[27] relationships between text and image, along with broader codicological analysis, can further help to nuance readerly perceptions, interpretations, and uses of these textual materials, particularly given the common interpretation of race as referring to visual processes of differentiation. In this sense, although genre has underpinned the selection of my primary corpus for practical reasons, like Saracen identity it is both made and unmade in the process of this study.

A good example of a text that challenges our use of genre to define racial representations can be seen in the tale of *Aye d'Avignon* from the medieval French Nanteuil Cycle of *chansons de geste*. This Cycle has received relatively little attention, especially as regards the presentation of racial difference. Such neglect is rather surprising given that, aside from being unusual in nature and genre, the most well-known text, *Aye d'Avignon*, contains a Saracen whose racial identity is decidedly uncertain. The cultural politics of this text are similarly worthy of greater attention. Though seemingly an epic tale, *Aye d'Avignon* contains features more commonly found in idyllic romance, which include a cross-cultural marriage narrative: a literary trope that reveals lines of difference and points of contact between peoples.[28] Likely composed around the late twelfth century, this work is therefore situated upon the divisional cusp noted above that takes the thirteenth century as a turning point in established social mentalities and practices.[29] As with several other works detailing intercultural contact in this period (such as the Old French idyllic romance of *Floire et Blancheflor*, or the *chantefable* of *Aucassin et Nicolette*), *Aye d'Avignon* does not seem to have enjoyed a wide diffusion, being extant in only one complete manuscript. Nevertheless, this text offers a means to set this potential shift in attitudes, especially where race is concerned, against later manifestations of similar material and recurrent characters across the Cycle as a whole, as will be discussed below. Far from reflecting the emergence of a stricter division of peoples through a nascent concept of nationalism, *Aye d'Avignon* muddies the waters: it presents an anamorphic social tableau of cultural crossings and treacherous liaisons, despite being stylistically identifiable as a *chanson de geste* and thus part of a genre evoking an ethics of crusade and conquest. In this text, intercultural contact and racial difference serve a different purpose, since the inadequacies of the Christian hero and the rottenness of the Frankish court are only perceptible when set in relation to a Saracen paragon of chivalry whose presence is felt throughout the Cycle.

This figure, Ganor, is the most important Saracen across the Cycle and his behaviour simultaneously reflects his oscillating status between exotic foreigner and 'romance hero'.[30] The plot of *Aye d'Avignon* is as follows: Garnier de Nanteuil has been raised at Charlemagne's court and is given the beautiful Aye d'Avignon as his bride, despite the fact that she has already been promised to Berenger, son of the infamous traitor Ganelon. Berenger's relatives accuse Garnier of plotting regicide, but the latter proves his innocence in a trial by combat. When Garnier leaves to serve in Charlemagne's army, Berenger's relatives capture Aye. She escapes and seeks refuge in an abbey, but is soon recaptured by Berenger himself at Avignon. When Charlemagne returns from Spain and hears what has happened, he lays siege to Berenger's castle at Grailemont. Berenger flees to Spain, taking Aye with him. It is here, on the island of Majorca, that they encounter the Saracen ruler Ganor, who is in want of a wife and so offers to purchase Aye from Berenger. When Berenger refuses, Ganor conveniently sends him away to the son of the Saracen king Marsile (Marsilon), who lavishes riches upon him for being the son of Marsile's old ally, Ganelon. Upon hearing of Aye's beauty, Marsilon then wishes to have Aye for himself and demands that Ganor surrender her. Ganor refuses and war ensues. Meanwhile, Garnier has heard of Aye's plight and so goes to Majorca in disguise, fighting in Ganor's army as a mercenary where he kills Berenger. After the battle,

Ganor leaves his lands in Garnier's hands (still unaware of his identity) and goes on a pilgrimage to Mecca, during which absence Garnier rescues Aye and returns to Avignon where they have a son, Gui. When Ganor discovers Aye's flight, he is devastated. He disguises himself as a pilgrim and goes to Avignon, where, after giving Aye gifts, he abducts her son and returns to Majorca. While Gui is caringly raised by Ganor, Garnier is killed by the traitors back in France. Ganor supports Gui in avenging his father's murder and is rewarded with Aye's hand. He converts to Christianity, marries the heroine and immediately engenders a son, Antoine, who will go on to help his brother against the treacherous lineage of Ganelon.

Ganor's identity in this text consists of a set of established personas that he is able to don or discard as necessary, performing the role of avenger, protector, opponent, and even suitor. Yet he equally exposes the possibility of pre-existing similarities between Frank and Saracen, reflecting the commonly held theory that Saracens are merely misguided Christians who could therefore achieve reintegration.[31] The specifics of Ganor's disguise ploys and their effect upon the representation of gender and genealogical progression will be analysed below. More generally, he reveals the problematic relationship between physical form or appearance and racial identity. Ganor is a shape-shifting Saracen, who, in *Aye d'Avignon*, conforms to 'the traditional portrayal of the hostile Saracen' and yet is later depicted as being 'wealthy, amorous, attractive', becoming 'the best partner the text can offer' to its heroine Aye.[32] We therefore witness in *Aye d'Avignon* an acknowledgement of the potential for identity to be assumed, constructed, and, conversely, deconstructed.

Ganor's chameleon-like identity is apparent from the outset. Despite the fact that his kingdom is exotic and opulent, containing 'de bones cités menant e replenies | de rouge or e d'argent e de pailes d'Aufrique' (vv. 1419–21) [good and powerful/rich cities filled with red gold and silver and African fabrics], Ganor's physical appearance does not, in many ways, reflect this. In keeping with Akbari's observation that medieval texts often present 'attractive, European-looking Saracens side by side with dark-skinned, grotesque Saracens',[33] we read the following description of him:

> Mais le vis de devant ot il cler con fin or,
> Par les espaules fu les, moult ot bien fet le cors,
> Grailles par la çainture, e de moult biau deport,
> Les mains beles e blanches, e si ot gros le col. (vv. 2317–20)

> [His forehead was as bright as pure gold, his shoulders were slim and his body well-formed, he was slender about the waist and of handsome bearing, his hands were beautiful and white and his neck sturdy.]

Ganor's body carries no obvious racial identifiers that might be called 'Saracen': not only does he not conform to Debra Higgs Strickland's assessment that in artworks, 'most [Saracens] are dark-skinned, some are ugly, and nearly all possess extraordinary size and strength' but he also does not typify the virtuous Saracen warrior such as Fierabras or Renoart.[34] These warrior figures, whilst possessing many identical traits to their Christian counterparts, such as skin colour, nonetheless have extraordinary distinguishing physical attributes, especially their size. This is often to ensure that the 'Christian victory would be all the more glorious if the vanquished were both dangerous and worthy'.[35] Ganor, however, is not the other to be bested on the battlefield, but rather the unlikely hero and saviour of the Frankish future generations; as such, he is very much a curiosity.

Even the terms used to refer to Ganor throughout the Nanteuil Cycle echo this status: while 'Mahon' or 'Mahom' are names commonly given to the Prophet Muhammad or to the Saracen gods and idols in medieval literary works, he is only once called 'Ganor de Mahon' (v. 1437) [Ganor of Mahon] when he first appears in *Aye d'Avignon*, as if it is necessary to clarify his religious identity for the reader. After this early introduction, he is frequently called 'Ganor l'Arrabi' (v. 1671) [Ganor the Arab]. The word 'Arrabi' in this sense seems to function more as an indicator of Ganor's geographical origins than his religious affiliation, as is the case with Christian characters such as 'Rainmon l'Espengnois' (v. 2429) [Raimon the Spaniard], suggesting a racial, or at the very least geographic, rather than a religious emphasis.[36] This is further evinced by the fact that he is still given the epithet after his conversion in the second text of the Cycle, *Gui de Nanteuil* (v. 2749),[37] and so the very language used to describe him seems to evoke the idea of a stable, conventional Saracen identity even as the narrative works to undermine this illusion.

Medieval Identity and the Body

Adopting an approach to medieval race that is rooted in literary works such as the Nanteuil Cycle is not to deny, however, the importance of scholarship focused on historical contextualization and the realities of contact, but to reinvigorate debate concerning the impact of literature and convention upon depictions of identity and by extension upon our conclusions regarding medieval social attitudes and categories. This re-examination of Saracen representations from a literary perspective is not an attempt to uncover 'real' Saracens, but rather explores how literature can function as a reservoir of broader social and cultural ideas. Axiomatic to this is the potential for such cultural productions to construct racial identity through stylistic processes, including narrative structure, thematic conventions, and rhetorical devices. Theoretical studies on identity and its construction thus enable me to situate these Saracens within conceptual frameworks as processes of representation rather than necessarily being reflections of lived experiences. Such frameworks in turn provide a way to consider the meaning of 'race' as a concept in the Middle Ages by bringing medieval representations of Saracens into dialogue with modern discourses of identity and race.

Too often seen as the primary locus of medieval identity, there is a particular need to reconsider the place of the body in relation to the study of race. Numerous recent works on medieval identity examine questions of plurality and fluidity rather than fixity, especially as regards gender identity and difference.[38] However, such studies do not usually engage with concepts of race. Perhaps the best-known analysis of identity in the Middle Ages that employs a theoretical methodology is Jeffrey Jerome Cohen's *Medieval Identity Machines*. Cohen uses the term 'identity machine' to emphasize that 'the body, medieval and postmodern, becomes [...] nonhuman, transformed via generative and boundary-breaking flux into unprecedented hybridities'.[39] He focuses upon the mutability of the body and the fragmentation of selfhood that occur when the body is no longer treated as a coherent site with a fixed, fleshly boundary. Although Cohen's study reminds us that the body is unstable and consists of 'machines', or movements that produce identity, it continues nonetheless to prioritize the physical body. This is visible in his discussion of a miniature in a fourteenth-century manuscript of the *Grandes chroniques* (Paris, Bibliothèque nationale, MS fonds français 2813, fol. 119) where armed Saracens are portrayed wearing demonic masks in an exaggerated conscious mimicry of themselves, seemingly in order to frighten their Christian counterparts.[40] He observes how the Saracens' adoption of monstrous disguises exposes the troubling acknowledgement 'that race can be performed, that dominant representations and the bodies grouped beneath them do not necessarily coincide'.[41] However, while he notes in reference to this image that there were 'no real Saracens' in the Middle Ages, in Cohen's view, the Saracen's nebulous state is tied to notions of monstrosity. Although he therefore importantly underlines the constructed nature of race and the importance of 'repetitive acts of representation', this is still 'always written on and produced through the body' — bodies that are also notably monstrous or abject.[42]

It is this emphasis on the body (coherent or hybrid) as the locus of identity that seems to have led to a narrower view of what medieval race more broadly may encompass. The analyses that follow therefore consider what happens to this master signifier when the body does not, or cannot, function as the site of visible difference and consequently as the site of racial identification. Physical factors remain important, but the body is treated as one among many elements of racial identity that may be seen as effects of performance: elements such as religion, language, and genealogy. In this respect, I both engage with more recent thinking about race in the Middle Ages as involving 'embodied practices' and 'lived differences', as pinpointed by Cohen himself in his 2015 article with Karl Steel,[43] and go one step further by decentring the body: race is not simply a physical state of being or embodiment but a multifaceted process of becoming, of acting, and being acted upon.

To lend too great a weight to the Saracen body in particular would be to overlook the ways in which that body is much more than just a physical support for identity. Tolan notes that the Saracen's status as 'flesh-bound' meant that he lacked the potential for an immortal soul: the body could act as a reflection of moral and religious identity.[44] When medieval visual depictions of other communities are also considered, such as those of Jews or Ethiopians, it seems that skin colour may have been just as much 'a common pejorative visual vocabulary' for Christian writers as the sign of specific racial, ethnic, or religious identities.[45] It thus becomes difficult to generalize as to the role of the body in determining race, as underlined by historian Thomas Hahn, who observes that in the context of cartographic representations at least, 'black physiognomy visually marks territorial distance and exoticism'.[46] While the bodies of Saracens were often differentiated from those of Christians, the means of such differentiation appear unstable. Recognizing this instability, Akbari, for instance, has posited a 'continuum' of corporeal difference, 'with the monstrous races found at the fringes of the ecumene located on one end, and the normative European body on the other'.[47] Even if the notion of there being two ultimate poles on the spectrum is potentially problematic, Akbari's suggested continuum is very valuable because it highlights the variety of possible representations of Saracen bodies as well as the fluidity that characterizes this identity in medieval depictions.

Emphasis upon the instability of the body is not only a feature of recent medieval scholarship but also of developments in contemporary race theory. Given the fundamental changes over the last half-century to the way we use and encounter the language of race in everyday life, it is no surprise that there has been a great deal of interest in understandings of race and racial difference. This interest has spanned disciplines and time periods, and literary theory is far from exempt from this trend, since engagements with the body and with skin colour as the ultimate site of difference have continued to haunt theoretical works. For instance, the legacy of Frantz Fanon's troubling of physical appearance and racial identity in *Peau noire, masques blancs,* published in the nineteen-fifties, is undeniable in terms of theorizing race and self-perception. One of the central concepts of this work is that the black subject identifies with the white colonizer, creating what M. Fakhry Davids has described as 'a racist relationship within the mind' that is dependent upon the visual nature of racial difference and most notably on skin colour.[48] However, the prioritization of the role of skin colour in identity formation has also been subject to recent criticism. In Davids' *Internal Racism*, a movement towards understanding the psychological processes of race beyond skin colour is evident, and this is additionally apparent in Kalpana Seshadri-Crooks' desire to understand how

> in a wholly racialized society [...] appearance or physical attributes have come to be more starkly vested, more consequential than anything else such as family, wealth, culture, education or personal achievement. The investment in bodies may differ, and their meanings and ordering may vary according to each society, but the fundamental significance of physical attributes remains constant.[49]

In this respect, contemporary race theory (in particular Critical Race Studies) is often characterized by a desire to un-think the emphasis upon physical appearance as part of a broader wish to counter racial (and racist) thinking, to understand the psychological processes of race, and ultimately to attempt to move away from social divisions or hierarchies based upon ideas of race.

Despite the general acknowledgement that physical appearance is overly emphasized in racial discourses,[50] bodily form — and especially its somatic features — has nonetheless endured as the main focal point for studies of race, whether based on the twentieth century or the medieval period.[51] Lately, however, theorists have called for approaches to race that look beyond materialism; that engage with questions of representation; and that bring race into an intersectional dialogue with other aspects of identity such as gender or class.[52] This book offers an initial response to these appeals within a medieval context: it reconsiders the role of the body in determining Saracen identity and contends that it is similarly time to draw out some of the processes of constructing identity that underlie and accompany the notion of race as physical difference, whether based upon religious thought, devotional gestures, dress, lineage, or gender. Understandings of racial identity that rethink the role of the material and the visual echo the move towards the internal workings of race in much contemporary race theory. Medieval literary depictions of the Saracen call for such an approach in that they do not usually prioritize skin colour. Whereas Seshadri-Crooks divides modern notions of race from ethnicity by noting that race is perceived as being 'not at all malleable' and bestowed by inheritance,[53] medieval race is characterized by greater fluidity. This fluidity is recognized, as previously noted, by Cohen in relation to the body itself, yet it also has the effect of unsettling the very vocabulary used to discuss 'race' and exposes both the exploitation and potential manipulability of the concept.

Why Race? Terminology and Medieval Studies

In the last few years, the international community of medievalists has begun to engage more deeply and more seriously with questions of race and racism and three broad strands of study seem to have emerged: the first explicitly and actively challenges modern prejudice and promotes greater equality within the present-day academy and higher education system; the second addresses the misunderstanding and misappropriation of the Middle Ages by contemporary political organizations; and the third engages in the study of race and racism in the medieval period itself. While these strands are often, of course, interconnected, the present book is very much situated within the third. It is hoped that my theoretical and conceptual exploration will resonate with many of the concerns addressed by these sister studies, yet it is not the aim of this book to enact a meaningful engagement with the sensitive contemporary contexts that scholars must navigate in such projects. That is for another day, another study, and perhaps, given the position from which I myself speak as a white, British woman at an historic university, also other voices. Instead, my study contributes to these larger discussions on race and medieval studies by emphasizing the non-homogenous concepts of race and race relations that lie behind and within medieval literary representations of one particular group and their racial identities.

Historically, terminological concerns among scholars have tended to dominate discussions of medieval race, which, I argue, stem precisely from the prioritization of the body noted above: if race is deemed to be bodily determined and the medieval body (and more importantly here, skin colour) did not have the same currency in determining difference as in later periods, then one could be forgiven for thinking that the term 'race' is somehow anachronistic or at best insufficient. Such interest in the transhistoricity of race as a concept and the depiction of racial attitudes endured for well over a decade. Somewhat ironically, while scholars in the fields of literature and linguistics were turning to the historical bedrock of primary sources, historians have been concerned with the language used to analyze these sources. For the medieval period, a comprehensive overview of the subject appeared in 2001 with the special edition of the *Journal of Medieval and Early Modern Studies* dedicated to questions of race.[54] This volume is a veritable handbook of criticism in this field, incorporating contributions from several renowned scholars: while Thomas Hahn, for instance, ponders the inextricable connection between skin colour and the semantics of race, William Chester Jordan questions the very usefulness of a term such as 'race' in a medieval context.[55] Equally, although Robert Bartlett rightly argues that race should be reclaimed from modern racist associations and suggests the tempting compromise that the terms 'race' and 'ethnicity' should be treated as synonymous, this may perhaps risk obscuring nuances of meaning and conceptual use.[56]

More recently, the use of the word 'race' within medieval studies has gained momentum, as seen in the 2015 special edition of *postmedieval*, a response, in a way, to that of *JMEMS* with its title: 'Making Race Matter in the Middle Ages'.[57] Over a decade on, Cohen and Steel's closing review article summarizes the often insufficient reasons that have been given for omitting 'race' from categories of medieval difference.[58] This return to the term 'race' has nonetheless maintained a general emphasis on physiognomy and skin colour. Lynn Tarte Ramey's *Black Legacies*, as the title may suggest, is primarily concerned with tracing relationships between medieval and modern ideas of race and racism: it highlights 'the legacy of the Middle Ages to the development of racial prejudice and ultimately black-white problems in the West'.[59] Her discussion of 'the color question' in a medieval context fundamentally focuses on 'the socially selected physical trait of skin color', examining 'color prejudice and anti-black sentiment' in an earlier period than that usually covered by race theorists.[60] However, there is so much more to concepts of race in the Middle Ages than skin alone, and while the body clearly participates in medieval racial identifications, especially in those involving overtly racist, monstrous, or exoticized representations,[61] what is at stake here is not the term 'race' but the assumption that the body is necessarily the *locus* of racial identity. Once identity is alternatively construed, contemporary race theory becomes more rather than less applicable, with its drive to bring into focus non-corporeal processes of identification — what Geraldine Heng calls 'culturalist forms of racing'.[62] From such continued terminological and semantic debates, it is clear that a piece-by-piece approach may be the only hope of determining the processes by which medieval society conceived of something that we might call racial difference. In this respect, in contrast to Heng's timely study, *The Invention of Race in the European Middle Ages*,[63] which provides a socio-historical survey of paradigms and case studies for thinking about race in this period and ranges widely in both temporal and geographical senses, I have chosen here to prioritize the specificities of literary, linguistic, and historical context.

In light of both the terminological minefield and modern tendencies to distinguish race from ethnicity (with the latter often regarded as more cultural and less biological) my adherence to the term 'race' at all may seem somewhat paradoxical, especially given my reassessment of the body. Nonetheless, to construe the Saracen according to a modern understanding of race as embedded within (pseudo-)

scientific principles and physiognomy is to misunderstand the workings of medieval difference. Maintaining the term 'race' therefore challenges the notion that the concepts underpinning this word apply only in those social and historical contexts that prioritized skin colour, for instance in the context of post-Enlightenment black-white relations. Furthermore, the use of an alternative term may actually risk feeding into the medieval exceptionalism that scholars have recently criticized.[64] As Ramey comments:

> coining a new word to apply to the medieval period [...] seems designed to force the medieval period into an uncomfortable dichotomy with the modern period. [...] the Middle Ages emerges as either a golden age of cohabitation or a time of hopeless infancy.[65]

For a similar reason, the term 'race' rather than a composite word such as 'race-religion' is preferable,[66] despite the fact that the interconnectedness of racial and religious identities permeates the texts under discussion here.

Like race, religious identity is often regarded as fixed in scholarship even though this stability is called into question by medieval texts. Racial attributes and religious identifications frequently appear together in medieval contexts, leading Bartlett to conclude that 'one was born a Christian, a Muslim or a Jew, just as one was born English or Persian'.[67] Geraldine Heng has also noted enduring, biologized attitudes towards religion in *The Invention of Race*,[68] and the inherited nature of religion is underlined in Tolan's pan-historical study of Saracens, where he observes that being born into a certain religious community had consequences for which legal system an individual came under.[69] Yet, Tolan does not differentiate explicitly between Saracen and Muslim in his sources in a way that erodes potential differences of understanding; the pagan religious customs described as 'sarrasin', for instance, often bear little resemblance to modern Islamic practices.[70] My own use of 'Saracen' to refer to characters supposedly of Arab, Eastern, or Middle Eastern origin that are also portrayed as non-Christian or as of 'Saracen' faith reiterates the connection between faith and race in the Middle Ages; yet doing so allows us to rethink the implicit essentialism that accompanies the notion of being born into a faith and/or a race. This essentialist understanding of race has in fact persisted even in recent studies such as Heng's *The Invention of Race* where, although recognizing that racial logic may 'stalk and merge with other hierarchical systems — such as class, gender, or sexuality', she nonetheless highlights that

> 'race' is one of the primary names we have [...] attached to a repeating tendency, of the gravest import, to demarcate human beings through differences among humans that are selectively essentialized as absolute and fundamental, in order to distribute positions and powers differentially to human groups.[71]

Conversely, both anthropologists and historians have noted the role of cultural representations in the construction of identity, and racial identity is no exception to this: referring to language use, for instance, Bartlett notes that 'culture creates ethnicity'.[72] If such identities are culturally constructed, identity performance also plays a role in creating and modifying categories such as 'ethnicity' or 'religion'.

In this respect, the theoretical concept of performativity provides a useful means of exploring the workings of literary convention as this manifests itself in representations of identity; it additionally sheds light on how such conventions may be remoulded to suit particular audiences and production contexts. Incorporating speech, act, and appearance, performativity is an appropriate concept to consider in relation to the literary Saracen, as it does not presuppose a binary view of identity; instead, performativity recognizes that although identity may be determined by conventions, it is the very conventionality of these features that also enables identity to be repositioned and reformed. Consequently, racial identity, as seen in representations of the Saracen, may be viewed as a product of repetition: a process, not a definition or an essence.

Identity Formation and Manipulation: Performativity

Performativity is a concept which challenges any suggestion of a coherent and fixed identity. As a methodological framework, it not only exposes the conventions through which identities may be formed, but also reveals how such conventions are established and potentially reworked. Originally a term used by J.L. Austin in the 1950s to refer to the power of language to enact rather than simply reflect a reality,[73] performativity has since been used by numerous theorists, from Jacques Derrida in his deconstruction of the boundary between real and fictional utterances, to Eve Kosofsky Sedgwick, who extended it into the realm of identity formation. Perhaps the most notable theorist to have engaged in detail with this concept is, however, Judith Butler in her work on gender and identity.

For Butler, performativity is a system through which to discuss 'the variable cultural construction of sex, the myriad and open possibilities of cultural meaning occasioned by a sexed body'.[74] In countering the supposedly normative binary division that has shaped understandings of gender difference, even among feminist theorists, Butler suggests that:

> Gender ought not to be conceived merely as the cultural inscription of meaning on a pregiven sex (a juridical conception); gender must also designate the very apparatus of production whereby the sexes themselves are established.[75]

Gender, far from being culturally imposed, plays an active role in the construction of identity due to the repetition and recognition of conventions; it is something that we assume within the dialogue of culture as 'a process, a kind of making and we are what is made and remade through that process'.[76] The acts that establish us as gendered individuals do so through the conventionalizing power of repetition, which renders identities recognizable. Performativity is therefore one of the ways in which the individual is bound within this normalizing system, in which he or she is confined within the conventional. However, Butler's theory of performativity also suggests that the normalizing effects of this process may be challenged through the performative process itself. Not only does Butler's theory challenge assumptions of normality, but the attribute of 'real' so often used in conjunction with gendered behaviour is consequently revealed to be an illusion, a 'felicitous self-naturalization'.[77] In this sense, Butler breaks down the supposed opposition between a real or original and an illusory gendered identity.

Gender may therefore be constituted by the 'forced reiteration of norms', yet it is also established through the individual's response to 'the interpellation of gender'.[78] Butler reconfigures the Althusserian concept of the individual as being 'hailed' into subjectivity by considering the effect of the naming of a child, whereby 'the naming is at once the setting of a boundary, and also the repeated inculcation of a norm'.[79] Since Butler contends that gendering is a kind of unavoidable act that is conferred upon a body, we might wonder if the same can be said of other definitions of identity, such as those based upon race. Although Butler does not look at the specific relation of performativity to race, she recognizes that other scholars have attempted to do so, notably cautioning that 'race and gender ought not to be treated as simple analogies'.[80] She suggests that we should not try to 'transpose' her theory of gender onto race, but to consider 'what happens to the theory when it tries to come to grips with race'.[81] Accordingly, while not treating gender and race as analogous, we may think of them instead in terms of shared processes of identity formation which expose similar if also diverging tendencies.

Even if Butler does not specifically extend her work on performativity to race, she does consider connections between concepts of race and sexuality in *Bodies That Matter* in a useful way. With a similar argument to that made for performativity, Butler suggests that it may be profitable not only to consider the 'convergence' of concepts of sex and race, but also 'the sites at which the one cannot be constituted save through the other'.[82] She does this with reference to Nella Larsen's twentieth-century novella *Passing*, whose heroine Claire's racial ambiguity is both essential to her status as erotic love object and to the white identity of her husband (Bellew):

> he cannot be white [...] without the lure of an association that he must resist, without the spectre of a racial ambiguity that he must subordinate and deny. Indeed he reproduces that racial line by which he seeks to secure his whiteness through producing black women as the necessary and impossible object of desire, as the fetish in relation to which his own whiteness is anxiously and persistently secured.[83]

It is such processes of reproducing lines of racial difference that will be explored here, rather than the question of the desire that such reproductions may engender or reflect, since competing sentiments of attraction and repulsion have been discussed elsewhere in relation to the medieval Saracen.[84] Likewise, medieval studies is no stranger to Butlerian theory. In his discussion of medieval identity Steven F. Kruger underscores the difficulties of distinguishing so-called 'real' or biological identities from those assumed or chosen, noting that:

> For the Middle Ages, sexuality, race, and religion are all constructed at least partly in moral terms — as choices that might be changed — and partly as biological difference, which would suggest perhaps a more determinate and unchangeable (sexual, racial, or religious) "nature".[85]

However, approaching identity as constructed has largely remained the preserve of gender-based medieval studies and has yet to be adopted specifically in discussions of medieval race.[86] In this book, I shall therefore explore how the racial identity of the Saracen can be seen as performative, and how race converges with other elements of identity such as gender and religious belief.

Even theoretical studies linking performativity and race in general are, at present, rather thin on the ground, with the notable exception of Ann Pellegrini. Pellegrini notes that other differences between individuals frequently tend to be 'absorbed into the framework of sexual difference', making it necessary 'to extend the concepts "performativity" and "citationality" to the experiences and idea of "race"'.[87] In this sense, it seems possible to consider performativity beyond gender by maintaining the Butlerian desire to challenge binary oppositions and by revealing the basic 'ideological strategies whereby culture seeks to pass itself off as nature'.[88] The term 'nature' in this sense is criticized by Butler for establishing the concept of an innate biological identity that has the power to determine identity overall.[89] This is also echoed in the work of theorist Bridget Byrne, who recognizes the power of repeated racialized practices to produce 'bodies and subjects that are raced'.[90] In such a light, the construction of racial as well as gendered identity stems from repetition, from the conventional; it also marries bodily form and the power of language.

For theorists of race as well as for gender theorists, the unavoidable imposition of identity through language is a central preoccupation, as can be seen in Frantz Fanon's analysis of a white cultural unconscious imposed onto a black subject. The centrality of skin colour to Fanon's work is underscored in his example of being racially interpellated as a phobic object by a child's reaction upon seeing him: 'maman, regarde le nègre, j'ai peur!'[91] In his formulation, this 'regard objectif' is what limits the black man to the position of the observed, as object not subject and reflects the fact that, as noted by Michael Vannoy Adams, it is the white man who reminds the black man of his skin colour and who constitutes his visually different identity.[92] This means of producing identity through language and representation reveals the potential for identity to be produced through the literary text, even if the prioritization of visual appearance in a medieval context cannot be assumed to operate in the same way.

Similarities in the way that both race and gender theorists have discussed the power of language should not, however, obscure key points of divergence between the treatment of identity in the works of Butler and Fanon. While Fanon's work challenges the stability of the body, of blackness and whiteness, he nonetheless relies upon 'the machinery of sexual difference',[93] consequently drawing other lines of exclusion in his approach to race. In this respect, the construction of gender difference seems to be overlooked by Fanon's own discussion of race. Caution must therefore be used when assembling discourses of gender and race so as neither to simply apply one to the other (as highlighted by Butler) nor to reinforce one by focusing upon the other (as with Fanon). In addition to Pellegrini's charge that Fanon ignored the black female subject, she also notes that he does not consider the possibility that racial conventions may in fact be subversively reappropriated, where 'misidentification and misrecognition play in the dialectic of self/other and eclipse the fundamentally ambivalent structure of all identifications'.[94] Notions of recognition and appropriation are in fact central to Butler's discussion of the drag queen, and so viewing questions of race through the lens of Butlerian performativity highlights the potential for conventions of Saracen identity to be reappropriated in, as well as produced by, the texts in question.

The common link between Butler, Pellegrini, and Fanon could therefore be summarized as their mutual recognition of the general 'nonreferentiality of representation' — a troubling of the body as the site of identity, whether gendered or racial.[95] In the context of the medieval Saracen, this theoretical troubling of the body destabilizes the notion that medieval race can only be deemed to have existed insofar as it was invested in physical appearance. In this respect, bringing together discourses of race and performativity helps to recognize not only the ambiguity of the body itself, but also the potential for identity to be produced by other processes of identification, exploring just when, where, and how racial lines are being drawn and what kinds of identities are produced or producible.

Using the concept of performativity in the context of racial identity therefore ensures that the Saracen is not essentialized into a mere body. To return briefly here to my example of the Saracen Ganor of *Aye d'Avignon*, his apparently 'natural',[96] inherited identity demonstrates the very performativity of identity and the illusory nature of visible appearance; he repeats the behavioural norms associated with the Saracen in literary works, despite his white, typically Frankish, body. Such conventional behaviours include, for instance, his use of a magic and exoticized ring and his initial mercenary attempt to purchase the Christian noblewoman Aye, an act that Berenger, the traitor, scorns as un-Frankish:

> N'est pas costume a nous en la terre de France,
> En la loi que tenons e en nostre creance,
> A nul bon crestien que il sa fame vende. (vv. 1478–80)

[it is not our custom in the land of France, according to our laws and beliefs, that a good Christian should sell his wife.]

Even before his act of disguise, Ganor is consequently an ambiguous figure in his unconcealed visible appearance, suggesting a blurring of the boundaries between the other and the self for the Christian characters. For instance, in contrast to this initially mercenary behaviour, he responds in an unexpected way to Aye's lament in this episode that he plans to disgrace her, which evoked a common conventional motif of Saracen lechery, by saying simply: 'ne vous esmaiez mie, belle seur, douce amie [...] Je vous prendrai a fame, que de moillier n'ai mie' (vv. 1516–18) [do not be alarmed fair sister, sweet friend [...] I will take you as my wife for I have none]. He therefore reassures her in very courtly language of his honourable intentions.[97] Unusual though it may seem, such behaviour is actually far from limited to Ganor in the Nanteuil Cycle. A similar example of this kind of behavioural crossing can also be found in the roughly contemporary sequel *Gui de Nanteuil* through the Saracen nobleman Grandoine (the Emir de Coine), who falls in love with a Christian woman (Flandrine) and woos her with a surprisingly passionate entreaty:

> Vos est ma vie, ma lux, moi entendiment,
> ma sperançe, ma joie, sans malvais pensament —
> Por vos morai lais, zaitis, dolent,
> Se da vos enn ai en breus confortament.
> (*Gui*, Venice, ll. 2809–12)[98]

[You are my life, my luxury, my understanding, my hope, my joy, and are without mean thoughts — I will die for you, weak, miserable, and suffering, if I do not receive brief comfort from you.]

As with Ganor, Grandoine's words successfully manage to reframe his Saracen origins by conforming instead to Frankish behavioural expectations, namely by evoking the language and customs of courtly love.

In the case of Ganor, Aye's failure to recognize his heroic identity stems from the confusion surrounding his initial performance of what could be termed 'racialized' Saracen behaviour. This echoes Bridget Byrne's assertion that, as an 'embodied performative', race is 'in the eye of the beholder'.[99] Byrne consequently emphasizes the importance of visual recognition in racial identity:

> It could be argued that visual differences are to 'race' as Butler argues that sex is to gender [...] So, for 'race', racial discourses serve to construct the visible differences on which they themselves are based. It is through raced categories that visual differences become apprehended. In this way, seeing or perceiving of visual differences is constructed as 'prediscursive', neutral or inevitable.[100]

Set within this paradigm, Ganor's physical appearance shows that visual difference may in fact *not* be indicative of race, and that in repeating acts that have become normalized for a certain race, Ganor is performing identity, constructing it through the familiarity of the scene (the Saracen treating the woman as an object to be purchased) rather than through his visible, physical presence. To Aye, it is his behaviour that produces him as Saracen and so arguably it is his behaviour that can also change this association.

In a sense, if the Saracen reveals a concept of race that encompasses various attributes and behaviours associated with those who were non-Christian/Frankish, Butler's theory of performativity seems even more relevant to racial identity in a medieval context than a modern one. It is possible to replicate the assumed binary divisions of male/female that are being deconstructed by Butler in the racial divisions believed to be at work in medieval texts, yet significantly, the binaries that emerge in this context are not necessarily limited to Christian/Saracen or black/white but also concern race/religion. Given the instability of the medieval body, this performative paradigm also needs to take into account other aspects of racial identity, such as religious worship or geographical origins. For this reason, my understanding of performativity is deliberately broad: a form of performance (whether act, gesture, dress, speech etc.) which, when repeated, constitutes identity in an active process. In fact, it seems more appropriate to refer to 'performativities' in the plural, since my analyses will weave through different articulations and developments of this concept seen in the works of theorists such as Judith Butler, Jacques Lacan, and Jacques Derrida. Each formulation of performativity brings the representation of race into relation with another aspect of identity (such as gender, genealogy, and religious belief) by highlighting the variety of processes that may be involved, from the idea of reciprocity that emerges in Lacanian logical time to the self-haunting of Derrida's spectrality. Although performativity is usually discussed in relation to a living subject, I do, of course, refer throughout this book to literary representations. In this respect, theories of performativity expose the fact that literary representation and the reception of literary works are themselves processes that engage with generic traditions, social conventions, and communal expectations, even with a writer's own agenda, to construct identities. In turn, the ways in which race is presented as a subjective process rather than an objective state of being begin to emerge.

Taking into account the status of a literary work as entertaining, as a cultural production, performativity further addresses how the Saracen may be used as a figure of opposition in the formation of communities. Just as Butler described the interdependence of 'normative' and 'non-normative' concepts of gender, whereby one creates the other, Pellegrini asserts the importance of the racial other in constructing the racial identity of the self, allowing for the establishment of oppositions and limits between individuals and communities. However, as she explains, this self-other binary is in itself problematic, since it reveals 'a self-identity that must always look anxiously outside for its confirmation, disavowing any relation between inside and outside, self and mirroring image'.[101] Seen in this manner, racial identity appears to hinge predominantly upon the identification or dis-identification present in the self-other relationship, even if, as she goes on to note, the experience of racialization in this way is 'by no means uniform or universal' and differs within as much as between groups. The denial or erasure of difference within groups lies at the heart of much early scholarship on the medieval Saracen: as Ramey observes, in such cases 'Saracens lose all ability to function as individuals'.[102] In this respect, Pellegrini's emphasis is slightly different to that of Butler, who focuses upon the constructive force of overarching cultural conventions or norms in the performativity of gender.

Combining both approaches means studying the relationship between literary, generic conventions and the broader cultural systems that establish them, as well as the interactions of particular individuals and groups. While performative paradigms may posit the hailing of the self into subjectivity, it is often far from easy to distinguish self from other in the medieval texts at hand. This is especially true when the mutable, racial identity of the Saracen exposes that of the Frank or Christian as fragile and contingent. Accordingly, the concepts of 'self' and 'other' are in no way immutable or universal and are often troubled in the performative processes at work. Pellegrini's model of racial performativity is thus a helpful starting point, as it proposes a much broader spectrum of possible identities than is the case with gender. She underlines, for example, the constantly shifting meaning of the concept within and between social groupings.[103] Yet her view of racial performativity as a process of identificatory exchanges between self and other is such that the exploitation of associated conventions would undermine these exchanges. As a result, this understanding of racial performativity may prove problematic for deliberately manipulated identities such as disguises: if we can indeed only 'catch ourselves in the act of becoming subject when we see ourselves as if through the other's "I"', then concealing the '"seen" of difference' prevents this mutual identification.[104]

In blurring aspects of difference, whether physical, behavioural, or otherwise, texts often recast normative behavioural expectations of the Saracen, especially those previously excluded as 'false, unreal, and unintelligible' in Butlerian terms or as indicative of 'self' and 'other'.[105] Although initially established through discussions of gender, performativity helps us to evaluate the role of conventions in understanding race and to recognize the effects of different forms of 'performance', from disguise to religious worship. To this end, *Theorizing Medieval Race* aims to expose the insufficiency of previous binaries between Christian/Saracen, East/West and above all race/religion.

Overview

This book is divided into four chapters and a conclusion that, broadly speaking, address areas commonly at the heart of essentialist views of the Saracen and which take, for instance, physical form or religious belief as defining characteristics. As regards the Saracen body, Chapter One explores the presentation and role of disguise in constituting Saracen identity in the Nanteuil Cycle of *chansons de geste*, focusing above all on *Aye d'Avignon* and *Tristan de Nanteuil*. The Saracen King Ganor shows how cross-racial disguise may expose and exploit the performativity of identity more generally; the body as the site of racial identity is destabilized by the exploitable nature of the very conventions that ensured its primacy. By extension, *Tristan de Nanteuil*, a much later epic work, presents examples of particularly fluid Saracen identities, where the figures of Aye and Blanchandine also provide the opportunity to consider the intersectionality of gender and racial-religious identifications. Overall, racial cross-dressing is shown to be part of an alternative conceptualization of mixed race lineage structures where the Saracen is not simply integrated by acts of military prowess and religious conversion but by marriage and the creation of multiple familial ties.

The second chapter continues discussion of the representation and role of the body and its relationship to genealogy through an examination of the spatial and temporal displacement of the Saracen in the Arthurian prose romance of the *Estoire del Saint Graal*. The heritability of racial identity is considered in relation to the Lacanian concept of logical time, where time is a product of reciprocal deductive processes and race, I argue, is similarly 'logical'. According to medieval theories of racial-religious identity, extremes of heat and cold fundamentally affected the qualities of the individual, so that skin colour could be regarded as the result of the sun's strength and lustfulness as the effect of imbalanced humours: in the case of the Saracen, this was usually an excess of cholera.[106] Since geographical origins could evoke climatic theories of physiognomy and thus of racialized physical features, this chapter explores the purpose and effect of not only relocating the Saracen but also of altering the very trajectory of the narrative itself, so that it becomes a move from east to west rather than west to east. In addition, spiritual experience in this text is shown to create alternative forms of lineage that are belied by geographical conventions and which invert conventional systems of blood-based genealogy.

Chapter Three continues to think about the temporal positioning of Saracens by considering the miraculous moments experienced in three miracle tales from Gautier de Coinci's *Miracles de Nostre Dame* (dated 1214–1246) and exploring text-image relationships across the manuscript corpus. Religious conversion in these tales calls the idea of religious essentialism into question; uniting narrative with visual renderings of the events brings the Saracen body into dialogue with religious identity to explore the extent to which religion can be deemed to mean race in this period. In these narratives of change, the Derridean concept of spectrality helps to consider the idea that Saracen conversion might be a return to a previous Christian state involving haunted and haunting identities. This concept also underscores the importance of gesture and its recognition in the construction of identities and reveals the Saracens' roles within the formation and education of the Christian community. They are not simply negative yardsticks to promote the internal solidarity of the Christian world but are exemplars in their own right. While repeating religious gestures — and the recognition of this repetition — may produce a kind of Christian identity, the convert is a means to highlight the fact that the Christian is also perpetually haunted; the repetition of such devotional gestures is always imperfect, so the devotee must always strive to achieve an identity as 'good' Christian. Through the spectrality of miraculous bodies and visionary experiences the body is shown to be central to Christian religious identity, rather than needing to be rejected as suggestive of an embodied (and possibly racial) otherness.

In Chapter Four devotional practice features alongside the performativity of religious gestures and even of faith itself in the *Roman de Mahomet*, a thirteenth-century adaptation of the life of Muhammad. As the earliest known Old French version of the Prophet's life, this text has been characterized in scholarship as responding to the literary legacy of Latin anti-Islamic treatises, such as Embrico of Mainz's *Vita Mahumeti* or Guibert de Nogent's *Gesta Dei per Francos*.[107] Yet when the literary devices used in this work are set in relation both to its manuscript context and to the understanding of faith and reason in this period, it appears less as an anomaly and more as a variation on a theme. While Islam is still clearly seen as heretical and Muhammad represented as a corrupter, the engagement with rationality speaks to broader intellectual and theological concerns, with the result that exemplarity is now what undermines rather than enforces Muhammad's credibility. As with Gautier's *Miracles*, the Saracen may be crucial to the formation of a community, but one arguably concerned as much (if not more) with wisdom in general and with the performative power of speech to construct identity as with Islam in particular. In the *Roman*, the misrecognition of Muhammad's exemplarity on the part of the community leads to his supposedly misguided elevation as a Saracen prophet and even to the construction of a Saracen race. As a result, Muhammad's eloquence is robbed of its power in this work; just as disguise exposes the citationality of convention, so the Prophet's words expose his faith as rational argument rather than true belief, as constructed by his exploitation of convention and therefore as performative.

Finally, my concluding section revisits the perception of bodies and racial identity and unites questions of performativity with the concept of racial passing via the narrative tradition of *La Fille du Comte de Pontieu*, which appears not only as a short thirteenth-century prose tale but also features in the Second Crusade Cycle and a fifteenth-century prose romance trilogy. Focusing on the ways in which the indeterminacy of racial identity is made readable via genealogical and historical visibility brings a return to notions of blood, causality, and cross-dressing and unites the various strands of identity explored across my primary texts. In the *Fille* tradition, Saladin's integration into a Christian genealogy is tied to both his own act of passing and that of his western ancestor, while the racial identity of the eponymous *fille* is shown to hinge upon, yet also challenge, her maternal and dynastic functions.

By uniting close literary analyses with theoretical studies, this book highlights throughout the need for a clearer overall picture of the vast panoply of literary depictions of the Saracen. Less well-known instances of Saracens have been specifically selected to counter the dominance in non-literary focused scholarship of epic representations of the Saracen. While the real Saracen may well have been both 'everywhere' and 'nowhere', I hope that by analyzing different literary interpretations of this racial-religious identity, these figures will at least no longer simply be viewed as part of the 'somewhere' of epic by default.

Notes to the Introduction

1. Sara Ahmed, 'Race as Sedimented History', *postmedieval*, 6.1 (2015), 94–97 <https://doi.org/10.1057/pmed.2015.5>, (p. 94).
2. I am grateful to John Trigg, Chair of the Saracens Supporters Association for his assistance and for suggesting that the name may have been chosen as there was no obvious London area or location after which the club might be named (private correspondence). It seems that there was also a general tendency for more flamboyant club names at this time. See Robert Huntley, *Saracens: 125 Years of Rugby* (London: Saracens Ltd, 2001).
3. See [Anon.], 'History of Saracens', *Saracens Amateur Rugby Football Club Ltd*, Information section, <http://www.saracensamateurrugby.com/a/history-of-saracens-9702.html> [accessed 2 December 2018]; Leana Kell, 'History of Saracens', *Centurion Rugby/Primo Play Ltd*, <https://www.centurion-rugby.com/blogs/rugby/93310785-history-of-saracens> [accessed 2 December 2018]; Bertrand Lagacherie, 'Finale de la Coupe d'Europe: Huit choses à savoir sur les Saracens', *L'Équipe*, 12 May 2017 <https://www.lequipe.fr/Rugby/Actualites/Sept-choses-a-savoir-sur-les-saracens/551375> [accessed 2 December 2018].
4. See Debra Higgs Strickland, *Saracens, Demons, & Jews: Making Monsters in Medieval Art* (Princeton: Princeton University Press, 2003).
5. Anthony Cutler, 'Everywhere and Nowhere: The Invisible Muslim and Christian Self-Fashioning in the Culture of Outremer', in *France and the Holy Land: Frankish Culture at the End of the Crusades*, ed. by Daniel H. Weiss and Lisa Mahoney (Baltimore: Johns Hopkins Press, 2004), pp. 253–82.
6. Norman Daniel, *Heroes and Saracens: An Interpretation of the Chansons de Geste* (Edinburgh: Edinburgh University Press, 1984), p. 8.

7. John Victor Tolan, *Saracens: Islam in the European Imagination* (New York: Columbia University Press, 2002), p. xv.
8. Yves Bonnaz, *Chroniques asturiennes: fin IXe siècle* (Paris: Éditions du Centre national de la recherche scientifique, 1987), pp. 1–9. For similar works dealing with Islam and the Prophet, see also Michelina Di Cesare, *The Pseudo-Historical Image of the Prophet Muhammad in Medieval Latin Literature: A Repertory,* Studien zur Geschichte und Kultur des islamischen Orients, 26 (Berlin: De Gruyter, 2012), pp. 55–56 and pp. 220–35.
9. *Chronica Prophetica*, trans. from the Latin by Kenneth Baxter Wolf, <https://sites.google.com/site/canilup/chronica_prophetica> [accessed 28 November 2018].
10. For understandings of the term 'Saracen', see also Jeffrey J. Cohen, 'On Saracen Enjoyment', in *Medieval Identity Machines*, Medieval Cultures, 35 (Minneapolis: University of Minnesota Press, 2003), pp. 188–222 (pp. 190–99).
11. Tolan, *Saracens*, pp. 126–34.
12. Tolan, *Saracens*, fn. 25, p. 287.
13. See Marianne Ailes, 'Chivalry and Conversion: The Chivalrous Saracen in the Old French Epics *Fierabras* and *Otinel*', *Al-Masāq*, 9 (1996–97), 1–21.
14. *Fierabras: Chanson de geste du XIIe siècle*, ed. by Marc Le Person, Les Classiques français du Moyen Âge (Paris: Champion, 2003).
15. See for instance, Lynn Shutters, 'Christian Love or Pagan Transgression? Marriage and Conversion in Floire et Blancheflor', in *Discourses on Love, Marriage and Transgression in Medieval and Early Modern Literature*, ed. by Albrecht Classen (Tempe: Arizona Centre for Medieval and Renaissance Studies, 2004), pp. 85–108; Robert Mills, 'Invisible Translation, Language Difference and the Scandal of Becket's Mother', in *Rethinking Medieval Translation: Ethics, Politics, Theory*, ed. by Emma Campbell and Robert Mills (Cambridge: Brewer, 2012), pp. 125–46.
16. For pan-European engagements with Saracens in this period, see Tolan, *Saracens*, pp. 171–275.
17. For translation from Arabic into Latin in this period, see Charles Burnett, *Arabic into Latin in the Middle Ages: The Translators and their Intellectual and Social Context* (Farnham: Ashgate, 2009).
18. William Wistar Comfort, 'The Literary Rôle of the Saracens in the French Epic', *PMLA*, 55 (1940), 628–59 <http://www.jstor.org/stable/458731> [accessed 6 December 2018] (p. 659).
19. Cohen, 'On Saracen Enjoyment', pp. 206–18.
20. Jacqueline de Weever, *Sheba's Daughters: Whitening and Demonizing the Saracen Woman in Medieval French Epic* (New York: Garland, 1998), p. xvi.
21. Lynn Tarte Ramey, *Christian, Saracen, and Genre in Medieval French Literature*, Studies in Medieval History and Culture, 3 (New York: Routledge, 2001), pp. 2–3.
22. *La Chanson de Roland*, ed. and trans. by Ian Short, Lettres gothiques, 2nd edn (Paris: Livre de Poche, 1990), v. 1015; to name but a few: Ramey's *Christian, Saracen and Genre* begins with the *Roland* and its importance for nation formation (p. 1); the *Roland* is the most frequently mentioned literary work in Avner Falk's psychoanalytic study, *Franks and Saracens: Reality and Fantasy in the Crusades* (London: Karnac, 2010); Carol Chase opens with a reference to the *Roland* in 'La Conversion des païennes dans l'*Estoire del Saint Graal*', in *Arthurian Romance and Gender: Selected Proceedings of the XVIIth International Arthurian Congress* [Masculin/Féminin dans le roman arthurien médiéval; Geschlechterrollen im mittelalterlichen Artusroman], ed. by Friedrich Wolfzettel, Internationale Forschungen zur allgemeinen und vergleichenden Literaturwissenschaft, 10 (Amsterdam: Rodopi, 1995), pp. 251–64.
23. See *laisses* 232–33.
24. See also Sharon Kinoshita's similar criticisms in 'Beyond Philology: Cross-Cultural Engagement in Literary History and Beyond', in *A Sea of Languages: Rethinking the Arabic Role in Medieval Literary History*, ed. by Suzanne Conklin Akbari and Karla Mallette (Toronto: University of Toronto Press, 2013), pp. 25–42.
25. de Weever, *Sheba's Daughters*.
26. Suzanne Conklin Akbari, *Idols in the East: European Representations of Islam and the Orient, 1100–1450* (Ithaca, NY: Cornell University Press, 2009), pp. 160–61.
27. For instance: Strickland, *Saracens, Demons, & Jews*.
28. *Aye d'Avignon: Chanson de geste anonyme*, ed. by S. J. Borg, (Geneva: Droz, 1967). All further references are to this edition.

29. Sharon Kinoshita discusses this turning point in *Medieval Boundaries: Rethinking Difference in Old French Literature* (Philadelphia: University of Pennsylvania Press, 2006), p. 2.
30. Ellen Rose Woods, *Aye d'Avignon: A Study of Genre and Society*, Histoire des idées et critique littéraire, 172 (Geneva: Droz, 1978), p. 31.
31. See for instance Akbari, *Idols in the East*, pp. 208–10.
32. Sarah Kay, *Chansons de Geste in the Age of Romance: Political Fictions* (Oxford: Clarendon Press, 1995), pp. 190–92.
33. Akbari, *Idols in the East*, p. 156.
34. Strickland, *Saracens, Demons, & Jews*, p. 173.
35. Strickland, *Saracens, Demons, & Jews*, p. 188.
36. For the names of epic Saracens, see Paul Bancourt, *Les Musulmans dans les chansons de geste du Cycle du roi*, 2 vols in 1 (Aix en Provence: Université de Provence, 1982), pp. 33–52.
37. *Gui de Nanteuil: Chanson de geste*, ed. by James R. McCormack, Textes Littéraires Français 161 (Geneva: Droz, 1970). Interestingly, by the final text, *Tristan de Nanteuil*, he is now called 'Ganor d'Auffelerne' (e.g. v. 906), with the epithet 'l'Arrabi' reserved for other Saracen figures, above all the enemy ruler Galafre.
38. *Representing Medieval Genders and Sexualities in Europe: Construction, Transformation, and Subversion, 600–1530*, ed. by Elizabeth L'Estrange and Alison More (Farnham: Ashgate, 2011); *Difference and Identity in Francia and Medieval Europe*, ed. by Meredith Cohen and Justine Firnhaber-Baker (Farnham: Ashgate, 2010); *Constructing Medieval Sexuality*, ed. by Karma Lochrie, Peggy McCracken, and James A. Schultz (Minneapolis: University of Minnesota Press, 1997).
39. Cohen, *Medieval Identity Machines*, p. xiii.
40. Cohen, 'On Saracen Enjoyment', p. 202.
41. Cohen, 'On Saracen Enjoyment', pp. 203–06.
42. Cohen, 'On Saracen Enjoyment', p. 189 and p. 193.
43. Jeffrey Jerome Cohen and Karl Steel, 'Race, Travel, Time, Heritage', *postmedieval*, 6 (2015), 98–110 <https://doi.org/10.1057/pmed.2014.39>, (p. 100).
44. Tolan, *Saracens*, p. 283.
45. Strickland, *Saracens, Demons, & Jews*, p. 165.
46. Thomas Hahn, 'The Difference the Middle Ages Makes: Color and Race before the Modern World', in 'Race and Ethnicity in the Middle Ages', ed. by Thomas Hahn, Special Issue, *JMEMS*, 31 (2001), 1–38 (p. 11).
47. This concept is devised by Akbari, *Idols in the East*, p. 160.
48. M. Fakhry Davids, *Internal Racism: A Psychoanalytic Approach to Race and Difference* (London: Palgrave Macmillan, 2011), p. 107.
49. Kalpana Seshadri-Crooks, *Desiring Whiteness: A Lacanian Analysis of Race* (London: Routledge, 2000), pp. 1–2.
50. See for instance Rachel Caspari, 'Deconstructing Race: Racial Thinking, Geographic Variation, and Implications for Biological Anthropology', in *A Companion to Biological Anthropology*, ed. by Clark Spencer Larsen (Oxford: Blackwell, 2010), pp. 104–23.
51. Most recently, Sophia Rose Arjana focuses on ideas of monstrosity and representations of medieval Muslims as part of her pan-historical study *Muslims in the Western Imagination* (Oxford: Oxford University Press, 2015). A non-medieval example would be Gail Ching-Liang Low's *White Skin/Black Masks: Representation and Colonialism* (London: Routledge, 1996).
52. See for instance, Penelope Ingram, *The Signifying Body: Toward an Ethics of Sexual and Racial Difference* (Albany: State University of New York Press, 2008); Intersection Theory is also at the heart of a recent edited volume: *Race, Gender, and Class: Theory and Methods of Analysis*, ed. by Bart Landry (Abingdon: Routledge, 2016 [Pearson, 2007]).
53. Seshadri-Crooks, *Desiring Whiteness*, p. 4.
54. 'Race and Ethnicity in the Middle Ages', ed. by Thomas Hahn, Special Issue, *JMEMS*, 31 (2001).
55. Hahn, 'The Difference the Middle Ages Makes'; William Chester Jordan, 'Why "Race"?', in 'Race and Ethnicity in the Middle Ages', ed. by Thomas Hahn, Special Issue, *JMEMS*, 31 (2001), 165–74.

56. Robert Bartlett, 'Medieval and Modern Concepts of Race and Ethnicity', in 'Race and Ethnicity in the Middle Ages', ed. by Thomas Hahn, Special Issue, *JMEMS*, 31 (2001), 39–56 (p. 41).
57. 'Making Race Matter in the Middle Ages', ed. by Cord J. Whitaker, Special Issue, *postmedieval*, 6(1) (2015).
58. Cohen and Steel, 'Race, Travel, Time, Heritage', p. 100.
59. Lynn Tarte Ramey, *Black Legacies: Race and the European Middle Ages* (Gainesville, FL: University Press of Florida, 2014), p. 1.
60. Ramey, *Black Legacies*, p. 1 and p. 28.
61. Examples of such monstrous racialized figures include, for instance, the giantess Amiete in *Fierabras* or the Saracen warrior Renoart in the Guillaume d'Orange Cycle.
62. Geraldine Heng, 'The Invention of Race in the European Middle Ages I: Race Studies, Modernity, and the Middle Ages', *Literature Compass*, 8(5) (2011), 315–31 <https://doi.org/10.1111/j.1741-4113.2011.00790.x>, p. 324.
63. Geraldine Heng, *The Invention of Race in the European Middle Ages* (Cambridge: Cambridge University Press, 2018).
64. Heng, 'Invention of Race I', pp. 322–23.
65. Ramey, *Black Legacies*, p. 27.
66. This term was previously proposed by Geraldine Heng to recognize this *'single indivisible discourse'* (her emphasis), See *Empire of Magic: Medieval Romance and the Politics of Cultural Fantasy* (New York: Columbia University Press, 2003), p. 234.
67. Bartlett, 'Race and Ethnicity', p. 42.
68. Heng, *The Invention of Race*, pp. 75–79.
69. Tolan, *Saracens*, p. xv.
70. Tolan, *Saracens*, pp. 105–34.
71. Heng, *The Invention of Race*, p. 3.
72. Bartlett, 'Race and Ethnicity', p. 48.
73. J.L. Austin, *How to Do Things with Words: The William James Lectures delivered in Harvard University in 1955* (Oxford: Oxford Scholarship Online, 2011) <http://dx.doi.org/10.1093/acprof:oso/9780198245537.001.0001>, pp. 6–7.
74. Judith Butler, *Gender Trouble: Feminism and the Subversion of Identity*, 2nd edn (New York: Routledge, 1990; repr.2008; Preface 1999), p. 142.
75. Butler, *Gender Trouble*, p. 10.
76. James Loxley, *Performativity* (London: Routledge, 2007), p. 118.
77. Butler, *Gender Trouble*, p. 45.
78. Judith Butler, *Bodies That Matter: On the Discursive Limits of "Sex"* (London: Routledge, 2011. First published New York: 1993), p. xvii.
79. Ibid.
80. Butler, *Gender Trouble*, p. xvi.
81. Butler, *Gender Trouble*, pp. xvi–xvii.
82. Butler, *Bodies That Matter*, p. 123.
83. Butler, *Bodies That Matter*, p. 127.
84. See most notably Cohen's 'On Saracen Enjoyment' and Michael Uebel, *Ecstatic Transformation: On the Uses of Alterity in the Middle Ages* (New York: Palgrave Macmillan, 2005).
85. Steven F. Kruger, 'Conversion', in *Constructing Medieval Sexuality*, ed. by Karma Lochrie, Peggy McCracken, and James A. Schultz, Medieval Cultures, 11 (Minneapolis: University of Minnesota Press, 1997), pp. 158–79 (p. 164).
86. Kruger treats race in conjunction with sexual identity, particularly focusing upon representations of Jews ('Conversion'); Cohen briefly touches upon racial 'passing' yet does not elaborate on the notion of performance (*Medieval Identity Machines*, pp. 203–06).
87. Ann Pellegrini, *Performance Anxieties: Staging Psychoanalysis, Staging Race* (New York: Routledge, 1997), p. 3.
88. Pellegrini, *Performance Anxieties*, p. 6.
89. Butler, *Gender Trouble*, pp. 50–51.

90. Bridget Byrne, *White Lives: The Interplay of "Race", Class and Gender in Everyday Life* (London: Routledge, 2006), p. 16.
91. Frantz Fanon, *Peau noire, masques blancs* (Paris: Seuil, 1995. First published 1952), p. 90.
92. Michael Vannoy Adams, *The Multicultural Imagination: "Race", Color, and the Unconscious* (London: Routledge, 1996), p. 167.
93. Pellegrini, *Performance Anxieties*, p. 109.
94. Pellegrini, *Performance Anxieties*, p. 111.
95. Pellegrini, *Performance Anxieties*, p. 9.
96. Where necessary, I use single quotation marks here for terms such as 'natural', 'real', 'true', 'illusion' and 'norms' (among others) to maintain a continuous focus on their problematic nature.
97. Other instances of Ganor's courtly vocabulary occur when he addresses Aye as 'suer gente' (v. 1726) [sweet sister] and swears he will protect her from Berenger (v. 1729).
98. Note that 'Venice' here refers to the Venice manuscript text (Venice, Biblioteca Nazionale di San Marco, fr. 10) in McCormack's edition of *Gui de Nanteuil*.
99. Byrne, *White Lives*, p. 16.
100. Byrne, *White Lives*, p. 21.
101. Pellegrini, *Performance Anxieties*, p. 7.
102. Ramey, *Christian, Saracen and Genre*, p. 3.
103. Ibid.
104. Pellegrini, *Performance Anxieties*, p. 11.
105. Butler, *Gender Trouble*, p. xxv.
106. See Akbari, *Idols in the East*, pp. 162–63.
107. See John Victor Tolan, 'Anti-Hagiography: Embrico of Mainz's *Vita Mahumeti*', *Journal of Medieval History*, 22 (1996), 25–41; for an overview of literary representations of the Prophet Muhammad, see Sini Kangas, '*Inimicus Dei et sanctae Christianitatis?* Saracens and their Prophet in Twelfth-Century Crusade Propaganda and Western Travesties of Muhammad's Life', in *The Crusades and the Near East*, ed. by Conor Kostick (London: Routledge, 2011), pp. 131–60. Kindle edition; See also Akbari, *Idols in the East*, pp. 221–35.

CHAPTER 1

❖

Race and Gender: Cross-dressing and Performative Identity in the Nanteuil Cycle

> We take the transvestite to be a potential figure of category crisis that not only blurs boundaries between male and female but also undermines the whole attempt to construct stable binary categories of oppositional difference, a figure onto which irresolvable crises of boundary definition (man-woman, Orient-Occident, gay-straight) can at specific historical and cultural junctures be displaced and (not quite) contained.
> CLARK and SPONSLER, 'Queer Play: The Cultural Work of Crossdressing in Medieval Drama'[1]

With his white skin but initial adherence to Saracen behavioural conventions, the Saracen king Ganor from the Nanteuil Cycle of *chansons de geste* enacts a form of cross-dressing even before adopting a deliberate disguise; like the character of Mossé the Jew from the *Miracle d'un marchant et d'un juif* [*Miracle of a Merchant and a Jew*] discussed in Clark and Sponsler's article, he is, in many ways, 'just a Christian in Oriental drag'.[2] Yet whether deliberate or unconscious, the legacy of Ganor's various forms of cross-dressing can be felt throughout the whole of the Cycle. From *Aye d'Avignon*, to the sequels *Gui de Nanteuil* and *Tristan de Nanteuil*, his identity acts as a prism through which both the disguises and supposedly true identities of other characters may then be viewed. Furthermore, the success of his own disguise in *Aye* not only reveals his apparent similarity to the Franks, but also prompts a more general consideration of the universal failings of visual identification.

As previously noted, the relationship between bodily form and racial identity in the Middle Ages is problematic, and in particular, acts such as cross-dressing and disguise obscure attempts to use the body as a reliable site of identification, to say nothing of cases involving racial 'passing', a concept to which I will return in my Conclusion. We have already seen how the initial portrayal of Ganor challenges identity constructs by breaking with conventional Saracen attributes of form and behaviour and his representation is complicated by his later, conscious assumption of other roles through disguise. This is especially true for his role as (surrogate) father, since his relationships with Aye and her son Gui connect the Nanteuil dynasty to both Frankish and Saracen realms and provide the roots for narrative frameworks replicated throughout the Cycle. His manipulation of identity in this manner is also exceptional because it leads to his integration into the Christian community via his fulfilment of genealogical rather than military roles; male Saracen characters rarely marry Christian women in medieval French texts, let alone have children with them, and so Ganor's participation in genealogical systems, as much as his religious conversion, facilitates his identity performance. In turn, the overarching concern for the matrimonial and genealogical in the Nanteuil Cycle reveals the different workings of gender and racial cross-dressings, notably in relation to the disguises adopted by women in the final text of the Cycle, *Tristan de Nanteuil*. Overall, the structural importance of Ganor's cross-dressing(s) and the ensuing revelation of conventions begin a chain of events that culminates, in *Tristan de Nanteuil*, in the establishment of a society of shape-shifters with mixed racial origins: a society which 'semble ne plus pouvoir se contenter des purs chevaliers de France' [no longer seems content with the pure knights of France].[3]

A central principle of Butler's theory of performativity is that identities are not simply reflections of social conventions but have the potential to challenge, exploit, and even rework them. Disguise ploys allow us to see such processes at work, as they rest upon the perpetrator's ability to exploit the expectations of those around him or her. Given that several incidents of disguise within the Nanteuil Cycle also present a form of racial cross-dressing, this chapter takes up Butler's challenge to consider how concepts of race may function within the paradigm of performativity, in this case in relation to dress and drag. While Butler's original formulation of cross-dressing was profoundly rooted in the study of gender, Clark and Sponsler have argued for the study of other kinds of cross-dressing that do not necessarily involve gendered cross-dressing and drag:

> [...] the very definition of cross-dressing should be expanded to include instances of dressing across the boundaries of race and class which do not involve transsexual drag but which do show the same kinds of desire and appropriation of the other which most often characterize dressing across gender boundaries.[4]

However, in the Nanteuil Cycle there are characters who combine different forms of cross-dressing at once and so it is also useful to consider the workings of racial and gendered disguise side by side. Questions of gender and race are not simply interchangeable, but Butler's study of gendered identity provides a window onto other important factors in identity formation by revealing general performative trends and raising important questions about the representation of identities, especially as regards the points where gender and race constitute one another.[5] In fact, the ways in which racial and gendered cross-dressing interact in this cycle are particularly significant because they allow for alternative conceptualizations of lineage structures which, in demonstrating both the limits and possibilities of biologically determined identities, comment upon the fragility and contingency of Christian, Frankish identity.

Cross-dressing and Race: Saracen King as Christian Pilgrim

For Butler, the figure of the drag queen presents 'ways in which the performance of gender might itself be not the participation in the normalising, dissimulating work of power, but instead a kind of enacted critique'.[6] The drag act thus exposes the illusion of a natural gendered identity.[7] Butler especially follows the work of anthropologist Esther Newton, who highlights the ability of drag to blur the boundaries of internal and external identities and cites the double bind that:

> Drag says "my 'outside' appearance is feminine, but my essence 'inside' [the body] is masculine". At the same time it symbolizes the opposite inversion; "my appearance 'outside' [my body, my gender] is masculine but my essence 'inside' [myself] is feminine".[8]

It is in this manner that drag can function as a sort of disguise, having the power to conceal the physical body beneath the attributes of another identity, in this case, a feminine one. Yet at the same time drag could also be considered to unveil identity. Rather than simply conforming to the expected norms of performance that would reflect the physical sex of the body, the individual reveals the self by following, or choosing to follow, a different set of norms, consequently undermining the perceived naturalness of gender identity. In this respect, the cross-dresser problematizes the presentation of reality and illusion and the very idea of an innate identity preceding performance. In cross-dressing, since we think we can distinguish between illusion and reality, we 'take the secondary appearance of gender to be mere artifice, play, falsehood, and illusion'.[9]

To recap, Butler's concept of performativity is rooted in the interplay between (presumed) bodily form and behavioural norms established through social convention. This relationship between 'reality' and 'illusion' is just as significant in a medieval context as a modern one, so that assumptions are similarly made according to the presumed physical nature of the body itself, or, for instance, based upon the clothes someone wears.[10] Consequently, even disguises based purely upon clothing rather than the adoption of physical attributes, such as skin colour, may prove effective in concealing, confusing, and even constructing the race of the individual that supposedly lies beneath. Ann Pellegrini notes in her discussion of racial performativity that the body is important as 'the last and first best hope of holding the line between nature and culture, "sex" and gender, and perhaps also "race" and ethnicity'.[11] Once the biological body is therefore problematized as this primary locus of identity, as occurs, for instance, through acts of drag and disguise, all identity, racial or otherwise, is revealed to be contingent and discursively produced. Disguise that crosses racial boundaries would in this sense expose the possibility of performing a racial identity that is taken for the 'real' thing and, by extension, the very confected nature of such 'real' racial identities.

It is important perhaps to reiterate here too that ideas of race (medieval or otherwise) are very much tied to socio-cultural concerns beyond the body, such as religious identity. Geraldine Heng has highlighted that medieval race may be determined by social customs 'as much as by phenotype',[12] underlining a tendency to conflate biological, ethnic, and religious concepts within an umbrella term.

Since racial identifiers in medieval texts may not necessarily correspond to physical features, but may also include attributes that signal, for instance, social customs, dress, or religious difference, parallels with the gender cross-dresser begin to arise. If outward appearances beyond human flesh influence both racial and gendered identity, the function of cross-dressing in Butler's discussion of the drag queen can therefore be extended to the unveiling and conscious manipulation of racial identity. Katrin Sieg, for example, has summarized the effects of what she terms 'ethnic drag' as follows:

> As a crossing of racial lines in performance, ethnic drag simultaneously erases and redraws boundaries posturing as ancient and immutable. [...] As a technique of estrangement, drag denounces that which dominant ideology presents as natural, normal, and inescapable, without always offering another truth. As a ritual of inversion, it purports to master grave social contradictions, yet defers resolution through compulsive repetitions. As a symbolic contact zone [...] ethnic drag facilitates the exercise and exchange of power. And as a simulacrum of "race", it challenges the perceptions and privileges of those who would mistake appearances for essence.[13]

Nonetheless, as with most scholarship on racial cross-dressing, Sieg refers primarily here to theatrical performances. A broader approach that takes into account the potential disparities between racial drag and racial cross-dressing used as disguise is therefore necessary. By repeating conventions in slightly different ways, the performative possibilities of such acts vary, as does their power to construct and manipulate racial identities.

For instance, this power of disguise to unveil as well as conceal is visible in the representation of Ganor, whose outstanding feature is that physically, linguistically, and culturally he is mostly part of the Frankish community from the outset: his change of clothes, paradoxically, dispels his initial otherness and renders his seemingly transgressive identity (that maintained through a kind of racial drag) more coherent. Rather than a disguise to conceal his 'true' Saracen identity, his change of clothes actually seems to allow his apparently Frankish qualities to shine through. The key disguise event in *Aye d'Avignon*, which occurs mid-way through the text, may be summarized as follows: Ganor, through love of the Christian noblewoman Aye, has been waging a war against the sons of King Marsile of Spain and the treacherous Frank Berenger, who wishes to have Aye for himself. Inadvertently, Ganor has enlisted the help of Aye's husband Garnier as a mercenary knight in the battle, and when they are victorious, willingly entrusts his kingdom to this faithful vassal while he undertakes a pilgrimage to Mecca. Garnier takes this opportunity to betray Ganor and rescue his wife, fleeing back to Avignon where the couple have a son, Gui. Upon his return, Ganor is extremely affected by Garnier's betrayal and the loss of Aye (whom he wished to marry), refusing to shave or bathe in his distress; Ganor then decides to travel to France 'por penitence faire' (v. 2329) [to do penance], going to Avignon disguised as a Christian pilgrim in order to meet Aye incognito. Although Aye thinks that Ganor is familiar, she does not recognize him, so he concocts a new identity and claims to have been a guest at her wedding in Laon. When he is given lodging for the night in the same place as Aye's son Gui, Ganor takes the opportunity to abduct the boy, leaving Aye his ring and glove as security and returning to Majorca where he raises Gui as he would his own son.

Ganor's choice of pilgrim's garb for his disguise is not in itself unusual, since pilgrims moved across vast spaces and foreign cultures; for similar reasons, merchant or *jongleur* disguises also feature frequently in literature.[14] Yet Ganor's disguise is striking as it crosses both religious and racial lines: he claims to the sailors transporting him to be 'de France la garnie, [...] de Saint Denise' (vv. 2344–45) [from glorious France [...] from Saint Denis].[15] More importantly, it is also successful. When he happens upon Aye returning from vespers, there is no longer mistrust on her part; she 'par poi nel reconnut' [only just misrecognized him] and, though he is familiar, she cannot place him (vv. 2398–2400), accepting his explanation that he was a guest at her wedding. Ganor even creates an entirely fictitious backstory for himself in his claim to be a knight from Vermandois who accidentally killed a relative during a tournament and who is subsequently travelling from Rome to Tours to seek penance. In so doing he claims an inherited identity here that positions him within a Frankish noble lineage and ties him to a geographical origin. At this point, his visible, external appearance as a Frankish, Christian knight is also confirmed by Aye, who refers to him as 'bien prodonme' (v. 2430) [a very worthy man]; his physical body and behaviour are conjoined, so that Aye perceives a coherent identity, in spite of the fact that this is all just a ruse. Indeed, the very fact that Aye perceives this identity as coherent at all may well be because it has been consciously constructed by Ganor to be so; their encounter therefore suggests that, if all identity is illusory, the only way to present a coherent identity is thus to produce one deliberately.

In the manner of Butler's gender cross-dressing, according to which there is no 'true' identity to be discovered, the use of disguise in Ganor's case produces a similar result. If Ganor's initial appearance before Aye provoked anxiety, the performance of his assumed disguise invites acceptance. The Saracen body that we would assume to be concealed beneath his disguise conforms instead to the identity Ganor performs, yet was apparently not enough in itself to determine his racial identity. Ganor's chosen disguise can consequently be regarded as an unveiling: an unveiling that reveals his conformity to Christian, Frankish norms to the medieval audience and, by extension, suggests that he was somehow just pretending to be Saracen. This is later confirmed by his conversion, which ultimately creates order by aligning visible and invisible markers of identity. Finn Sinclair notes that Ganor's conversion merely emphasizes his 'innate nobility of spirit' and demonstrates his 'epic worth'.[16] However, the problem is that Ganor's performances of identity fundamentally challenge any idea of innate qualities preceding racial or religious adherence: since he is potentially both Christian acting as Saracen, and Saracen acting as Christian, these qualities are shown to be effects of his successful repetition of identity conventions at particular moments, in particular contexts.

In Ganor's disguise we see an example of how a perceived racial identity may both reveal, yet also diverge from, internal qualities and visible traits (physical or otherwise). This notion is evident on a broader scale in the final battle with the

Frankish traitor Milon in *Aye d'Avignon*. Arriving to besiege Avignon, Milon sends a spy to the city who, upon seeing Ganor's encamped forces, labels them as 'Sarrazin' (v. 3930) and presumes that 'il sont venus par mer, aus estoiles nagent | por destruire dame Aye e tot le tenement [...] il iront assaillir la ville maintenant' (vv. 3931–35) [they have come by sea, sailing under the stars | to destroy lady Aye and all her lands [...] they are now going to attack the town]. The impossibility of correlating external visible appearance with racial identity is therefore dramatically exposed, as Milon's forces assume that the amassed Saracens led by Ganor will conform to expected norms and will destroy the city as invaders. This moment — which is, after all, a deliberate ruse by Ganor — is especially reminiscent of the Saracens depicted in a miniature of the *Grandes chroniques* discussed by Cohen, where the Saracen army wear masks in an exaggerated conscious mimicry of themselves in order to frighten their Christian counterparts.[17] Both examples demonstrate the performative nature of identity, but in addition to being unconsciously constructed, they stage how identity may be self-consciously assumed, exploited as disguise in the manner of drag.

In her reflections upon truth and reality, Butler uses the example of drag to consider the relationship between an 'original' and an 'imitated' identity, isolating three spheres of performance: 'anatomical sex, gender identity, and gender performance'.[18] Each of these is sharply at odds with the other in the drag performance, which reveals both the separation of these qualities and the problematic attribution of the label 'woman': *'In imitating gender, drag implicitly reveals the imitative structure of gender itself — as well as its contingency'*.[19] The resulting inability to distinguish true from false, or original from imitation, provokes anxiety in those observing the act, where the realization that gender is repeatable, or 'citational', is born: if drag is something enacted by all, then 'all gender acts are an imitation of an unreachable ideal'.[20] Thus drag exposes 'the imitative structure of gender' in attempting to replicate an original that was only ever illusory anyway.[21] In this respect, there is a fundamental difference between the drag act and the incidents of disguise outlined in the Nanteuil Cycle. For the drag performer, the artificiality of society's conventions is exposed flamboyantly, creating an obvious spectacle, the success of which relies upon others finding the mismatch of external and internal identities troubling. Disguise in the Nanteuil Cycle, however, is instead a way for the Saracen to be legitimized and integrated, even offering a way to heal social flaws; it allows a chosen identity to be tested out secretly and its success is rather proved in the preservation of the 'illusion' rather than the dénouement.

The success of Ganor's disguise ploy subtly reveals that identity can be deliberately assumed and upheld, as his scheme is not suspected by Aye. The destabilization of social boundaries that one might expect through the use of deception does not occur, as Aye does not experience the troubling realization that Ganor is a Saracen dressed as a Christian when she sees him. His disguise is not perceived as such but is instead taken as reality. However, though there is no troubling mismatch as in drag (since Ganor's disguise actually appears to unify his various attributes) he nevertheless exposes the illusory nature of a coherent Frankish identity in a different way. Whilst Ganor, as a cross-dressing Saracen, is welcomed by the Franks and given lodging, Aye's first husband, Garnier, who is a 'true' Frank, is accused of being a traitor: a threatening other figure whose internal loyalties and external appearance cannot be trusted. Disguise in such an environment consequently ceases to be a disguise, so that characters possess no single, underlying identity but enact multiple identity performances.

Crucially, it is not only Saracen characters who are able to manipulate conventions in this manner, as the universal failings of visual identifications are clearly shown by the mirroring acts of Garnier and Ganor in *Aye d'Avignon*. Although it is not cross-racial, Garnier's own use of disguise is potentially more troubling than that of Ganor. Early in the text Aye is abducted by the Frankish traitor, Berenger, who, fleeing the wrath of Charlemagne, arrives in Ganor's Majorcan territory. Ganor falls immediately in love with Aye and wishes to keep her in his city, Aigremore, planning to marry her after one year. Upon subsequently learning of his wife's whereabouts from a pilgrim, Garnier disguises himself and his men as mercenary soldiers in order to get close to Aye in Ganor's kingdom.[22] As with Ganor, appearance is deliberately manipulated in this instance for personal gain, and the physical changes undergone are described in detail:

> Les barbes firent rire, n'i laissierent grenon,
> E le chief trestuit rere e li *noir* et li blont;
> Coifes orent vermeilles de paille e d'aqueton:
> En quel terre qu'il viengnent ne les connoistra on. (vv. 1854–57)

[They had their beards shaved and left no stubble and whether dark or blonde they shaved their heads; they had red caps made of cotton fabric: wherever they go no-one will recognize them.]

In contrast to Ganor's disguise as a pilgrim, Garnier chooses to pretend to be a mercenary knight and, in doing so, dissociates himself from his lands and his inherited identity. His disguise allows him to move from the realm of allegiances predicated upon loyalty, into that of economic exchange, echoing the corruption of such principles achieved by the traitors at court who had betrayed him earlier in the text (vv. 205–95). Not only does his ruse lead him (temporarily) to abandon his hierarchical position as lord, but also to betray Ganor, who has trusted him with his lands. It is this act of betrayal that, in turn, prompts Ganor's own act of disguise. In a sense, Garnier's disguise seems to make him the traitor he is accused of being and, instead of providing stability, facilitates the return to Nanteuil that leads to his death.

Rather ironically, Aye's initial Frankish abductor, Berenger, who is being held prisoner by Ganor, is unable to recognize Garnier and even tells Ganor that 'Li sodoier qu'i sont | ne sont mie de France, dou roiaume Karlon | ne de la cort roial' (vv. 2115–17) [The soldiers that are here | are not from France, from the kingdom of Charles or from the royal court]. His pronouncement on their identities is based upon their geographic and social provenance, echoing Ganor's use of such Frankish reference points in his own disguise. Berenger appears as the opposite of Ganor, since while Ganor seems to be a Saracen performing Christian identities, Berenger is a Christian performing those qualities associated with Saracens: not only can

Berenger speak the Saracen language (vv. 1631–32) but he also lusts after Aye (vv. 1229–32) and goes on to marry the Saracen sister of Marcilion, son of the infamous Marsile from the *Chanson de Roland*.[23] In this respect, Berenger's failure to perceive the ruse seems to be a way to dissociate him further from the Frankish community, whereas Aye's failure to recognize Ganor's signalled his integration. The contrasting disguises used by Christian and Saracen, coupled with parallel identity performances and a general emphasis on processes of recognition, reveal the risks of basing social stability upon the perception of coherent identities. Instead, new forms of social bonds begin to emerge through the recognition and exploitation of performative identities, as seen, for instance, in Ganor's cross-cultural marriage to Aye, adoption of Gui, and subsequent procreative power.

The parallel disguises in *Aye d'Avignon* trouble the idea that racial identity is performed primarily through the body, since visible, physical appearance is easily disregarded or transformed and bodies appear to be just as manipulable as behavioural conventions. The respective victims of the tricks, Ganor and Aye, are even given mirroring lamentations:

> Ahi! Gent crestienne, con par estes felon!
> Qui se seüst garder de tel subducion?
> (Ganor in *Aye d'Avignon*, vv. 2305–06)

[Oh you Christians, how you are wicked! Who could protect themselves from such deceit?]

> Hay! Gent sarrazine, conm este[s] souduiant!
> Qui se seüst garder de tel enchantement?
> (Aye in *Aye d'Avignon*, vv. 2554–55)

[Oh you Saracens, how you are deceitful! Who could protect themselves from such enchantments?]

This echo recognizes that embodied identity is problematic for both Saracens and Christians as it can be manipulated for personal gain. As an almost exact replication of Ganor's words, Aye's speech, though seeming to pit Christians against Saracens, simultaneously displays the arbitrariness of such racial division, because the positions of Saracen and Christian may be easily inverted.

In spite of its unsettling potential, cross-dressing may nonetheless function to reassert the system of norms in medieval texts; the bringing of the racial other into the community through religious conversion, for instance, can be regarded as 'just another case of impersonation'.[24] Clark and Sponsler have suggested that often such conversions must also involve physical transformations 'if the former outcast hopes to pass as an insider'. They argue that racial cross-dressing in late medieval texts 'results in the marking of bodies as "other" in ways that demonstrate the performativity of racial categories and the deployment of racial thinking'.[25] In this context, they conclude that racial cross-dressing may even constitute a more transgressive act than gender crossing, as it involves the 'highly ambivalent desire and appropriation of the other'.[26] However, the various uses of disguise throughout the Nanteuil Cycle evince a rather different relationship between gender and race: while race appears to be fluidly interpreted and variously determined, gender identity always requires recourse to the body. Disguises in the Cycle that combine both gender and race thus require intersectional analysis, and highlight the need to remain mindful of Butler's warning about the direct application of gender performativity to race.

Gender, Race, and Disguise: Aye and Blanchandine

In medieval scholarship, discussion of cross-dressing has, as previously mentioned, prioritized questions of gender, which is evident, for instance, in Lynette Muir's comment that: 'a change of sex is perhaps the ultimate disguise'.[27] This is true even when such cross-dressing is enacted by Saracen characters.[28] Furthermore, studies on cross-dressing have also tended to centre upon the inherently theatrical nature of gender cross-dressing and role reversal.[29] For Clark and Sponsler, the medieval theatre was 'the site of intense cultural and ideological negotiations' where cross-dressing produces 'queer moments' which are never completely dispelled with the return to conventional structures, reminiscent of Butler's notion of drag.[30] To gain success through the mechanism of disguise, the female character must often reject her femininity and display exemplary manly behavioural norms.[31] This is apparent, above all, in texts where the woman is anatomically transformed by supernatural means, such as in the *chanson de geste* of *Yde et Olive* and, as discussed here, *Tristan de Nanteuil*.[32] However, in examples of cross-dressing that lack this biological transformation, the body in drag is potentially a destabilizing presence, as it highlights that external appearances cannot solely be relied upon to signify identity or reinforce hegemonic ideals.

In the last text of the Nanteuil Cycle, *Tristan de Nanteuil*, it is Aye herself who exploits racial norms through disguise by pretending to be a Saracen knight, Gaudion, a kinsman of the Saracen King Galafre d'Arménie. This is a vast narrative of some 24,000 lines, but to summarize briefly the initial events surrounding her ruse: Aye and Ganor are besieged at their fortress of Aufalerne by the Saracen Galafre and call for aid from their son Gui de Nanteuil, who sets sail along with his wife Aiglentine. Their arrival unfortunately is thwarted by a sudden storm, which deposits the couple and their new-born son Tristan on the coast of Babylon. Ganor and his two sons with Aye, Antoine and Richer, are captured by Galafre's forces and Aye escapes from the city via a secret door. At some point when leaving the city, or soon after, we assume that she disguised herself as Saracen. Unfortunately, the description of her initial transformation is lost due to a manuscript lacuna, so we only learn of her ploy through her subsequent accounts of the event to her imprisoned husband and sons:

> Je me fis chevalier, Gaudïon fuy clamés,
> Et poursuyvy les guerres et les estours mortelz.
> Tant fis par ma proesse que le roy couronnés
> Me retint a sa court, jamés nel mescrées. (*Tristan*, vv. 3059–62)

[I made myself into a knight called Gaudion and took part in wars and mortal frays. I achieved so much through my prowess that the reigning king kept me at court and never suspected a thing.]

Aye does not merely conceal her physical appearance, but also follows Saracen behavioural conventions, such as by praising their gods (v. 1924). Her replication of conventional acts of warfare, along with culturally normalized behaviour, means that she presents an identity that conforms to the expectations of her Saracen allies and so, like Ganor, she is consequently successful. In fact, as she states in this quotation, her prowess is so highly respected that the king retains her at court and does not question her identity (*Tristan*, vv. 3059–62). As Perret comments about female-male disguise, 'c'est bien l'attente créée par les signes extérieurs qui permet que la réalité ne soit pas discernée et qui fausse la perception' [it is the expectation created by exterior signs which allows reality to go undiscerned and which distorts perception].[33] Nonetheless, although Aye has assumed a completely different identity by altering her appearance, both in terms of gender and race, the author most frequently refers to her as 'Dame Aye d'Avignon' (e.g. v. 1966, v. 2769, and v. 3725) rather than by her Saracen alter ego. These references preserve her Frankish, noble, and gendered identity throughout.

Although her behaviour appears to sustain her cross-racial disguise, when Aye visits Ganor and her sons in prison, she is recognized by Antoine because of her feminine physical appearance, particularly her lack of a beard.[34] This is also the case when Aye reveals her identity to Aiglentine (her daughter-in-law), where it is once again her appearance, in particular her mouth and chin, that identifies her (v. 3359). Yet the most striking example of the gendered body being used to confirm identity occurs when Aye is later betrayed by one of her Saracen allies and imprisoned with her other son Gui, who initially fails to recognize her:

> Guyon voit la roÿne, qui .ix. mois le porta
> En abit de paien, dont moult s'esmerveilla.
> Les mamelles lui monstre dont elle l'alaitta,
> Et trestout son affere lui dist et recorda. (*Tristan*, vv. 3727–30)

[Guy saw the queen, who bore him for nine months, wearing pagan clothes, which greatly surprised him. She showed him her breasts from which she had fed him and told him absolutely everything about her situation.]

Here, Aye's identity is revealed via her breasts, which are clearly gendered as female by the emphasis on her nurturing, maternal body.[35] Peggy McCracken has recently shown how gendered anatomy in this text 'articulates something more than gender'.[36] Earlier in the text, Aye comes across her infant grandson, Tristan, who has been raised in the forest by a supernatural deer after becoming separated from his parents during the opening shipwreck, and similarly bares her breasts. This episode leads McCracken to suggest that: 'Aye d'Avignon's human breasts recall the wild child to what the text represents as his humanity [...] the suckling breast is a marker both of gendered identity and of human identity'.[37] Despite the almost identical wording of these narrative episodes, however, Aye's second revelation to the imprisoned Gui is not about recalling him to humanity, but uses her maternal biology to evidence her own lineage and race. As a result, it seems as if a more coherent identity in this text can be constructed via the gendered rather than racial body and, furthermore, that this is a gendered body profoundly marked by its reproductive role.

This emphasis is in keeping with Aye's apparent motivations for adopting her disguise as a Saracen knight. While we might assume that the most logical reason for such a ploy would be as a means of self-protection when the Saracens attack Aufalerne, her explanations repeatedly underline that the disguise enables her to fight and to rescue her imprisoned family, with the narrator commenting:

> Dame Aye d'Avignon y fiert hardïement,
> Ains dame ne fit ce, sachés certainement,
> Que fist celle roÿne dont je fais parlement;
> Mais s'estoit pour aquerre honneur parfaittement
> Que de son seigneur puist fere delivrement
> Et de ses deux enffans qu'elle ama loyaument. (*Tristan*, vv. 2840–45)

> [Lady Aye d'Avignon fought bravely there; know for certain that never before had a lady done what this queen I'm speaking of did; but it was entirely to gain honour so that she could rescue her lord and her two children, whom she loved loyally.]

In this respect, Aye's adoption of a cross-gendered disguise is motivated by the access it provides to military activity and thus by the fact that it enables her to rescue her family. It could even be said to enact a militarization of her already prominent role as matriarch in the earlier *chanson de geste Aye d'Avignon*. While Woods notes that in *Aye* 'the *miles Christi*, the knight in service of Christ, becomes a woman' through the use of romance morality to frame a crusading ethos,[38] the love plot of *Tristan* is one based more upon familial affection than heterosexual desire or courtly love. In turn, such oftentimes biological bonds demand an equally physical, rather than figurative, involvement from Aye. Now wielding arms on the battlefield, she situates her actions alongside those of her (male) descendants:

> Quant nous venrons aux champs, dessus l'erbe florie,
> Vous en occirés deux a l'espee fourbie.
> Et vo filz aultretant ne s'y faindera mye,
> Et j'en occiray bien toute l'aultre partie. (*Tristan*, vv. 16669–72)

> [When we get to the (battle)field, on the verdant grass, you will kill two with your gleaming sword and your son will equally not be half-hearted, and I will easily kill the rest of them.]

She then explicitly repeats the crusading rhetoric of Christian versus non-Christian warfare common to the wider *chanson de geste* tradition, telling Gui:

> Quant je seray montee sur le destrier gascon
> Et j'aray en ma main ou espee ou baston,
> Pour quatre Sarrasins ne guerpiray tençon,
> Car j'ay d'eulx a destruire telle devocïon
> Que ne pourray dormir ennuyt se petit non. (vv. 16674–78)

> [When I am mounted on a Gascon war horse, and I have a sword or club in my hand, for four Saracens I will not abandon the battle, since I am so devoted to destroying them that I will scarcely be able to sleep at night.]

In this respect, disguise in *Tristan* allows religious warfare to be presented as a cross-generational and cross-gendered affair, where the survival of the family is set alongside the need to defeat the enemies of Christianity. When we take into account the context of a fourteenth-century crusading rhetoric of loss and dwindling hopes of reconquering the Holy Land, we should not forget that by becoming 'tout le plus souffisant | qui soit en paiennye jusques en Oriänt' (vv. 3250–51) [the worthiest [knight] in the pagan world as far as the Orient] Aye's disguise also suggests that if a cross-dressing Christian woman is the best warrior that the Saracens have, then perhaps all is not lost for Christendom!

Although Perret argues that transvestism in this text relies upon the key identity markers of 'le vêtement et le nom' [clothing and name],[39] it is actually the body that proves to be undeniable, non-disguisable, and thus the bearer of a conventionally recognizable identity. However, while the inability to grow a beard proves an insurmountable hurdle for Aye to overcome in her change of gender, at no point is her disguise as 'Gaudion' betrayed by a lack (or presence) of racialized physiognomic features. In consequence, Aye's racial *and* gendered disguise suggests that, when gender is involved, physical distinctions between the sexes are revelatory. In theoretical terms, Catherine Rottenberg has noted that a key difference between race and gender performativity stems from the fact that while compulsory heterosexuality relies upon two idealized genders, racist regimes rely upon a single ideal of race predicated upon whiteness.[40] While her assessment that race is 'a modality of performativity' holds well for a medieval context, the distinction between gender and race performativity here operates somewhat differently: in the twentieth-century American context of her study, she notes how, in heteronormative societies, femininity is presented as desirable, not something to be discarded; this contrasts, she argues, with black subjects who are encouraged to desire to be white in a white, racist society.[41] In the medieval period, not only is the assumption of heteronormativity problematic, but the relationship between gender and desire must be set in context: for instance, religious teachings held that Eve was made of Adam's rib, a concept that fundamentally affects what we might read as 'feminine' or 'masculine' behaviours. Being a woman could therefore mean desiring to emulate masculine ideals in a time where women were often perceived as inferior versions of men.[42] What we see in the Nanteuil Cycle is that the modalities of race and gender performativity differ in the ways that they make recourse to the body, rather than perhaps in the systems of desire involved. It seems that the idealized association of binary gender identities with reproductive roles exists alongside a multifaceted (if still racist) ideal of racial hegemony that includes, but is not determined by, skin colour alone.

The significance of the body to gendered identity is further underlined in *Tristan de Nanteuil* by the character Blanchandine. Blanchandine is a Saracen princess who becomes the wife of Tristan de Nanteuil (son of Gui and Aiglentine, grandson to Aye). Imprisoned by her pagan father in Armenia, she disguises herself upon Tristan's advice as a Christian knight (Blanchandin) in order to escape with him to the court of the Sultan of Babylon, whom Tristan has been serving. When she is later recognized at the Sultan's court by a messenger sent to look for her, it is in spite of her change of dress and manner. Even though we are told that 'elle embrunche son vis' (v. 15593) [she hides her face] the messenger quickly realizes that 'cë est une femme' (v. 15650) [this is a woman]. In terms of gender therefore, Aye and Blanchandine both suggest that the female body is treated as the core of identity and so cannot ultimately be concealed through disguise.

This is also evident in the attitude of the Saracen princess Clarinde, daughter of the Sultan of Babylon, who becomes engaged to the disguised Blanchandine. Understandably, Blanchandine tries to delay this wedding and the ensuing need to consummate her relationship with Clarinde, but the latter grows impatient and plans to expose how Blanchandin/e is 'figuree' (v. 15695) [figured, made] in a public bathing scene, resorting to anatomical form to define her reluctant fiancé's identity. Faced with the ordeal of having to reveal herself, Blanchandine is rescued by divine intervention and an angel gives her the choice to remain as a woman or to be transformed into a man. Thinking her husband (Tristan) dead, Blanchandine chooses to be physically changed, which turns her temporary disguise into her new, permanent identity. The process of Blanchandine's identity formation is thus closer to that of another Saracen in *Tristan*, Garcion (discussed below) than to that of Ganor, since her inherited biological identity is brought in line with her disguise. Yet while Garcion's identity is imposed upon him by another, Blanchandine has chosen to adopt an initially temporary disguise as her permanent form: a form which, significantly, now allows her to take on a new genealogical role by engendering a son, Gilles, who goes on to become the very embodiment of anti-Saracen ideology. He is not only pious and resists the sexual temptation of the devil but is a successful warrior, can channel divine aid to heal others, acts as confessor to Charlemagne, and even baptises pagans. From the narrative of *Tristan de Nanteuil*, it seems that a supernatural body is needed to create a supernatural warrior in imagined Christian-Saracen conflicts of the fourteenth century.

When Doon, son of Gui and thus Tristan's half-brother, accidentally comes upon Blanchandine shortly after her transformation, he is shocked by what he sees: she 'lui monstra sa char qui toute estoit changie | Par dessoubz le braiel sy con par felonnie' (vv. 16240–41) [showed him her flesh which had been completely changed | below the belt as if by devilry]. In the end, it is this physical change — and in particular the changing of her sexual organs — that has ensured her complete transformation of identity.[43] Through her physical transformation, she no longer provokes anxiety as a woman dressed in male clothing in an apparent imitation of gender, because her female body is erased. Nevertheless, the supernatural process involved somewhat undermines the notion of physical determinism, as this identity is consciously chosen and constructed by the heroine herself in conjunction with the divine.

Once again, the physical signs that risk undoing Blanchandine's disguise, like that of Aye, are gendered markers of the procreative body. This dominance of gender is especially visible in the extreme measures needed to preserve Blanchandine's male disguise. When we consider Aye's cross-gendered *and* cross-racial disguise in light of other cross-dressing women in medieval literature, this suggests that, for women, becoming Saracen (or in many cases, becoming *more* Saracen) was associated with becoming male.[44] As a result of this simultaneous gender shift, the female Saracen is not an identity that may be assumed but only discarded.[45] We might legitimately wonder why texts such as these include a change of racial identity at all. One possibility is that while there are more specifiable (if pluralistic) concepts of what male Saracen identity would be, which are nonetheless repeatable and exploitable, there is no comparable element of *female* Saracen identity that may be imitated through disguise: Saracen women are, after all, characterized by their easy assimilation into Christian society in medieval European literary productions. This theory runs counter to the argument of Vern and Bonnie Bullough that the infrequency of male transvestites in medieval literature shows the interconnection of cross-dressing and change of status. Accordingly, medieval women cross-dressing as men demonstrate a wish to better themselves through this imitation, whereas men dressed as women would lose social status.[46] While this may explain an absence of men who combine gendered and racial disguises, the concept of status being the key motivation does not apply in the same way to gendered and racial disguises used by women. If the status argument held true here, there would be no real need for racial cross-dressing from Christian to Saracen; in many cases any increase in status gained by women disguised as men would be nullified by the effects of cross-racial disguise. In fact, it is often true that gendered and racial disguises also involve a deliberate lowering of social class, as with the commonly used minstrel guise.

Instead, the relative motives and outcomes of such acts for the protagonists shed new light on the combination of gender and racial cross-dressing. If, as Perret has noted, the motive for male gender cross-dressing is usually to gain sexual access to women,[47] this does not necessarily apply to racial cross-dressing in the same way. In *Aye*, Ganor's disguise and his ensuing change of race does not initially provide sexual access to a woman but does leave him with an heir. In fact, the question of genealogy raised here proves to be the connecting factor for the disguises used by the different sexes across the Cycle and reveals the different manners in which identities are produced. For Blanchandine, sexual union — and specifically the procreative process — is hindered by her gendered disguise, as she cannot consummate her union with Clarinde as a husband. Similarly, for Aye, while she is disguised as the knight Gaudion, the Sultan promises her Aiglentine (her own daughter-in-law) in marriage, which would threaten genealogical norms (although the union does not ultimately occur). In a sense, cross-racial disguise could be characterized by the role it plays in constructing and/or maintaining alternative and, more importantly, mixed-race lineages, a motivation which is thus thwarted and must be rectified when gender is also involved. This is the case for Aye, whose racial cross-dressing reveals the contingency of ideas of race and gender.

The idea that lineage structures are the primary motivating factors behind the representation of such crossings would be unsurprising, given that while men are usually portrayed as the root of lineage, the guarantors of genealogical continuity, women do not actively tend to found bloodlines.[48] Identity seems to be equated here with genealogical roots; women cannot sustain their intersectional disguise, as their gender means that they cannot create new lineages in the manner of men, yet they can move between those that already exist. As Peggy McCracken observed in relation to the eponymous, cross-dressing heroine of the *Roman de Silence*: 'ambiguous gender threatens the disruption of dynastic structures — a woman dressed as a man cannot engender a child'.[49] However, if, as McCracken has also discussed in relation to *Tristan de Nanteuil*, late medieval epics represent such concerns somewhat differently through an 'occlusion of the biopolitics of lineage',[50] cross-dressing instead imagines alternative kinds of biopolitics. While participation in a noble lineage is indeed a key concern in this text, the problematizing of lineage does not only occur via cross-species social models, as explored by McCracken, but also via mixed-race unions. Furthermore, these unions involve the active participation of both men and women in the creation of new bloodlines via gender crossings and in so doing present different methods for appropriating and claiming those of another culture/religion than those seen in earlier epic texts: Blanchandine's creation of a new gender identity as Blanchandin enables her to marry a converted Saracen princess as well as to engender a child. In this respect, it is tempting to situate this narrative within broader discussions surrounding mixed-race unions and missionary practices in this period, such as the writings of Pierre Dubois, who advocated the role of Christian women in educating and converting pagan populations through marriage.[51]

Tristan de Nanteuil therefore demonstrates that race is profoundly connected to genealogy and that genealogy in turn relies upon the gendered body. Nonetheless, when racial disguise is used independently of gender crossings, it is clear that so many shifts in identity occur that visual markers completely fail to be useful. While she is primarily discussing female cross-dressers, Perret's assertion that 'un dire fausse le regard' [what is said can distort what is seen] and that, as such, 'seul le langage permet de dire et de penser l'ambiguïté' [only language allows ambiguity to be spoken of and thought about] could equally apply to those crossing racial identities.[52] This is most evident in the episode when Tristan has been taken prisoner by another Saracen ruler, Guintelin de Trémogne. Upon hearing Guintelin and his men conversing, Tristan recognizes their language and so praises 'Mahon le mien dieu' (v. 10905) [Mahon my god] to convince them that he is in the service of another Saracen, Murgafier, and to engineer his release. We learn that 'il sot sarrasinois le languaige parler' (v. 10874) [he knew how to speak the Saracen language]. The power of language is even introduced in the opening scene of *Tristan de Nanteuil*, where Gui and Aiglentine arrive in Babylon and recognize the tower of Babel (vv. 79–88). It has been argued that this tower represents the myth of a movement from 'une communication première, instinctive' [an initial, instinctive communication] to different languages which unavoidably 'masquent la vérité qu'elles cherchent en vain à exprimer' [mask the truth that they seek in vain to express]; such a myth consequently echoes a notion that pervades the text more generally, according to which seemingly innate identities can in fact hide qualities rather than reveal any kind of inner truth.[53] Knowledge of cultural conventions such as language and behavioural norms thus comes to the fore in such brief examples of racial crossings in *Tristan*, so that for men at least, race (in the sense of appearance, religion, laws, and customs), appears to be a flexible element of identity, openly admitted as artificial and even banal. In contrast to Cohen's placing of the body at the centre of medieval identity,[54] in the Nanteuil Cycle, language and behaviour alongside physical appearance all have the power to position racial identity, even if this is complicated when gender crossings are also involved.

There is one specific social function undertaken by Saracens from across the Cycle as a whole that interrogates further the link between racial cross-dressing and genealogy: the role of surrogate father. These paternal figures are able to exploit the performativity of identity conventions in order to be successful, while also demonstrating the transformation of blood-based lineage. This process, however, necessitates a certain transparency. Above all, it is the notion of paternity that unveils the fundamental difference between shifts in identity performed by women and involving gender, and those involving race alone as enacted by men.

Disguise and the Surrogate Father: Ganor, Garnier, and Guintelin

In the first complete *chanson de geste* of the Cycle (*Aye d'Avignon*),[55] Ganor reveals the performative nature of identity by being unconsciously subject to the conventions of the society in which he lives, as well as by exploiting disguise to establish his own social position within the Frankish community. His racial and religious ruse as Christian pilgrim is crucial for the development of the text, since it not only allows him to avenge the wrong done to him by Garnier's betrayal, but also to gain an heir for his lands. It further suggests, as Thelma S. Fenster has discussed, the fantasy of a greater surrogate father figure and the rejection of the biological patriarch.[56] While it is true that the theme of non-biological paternity also characterizes the *Estoire del Saint Graal*, as I shall discuss below, this does not involve the parallel rejection of biological heritage. In the *Estoire*, the fantasy of fatherhood is more about revelation and discovery than replacement, where paternity goes mis- or unrecognized until the nature of racial-religious similarity is unveiled. In *Aye d'Avignon*, Ganor's adoption of disguise underlines his pre-existing likenesses to the Christians and demonstrates his devotion to Aye, despite also implying the inferiority of an alternative, Frankish paternity.

Without the successful removal of Gui from the Frankish community, the cycle of treacherous vassalic relations begun by Berenger would have eliminated the future of the family, as is evinced by Garnier's later demise at the hands of Berenger's kinsmen. This creates the paradox that 'the son moves away from his natural father in order to come closer to him, that is, to grow up'.[57] Ganor's resulting bond with Gui not only enables him to marry Aye but also places Gui in a position of power that crosses the racial/national divide, where he becomes 'something of an ersatz father himself to a new hybrid society of loyal, neo-Christian warriors'.[58] Ganor's controversial act consequently has a positive effect upon society; this is a common outcome of medieval disguise plots, as cross-dressing often presents a way to avoid the breaking of moral boundaries, such as through incestuous marriages and unwanted sexual advances.[59] Even though his disguise enables him to steal Gui from Aye, this abduction ultimately serves to reinforce order in the text, as Ganor removes him from the treachery of the Christian court that ensured the downfall of his biological father, Garnier. As a result, genealogical progression is maintained. In this respect, Ganor's successful disguise might be seen to form part of an emerging tendency in *chansons de geste* to resituate the enemy within Frankish society. Sarah Kay has noted that

> as the identification of the Saracen with 'the enemy' loses some of its force, we see the rise to prominence in the *chansons de geste* of plots where the 'true' enemy is located not at the periphery of the realm but at its very heart: in the person of the traitor at the royal court.[60]

In essence, the way that identities are shown to relate to perceived threats is changing in late twelfth- to early thirteenth-century texts, which also relocates dividing lines between Christian Franks and non-Christian Saracens.

The success of Ganor's surrogacy in *Aye* is, however, set in stark contrast to the events of *Tristan de Nanteuil*, the last text of the Cycle, where several substitute fathers fail miserably in their roles. Doon, for instance, Tristan's half-brother (they are both the sons of Gui) is initially rejected by his adoptive father Duke Garnier de Valvenise who refers to him as 'ung estrange enffant' (v. 1021) [a foreign child] and abandons him in the forest. It is striking that his name, Garnier, recalls the ill-fated hero of *Aye d'Avignon*, whose son (Doon's own father Gui) was successfully fostered by Ganor. In this later case of adoption, the Christian Duke is unable to accept a child who is not 'de sa lignye' (v. 1019) [of his line] as he realizes that this would disinherit any of his own bloodline, connecting legitimacy and inheritance to biology. For the Christian patriarchy, as represented by the Duke of Valvenise, Doon's unconventional identity as an illegitimate half-Saracen child troubles a social structure reliant upon a vertical axis of inheritance passed from father to son. Nonetheless, such an attitude does appear as rather ironic given that Doon is actually much more of a 'true' Christian than his legitimate and supposedly Christian half-brother, as it is he who teaches Tristan about Christianity and Christian values (vv. 6430–95): Tristan is of Frankish descent, yet is raised in the forest by a deer after being separated from his parents, Gui and Aiglentine. His lineage and thus his 'natural' identity do not guarantee an identity conforming to racial-religious conventions; these must be assumed and learned, chosen in a process that aligns his physical heritage with visible form. R. Howard Bloch observes of post eleventh-century texts that

> the lineal family model is predicated upon the principles of partial resemblance, contiguity, and, above all, continuity. Thus the son reproduces the father, accedes to the paternal name, title, heraldic sign, and land.[61]

This social structure is also recognized in later *chansons de geste* by Michael Heintze, who notes that in the earlier periods laterally constructed relationships were key, 'während in jüngeren Liedern der Vater zunehmend an Bedeutung gewinnt' [while in later songs the father increasingly gains significance].[62] As the repetition of identity through bloodline, genealogy is represented here as the continuity of a supposedly true, biological identity. Yet it is this emphasis upon replication that also reveals the illusory nature of lineal genealogy; the lasting bonds portrayed in the Nanteuil Cycle are those consciously made through the rejection or reworking of biological ties and the simultaneous reimaginings of Chirstian-Saracen unions, as is displayed through the bond between Gui and Ganor or in the marriage of the newly transfigured Blanchandin to Clarinde.

Tristan's turbulent relationships with his blood relatives in *Tristan de Nanteuil* further demonstrate the social failings of heredity based on bloodlines. Not only does Tristan fight against his own father (albeit unknowingly), but he is also killed by his own son, Garcion. Garcion is Tristan's son by a Saracen princess, Clarisse, and is abducted by Guintelin, a neighbouring Saracen, to be raised as a Saracen. In contrast to Ganor's nurturing of Gui, we are told that Guintelin 'tint l'enffant a filz, mais c'estoit sans raison' (v. 17752) [took the child as his son, but he had no right to do so] and that Garcion, before his conversion to Christianity, 'ot ceur sy felon' (v. 17759) [had such a disloyal heart]. The effect of Guintelin's role as father has clearly been a negative one, culminating in patricide (vv. 22950–23016). In this scenario, the biological father (Tristan) is destroyed by his own flesh and blood, the replication of his physical identity, as a direct result of the falsely adopted identities of first Guintelin then Garcion. Rather than acting as a surrogate father (an openly assumed and constructed role) Guintelin claims a 'true' paternity for himself by taking and naming Garcion his own 'filz' [son]. By assuming a false genealogical position, Guintelin has also imposed a false Saracen identity upon Garcion and though this identity alone is not destructive, the associated concealment of Garcion's true heritage is catastrophic. Garcion is more than willing to convert to Christianity when he discovers the nature of his birth at the end of the text. However, Guintelin's deception has left Garcion unaware of the illusory nature of his Saracen identity and so a false identity is taken to be natural or somehow innate. Garcion's unconscious disguise has determined his identity; this is in contrast to Gui's active choice to become Ganor's son and to confect an identity that exploits, rather than conceals, racial difference.

In *Aye d'Avignon*, it is clear that Ganor maintains Gui's birth identity while raising him, as he is consistently referred to as 'le fil Garnier' (*Aye*, v. 3275) [Garnier's son] and it is only upon Garnier's death that Gui declares: 'Je le weil e otroi que soie vostre fiz' (*Aye*, v. 3457) [I wish and consent to be your son]. Gui therefore constructs for himself a new identity by choosing to be recognized as the son of Ganor and, in doing so, he assumes a new social position, as commander of Ganor's (Saracen) forces. This consciously chosen identity does not seem to be a problem, owing to its open admission rather than concealment or forgery. In *Tristan*, however, the potentially problematic nature of concealed identities is raised even before Garcion's birth by the manner in which he is conceived. While visiting his ancestral lands around Nanteuil, Tristan is attracted to the Saxon (Saracen) noblewoman Clarisse, who has been promised to the treacherous local governor, Persant. He sneaks into her bedchamber at night disguised in Persant's clothes (v. 10189) but, the following morning the two discover that they are in fact related:

> Car vos mere Aiglentine est mon ante clamee.
> Vos cousine germaine avés huy vïolee. (vv. 10325–26)

[For your mother Aiglentine is my aunt. You have violated your first cousin today.]

When disguising the physical body conceals a character's lineage, whether through a lie (Guintelin), or clothing (Tristan), this creates a threat to society by disrupting not just convention but the very moral codes that depend upon it.

In contrast, the disguise adopted by Ganor in *Aye d'Avignon* gives him the opportunity to become a surrogate father to Aye's son Gui, subsequently ensuring that his fate is tied to that of the boy. As Woods notes, 'the two outsiders both must return to France, one to marry Aye, the other to assume his rightful position in the community'.[63] By the end of the text, Gui's new identity allows him to pass from one community to another; he commands forces from both Avignon and Majorca on the path to resuming his rightful position as the biological son of Garnier, yet also maintains his role in Saracen society through his adoptive ties to Ganor. Since Gui chooses his lineage, he has established a fluid racial identity. Yet as both Christian heir and Saracen commander, his plural identity (like that of Ganor) is clearly not readable through corporeal or visible form alone, epitomized at the end of *Aye* in the traitor Milon's confusion upon seeing the amassed Saracen forces under his command.

Ganor's positive paternal influence is perpetuated in the subsequent text in the Cycle, *Gui de Nanteuil*, where Gui once again calls upon the support of his surrogate father to defeat traitors at court. Although this plotline echoes Garnier's struggles in *Aye*, this time Gui is able to defeat his foes successfully with help from his half-brothers, Antoine and Richer, and his stepfather Ganor. Ganor has made himself indispensable to the cyclical framework, as it is repeatedly necessary for him to rescue Gui and by extension the Nanteuil dynasty from enemies in the Frankish kingdom. This Saracen figure has consequently created a new future for the family by preventing history from repeating itself and the bonds that he constructs actually maintain rather than threaten biological succession. Finn Sinclair suggests that Ganor's otherness

> lies not in his ethnicity and religion, but in his genealogy [...] it is Gui who is Garnier's legal and genealogical heir; the masculine focus of the text ultimately lies with him.[64]

However, Ganor's identity could be viewed as rooted in a forward-looking genealogy, rather than in an inherited one. As a surrogate father to Gui, and new husband to Aye, Ganor's position in society, just like his identity, is constructed through the acts and gestures he performs, the most significant of which is his immediate engendering of a son:

> Seignor, icele nuit dont vos m'oez conter
> Engenra .i. enfant dont vos m'orrez parler:
> Entoine le fist puis rois Ganor apeler;
> Puis aida il Guyon, a son frere le ber,
> Vers le parenté Ganes sa terre a delivrer.
> L'andemain va Ganor le servise escouter,
> E si vit *le cors Dieu* e couchier e lever;
> Moult li plet *Jhesucrist*, Diex conmence a loër
> E la loi Mahonmet du tot a adosser. (vv. 4121–29)

[Lords, on the night you are hearing described he engendered a child and I will tell you of him: King Ganor had him named Antoine; he later helped Gui, his noble brother, to free his lands from Ganelon's relatives. The next day Ganor goes to hear the service and sees the body of God raised and lowered; Lord Jesus delights him, he begins to praise God and to abandon completely the law of Muhammad.]

Ganor's successful procreation with his Frankish wife Aye not only demonstrates his assimilation into Frankish society but also both looks to the future role of his bloodline in Frankish politics and asserts his conversion to the Christian faith. While chivalrous Saracen heroes may be stock character types of the *chansons de geste*, it is somewhat unusual for them to be integrated via marriage in this way — particularly via a fertile marriage. In fact, a feature of mixed-race unions in medieval literary works, even those between Saracen princesses and Christian knights, is generally their sterility, as has been observed, for instance, in relation to the Saracen queen, Orable, of the Guillaume d'Orange Cycle.[65] Ganor therefore represents a counterexample to Kruger's theory that in medieval literature conversion to Christianity did not provide integration into Christian familial structures but rather a rejection of matrimony and all its social obligations in favour of chastity.[66]

By openly assuming a surrogate role, Ganor, though inadvertently revealing the artificiality of conventional genealogical and racial identity, does not overhaul the social structure, as his disguise exploits coexisting, rather than contrasting, biological and behavioural identities and provides alternative familial networks. His establishment of a genealogy is therefore much less problematic than that of Guintelin, despite their parallel situations: whilst Ganor openly forges his position as patriarch through new bonds of loyalty and marriage, Guintelin attempts to do this through subterfuge, claiming a constructed identity (as father to Garcion) as biological and a disguise as inherited. Ganor's Saracen roots have consequently ceased to be a barrier to his incorporation into the Frankish community, as he participates in a new, multi-racial social framework that is nonetheless respectful of conventions involving marriage and bloodlines. Conversely, Guintelin's creation of an illusory racial identity for Garcion proves to be a threat to genealogy, ultimately leading Garcion to kill his own father. Believing himself a Saracen and Tristan a Christian, Garcion possesses a false concept of racial difference which destroys, rather than founds, lineage.

Conclusion

The racial cross-dressing present in the Nanteuil Cycle shows 'a clear fascination with trying on and rehearsing an alien, proscribed, and demonized other'.[67] It is this 'trying on' that facilitates the necessary cultural and racial repositionings that occur, allowing Gui to achieve power in Saracen lands, Ganor to gain a new wife and religion, and Tristan and Doon to move between realms, developing their chivalric prowess along the way. However, there are subtle differences in the workings of disguise across the Cycle as a whole, especially when gender crossing is also involved and genealogical structures are at stake. In addition, the uses of disguise throughout the Cycle reveal significant changes in how identity is depicted. In the earlier texts *Aye d'Avignon* and *Gui de Nanteuil* identity is individually assumed and transformed by replicating behavioural conventions. This exemplifies Butler's theory that identity — regardless of whether or not it is self-consciously performed — is determined through the citational performance of convention. Characters in these texts such as Ganor and Grandoine (another Saracen nobleman) are able to exploit recognized forms and behaviours successfully; rather than threatening the stability of the Frankish community, their performed identities ultimately allow them to choose their racial affiliation and their racial crossing reinforces hegemonic structures.[68] Ganor also establishes a new form of lineage constructed through chosen bonds as well as biological paternity, which does not usurp conventionally inherited genealogy, but rather protects it. Even if Ganor's disguise temporarily unsettles behavioural conventions, its effects are fundamentally conservative, as he maintains and extends systems of heredity.

As a result, genealogical conventions reveal the different workings of racial and gendered cross-dressing. Whereas the behavioural repositioning of race can be ratified by religious conversion and sexual union, gender crossings ultimately require a change in physical make-up to be sustainable and for the bodies involved to be reproduced through the engendering of children. Nonetheless, it is perhaps precisely because gender roles in *Aye d'Avignon* are so unstable from the outset that conventions of racial identity are also able to be brought into question and reworked. With a focus on the antics of a heroine rather than hero, this *chanson de geste* allots a different role to its Saracen protagonist; Ganor becomes not the chivalrous warrior to be bested and convinced to convert, but conforms instead to literary conventions associated with the beautiful Saracen princess, converted for love and assimilated through marriage. Of course, while the early thirteenth century brought new ways of representing relations between Christians and Saracens, such as through the growing interest in the reputation of Saladin, the chivalrous Saracen, and Saracen princess motifs,[69] it was also a period where romance narratives and their prioritization of love began to flourish.

In *Tristan de Nanteuil*, however, both constructed lineage and inherited bloodlines repeatedly fail in a tangle of misidentifications, where gender performances may hinder new forms of mixed-race lineage and Saracens are both militarily defeated and impregnated by women. Guintelin, for instance, attempts to replicate a conventional lineage based on biological paternity by disguising Garcion, Tristan's son, yet is ultimately unsuccessful. Similarly, Blanchandine's disguise cannot be maintained without divine intervention as it cannot produce a lineage. The attempts to resituate identity in *Tristan de Nanteuil* seem to fail primarily because disguise or constructed identity is used to make alternative biological claims, even as characters are pretending to be something they are not. Disguises may permit various identity performances (whether unconscious or chosen), but such new identities are time-limited and cannot be replicated without supernatural intervention; any attempt to pass them off as permanent threatens familial and social order. This is because conventions of descent are simultaneously shown to rely upon the replication of physical identity, while also being destabilized by the potential concealment and (re)construction of bodies, especially where the gendered body is concerned. Fatherhood, perhaps more so than marriage, is thus a way to establish conformity. Yet, significantly, this need not only be through procreation and physical replication, but can also occur through the assumption of a paternal role — a role that is forward-looking and positively produces new genealogical chains.

Aside from its role in producing genealogical identities, the Nanteuil Cycle reveals that the body, though used to evoke biological lineage, is not always the main signifier of race and the combination of Ganor's physical and behavioural identities demonstrates this. He actually provokes more anxiety before he is disguised by possessing a physically white, beautiful body yet displaying Saracen behaviour: something which makes him an interesting counterpart to Butler's transvestite. His cross-dressing is no longer contained by a ruse, a temporarily assumed disguise, but is instead his everyday, visible identity. Ganor's internal and external identities must ultimately be brought into line in order for him to find his place in society and this is finally achieved through his marriage to Aye and conversion to Christianity, which both ensure his integration into the Frankish community: he is now the surrogate father of the new lord of Avignon and able to make a valuable match in the niece of Charlemagne.

Ganor's performances of identity, whether deliberate or not, consequently underline the unreliability and inconsistency of the body in medieval identity construction; this is a phenomenon reiterated in both *Gui de Nanteuil* and *Tristan de Nanteuil* through the tropes of courtly lover, disguised knight, and surrogate father. In attempting to rely upon physiognomy and external signs to define identity, the depicted society is left vulnerable to deception by disguises in which appearances may be exploited. Knowledge of behavioural conventions (such as religious custom, gender relations and language ability) is most often revealed to be just as significant as bodily form for the establishment of racial identity and, like visible appearance, these conventions may be exploited if needed. This departs somewhat from previous scholarship situating medieval understandings of otherness within a predominantly physical context. For instance, in his study 'On Saracen Enjoyment', Cohen's aim is 'to trace briefly the genealogy of a violent, racializing identity machine rooted in corporeal otherness that spreads the body across environment and objectal world', while Jacqueline de Weever's *Sheba's Daughters* similarly focuses upon the visible nature of race through ideas of blackness and bodily form in relation to Saracen women in epic narratives.[70] Such a prioritization of the body is also found in many modern theoretical discussions of racial difference, as testified for instance by Bridget Byrne's notion of race as 'a particular kind of seeing the human body'.[71] In *Aye d'Avignon*, no-one questions Ganor's appearance as a Christian, Frankish pilgrim because he looks *and* acts the part.

Perhaps one of the reasons why the concept of performativity in relation to race has often been overlooked is that studies on racial identity have tended to place most emphasis upon the body, whereas Butler's performativity relies upon the premise of co-existing if not conjoined physical and behavioural identities. In the Nanteuil Cycle the role of the body in disguise episodes reveals a key difference between racial and gendered identity, as in gender cross-dressing it is the body that ultimately betrays the performer. Byrne argues in relation to modern concepts of race that 'the fact that there are numerous possible descriptions of race — rather than the neat duality of male/female — does not mean that it is somehow less obligatory or coerced';[72] this contrasts with the varying success of racial and gendered disguise present in *Tristan*, as gendered disguise ultimately appears to be restricted by the physical body in a way that seems not to be the case for the assumption of racial identity.

Overall, a general sense of the performativity of identity emerges across the Nanteuil Cycle: disguise challenges the norms of expected behaviour, whether racial, gendered, or even class-based, acting as a leveller and allowing identity to be chosen by removing restrictions that we might assume to be imposed by physical form. Just as Butler suggests that boundaries between 'the natural and the artificial, depth and surface, inner and outer' in gendered discourse are destabilized by drag performances,[73] so the racial cross-dressing in these texts has a similar effect upon the means of racial identification, although the obvious critique achieved by drag has been seen to contrast with the necessary concealment of disguise.

To return briefly here to the definition of a Saracen and the interconnection of race and religion that it espouses, just as the body had to be changed for gender crossings to be maintained, so religious conversion must occur for racial crossings to stick. In the fourteenth-century *Tristan de Nanteuil* for instance, mixed-race unions abound, even if baptism is always achieved before marriage itself.[74] However, it is interesting that Tristan and Blanchandine's son, Raimon, is never clearly baptized in the text, despite becoming the lord of Avignon (he is born in the forest to a savage Tristan and pagan Blanchandine, and then raised by his Christian grandmother, Aiglentine, at a Saracen court). Such cases would suggest that even religion does not always constitute an ultimate and essential difference between Christian and Saracen, or perhaps may sometimes be taken for granted.

In the Nanteuil Cycle, it seems that Saracens gain intelligible and acceptable identities in Frankish society when they conform to recognizable identity conventions, even before conversion, and even if these cross boundaries of gender or race. Yet, in doing so, these Saracen characters simultaneously expose the instability and unreliability of all such norms. Indeed, by the time we reach *Tristan de Nanteuil*, society is in a constant state of flux: everything is not always as it seems in the realm of the visible, where identity is constructed by, on the one hand, exposing the illusory and on the other, concealing and manipulating difference. Nevertheless, although characters perform a range of identities in this Cycle, often replicating and exploiting conventions as context requires, they are ultimately unable to maintain them if they trouble genealogical continuity. The Nanteuil Cycle therefore reveals a flexible view of race as manipulable and performatively constructed, yet one that relies upon genealogical identities in a context where these are themselves being called into question and repositioned in relation to (biologically) inherited identity and gender. This means that a new form of Saracen lineage may be established by alternative social bonds, but must not threaten existing biological inheritance in the process. Crucially, however, the concept of bloodlines was itself neither essentially understood nor consistently applied in literary works, and while evoked in the context of racial identities it may appear in many different guises. Whereas I will return to the relationship between blood and racial crossings in my Conclusion, in Chapter Two I shall further set notions of bloodline in the sense of genealogy in relation to racial thinking. Instead of an alternative anchor to align appearance and reality and ensure temporal continuity, as was the case with Ganor, in the *Estoire del Saint Graal* we will see how genealogy can be constructed via logical processes and narrative technique: like disguise, it produces bodies that reveal the performativity of racial identity conventions and may even engender the Saracen through his descendants.

Notes to Chapter 1

1. Robert L.A. Clark and Claire Sponsler, 'Queer Play: The Cultural Work of Crossdressing in Medieval Drama', *New Literary History*, 28 (1997), 319–44 <http://www.jstor.org/stable/20057418> [accessed 16 November 2018], (p. 321).
2. Clark and Sponsler, 'Queer Play', p. 329.
3. Jean-Louis Picherit, 'Les Sarrasins dans Tristan de Nanteuil', in *Au carrefour des routes d'Europe: la chanson de geste: Xe Congrès international de la Société Rencesvals pour l'étude des épopées romanes, Strasbourg, 1985*, Sénéfiance, 20–21 (Aix-en-Provence: Publications du CUERMA, Université de Provence, 1987), pp. 941–57 (p. 954).
4. Robert L.A. Clark and Claire Sponsler, 'Othered Bodies: Racial Cross-Dressing in the Mistere de la Sainte Hostie and the Croxton Play of the Sacrament', *JMEMS*, 29 (1999), 61–87 (p. 62).
5. Butler, *Bodies that Matter*, p. 123.
6. Loxley, *Performativity*, p. 125.
7. Ibid.
8. Esther Newton, *Mother Camp: Female Impersonators in America* (Chicago: University of Chicago Press, 1979), p. 103. Butler discusses this paradox of internal and external identity in *Gender Trouble*, p. 186.
9. Butler, *Gender Trouble*, Preface (1999), p. xxiii.
10. Kruger, 'Conversion', p. 164.
11. Pellegrini, *Performance Anxieties*, p. 6.
12. Heng, *Empire of Magic*, p. 14.
13. Katrin Sieg, *Ethnic Drag: Performing Race Nation, Sexuality in West Germany* (Ann Arbor: University of Michigan Press, 2002), pp. 2–3.
14. See for instance, the *chanson de geste Daurel et Beton* for the use of *jongleur* disguise and *La Prise d'Orange* for Guillaume d'Orange and his men masquerading as merchants to enter a Saracen city.
15. Note that St Denis is particularly evocative of a nascent French national identity around the twelfth century and acts as an important spiritual centre for the Frankish kingdom.
16. Finn E. Sinclair, *Milk & Blood: Gender and Genealogy in the 'Chanson de Geste'* (Oxford: Peter Lang, 2003), p. 264.
17. Cohen, 'On Saracen Enjoyment', p. 203.
18. Butler, *Gender Trouble*, p. 187.
19. Ibid (original emphasis).
20. Loxley, *Performativity*, p. 126.
21. Judith Butler, *The Psychic Life of Power: Theories in Subjection* (Stanford, CA: Stanford University Press, 1997), p. 145.
22. Even though he maintains his Frankish identity throughout his disguise, as a mercenary rather than a landed knight, Garnier nonetheless crosses class boundaries, which may provide parallels

to Clark and Sponsler's discussion of the popularity of Robin Hood disguises. See 'Queer Play', pp. 322–23.
23. See Woods, *Aye d'Avignon*, pp. 18–21.
24. Clark and Sponsler, 'Queer Play', p. 329.
25. Clark and Sponsler, 'Othered Bodies', p. 74 and p. 61.
26. Clark and Sponsler, 'Othered Bodies', p. 62. The authors focus, however, on the later medieval period and suggest that there was a 'sharpening of racial boundaries' (p. 62).
27. Lynette R. Muir, *Literature and Society in Medieval France: The Mirror and the Image 1100–1500* (London: Macmillan, 1985), p. 105.
28. Note that the disguise used by Nicolette in *Aucassin et Nicolette* has, however, attracted the attention of several scholars. For instance: Jacqueline de Weever, 'Nicolette's *Blackness*: Lost in Translation', *Romance Notes*, 34 (1994), 317–25; Maria Rosa Menocal, 'Signs of the Times: Self, Other, and History in *Aucassin et Nicolette*', *Romanic Review*, 80 (1989), 497–511. A recent exception is also Saladin's disguise in Boccaccio's *Decameron*. See Ana Grinberg, 'Robes, Turbans, and Beards: "Ethnic Passing" in *Decameron* 10.9', in *Medieval Clothing and Textiles*, 13, ed. by Robin Netherton and Gale R. Owen-Crocker (Woodbridge: Boydell, 2017), pp. 67–81.
29. For example, Clark and Sponsler's analysis of medieval Marian miracle plays and Early Modern Robin Hood performances in 'Queer Play'.
30. Clark and Sponsler, 'Queer Play', p. 320.
31. Valerie R. Hotchkiss, *Clothes Make the Man: Female Cross Dressing in Medieval Europe*, Garland Reference Library of the Humanities, 1991 (New York: Garland, 2000. First published 1996), p. 4.
32. For female cross-dressers in medieval French, see Michèle Perret, 'Travesties et transsexuelles: Yde, Silence, Grisandole, Blanchandine', *Romance Notes*, 25 (1985), 328–40.
33. Perret, 'Travesties et transsexuelles', p. 333.
34. Antoine observes that 'la bouche petite n'ot barbe ne grenon' (v. 3028) [her little mouth had neither beard nor stubble].
35. See Peggy McCracken, *In the Skin of a Beast: Sovereignty and Animality in Medieval France* (Chicago: University of Chicago Press, 2017), p. 147.
36. McCracken, *Skin of a Beast*, p. 148.
37. Ibid.
38. Woods, *Aye d'Avignon*, p. 70.
39. Perret, 'Travesties et transsexuelles', p. 332.
40. Catherine Rottenberg, '"Passing": Race, Identification, and Desire', *Criticism*, 45 (2003), 435–52 (p. 436). Rottenberg expands this study in: *Performing Americanness: Race, Class and Gender in Modern African-American and Jewish-American Literature* (Hanover, NH: Dartmouth College; University Press of New England, 2008), (e.g. p. 62).
41. Rottenberg, *Performing Americanness*, pp. 34–35.
42. See, for instance, Jane Gilbert's discussion of gender identity in 'The Practice of Gender in Aucassin et Nicolette', *Forum for Modern Language Studies*, 33 (1997), 217–28.
43. See McCracken's discussion of Blanchandine's sexual body in *Skin of a Beast*, pp. 152–54.
44. Examples include for instance Nicolette in *Aucassin et Nicolette*, Maugalie in *Floovant* or Josiane in *Beuve de Hantone*. See Ramey, *Christian, Saracen, and Genre*, pp. 83–93.
45. There are numerous examples of female Saracens who convert to Christianity, possibly the most well-known being Bramimonde from the *Chanson de Roland*. There are also examples of Saracen women using disguise to reject their Saracen heritage, such as Nicolette in *Aucassin et Nicolette*, or Maugalie in the *chanson de geste Floovant* who both blacken their faces and travel as minstrels.
46. Vern L. Bullough and Bonnie Bullough, 'Cross Dressing and Social Status in the Middle Ages', in *Cross Dressing, Sex, and Gender* (Philadelphia: University of Pennsylvania Press, 1993), pp. 45–73 (p. 46 and p. 68).
47. Perret, 'Travesties et transexuelles', p. 329.
48. The fairy Mélusine is a key exception, since she acts as founding mother to the Lusignan family, although this narrative again includes the influence of the supernatural. See for example, Jean d'Arras, *Le Roman de Mélusine ou La Noble Histoire de Lusignan*, ed. by Jean-Jacques Vincensini

(Paris: Livre de Poche, 2003).
49. Peggy McCracken, 'The Boy Who Was A Girl: Reading Gender in the *Roman de Silence*', *Romanic Review*, 85 (1994), 517–36 (p. 517).
50. McCracken, *Skin of a Beast*, p. 156.
51. See Sylvia Schein, 'Women in Medieval Colonial Society: The Latin Kingdom of Jerusalem in the Twelfth Century', in *Gendering the Crusades*, ed. by Susan B. Edgington and Sarah Lambert (Cardiff: University of Wales Press, 2001), pp. 140–53.
52. Perret, 'Travesties et transsexuelles', pp. 336–37.
53. Perret, 'Travesties et transsexuelles', p. 340.
54. Cohen, 'On Saracen Enjoyment', pp. 92–93.
55. There are also fragments of a thirteenth-century manuscript of *Doon de Nanteuil*, which deals with the ancestors of Garnier de Nanteuil.
56. Thelma S. Fenster, 'The Family Romance of Aye d'Avignon', *Romance Quarterly*, 33 (1986), 11–22 (pp. 11–13).
57. Fenster, 'Family Romance', p. 11.
58. Fenster, 'Family Romance', p. 12. Note though that there is no tolerance of religious divide and all must convert to Christianity by the end of the text.
59. Clark and Sponsler, 'Queer Play', p. 326. See also the figure of Yde in *Yde et Olive* for this disguise mechanism, and Blanchandine in *Tristan de Nanteuil*.
60. Kay, *Chansons de Geste*, p. 178.
61. R. Howard Bloch, *Etymologies and Genealogies: A Literary Anthropology of the French Middle Ages* (Chicago, IL: University of Chicago Press, 1983), p. 86.
62. Michael Heintze, *König, Held und Sippe: Untersuchungen zur Chanson de geste des 13. und 14. Jahrhunderts und ihrer Zyklenbildung*, Studia Romanica, 76 (Heidelberg: Winter, 1991), p. 495.
63. Woods, *Aye d'Avignon*, p. 36.
64. Sinclair, *Milk & Blood*, p. 264.
65. Philip E. Bennett and Leslie Zarker Morgan, 'The Avatars of Orable-Guibourc from French *chanson de geste* to Italian *romanzo cavalleresco*. A Persistent Multiple Alterity', *Francigena*, 1 (2015), 165–215.
66. Kruger, 'Conversion', pp. 166–67.
67. Clark and Sponsler, 'Othered Bodies', p. 80.
68. Rottenberg discusses how racial crossing, in particular passing, relates to hegemonic ideals in '"Passing"'.
69. See for instance, Ailes, 'Chivalry and Conversion', p. 18.
70. Cohen, 'On Saracen Enjoyment', p. 189; de Weever, *Sheba's Daughters*.
71. Byrne, *White Lives*, p. 21.
72. Byrne, *White Lives*, p. 18.
73. Butler, *Gender Trouble*, Preface (1990), p. xxxi.
74. See for instance the relationships between Gui and Honorée and Tristan and Blanchandine.

CHAPTER 2

Race and Time: Genealogy and Logical Race in the *Estoire del Saint Graal*

'Il n'estoit nule rien terriene que je tant desiraisse a oïr comme la counissanche de mon lignaige' [there was nothing on earth I desired so much as hearing about my lineage]:[1] this is the reaction of the *Estoire del Saint Graal*'s narrator to the celestial book that details his lineage. With this comment, however, he also evokes the role of this text as the very guarantor of genealogy. For, sandwiched between this narratorial insight and an extensive genealogical summary leading into the rest of the Vulgate Cycle, lies a tale of origins, destiny, and heredity depicting the Saracen ancestors of Arthurian heroes. In contrast to those medieval works that represent the genealogy of the Saracen race as dictated by biblical history and theories of climatic variation,[2] Saracen identity in the *Estoire* is tied to processes of deduction that defy linear chronology and geography. Such processes expose racial identity as performative in the sense that it is shown to be reliant upon prolepsis and retrospective attempts to naturalize what has been constructed; in turn, this reformulates not only conventional Saracen conversion fantasies but also ideas of race as inherited and as produced through bodily repetitions and geographical provenance. The central Saracen king, Evalach/Mordrain, is only able to lose his epithet 'li Mesconneüs' [the Unknown] through the narrative of his spiritual birth as a Christian. His brother-in-law, Seraphe/Nascien, both gains and provides genealogical origins while temporally suspended between Christian and Saracen identity and spatially removed to a revolving island.[3] With its focus on genealogical causality as non-linear, the *Estoire* therefore explores alternative ways in which the transmission of race and racial identity may occur; by extension, it reveals how this identity might be repeated and repeatable in a variety of ways and how Saracen racial identity is understood as constructed rather than essential.

Referring to racial thinking today, anthropologist Rachel Caspari underlines that, despite our general association of race with genealogy, elements of identity that we take to mark race can also conceal ancestry, since a person's biological heritage may be obscured by their outward appearances.[4] Just as racial identity can intersect with ideals of gender and procreative acts in different ways, Caspari's observation calls into question the causal relationship between ancestry or genealogy and race.

While in the Nanteuil Cycle the preservation of genealogical continuity restricted the role of the body in shifts of racial and gendered identity, in the *Estoire*, narrative progression and spiritual awakening — above all processes of religious conversion — actually determine genealogy. Miranda Griffin has demonstrated that although causality is a central concern of medieval French literature in general, temporality in the Vulgate Cycle is very particular and can be read in terms of Lacan's notion of logical time, which insists on subjective processes of hesitation and reasoning instead of linear sequences of events.[5] This formulation of time and causality as produced through the repetition of conventions shares principles with the concept of performativity and relies upon similar structures. Performativity exposes how there is no pre-existing, or underlying truth to identity and how identities are instead produced through the repetition and recognition of conventions via discourse, behaviour, dress, and more besides. In a similar way, the repetition that characterizes the *Estoire*'s temporality not only produces particular kinds of genealogical identities but, in the process, reveals the very conventions upon which those genealogical aspects of race are founded; for instance, the convention that race is understood as being passed from father to son through bloodlines is inverted at moments where the actions of future characters in the Cycle determine the nature of their ancestors. As a brief example, one such case is when the converted Saracen Nascien is told of his illustrious descendant (Galahad) and consequently of his own role as part of a sacred lineage by the angel announcing the Grail quest (*ESG*, p. 168). The angel first explains that the man who will see the marvels of the Grail will be full of all goodness and prowess (*ESG*, pp. 167–68) then clarifies that this great man will also be the last of Nascien's lineage. In this respect, Galahad's predetermined qualities and role within the Grail tradition dictate Nascien's identity, as they confirm the credibility of Nascien's conversion to Christianity, marking him as belonging to such a tradition.

Combining logical time with the performativity of identity, this chapter examines how the troubling of linear chronology affects the representation of race. In particular, the retrospective prologue to the Cycle, the *Estoire del Saint Graal* reveals that there is neither a linear genealogical progression from Saracen ancestor to Christian descendant nor a fixed geographical trajectory from east to west. Furthermore, this lack of geographical fixity decentres any attempt to make Britain into a new Jerusalem and exposes the citationality of any associated crusading rhetoric. As a consequence of this, I argue that race, like time, may likewise be regarded as 'logical': it does not reflect a universalized understanding of genealogy, but is formed through intersubjective, reciprocal processes whereby ancestry and geography are deduced. While characters are not, of course, capable of independent thought in some way, the term 'intersubjective' recognizes that their comprehension of genealogy nonetheless occurs via reciprocal processes.

The *Estoire*'s Genealogies in Context

The Old French Vulgate Cycle (*c*.1215–1235) refers to an expansive group of prose romances that provide a comprehensive history of the Grail, covering its place in the Passion of Christ, the discovery of King Arthur, the Grail quest, and the demise of the Arthurian world, thus building upon earlier works such as those of Robert de Boron. One particular narrative, the *Estoire del Saint Graal* (dated to around 1225–30)[6] focuses upon Saracens, depicting them as the ancestors of the Arthurian knights, and consequently incorporates them into a highly Christianized chivalric community as the relatives of even Galahad himself. Although it is the first text in narrative terms in the Cycle, which comprises the *Estoire*, the *Estoire Merlin*, the *Lancelot*, the *Queste del Saint Graal* and the *Mort Artu*, in terms of composition, it is usually placed after the *Mort*, or at least as being contemporaneous with the *Queste*.[7] The position of this text within the genealogy of the Cycle is therefore far from clear-cut, with episodes that seem to be produced retroactively by those yet to come in other works. Most importantly, the *Estoire* also problematizes the relationship between genealogy and race.

The events of the *Estoire* may be summarized as follows: after an introductory section detailing the finding of a source book by the narrator and the commencement of his copying process, the narrative proper begins with Joseph of Arimathea, his catching of Christ's blood in the Grail, healing of the leprous Vespasian and travel to the Saracen city of Sarras. There, Joseph and his son Josephus meet and convert King Evalach (baptized Mordrain), along with the King's brother-in-law Seraphe (baptized Nascien) and the rest of the kingdom. An angel appears and announces the Grail quest before all and, after various visions and spiritual abductions to far-flung isles to test the faith of the new converts, Mordrain and Nascien return to Sarras. A series of relocations to the realm of Britain ensue, which begin with Celidoine (Nascien's son) then continue with Joseph and Josephus, Nascien, and finally Mordrain and his wife Sarracinte. Once in Britain, the migrants convert the local Saracen population, which involves a series of military skirmishes. Mordrain is punished with blindness and impotence for approaching the Grail and asks to live until the last in Nascien's line should come before him. The text ends by detailing the successive protectors of the Grail and the subsequent descendants of Nascien, Joseph, and his relatives.

Despite the substantial scholarly attention that this work has attracted, the relationship between Saracen identity and the unusual genealogical roles fulfilled by Saracen characters has only received cursory treatment.[8] The *Estoire*'s Saracens provide illustrious origins for the well-known Arthurian heroes of the Cycle and their depiction is connected both to questions of narrative repetition and hesitation, and to the tensions between genealogy as history and genealogy as involving descent and prophecy. A straightforward chronology of lineage does not exist in a text where Arthurian heroes such as Lancelot and Galahad determine the nature of their ancestors (Celidoine, Nascien, and to a certain extent, Mordrain). This inverted process of genealogical repetition, with descendant producing ancestor, therefore reveals an alternative understanding of lineage, which nonetheless engages with genealogical conventions involving parentage or geographical provenance. Since such conventions are implicated in the construction of racial identity, the nature of genealogical progression in the *Estoire* sheds light upon the representation of race through the Saracen.

The lineage of the Saracen Evalach/Mordrain usefully illustrates the way in which race and genealogy are connected in this work. Evalach/Mordrain's lineage is simultaneously rediscovered and produced by the narrative, which is most visible when Josephus describes it to him. Firstly, the tenses in this episode interconnect where Josephus explains:

> Or te dirai dont ke tu feras: che te mande li Diex des crestiens ke tu soies ramembrans qui tu iés et comment tu venis a si grant hauteche com tu as eüe jusc'a chi; tu quides ke nus ne sache qui tu es et de quel lignaige, mais je le sai bien par la grasce et par la virtu del haut Signour, a qui nule repostaille ne puet estre chelee. (*ESG*, p. 98)

> [Now I will tell you what to do. This is what the God of the Christians tells you: you are to remember who you are and how you came to such great dignity as you have had until today. And you believe that no one knows who you are, or of what lineage. But I know it well, by the grace and power of the great Lord from whom no secret can be kept.]

Here Josephus says that he will tell Evalach ('dirai') what no-one else knows ('sache'), so that Evalach will be able to remember how he achieved his present state, suggesting that the memory of the past is a process dependent upon its future recounting. Secondly, Josephus also uses the term 'repostaille' to refer to Evalach's lost identity, which signifies something that is a deeply hidden secret as well as a potential mystery of faith.[9] This consequently establishes a link between the exposure of Evalach's hidden lineage and God's discernment of faith, suggesting that lineage cannot be known without belief. Subsequent to this episode, Evalach is also retroactively connected to the yet unborn (but already well-known) Galahad through the narrative legacy invoked by the visions he is granted.[10] In the pre-existing narrative of the *Queste*, the meeting of Galahad and Mordrain signals the end of the latter's divine punishment, so the depiction of the initial inflicting of Mordrain's wounds has been determined by this subsequent encounter. While not a blood relative, Mordrain is nonetheless connected to Galahad in a spiritual sense, since, in the *Queste*, it is the arrival of Galahad on the Grail quest that liberates Mordrain from his divine punishment.

Zrinka Stahuljak argues that Arthurian romance is the quest for, rather than proof of, the father: it establishes a linguistic process of recognition that is marked by an 'inherent fatherlessness'.[11] For Stahuljak, Arthurian genealogies are bloodless to the extent that paternity is a question of spiritual knowledge achieved through the Grail quest, not a matter of biology; paternity is ultimately a question of belief not procreation.[12] In the *Estoire*, this spiritualization of genealogy unsettles conventional causality, so that the link between ancestor and descendant is exposed and challenged by Saracens who seem to be engendered by their faith. Positioned thus as Christian converts, their connection to the Grail quest is what determines their Saracen heritage. For instance, Galahad's participation in the Grail quest narrative places him within the *Estoire*'s genealogy and so retrospectively determines his connection to Mordrain. As a result, the alternative lineage structures created by this work challenge the relationship of race to linear definitions of ancestry.

Genealogy is likewise intimately connected to geography in this text. Not only are genealogy and geography often represented concomitantly in the *Estoire*,[13] but they are also fundamentally interconnected in theories of race, both medieval and modern. In the Middle Ages, this interconnection is perhaps most visible in attitudes towards the Christian loss and potential recovery of the Holy Land, a discourse which forms a backdrop to the evangelizing missions of the *Estoire*. For instance, upon arrival in Britain, Josephus, son of Joseph of Arimathea, tells his followers that: 'vez ci la terre qui nos est pramise et a noz ancesors' (*ESG*, p. 418) [This is the land that is promised to us and our descendants]. Britain is not simply the land to be colonized and converted; it is the land that has been promised to this group. Nonetheless, the non-linear time of the *Estoire* and its alternative geographical trajectories complicate a reading of Britain as a new Jerusalem. Significantly, Ponceau comments in relation to this statement that while 'ancesors' appears in some manuscripts, there are also the terms 'oirs' or even 'successors' used.[14] Besides suggesting a certain confusion between the exact nature of the heritage being acquired, this underlines that perhaps the boundaries between past, present, and future members of the community are unimportant: what matters is that the land is theirs by right, so that genealogy as a non-linear relation between people guarantees their geography.

At first sight, this association of geography and lineage may seem unexceptional, as not only are characters in literary works frequently identified by where they come from (e.g. Aye d'Avignon) but also medieval attempts to describe and explain different peoples are marked by theories of climatic disposition and of the biblically determined distribution of territory.[15] However, it is far from the case that in the medieval period genealogy was consistently equated with specific locations or vice versa. Akbari, for instance, reminds us that while mappaemundi present both the division and unity of the world, depicting as they do notions of common descent yet separate lineages, any 'simplistic effort to align genealogical descent with geographical region' is futile.[16] Yet if, as Akbari also suggests, 'the Saracen body was understood in terms of fixed locations',[17] confused and even inverted geographies must surely impact upon Saracen identities, as must also be the case when descent is determined by non-chronological narrative legacies, not underwritten by blood. The points of intersection between geography, chronology, and genealogy in the *Estoire* thus trouble the frequently assumed stability of these categories, a stability which underwrites an essentialist reading of race.

Relationships between the psychoanalytic concept of logical time and lineage encourage us to reconsider the assumption that genealogy is a linear progression from ancestor to descendant in the *Estoire*. This causal link is reworked by the structure and ordering of the *Estoire*'s narrative and by its position within the Cycle more broadly. Genealogies that result from narrative processes interact with conventional understandings of genealogy as determined by flesh, blood, and geographical origins, revealing alternative forms of racial identity, above all, for the Saracens Nascien and Mordrain.

Lineage, Logical Time, and Performativity

In her study of genealogy and historical narrative, Gabrielle Spiegel states that 'genealogy necessarily fashions history as linear narrative, for what, after all, is a *lignage*, if not a line?'[18] Yet temporality in the *Estoire* does not operate in a linear way. As Miranda Griffin has shown, in the Vulgate Cycle as a whole, time functions in a 'logical' manner: a notion that draws upon the Lacanian definition of logical time.[19] Lacan's primary example of this theory is a sophism involving three prisoners, who each have either a black or white disc placed on their back. Knowing that there are two black and three white discs possible, they must deduce what colour they have been given without speaking, using only silent reactions and hesitations to guide them.[20] Griffin explains that: 'logical time, then, as distinct from chronological time, involves a notion of temporality which is conceived of in subjective terms, understood and structured by the subject's own mental and emotional processes rather than an external, historical representation of the passage of time'.[21] The logical timeframe of romance does not mean that there is simply 'a more circular time-frame' in the Vulgate, but that this time is structured through a process, a temporal as well as thematic *entrelacement*.[22] It is this use of parallel times and plotlines that creates a sense of repetition rather than narrative progression.[23] In turn, the retrospective causality that results from these logical processes is reminiscent of the way in which identities are more generally contingent upon the repetition of conventions, an idea central to the concept of performativity.

In the *Estoire*, the sense of repetition produced by references to previously written (yet narratively subsequent) works or characters is perhaps clearest in the revelation of prophecies, such as when the Saracens are granted visions of their geographical destiny. Flegetine, wife of Nascien, sees that she should go to the land that would be populated by 'sa semence' (*ESG*, p. 392) [his seed][24] and when his son Celidoine is cast off in a boat, Nascien is reassured by a hermit that he will soon see him 'sein et haitié en la terre que Dex a pramise a toi et a ton lingnage' (*ESG*, p. 389) [safe and sound, in the land God has promised you and your lineage]. In this respect, it seems that lineage guarantees geographical destiny, a lineage of faith not of blood that is not reliant upon the idea of racial or religious origins and is instead produced by future events. If, as a result of this guaranteed future, time is to be treated as non-linear, the repetition inherent to genealogy is also non-linear and does not simply pass from ancestor to descendant. Equally, if genealogy functions as a logical process of deduction, this would trouble the conventional geo-chronologies of the Saracen race that strive to assign to this group both a spatial origin and temporal trajectory. Conventions of bloodlines, provenance, and lineage are aspects of racial identity that are not fixed by chronological family structure, but span past, present, and future at once in an eternal present of narration.[25] The result is a suspended narrative temporality akin to the hesitation that characterizes Lacan's example of the three prisoners. Narrative hesitation leaves race subjectively and retrospectively construed rather than objectively defined, and viewing temporality through the lens of Lacanian logical time highlights how identity is contingent upon proleptic processes and is consequently performative. In short, Saracens will become Christians because they are always-already Christians.

Whilst some scholars have suggested that social changes in this period produce a crystallization of vertical lineage,[26] the preoccupation with genealogy in the *Estoire* presents lineage less as a line and more as a web or map. As narrative temporal order admits the transmission of events past and yet to occur, so it is the descendants who create the ancestors, their exemplarity acting as the proverbial carrot with which to lead the Saracens to conversion. The revelation to the Saracens of the Grail quest and their destined move to Britain is, for example, accompanied by details of Galahad's status as 'plains de toutes les bontés' (*ESG*, p. 168) [filled with all goodness] and as the privileged final viewer of the Grail. As a result, the significance of the Grail quest in shaping genealogy in the *Estoire* is evident from its inauguration. When the Grail quest is revealed to the assembled Christians, the angel is the first to mention the great destiny of Nascien's lineage: namely that the last in his line will be the one to see the marvels of the Grail. A sense of continuity is created through the explanation given, as the angel conveys God's decree that:

> Et tout ausi com Nasciens a esté li premiers hom qui les mervelles du Graal a vees, autresi sera chil li daerrains qui les verra, car che dist li vrais Cruchefis: "Au premier home du precieus lignaige et au daerrain ai jou devisé a demoustrer mes mervelles." (*ESG*, p. 168)

> [Just as Nascien was the first man to see the marvels of the Grail, he [Galahad] will be the last to see them, for The True Crucified One said this: "I promised to demonstrate My marvels to the first and last of the precious lineage."]

Nascien is therefore established as the *beginning* of this so called 'lignaige', despite the effort that the text later makes to relate both him and his descendants back to biblical figures. Two aspects of Galahad's genealogy are consequently emphasized: one places Nascien as the first in this lineage; the other positions Galahad more broadly in relation to biblical ancestors and by extension to a biblically structured timeframe, a universalizing history. Further evidence that genealogy is manipulable is later provided when Josephus describes the Tower of Marvels to the newly converted Duke Ganor in Britain. Here Galahad is referred to as 'le desreain chevalier del lignage Nascien' (*ESG*, p. 444) [the last person in Nascien's line], clearly placing Nascien as the critical point of origin for this lineage instead of highlighting the broader line that we know extends back to Solomon and the Virgin.

In this respect, lineage in the *Estoire* is not a question of lines, whether of blood or of geographical movement, but a matter of spiritual experience and more particularly, a matter of the Grail. While Bloch concludes that 'linearity is the defining principle of the noble house, dynasty, and — the partial homonymy is striking — of lineage',[27] the *Estoire* focuses on family connections that although expressed in genealogical terms, are nonetheless dictated by divine decree, characterized by atemporality, and rooted in geographical positionings (or repositionings). The matter of genealogy here is not just a case of creating new connections between peoples but also of creating new temporalities. This genealogical flexibility in turn reveals the performativity of racial identity, as lineage can actually construct race as well as be evidence of it. Furthermore, the race constructed in the *Estoire* proves to be tied to the logical processes at work in the literary text rather than to any essentialized concept of Christian or Saracen.

The idea that race, as articulated through genealogy, can be seen as logical in this way provides another angle on the performativity of identity, since performativity recognizes the productive potential rather than descriptive power of social systems and conventions. For Butler, genealogy

> investigates the political stakes in designating as an *origin* and *cause* those identity categories that are in fact the *effects* of institutions, practices, discourses with multiple and diffuse points of origin.[28]

In this respect, to examine genealogy from a Butlerian perspective is to consider the genealogy of genealogy itself: to question what we take as an origin and rethink the processes by which an identity may be constituted, moving away from essentializing, materialist interpretations of bloodlines. The artifice of cause and effect sequences exposed in Butler's theory of performativity thus constitutes a particular point of convergence with Lacan's concept of logical time, since both underscore the power of subjective processes of deduction and perception and expose the facticity of externally or socially imposed systems. In the medieval period, intergenerational bonds did not always necessitate a direct tie of blood and could instead rely upon surrogate relationships.[29] We saw in *Aye d'Avignon* how the Saracen may acquire a whole new family unit by exploiting the performativity of visual and behavioural identity conventions and the citationality of conventions is also exposed in the genealogies of the *Estoire*. For, if there is no strict chain of causality between the physical body and genealogical identity, then ancestry cannot be said to determine race and/or race cannot be said to originate in the body. Other conventions of identity affecting the representation of race may emerge as influential, such as the association of race with place. Moreover, it becomes clear that the logical processes at work in the narrative of this text determine the constitution of race, since Saracen identity is formed by both Christian ancestors and descendants, leaving this identity temporally suspended between a biblical past and an Arthurian future.

Reworking Blood and Lineage Conventions

The Saracen religion was commonly connected to a kind of biblical genealogy based upon descent from the Prophet Muhammad. This association appears in the *Estoire*, where the narrator comments that the idea that Saracens are descended from Sarah is 'controvaille' — an invention or lie (*ESG*, p. 42). Saracen heritage is instead made relative to that of Jews, and the narrator's comments reproduce but rethink the common association between Sarah and the Saracen people.[30] The concept of a Saracen race here is logical in the Lacanian sense, being deduced through a process of reasoning — a process that reaches beyond simply the Arthurian literary context at hand. As the narrator concludes, Sarah was a Jew and her son was a Jew along with all his descendants, so it does not make sense that the Saracens were the ones to take their name from her (*ESG*, p. 42). The implication is, therefore, that because the Jews stemmed from Sarah, the Saracens did not, with the narrator once again using a point of comparative reasoning to support his own theory. This reasoning may stem from the form of race being presented here. While the term 'Jew', like that of 'Saracen', is similarly problematic to define in terms of its racial/religious uses and emphases in the Middle Ages, in this context it is tempting to see it as an example of a religiously determined lineage system. The narrator additionally explains how the Saracens instead take their name from the city of Sarras because 'la fu controvee et establie la secte ke Sarrasin maintinrent puis juc'a la venue de Mahomet' (*ESG*, p. 42) [in this city was founded and established the sect that the Saracens maintained until the coming of Mohammed]. In this respect, Saracen genealogy is a question of religious descent that nonetheless makes use of geographical details as support, along with mentions of familial descent. Saracen race is thus not so much a bloodline, but a 'faithline' in this case, where Christian conventions of lineage are cited, yet repositioned to tie together faith, blood, and geography.

Although biblical scripture was commonly used as a basis for the descriptions of Saracen origins in Christian texts, such descriptions were, nonetheless, far from consistent, as Benjamin Braude highlights with reference to the common descent of man through the sons of Noah.[31] While it is most often assumed that Japheth is connected to Europe, Shem to Asia, and Ham to Africa, this is not always the case in medieval sources: in the twelfth century, Peter Comestor in his *Historia Scholastica*, for instance, notes the conflicting theories of dividing the sons between the three continents, and there are early representations of T-O maps that suggest the sons could be allocated to regions of the world without the accompanying place names.[32] In this respect, although biblical figures are frequently used to structure genealogical discussion, the way in which this is achieved does not guarantee a stable understanding of race; likewise, the assumption that geographical provenance was somehow codified or consistently tied to these concepts of descent is misleading. Even texts with a classificatory approach to genealogy show that conventions, while present and acknowledged, could be variously interpreted, and the Bible itself is no exception: there was no definitive edition of the Bible in this period and the concept and presentation of biblical genealogy was (and indeed still is) far from unproblematic. Apart from confusion surrounding the locations of the subsequent descendants of Japheth, Shem, and Ham, one of the more controversial genealogical questions appears in the case of Christ's siblings. Although the Bible does state that Christ had brothers and sisters, this was potentially problematic if Mary remained a virgin throughout her life.[33] In this sense, the use of biblical genealogy does not in itself enact a tightening up of lineage structures, and it is unsurprising that we should find complex and even contradictory genealogical ties posited in the *Estoire*.

Alongside the instability of conventions surrounding biblical lineage, genealogical time in the *Estoire* is also constructed in an unconventional way. Lineage in this work is motivated less by notions of past heritage than by future succession, despite the impression of historical continuity created by genealogical themes and the inclusion of ancestral characters. The nature of this forward-looking focus is noted in the letter that Nascien receives when he experiences a vision of his descendants on the ship of Solomon: 'vez ci la branche et la hautesce de ton lingnage, non pas celui dont tu iés descenduz, mes celui qui de toi descendra' (*ESG*, p. 402) [here is the noble branch of your lineage, not the one from which you are descended, but the one that will henceforth descend from you]. This reversal of conventional ancestry into descent (or rather, ascent, given that Galahad is the best-of-the-best) both situates the Saracen in relation to his future relatives and goes on to place him in relation to the Arthurian heroes of literary tradition. The result is the construction of a new temporality for the Saracen where he is now in a time beyond time within legend: just as Galahad is better than all those who came before him and those yet to come, so Nascien is simultaneously the future of the biblical Solomon and the past of the Arthurian Galahad. The Saracen is thus the link between two literary traditions: a stopping point between biblical history and Arthurian questing narrative. His intermediary function in this work would suggest that he is both seen as 'historical' and 'literary': historical, as his role evokes a place in the established biblical trajectory of humankind noted by numerous encyclopaedists; 'literary', since he both facilitates, and is constructed by, the development of the Vulgate literary tradition. It is in Nascien's reading of this letter that we encounter Galahad's name, evoking the later texts (previously written) in the Cycle. Given that Galahad does not supplant Perceval as the Grail knight until the Vulgate Cycle, perhaps the addition of these Saracen ancestors could even be seen as a way to legitimize his status as the most Christian of knights as much as to legitimize their position as Christian converts.

Nascien's suspension in time is also reflected in his geographical location in this episode, as he has been taken to the Turning Isle far from his homeland where he undergoes a test of faith. Geography and history do therefore come together to determine racial identity, but not in the way we might expect, since this occurs in a moment of stasis, or even of suspended animation, rather than through linear progression. The unsettling of chronological time revealed by the logical process of forming genealogy in the *Estoire* means that race cannot be thought of as temporally definite; it is not a case of characteristics (physical or otherwise) passed from father to son but in fact of a subjective system of recognition.

In the Nanteuil Cycle, processes of disguise showed how familial units are far from fixed and this fluidity has parallels in the *Estoire*. Contrary to conventional connections between genealogy and history, Griffin notes that in the *Estoire*, 'genealogy is an inscription which is structured around logical time'.[34] Through its reliance upon genealogy, race similarly becomes logical and relative: more importantly, this logical quality is very much determined through reference to descendants that are part of a broader literary tradition.

Beginnings in the Middle: Questioning Causality

Somewhat predictably, lineage patterns in the *Estoire* quickly reveal that not only are genealogies often in conflict with those in the wider Vulgate Cycle but that different elements are emphasized for specific narrative reasons at specific points,[35] leaving us with lineages that do not begin and end according to blood relations. Of particular note in this regard is Galahad, who provides a model for the clash between conventional biblical descent and techniques of *entrelacement* common to the Vulgate Cycle. Galahad's genealogy constructs race through a narrative and logical process, since his overall significance as Grail knight and connection to the *Estoire*'s protagonists exposes a lack of linear time. The nature of time as logical is most visible at the point when the question of genealogy as lineage seems to fail, and rather than being a line from ancestor to descendant, it appears instead as both predicted and predictable: determined in relation to other people and places and lacking a stable chronological basis.

After his conversion, Mordrain is taken away to an island by celestial hands to test his faith and, when his disappearance is discovered, Nascien is accused of killing him and is imprisoned. Nascien is rescued and similarly transported, though unlike Mordrain he is left on the Turning Isle. While there, a marvellous ship arrives, which prompts the narrator to describe the tree of life, the story of Cain and Abel, and the building of the boat itself by Solomon as a way of communicating with his descendants. Chronological time is therefore troubled in this episode since, as explored by Griffin, the discovery of the ship is what prompts the tale of its creation.[36] In a sense, the ancestor is consequently able to orchestrate the telling of his own tale, as he is informed that his descendant will enter the ship (*ESG*, p. 289). Though this entire section appears to be conventional in the ordering of human genealogical history, which moves from Adam and Eve in Paradise, to their children, and then to their later descendant Solomon, narrative progression here is far from linear. The ancestor (Solomon) sees a vision of the final descendant (Galahad); meanwhile, the intermediate descendant (Nascien) simultaneously prompts the narration of the final descendant's coming and the description of his own ancestry. Genealogy is thus constructed not through new forms of familial ties (as we saw in *Aye d'Avignon*) but through narrative structure and the erosion of chronologically ordered time. In this case, the narrative itself, rather than the manipulability of visible identity, renders racial identity unstable.

During this episode, when God speaks to Solomon in a vision, he explains that the Virgin will be his descendant (and ultimately Nascien's ancestor), but that the end of his lineage will be brought about by a knight who will exceed all who came before him and come after him, as well as his contemporaries (*ESG*, p. 282). A fusion of biblical and Arthurian genealogies occurs, as Galahad is clearly linked to the Virgin by this biblically-focused narrative section. The organization of time within a biblical paradigm has the further effect of placing Nascien within a Christian eschatology, so that Saracen identity becomes instead simply an isolated detour along the path to a Christian future, which has not only been inherited from Nascien's ancestors but also foretold for his descendants. Time is structured through the relation of biblical events to other events in the present, past, and future of the text. This interweaving of timeframes ultimately leaves a closed-loop universe in which there is a limited number of events or objects (such as of Solomon's ship or the vision of Celidoine's descendants) that are continually repeated and repositioned to unfold the narrative. The placement of Nascien between the exemplary figures of Galahad and the Virgin makes him part of this Christian, Arthurian race, as his identity is defined by his association with these figures more than by the conventions frequently used to identify Saracens in medieval texts. In turn, however, it is Nascien's status as a Saracen convert that leads to his stay on the Turning Isle and to his subsequent discovery of the ship of Solomon: if Nascien had not been a Saracen convert, his faith would not have needed to be tested on the ship of Solomon, an event which prompts the description of Galahad's lineage. The descriptions of the Virgin and Galahad are therefore reciprocally reliant upon Nascien's racial-religious identity, echoing the principle that 'logical time is interactive [...] characters inevitably arrive at knowledge (of self) only via others'.[37] Yet as a test of faith, Nascien's stay on the island also shows that genealogy is a matter of faith not blood, as it only becomes visible at the moment when he must affirm his Christianity.

This concept of lineage as exceeding linear, biological blood ties equally appears in the vocabulary used to describe the biblical ancestors of the Saracens in the *Estoire*. Reflecting on the difference between Eve and the Virgin, Solomon concludes that one should be referred to as 'mere' [mother] and the other as 'marastre' (*ESG*, p. 282) [stepmother]. The text does not specify which term should be used for which woman, so, at first sight, it would be tempting to see the mother as Eve, from whom all are ultimately descended, and the Virgin as a form of new mother figure in the sense that she is married to God the Father. However, the *marâtre/mère* parallel appears in other works of the period, such as in Gautier de Coinci's *Miracles*, where the idea of the stepmother is pejorative.[38] If this is the case here, then genealogical vocabulary would be reliant as much upon an identification with certain character traits as upon blood, since Mary would be considered the true 'mother' rather than the stepmother of mankind despite not being the biological ancestor. The influence of character traits upon genealogical positioning is also suggested by the message left on the hilt of the sword on the ship, which does not explicitly refer to the lineage of Galahad but to the fact that he will be the best knight (*ESG*, p. 264). Galahad's identity as descendant is therefore associated with his chivalric abilities and these abilities are themselves positioned within a narrative series of events to come so that he is 'retrospectively called into being by the space in the text he is required to fill':[39] the narrator tells us that Solomon's letter was for the knight who would perform such great feats of chivalry in Logres and beyond 'come li contes le devisera ça avant' (*ESG*, p. 288) [as the story will tell farther on].

In this manner, the tale becomes the guarantor of lineage, since, if the narrative of this knight's exploits is not related, then he will not be recognized as this foretold descendant. The reception of the text is a process of filling in the gaps to reach the pre-concluded end of this great lineage, so that it is the adventures recounted in the tale that determine who is considered part of the privileged genealogy, rather than blood connections. As we saw at the announcement of the Grail quest, race seems to be similarly determined by narrative events, given that Galahad is linked to Nascien by their roles within the Grail narrative rather than by geographical origins or any apparent specifics of appearance. In the Turning Isle episode, while Nascien prompts the narration of past events (such as the Fall from Paradise and the building of Solomon's boat), this simultaneously emphasizes his future trajectory to the reader (if not yet to Nascien himself) as connected to Britain and the Arthurian realm. Consequently, Nascien's genealogical identity is produced by a kind of 'thinking on the spot', a period of comprehension where, in this case, both the reader and Nascien move backwards and forwards 'without progressing to a reasonable solution';[40] this period is produced during the reading of Solomon's letter, which connects Nascien to past and future others. Such narrative hesitation is underscored by the fact that after setting sail in the ship, Nascien's disbelief quickly causes the ship around him to disappear. Deposited in the sea, he is carried back to the island, so that his inability to journey onwards echoes how incredulity has similarly hindered his access to genealogical knowledge.[41] Once more this would seem to be evidence of the connectedness of genealogy and faith (rather than blood-based race), as it is only later, when he has followed God's instructions and is once more in the ship of Solomon, that Nascien can learn of his descendants (*ESG*, pp. 402–04). Although Solomon does not state that Nascien will find the boat, as readers we know from the announcement of the Grail quest that Nascien will be the ancestor of the perfect knight (*ESG*, p. 168). After reading the episode with Solomon's ship we know by extension that Nascien must also be related to Solomon, since the perfect knight is also the latter's descendant (*ESG*, p. 282). In this respect, Nascien's lineage is not revealed chronologically through reference to his forebears, but logically in a process where Galahad as descendant is both created and anticipated by the position of this text as a prequel-yet-sequel in the Vulgate Cycle.

Since Nascien is both in the middle of a biological line and at the start of a new literary and spiritual race, I suggest that the lineage constructed in the *Estoire* can be regarded as a 'Grail race', where genealogical ties are formed less by blood or geographical origin than by relationship to the Grail in a performative network of repetitions and recognitions. This concept of race would mean that, in the *Estoire*, race cannot be reduced to religious difference and this can clearly be seen, for instance, in the episode where Nascien departs for Britain to rejoin his son Celidoine. Expressing a wish to die in the land where his 'semence' will multiply, Nascien hears a voice telling him to leave, so he thanks God for sending him 'aprés Celydoine por puepler la terre et le païs qui estoit repleni des mescreanz' (*ESG*, p. 393) [after Celidoine to populate the land that was full of unbelievers]. It seems that the purpose of his removal to Britain is both to fulfil his wish to find his son and to populate the land: the emphasis is upon the repopulation of Britain rather than upon religious crusade, even if conversions do also occur.[42] A notion of genealogy defined through blood is therefore present in the *Estoire*, yet it seems to be used in support of the religious lineage being created.

Further support for the idea that race (as lineage) cannot be equated to religious difference is provided in the episode where Nabor, one of Nascien's knights, tries to persuade Nascien to return to his kingdom rather than leave for Britain. Nabor is presented as corrupt even though he, like all of Nascien's people, is Christian: he lied to Nascien about his lineage by claiming to be the son of a king, when in fact 'non ert, ainz ot esté filz d'un vilein chiens de male estrace et de mal grein' (*ESG*, p. 394) [he was not; rather, he was the son of a vile peasant, descended from a bad line and bad seed]. His poor heritage apparently condemns him to being 'felon' [evil], an impression reinforced by the comment that he is 'estraiz de lingniee malvese' (*ESG*, p. 396) [descended from an evil lineage]. Religious belief is therefore not the sole guarantor of worthiness, as heritage can still have an influence. The problem is not that Nabor is (or was) a Saracen, or that he has abandoned his new faith, but that his line was bad, which admits the idea that behaviour may be transmitted through one's bloodline. Yet Nabor's poor lineage also serves to demonstrate God's omnipotence, as he is miraculously struck down when he tries to prevent Nascien from leaving: a fate that soon after befalls another knight Karrabel, who, we are told, killed his father in order to inherit his lands. Although Karrabel claims that there is no worse crime than a crime against one's lord, God would not seem to agree, as a voice explicitly says that his crime is worse and that the punishment will be eternally remembered (*ESG*, p. 398). Both Nabor and Karrabel are punished for crimes against, or resulting from, genealogy, so that although, as Stahuljak notes, 'seminal procreation is thus rejected in favor of spiritual paternity',[43] in this case blood-related crimes have the power to incite spiritual retribution. In this respect, flesh and blood genealogies are not necessarily rejected but rather produced by faith. Stahuljak regards the aim to establish 'procreation as paternity' as a key motivating force in romance,[44] yet in the *Estoire*, there is in fact a levelling of these two concepts: procreation and paternity (in the spiritual sense as set out by Stahuljak) become synonymous, so that crimes related to blood genealogy are treated as crimes against God the Holy Father. Bloodlines have clearly not been forgotten in the *Estoire* even if the Grail race seems to prioritize lineage as literary and spiritual.

Prediction, Genealogy, and Inheritance

If bloodlines may be non-linear and retrospectively constructed in the *Estoire*, prophecy may also play a role as a guarantor of 'logical' genealogy. Saracens were often situated as part of a divine ordering of geographical and historical knowledge, which meant by extension that they were set in relation to a biblical chronology as well as biblical genealogy. This may partly have been, as Tolan notes, a means to explain their contemporary military successes within a longer-term Christian perspective, which would ultimately culminate in the resurrection and rapture of the faithful.[45] To a certain extent, terrestrial time ceases to have meaning when the status of the soul is the guarantor of an eternal location among the chosen and the notion of prophecy comes to the fore. The misinterpretation of prophecy and of prophetic skills was also one of the charges laid against the followers of Muhammad by their Christian opponents.[46] In such adversarial contexts prophecy can be used as much to denigrate opponents as to glorify one's own cause: Rodulfus Glaber for instance, writing between the mid-tenth and mid-eleventh centuries, underscores that the Saracens misinterpret the Old Testament so that all prophecies are realized in Muhammad, which leads to their erroneous creation of a genealogy for him similar to that of Christ.[47] Of course, Muhammad himself was portrayed as the false prophet *par excellence* for medieval Christians,[48] so that his entire being is often defined by false predictions. But such criticism is not just limited to the matter of false futures: the Saracens also stand accused in the works of many medieval thinkers of confusing their own genealogical roots, as can be seen in the *Chronica Prophetica* mentioned previously. In this sense, Saracens seem to be suspended between, on the one hand, genealogy as history and, on the other, genealogy as descent and prophecy, which plays out in the *Estoire* through the retrospective causality that is so central to its narrative technique.

Just as genealogy is figured through projected descent as much as through ancestry in the *Estoire*, so the question of future inheritance is as important as past provenance for the Saracens. However, whereas Carol Chase asserts that overall, 'the goal is to wipe out the infidel and to purify the land for Christian occupation',[49] the dual purpose of the move to Britain enacted by Josephus and the Saracen converts is arguably the rediscovery of a lost heritage and the fulfilment of a prophecy: the Saracens in Britain seem simply to be converted along the way. This lack of crusading zeal where the Grail is concerned is observed by Jon Whitman, who sees Galahad's Grail quest as 'a rapturous individual achievement' rather than a communal crusade.[50] The status of Britain as the realm of a lost heritage is also clear in the numerous comments linking the fertilization and cultivation of land with lineage and inheritance. For instance, Josephus is told by God that the land of Britain is promised to his companions for the express purpose of repopulation: 'Et saches que ceste terre ou tu iés venuz est la terre qui est pramise a ton lignage por escroistre et monteploier le païs de gent plus convenable a Damledeu qu'il n'i a' (*ESG*, p. 418) [and you can be sure, truly, that this land where you have come is promised to your descendants, who are to increase and to fill the country with people more fitting than those who are there now]. The destiny of the Saracens to inhabit Britain guarantees them a future genealogy, yet genealogy is also the motivation for this land being promised to the group. Genealogy and geography thus function logically, as their interaction creates a moment of suspense between ancestry and descent, which connects the figures of the *Estoire* with those who inhabit the Arthurian Britain of the future.

Despite the importance of genealogy, the geographical future of the Saracens is also very much tied to their religious conversion, and the Saracen ruler Evalach provides a good example of this mechanism. Recalling Nascien's knowledge of lineage, it is only once Evalach has converted and become Mordrain that he is granted the vision of his nephew Celidoine and the lineage that will stem from him, so that his rebirth as Christian occasions his vision of future generations. In the vision, a large lake springs from Celidoine's stomach and nine rivers come from this, representing the descendants that will be born from him (*ESG*, pp. 176–77); this is the descent that culminates in Galahad. Mordrain's vision therefore situates lineage within the context of geography and spirituality simultaneously, since, although water is key to most of the travelling in the text, Mordrain also sees a man (who he later discovers is Christ) bathe in this river in recognition of Galahad's supreme goodness, in a scene reminiscent of baptism. In this respect, the concept of prophesized inheritance goes hand in hand with the creation of a spiritual genealogy: a new form of lineage uniting bloodlines, perception of place, and divine predestination.

Both time and geography in the *Estoire* would seem to be subjective concepts experienced through processes of prediction, revelation, and fulfilment. As A. J. Gurevich notes, 'man is not born with a "sense of time"; both his temporal and spatial concepts are invariably conferred upon him by the culture to which he belongs'.[51] The *Estoire* makes the time experienced by the Saracens part of a timeframe where the end of their narrative is also the beginning of another, a timeframe which brings with it a need for characters to discover their destiny. The Saracen in this work is not a figure who must be colonized, converted, or crusaded against, but one who is mistaken, misplaced, and consequently repositionable. In many ways, the flexibility of the spatially and temporally determined identity of the Saracen — his prophesized identity — is a reflection of the broader status of paternity and genealogy in this Arthurian romance. The roles of genitor and father are, as Stahuljak shows, separated in the Arthurian tradition so that fatherhood requires a process of recognition between father and son, which is figured linguistically.[52] Such a division between procreation as physical engenderment and fatherhood as the bestowal of a kind of legitimacy can be seen in the *Estoire* in the differing way in which Nascien and Mordrain experience visions of genealogical structures.

These two Saracens both experience revelations of the same lineage, albeit in different forms, despite not being related to one another by blood (Nascien is Mordrain's brother-in-law). Nascien occupies the role of genitor, being significant as the biological father of Celidoine and also as the ancestor of Galahad; fittingly, Nascien's vision of his future lineage takes the form of nine men (although one of whom, Lancelot, is shown in the form of a dog for his sinfulness) (*ESG*, pp. 402–03). After seeing the men walk before him, Nascien then reads a letter detailing their names and qualities and, upon awakening, finds this very letter in his hands. Mordrain, on the other hand, sees the metaphorical vision mentioned above revolving around Celidoine — his nephew by marriage (*ESG*, pp. 176–77). Mordrain's long-suffering wait for Galahad in the narrative of the *Queste* associates him with Stahuljak's notion of the father, as he recognizes Galahad's genealogical identity as the great knight who is ninth in Nascien's lineage: a recognition that bestows a certain narrative legitimacy.[53] Nascien, in contrast, is biologically connected to Galahad and, although he learns about him (and indeed is the first to discover Galahad's name) Nascien does not have the opportunity to meet him. As Stahuljak observes, genealogy here is thus about more than procreation.[54] Galahad's genealogical identity is not confirmed by someone in his bloodline but is still recognized by a father figure; yet this father figure is in fact reciprocally produced by his descendant, in the manner of Solomon who sees that his letter is received by Galahad before he actually sends it.[55]

Significantly, it is Mordrain's conversion that allows him to assume the role of father in this way, as he undergoes a process of spiritual engendering. While Stahuljak rightly reminds us that spiritual engendering is presented as beyond blood and seminal procreation, she also suggests that 'spiritual paternity signifies the moment of the recognition of the son(s) by the father'.[56] However, where Mordrain is concerned, conversion represents the moment in which the son recognizes God the Father as part of a process which establishes spiritual paternity. Moreover, conversion in this case equally involves the revelation of Mordrain's own blood connections: the revelation (or rather reminder) of his carnal, biological engendering. It is the construction of Mordrain's role as 'father' to Galahad that presents his genealogy as part of a logical process rather than a chronological sequence. Mordrain learns about the genitor through the father and vice versa: Josephus reveals God's knowledge or recognition of Mordrain, then reveals Mordrain's genitor, and Mordrain then subsequently recognizes God. This process is aptly contained in Moira Gatens's assessment that remembering is crucial for the construction of history since: 'we need to understand and remember how we became what we are, not in order to live what we have become as our 'truth' but rather as our conditions of possibility for that which we may become'.[57] For Mordrain, as with Nascien, procreation is not rejected in favour of spiritual paternity but rather created by it, which is also in keeping with the idea that faith can determine blood genealogy; this is an idea frequently expressed in the relationship between Muhammad, as the Saracen religious leader, and the Saracen people more generally. Asserting conventions of religious enlightenment, such as the revelation of God's omniscience, ensures that race is not repeated physically but spiritually. Similarly, although the Saracen is still part of what can be deemed to be a 'race', conventions of lineage as both blood-based (in the sense of biological) and bloodless are reworked in order to create alternative fathers and thus alternative genealogies. While for Ganor in *Aye d'Avignon* successful fatherhood — in particular, procreative ability — confirmed racial identity, in the *Estoire* it is faith in God the Father that produces lineage and to a certain extent trumps race, showing Mordrain to be far more Christian that Saracen.

Even so, it is not just that material or procreative bonds are translated into the spiritual in the visions given to the Saracens, but that geographical reality is also figured in relation to spiritual destiny, creating a retrospective genealogy for the Saracen people which simultaneously dictates their future location. For instance, if we return to the *Genealogia Sarracenorum* within the *Chronica Prophetica*, the author attributes the coming into Spain of the Saracens as fulfilling a prophecy made by the Prophet Ezekiel that Ishmael would 'enter the land of Gog' then kill Gog with his sword and make the people his slaves. Yet the Prophet also told Ishmael: 'Because you forsook your Lord God, I will forsake you and surrender you to the hand of Gog and you and all your people will fall victim to his sword. After you have afflicted them for 170 years, he will give retribution to you as you gave to him'.[58] There is an end in sight to the Saracen presence in Spain, so the author of this ninth-century work believes, as there has been a prophecy to this effect. Consequently, in the *Chronica Prophetica*, geographical location is explained in relation to a spiritually determined temporality. In the *Estoire*, however, the future destiny of Britain is guaranteed by retroactive rather than forward-looking narrative processes. The author of the *Chronica Prophetica* optimistically rationalizes the past and present of Spain in relation to a *desired* future; conversely, by situating the Saracen future in Britain, which is neither conventionally Saracen in the Arthurian tradition nor indeed in the real-time of composition, Saracen genealogy in the *Estoire* is logically limited by a *known* future. This is therefore an example of the narrative future perfect, which, as Griffin puts it, is 'the state of becoming what one always-already was'.[59] Britain is always-already a non-Saracen realm, so the associated prophecies are not merely hints at a possible future but are foregone conclusions, which then ensure that genealogy is appropriately deduced.

The co-dependence of time and space found in the *Estoire* is far from limited to the realm of literary representation in the twelfth and thirteenth centuries. As Whitman succinctly comments, there was 'a conspicuously elusive Holy Land' in this period, provoking what he terms a 'spiritual slippage' where 'medieval Christians tended to conflate time and space in the Crusader milieu with the temporal and spatial dimensions of the Hebrew Bible'.[60] One of the most significant attitudes circulating at this time with regard to space and inheritance concerns the question of a lost inheritance situated in the Holy Land. Given the fact that the late twelfth to thirteenth centuries had seen the crusader defeat at Hattin (1187), the loss of Jerusalem to Saladin, and the controversial Fourth Crusade leading to the sacking of Constantinople in 1204, it is unsurprising that anxieties surrounding the status of the Holy Land thoroughly permeate religious discourse. As evidence of this widespread anxiety, Whitman cites examples of penitential measures that were imposed by the Church in the hope of rectifying crusader losses, such as the insertion into the daily mass (Psalm 78 [Vulgate 79]) of a lament to God that 'gentes' have come into 'haereditatem tuam' [thy inheritance] and 'polluerunt templum sanctum tuum; posuerunt Jerusalem in pomorum custodiam' [have defiled your holy temple and laid Jerusalem on heaps].[61] Consequently, the loss of the holy city was not simply a defeat, but usurpation: a loss of what belonged to the Christians. In contrast, the slippage between past and present in the *Estoire* prevents a direct equation of Britain with Jerusalem, since there is no consistent geographical point of origin or destination that characterizes the movements in this text compared to the consistent spiritual currency of Jerusalem. In this respect, Britain is not marked by the melancholia that surrounds Jerusalem during this period, since it is not just a promised land but is always-already won.

Genealogy and Geographical Provenance

Alongside genealogies that are determined both physically (through flesh and blood) and temporally (through narrative structure and predictions) in relation to the Saracen, questions of geography are also associated with notions of the Saracens as a race. If ancestry in the Vulgate Cycle is a process of deduction that occurs in a hiatus between a universalizing biblical history and the literary formation of a

Grail race, the representation of geography potentially contributes to and conflicts with this process. Nascien's experience of the Turning Isle has already revealed that geographical location can suspend the Saracen between chartable territories and reflect the pausing of chronological narrative progression. However, the *Estoire*'s spaces also challenge causal links between geography and race.

Medieval understandings of the history of humankind illuminate both Saracen origins and how Saracens may themselves act as origins in the *Estoire*, especially since, biblically speaking, geographical provenance was determined by genealogical descent. John Tolan reminds us that in the Middle Ages 'to study the universe was to study God's reason. History, too, had a rational, divinely ordained structure'. Referring to Isidore of Seville's *Etymologies*, he comments that the overall drive was 'to offer an organized, coherent summary of human knowledge'.[62] This categorizing tendency is also discussed by Akbari, who, placing prose works alongside cartographic practices, observes a will 'to divide, hierarchize, and order the various parts of the world', which goes hand in hand with the allocation of the sons of Noah to the three continents of Asia, Africa, and Europe.[63] Most commonly, Ham is linked with Africa and so with southern heat, Japheth is associated with the north, or Europe, and Shem is identified with the east. However, these territorial allocations and the resulting genealogies of each brother have been shown to shift according to the writer's own frame of reference as well as the time in which he writes.[64] This would be a prime example of genealogy as logically rather than chronologically determined: lineage here is a deductive process rather than a fixed trajectory. Tolan sees Isidore's use of the genealogies of Genesis as reflecting his desire to show that 'the confusing diversity of humanity was rationally explicable and could (at least in theory), be traced to a unified origin, to a human ancestor, Noah';[65] yet we should not assume that Isidore's paradigm provided a stable model for all subsequent medieval writers. To note but one example, Braude discusses the errors and alterations made to biblical chronology and genealogies in the fourteenth-century *Travels* of Sir John Mandeville, so that, for instance, Ham becomes associated with Asia as the ancestor of the Khan and Mongols.[66] Writers were inevitably limited by the sources available to them for consultation, but it would be reductive to ignore the potential for subjective interpretation of conventional biblical, climatic, and geographical associations to promote the writer's own homeland. Even if for Isidore, 'human geography is a consequence of human history',[67] for many writers human history seems to have been shaped by a geography that was relative, rather than being cartographically or genealogically fixed. What is nonetheless clear is that race as lineage was continuously associated with place: birth was frequently said to determine which of Noah's sons gained which continent, while climate and geography could dictate the qualities of the peoples found in different regions.[68]

In the context of the *Estoire*, the inability to establish a fixed geography has implications for the depiction of genealogy, echoing the way in which narrative time may reverse and reorder lines of descent in this work. While this text does indeed involve interaction between a vague east and west, these should not be assumed to be 'the East' and 'the West' of an essentialized orientalizing or crusading world-view. The *Estoire* is a text of confusing yet often precise geographical detail. While numerous characters are removed to unknown lands with the narrator giving only their travel time as a point of reference,[69] specific directions and cities are also mentioned: the city of Sarras, for instance, is situated 'entre Babilone et Salamandre' (*ESG*, p. 42) [between Babylon and Salamander]; King Label hails from the 'roiaume de Persse' (*ESG*, p. 300) [kingdom of Persia]; and the Rock of the Perilous Port is 'en la mer Occeane' [in the ocean] on the route from 'la terre de Babiloine en la terre d'Escoche et d'Islande et es autres parties d'occident' (*ESG*, p. 187) [Babylon to Scotland, Ireland and other western parts]. For Szkilnik, the geography of the *Estoire* is an archipelago: 'traversée par de multiples bateaux, agitée par des tempêtes, l'*Estoire* est le récit de voyages en mer, d'île en île, de terre inconnue en terre inconnue' [crossed by numerous boats, shaken by storms, the *Estoire* is the tale of sea voyages, from island to island and from unknown land to unknown land].[70] However, since the text is also marked by crossings that defy linear structure, despite the drive to create a coherent universe, the representation of space leaves 'un monde mouvant, à la géographie incertaine' [an unstable world with an uncertain geography].[71] Ultimately Britain is the geographical west of the narrative, but when placed in the context of genealogy, it is clear that east and west determine one another. Furthermore, even the spiritual significance of the east is unstable in this work, as while characters pray to the east, their divine calling is to move westwards.

The lack of fixity regarding spiritual locations is also apparent in the characters' own perceptions of space. When stranded on the Rock of the Perilous Port, Mordrain is tested by the visits first of a good man, then of a devil in the form of a woman. When the woman returns a second time, Mordrain 'se tourna vers orient et enclina chele part de mout bon cuer en l'oneur de la glorieurse cité de Jherusalem' (*ESG*, p. 215) [turned toward the east and knelt in this direction with heartfelt emotion, in the name of the glorious city of Jerusalem]. The east is here associated with Jerusalem, and thus with Christ, providing comfort to Mordrain in his hour of need. Faith is figured geographically — though there is some confusion in this episode: the cardinal direction of the 'galerne' [the north-west wind] is described initially as being 'a destre' (*ESG*, p. 187) [to the right] yet Mordrain subsequently sees the lady's ship arrive 'a senestre partie, devers galerne' (*ESG*, p. 201) [to his left, toward Galerne]. Since we are not on the Turning Isle here (and as far as the 'galerne' can be assumed to hail from one recognizable direction) it would seem that what is more important is to designate locations in relation to Mordrain himself, rather than to any kind of empirical geography. Geographical detail does not therefore provide static locations but instead reveals the subjective conception of space in relation to others and in relation to symbolic conventions. In this respect, Szkilnik's division between an Orient 'non seulement associé au luxe et à la richesse mais aussi au diabolique' [not only associated with luxury and riches but also with the demonic] compared to an Occident that is 'le lieu du divin' [the place of the divine] is perhaps a little too binary given the attitudes revealed in the text and the complicating factors of genealogy and temporality.[72]

There is nevertheless a sense in the *Estoire* that movement, as well as geography can have a purifying influence over the converted Saracens, and this is not just because islands provide an arena in which to test the faith of the new converts. For example, a hermit tells Nascien that ships carry people across the sea like the Church carries man throughout the world:

> En la nef doiz tu entendre Seinte Yglise; en la mer le monde [...] Sainte yglise fait son buen serjant, son buen ministre, aparoir par desus toz pecheors net et espurgié de totes vilenies, ausi come li ors recuiz par set foiees apert a estre esmerez desus toz autres metauz et autresi come li soleuz apert en resplendissor par desus totes les estoiles. (*ESG*, pp. 295–96)

> [By the ship you should understand the Holy Church, and by the sea, the world [...] Holy Church makes her good servant, her good minister, rise above all sins, clean and purged of all baseness, just as gold that is refined seven times emerges pure above all other metals, and just as the sun appears in splendor above all the stars.]

The ship is not simply a symbol of the Church here: the travels undertaken by the Saracens with the aid of this vessel reflect a process of purification and ultimately a refinement of their beliefs, a process evident in the use of the metallurgic metaphor. Given that Christ appeared to Solomon and told him that the ship represented the house of God (*ESG*, p. 289), ships could also represent the process of conversion. In addition, as Szkilnik notes, 'la nef est ainsi le lieu d'un complexe jeu d'échos. C'est en elle que se dévoilent les secrets du passé et de l'avenir' [the ship is thus the location for a complex play of echoes. It is there that the secrets of the past and the future are revealed].[73] The fact that Nascien learns of his descendants while in this boat therefore links his genealogical role to spiritual conversion, as he drifts between realms, between times, and between religions.

Perhaps the clearest example of the instability of geographical identities can be seen in Evalach/Mordrain, King of Sarras. Initially, as previously noted, this character is referred to by all as 'Evalach li Mesconneüs' (Evalach the Unknown) since 'nus hom de toute sa terre ne savoit de quel terre il estoit nes, ne de quel lieu il estoit venus ne onques par nului n'en avoient oï enseignes en la terre' (*ESG*, p. 44) [no man knew in what country he was born, nor where he came from, or had they ever had news from anyone who had seen or heard of him in the land].[74] It is not that he does not know his *name*, as so often happens in romance, but that no-one knows where he was born or came from, or indeed knows anything of him. It is his geographically determined identity that is missing, and with it his apparent familial descent. This is rectified by Josephus, who reveals the king's origins to him before he battles the Egyptian Tholomer. In Evalach's case, genealogy is therefore a process that may be constructed retroactively and which, as we have seen, exposes the omnipotence of the Christian God who knows all things and all secrets (*ESG*, p. 100). Evalach's name as the indicator of his inherited identity is a reflection of his inability to recognize the true God: his lack of recognition of his spiritual father has led him to forget both his genitor and his place of birth. Josephus even evokes Evalach's epithet directly when he uses the same word — 'mescounoist' — to criticize his failure to recognize God (*ESG*, p. 92). However, although Bloch observes that 'in Arthurian literature the proper name is synonymous with — a kind of map of — lineage',[75] the narrative restaging of Evalach's lineage by Josephus does not result in his change of name. In Evalach's case, it is his conversion to Christianity rather than his bloodline that is mapped by his proper name, underlined by the fact that his new name, Mordrain, is described as a Chaldean word meaning 'tardieus en creanche' (*ESG*, p. 155) [late to believe]. No similar explanation appears for Nascien, and whereas his identity was determined by his temporal positions between Solomon and Galahad, Mordrain's is primarily figured through his name. Yet this name also epitomizes the process of religious enlightenment and his rebirth as part of the Christian community, emphasized by Mordrain's metaphorical rather than physical connection to Galahad. While self-discovery and spiritual enlightenment is hardly an unusual pairing, the addition of Evalach's unknown geographical origins adds a different dimension, evoking associations of the terrestrial categorization of peoples and by extension of what we might term 'race'. However, since this race is performatively constructed through the demonstration of divine knowledge, it seems more appropriate to speak of a concept of 'religion as race' in this case, that encompasses but does not equate racial identity and geographical provenance.

Genealogy is also shown to be understood through a logical process of religious experience by the fact that the revelation of Evalach's identity only occurs after a lengthy attempt by Joseph (Joseph of Arimathea, Josephus's father) to explain the Immaculate Conception and the mystery of the Trinity to the Saracen. Emphasizing that God has neither beginning nor end, Joseph explains how Jesus could have been conceived through the idea of 'esperitel engenrure' [spiritual engendering]:

> Ichil Diex, si est apielés Peres, pour chou ke chil de qui je te parole est ses Fiex, car il l'engenra des devant le commenchement de tous les aages; et si ne l'engenra mie carnelment, mais esperituelment. Ne li Peres ne fu onques fais ne criés ne engenrés ne onques ne nascui; ne li Fiex meïsmes ne fu onques ne fais ne criés, mais il fu engenrés, si com vos avés oï ke j'ai dit, de l'esperitel engenrure. (*ESG*, p. 52)

> [This God is called Father because the One I am telling you about is His Son, for He engendered Him before the beginning of all time; He did not engender Him carnally, but spiritually. The Father was never made or created or engendered, nor was He ever born. Nor was the Son ever made or created but He was engendered, as you have heard and I have told you, by spiritual means.]

Although Saracens in literature often question the Immaculate Conception, when combined with the emphasis on origins and inherited identity through the figure of Evalach, the notion of a spiritual lineage is particularly *à propos*. Evalach is spiritually reborn once his identity is uncovered, not least because it transpires that he actually hails from France and not from the east at all. Born in 'Miaus' [Meaux] to a poor cobbler, he was sent as part of a tribute to Rome. His appearance led people to believe he was 'de plus haut lignaige' (*ESG*, p. 99) [of nobler lineage] and he was placed in the service of the Count of Syria before earning his lands from his overlord Tholomer. As he closes this revelation, Josephus says that God wished to remind Evalach that he has come from nothing to something (*ESG*, p. 100) and this reminder serves to underscore the link between religious enlightenment and the origins of identity, which are concomitantly reconstructed as part of this experience. Significantly, Evalach does not attempt to apply reason or proof to achieve an understanding of the Christian God in this episode, which could be problematic because it suggests that faith itself is performative; instead he learns of Christ's origins along with his own. Just as the ship of Solomon is received in the narrative by Nascien (and Galahad) before its sending is detailed, so Mordrain is reminded of what he is in order to then become, through conversion, what he already was though birth: a western Christian. As a result, there is a much greater emphasis placed upon the process of finding faith than upon the moment of baptism, which is achieved rather rapidly (*ESG*, p. 155). If, as Griffin notes, the content of Solomon's letter to Galahad is not as important as the fact that 'Solomon knew that Galahad would receive the message',[76] for Evalach geographical and hierarchical origins are important only insofar as they are a yardstick to demonstrate the power of God. Even where faith is concerned, it is the process of coming to believe rather than the state of being a believer that is prioritized in this work and the body as the site of procreation and descent is similarly treated as part of this process rather than as an end in itself.

Following the explanation of his provenance, Evalach's identity continues to be evoked in the topography of his realm. His battle with Tholomer occurs at a castle, 'Evalachin', which is both beautiful and impenetrable (*ESG*, p. 103); we are told that Evalach chose the site because of its strategic potential and that he wanted 'tout chil qui jamais le noumeroient i ramenteüssent le non de lui en ramembranche de che qu'il l'avoit fait' (*ESG*, p. 104) [all those who would use its name to remember his name and what he had done]. Just as Evalach's identity is inscribed into the land around him, it is now assaulted in a parallel of Tholomer's assault upon his castle. Since it takes an ethereal white knight to come and assist Evalach before the battle is won, the protection of Evalachin the place runs parallel to the salvation of Evalach the person, who must similarly reclaim his spiritually destined British lands as part of his conversion. At this moment, the militaristic aspect of Evalach's identity is conveyed through the association of his name with the castle; as a result, although his geographical inheritance is reliant upon divine intervention, the connection of name and castle echoes the earlier comment made by Josephus that what he has gained on earth is not eternal and has been granted by God. While Evalach may have tried to fuse his name with his geographical surroundings, and while his name may bear witness to the need to connect lineage and geography, the *Estoire* also reveals this link to be dependent upon personal, religious experience and limited by divine predestination. The relationship with God is the ultimate determiner of land and lineage, which are merely constructed in the process.

Finally, naming is significant for Evalach when he is tested by being stranded on the Rock of the Perilous Port after his conversion and adoption of the new name Mordrain (*ESG*, p. 155; p. 186). During this episode, the correct or incorrect naming of the King once again shows his racial-religious identity to be logically ascertained.

Just as the narrator claims that the Saracens were called such because Sarras was the city where their faith emerged (*ESG*, p. 42) so the bestowing of Evalach's name is used to signify a specific religious identity. While on the rock, Evalach has gone from having an unknown lineage to being in an unknown place, to a state where he knows nothing for certain, not even if he is awake or asleep (*ESG*, p. 200). The change of geography does not simply take him away from others, but removes him from subjective consciousness. During this time, a silver ship and a black ship come to him. The first is the silver, which brings with it a handsome man called 'Tout en Tout' (*ESG*, p. 198) [All-in-All] who encourages him to stay true to his faith; the second is the black ship, which brings a very beautiful woman who tries to get him to leave the rock with her. When Tout en Tout asks Mordrain who he is, Mordrain replies simply that he is a Christian (*ESG*, p. 198). The woman however, as soon as she steps from the ship, addresses him as 'Rois Evalach' (*ESG*, p. 201) [King Evalach], clearly repeating his pre-baptismal appellation. This repetition reminds us that race is a question of perspective.[77] Evalach's identity as a Saracen is performatively produced in this moment of interpellation by another: the moment he is hailed, when his status as Christian or Saracen hangs upon whether or not he recognizes himself as such. In addition, Evalach's baptismal name is crucial to rendering lineage spiritual; in this liminal space, the name is not a way of repeating physical bloodlines, or of mapping out genealogical conventions, but provides an opportunity for the Saracen to confirm his new beliefs. Spiritual lineage is thus relative rather than fixed, as it is dependent upon either confirming or denying one's identity. The intersubjective nature of race and identity in the *Estoire* is also emphasized in this episode by the role of the ships which, alongside their importance as the sites of spiritual experiences, are also used to connect people rather than places, bringing figures of salvation and temptation to Mordrain. This once again undermines any attempt to fix racial or spiritual identity in geographical locations, since the continuity of experience provided by ship motifs in the *Estoire* and in the Cycle more broadly seems to have replaced the inheritance of material lands.[78] Not only are similar crossings made by ancestors and descendants between the *Queste* and the *Estoire* but, as seen in the case of Nascien, who sets off in the ship of Solomon to find Celidoine, transitory maritime experiences both maintain and produce genealogical ties.

Conclusion

Although, as Chase notes, the Saracen ruler Evalach could be regarded as the spiritual ancestor of Celidoine and thus of Galahad,[79] Evalach's identity lacks a definite chronology, thereby dissociating genealogy from linear time. The result is that genealogy does not progress from ancestor to descendant, but instead continuously repeats, a repetition that recites features and recasts events that were already present in the narrative, while also bringing about what has been prophesized. Genealogy is consequently an effect of narrative, of repetition, not a guarantee of origins; it does not fix the Saracen into a blood-based lineage structure but rather can be constructed through experiential processes. Just as Gatens has questioned the stability assigned to 'women' as a category of historical study,[80] so the stability of 'Saracen' as a category within a chronological line of descent is shown to be entirely flexible in the *Estoire*, above all because there is no consistent line. Even if medieval thinkers often tried to place the Saracen in a biblically determined and predictable sequence of history, this text suggests that the acceptance or at least use of these theories was not blanket and that the label 'Saracen' may in fact obscure inherited identity in this particular case. Seen here through the notion of bloodlines, taking the body as paramount for Saracen identity is just as problematic as our own modern tendency to seek physical determiners for racial ancestry.[81] If the body itself was seen to be manipulable, in the *Estoire* the determination of identity shifts to emphasize other factors. The Saracens in the *Estoire* give the impression that faith is more important than either geographical origins or genealogy, so that although there is a form of inheritance at work, this is less a matter of procreation than of spirituality. This suggests that without faith, genealogy would in fact be meaningless; the importance of faith in the establishment of lineage encourages us to question the extent to which either religious or racial identity might be viewed as bodily bound. Indeed, faith and its relationship to the body relates both to matters of conversion and the rhetorical construction of communities.

Stahuljak argues that relations between fathers and sons in Arthurian literature are based upon the sharing of non-physical characteristics such as 'linguistic alliance' rather than upon blood ties.[82] The presentation of history and geography in the *Estoire* reveals that race — as genealogy — is similarly untethered from blood inheritance. As Griffin suggests, the branches of lineage in the Vulgate eventually come together in the form of Galahad, who then becomes 'the culmination and convergence' of three different lines.[83] This merging of corporeal, geographic, and spiritual origins is similarly applicable to the identity of the medieval Saracen. Akbari notes in other contexts that while 'geographical location determines the nature of bodily diversity [...] Spiritual orientation [...] was similarly articulated in terms of place and location'.[84] Yet in the *Estoire*, both body and spirit seem less determined by fixed loci than by the temporal processes that structure the narrative. Consequently, faith, biology, and geography in the *Estoire* are not divided between essentialist notions of religion, on the one hand, and race on the other, but rather seem to converge within Saracen identity and concepts of origins, with conversion enacting a kind of second birth and engendering new lineage structures. The use of the term 'Saracen' may well distinguish between Christian and non-Christian people. However, by evoking conventions of identity that are not borne out by the revelations and reiterations of identity in the text, the term is also performative, demonstrating the confusion and coexistence of ideas of genealogy, geography, and belief. Since there can be no clear linear history in the *Estoire*, genealogy as a record of history — a temporalization, as it were, of blood — becomes detached from the notion of race as bestowed and inherited by biology; faith instead seems to determine the presentation of genealogical connections. Since faith is both eternal and atemporal, it is not a way to pigeonhole the Saracen but is actually the roadmap to his place within Arthurian literary tradition, with the Grail providing the canvas upon which to draw this cartography of becomings rather than origins.

The sacredness that characterizes the writing of the Grail legend, which is established by the narrator in the description of the book given to him by God, proposes a lineage of transmission for the narrative itself from celestial book, to narrator, to his copy (our narrative), and ultimately to the reader. However, just as Galahad's status as perfect descendant is retrospectively used to determine his ancestors, the existing Vulgate narratives have determined the writing of the *Estoire*. Even if, as Stahuljak notes, 'literature is a bastard covering its own fatherless origin',[85] the *Estoire*'s lineage is both spiritual and material, like its represented heroes, as it is both reliant upon a book gifted from God and upon the temporal and thematic threads that course like blood through the Cycle more broadly. The evocations of the Arthurian heroes that occur through the depiction of their ancestors thus leave us with literary repetitions disguised as origins and construct the Saracen backwards, looking from a point where he is Christian back to his plural beginnings. Nascien, as we have seen, is both the physical starting point of the Grail lineage and also mediates in the narrative between the biblical heritage of Solomon and the Arthurian future embodied in Galahad; Mordrain's process of uncovering both his own genealogy and that of his spiritual descendants suggests an alternative way to view legitimacy and exposes the problems of using geography, belief, and ancestry to determine racial difference. From this perspective, Saracen identity only becomes visible in this text from a point where it has been transformed into Christian identity. Presented as realizing their 'mistake' and fulfilling their destinies, these Saracens epitomize Christian fantasies of conversion, yet in so doing they trouble any attempt to base racial identity upon biological inheritance.

Significantly, it is the narrative structure of the *Estoire*, its sometimes giddying *entrelacement,* that allows us to see Saracen identity differently. Instead of being physically inherited, genealogy is pieced together by the manipulation of past and present in the text, positioning the Saracen in relation to what I have described as a 'Grail race'. The appearance of the Grail brings the angel's explanation of Celidoine's precious lineage, leaves Mordrain in a suspended state awaiting Galahad's arrival, and provokes the end of this lineage through the virginal Galahad's death. This leaves a romance that differs from those discussed by Geraldine Heng, where in medieval England concepts of race emerge in such works as part of a nationalizing myth.[86] Instead, the *Estoire* is a romance that connects peoples spiritually as much as politically, where characters determine the nature of the realm rather than the other way around. Britain is not used in the *Estoire* as some form of new Holy Land to compensate for contemporary military defeats, but rather its status as 'always-already' Christian and 'always-already' crucial in the Grail legends means that the Saracen movement from east to west is a return rather than an exodus — a movement that confirms a common genealogical ancestry based upon faith.

The restructuring of time in this text fundamentally impacts upon our ability to read geography as coherent: in the *Estoire*, Britain is both a lost heritage and a destined inheritance, the space of a guaranteed future but also a place of narrative return. The use of prophecy creates a sense of the future in the present (or even in the past) and given that in the *Estoire* these prophecies centre upon genealogy, the result is a common lineage where all characters are ultimately joined by their connection to the Grail and to God. Instead of providing an origin, geography is used to confirm the instability of time, as the act of return proves an act of self-recognition on the part of the Saracens who are members of a sacred lineage. The move to Britain places the Saracen within the familiar space of the Arthurian tradition and consequently legitimizes the future of the Grail quest in the present of the *Estoire*'s narrative. Mordrain abandons his lands, including the city named after him, as do the rest of the Saracens. If, as the narrator informs us, the Saracens took their name from Sarras, the abandonment of this realm is also an abandonment of the origins of their racial identity and acceptance of their destiny. However, this is a destiny determined as much by what they *were* as what they will become, as Saracen identity is produced in moments where the narrative does not progress but recapitulates events. To the extent that identity is based on a series of repetitions and non-conventional conventions, the narrative suggests that Saracen identity is performative: Evalach is not just the Arthurian knight who cannot remember his lineage or his name, but one whose very status as Saracen is produced by this misrecognition of his racial and/or religious identity. It is the logical processes by which the narrative allows him to reconstruct his identity (through dream visions, prophecies, revelations etc.) that create a new spiritual race, reflecting the way in which, as Bloch notes, the Vulgate Cycle texts work to 'detour consistently the continuity of the story line that we have identified with genealogical continuity'.[87]

In turn, the concept of geographical return relates to the idea that racial identity may be performative. If, in relation to drag, Butler considered the illusion of an innate identity, she also briefly mentions the problematic recourse to essences in determining race and origins. In an interview published as 'On Speech, Race and Melancholia' — one of the rare instances where Butler explicitly engages with the question of race and subjectivization — she considers the possible parallels between how the melancholia of heterosexuality relates to the origins of racialization that are foreclosed in diasporic cultures (her examples being slavery or emigrations from Africa). Since, she suggests, it is not possible to return to 'any pure notion of race',[88] this causes a certain melancholia where 'there is, as it were, inscribed in "race" a lost and ungrievable origin, one might say, an impossibility of return, but also an impossibility of an essence'.[89] However, in spite of the multiple movements of characters in the *Estoire*, it does not seem that the diasporic effect Butler evokes in modern racial thinking finds a parallel in this medieval work. A diaspora relies upon the idea of an ancestral or collective space to which a group will or wishes to return. By contrast, in the *Estoire*, despite the narrative and geographical return to Britain, the logical time of this romance means that the melancholia that characterizes the modern diaspora in Butler's comments is absent, as return is not impossible, not ungrievable, but instead is guaranteed. Equally, medieval geography is such an unstable concept in itself, and the medieval understanding of the connections between geography and genealogy is such that there is no one fixed point that is either lost or reclaimed — even Jerusalem does not fulfil this function in the *Estoire*, since the subjective geography that places Britain at the heart of the Arthurian world is westward looking. Likewise, the return enacted in the *Estoire* is fundamentally a question of narrative: a return to a Grail race rather than to a race that is Frankish or British, Eastern or Western, and furthermore it is as much a relocation as a return in its temporal instability.

In summary, while this text shows traces of conventions surrounding origins or provenance, these are left unstable, as time and space are merged. Bloodlines are posited, yet lineages appear to begin *in media res*; geographical position is both troubled and guaranteed; literary ancestors may be genealogical descendants. In this sense, genealogy is not simply a matter of linear bloodlines or flesh-bound ties but is created by the Grail, by the experiences of the first and the last to see it. Given that logical time stems from the merging of past, present, and future, we can thus talk of a 'logical' race in this text that is similarly dependent upon subjective experiences that are reliant upon reciprocity. As in Lacan's example of the three prisoners' deductive process, the *Estoire* shows that the Saracen race is defined intersubjectively, rather than being a series of essential qualities or traits; conclusions are made based upon both the narrative use of retroactive genealogies and the guaranteed future provided by a geographical inheritance. Above all, these processes are enabled by the spiritual awakening undergone by the Saracens. The logical ordering of time that occurs in the *Estoire* does not just mean that 'the genealogical narrative must be reconstructed',[90] but, more importantly, that it may be constructed differently in this process; like notions of performativity, it depends upon processes of retrospective causality and so does not simply refer to a slavish conformity to convention but recognizes the power for conventions to be repeated differently. Although the Saracens therefore seem to be the 'origins' of the Christians in a genealogical sense, the Christians are also the narrative ancestors of the Saracens, since the interlaced temporalities of this work are what underwrite lineage. The text accepts the non-linear narrative chronology that engenders the Saracens at the same time as it places them at the head of a new spiritual genealogy based upon the experience of the Grail. Ultimately, this *entrelacement* creates a guaranteed racial future for the Saracens of the *Estoire* — spiritual race can be formed through a series of logical processes, produced both through hindsight and prediction: here, a Saracen is not simply determined by where he comes from, but may be retrospectively rewritten by where he is going to.

Notes to Chapter 2

1. *L'Estoire del Saint Graal*, ed. by Jean-Paul Ponceau, Les Classiques français du Moyen Âge, 120–21, 2 vols (Paris: Champion, 1997), p. 6. All further references are to this edition.
2. See Tolan, *Saracens*, pp. 3–21 and 105–35.
3. I have kept both pre- and post-baptismal names for these Saracens here (e.g. Evalach and Mordrain), but will use these more precisely as the chapter progresses.
4. Caspari, 'Deconstructing Race', p. 116.
5. Miranda Griffin, *The Object and the Cause in the Vulgate Cycle* (London: Legenda/Modern

Humanities Research Association; Leeds: Maney Publishing, 2005), p. 1.
6. For the dating of the *Estoire*, see Michelle Szkilnik, *L'Archipel du Graal: Étude de 'l'Estoire del Saint Graal'*, Publications romanes et françaises, 196 (Geneva: Droz, 1991), p. 1.
7. I have followed Griffin in my use of 'Vulgate' rather than 'Lancelot-Grail' to refer to the Cycle as a whole. See Griffin, *Object and the Cause*, pp. 2–3, where she also summarizes some of the debate surrounding the order in which the texts were composed. See also Ponceau, 'Introduction' in *ESG*, pp. xii–xiii.
8. Carol Chase has produced several studies on Saracens in this work but does not focus on race and lineage: 'La Conversion des païennes'; Carol Chase, 'Des Sarrasins à Camaalot', *Cahiers de recherches médiévales et humanistes*, 5 (1998), <http://dx.doi.org/10.4000/crm.1372>; and Carol Chase, 'The Gateway to the Lancelot-Grail Cycle: *L'Estoire del Saint Graal*', in *A Companion to the Lancelot-Grail Cycle*, ed. by Carol Dover, Arthurian Studies, 54 (Cambridge: Brewer, 2003), pp. 65–74.
9. See the entry in Algirdas Julien Greimas, *Dictionnaire de l'ancien français*, 3rd edn (Paris: Larousse, 2004).
10. For Evalach/Mordrain's visions, see *ESG*, pp. 60–65 and pp. 175–77.
11. Zrinka Stahuljak, *Bloodless Genealogies of the French Middle Ages: Translatio, Kinship, and Metaphor* (Gainesville, FL: University Press of Florida, 2005), p. 109.
12. Stahuljak, *Bloodless Genealogies*, especially pp. 94–111.
13. See Carol Chase, 'Conversion des païennes', for the concept of spiritual inheritance and the importance of the female Saracens in the depicted lineages.
14. *ESG*, fn. 660b, p. 418.
15. For the climatic theory of medieval racial difference, see Akbari, *Idols in the East*, pp. 24–50.
16. Akbari, *Idols in the East*, pp. 36–37.
17. Akbari, *Idols in the East*, p. 155.
18. Gabrielle M. Spiegel, 'Genealogy: Form and Function in Medieval Historical Narrative', *History and Theory*, 22 (1983), 43–53 <http://www.jstor.org/stable/2505235> [accessed 28 November 2018], p. 51.
19. Griffin, *Object and the Cause*, pp. 22–24.
20. Jacques Lacan, 'Le Temps logique et l'assertion de certitude anticipée. Un nouveau sophisme', in *Écrits* (Paris: Seuil, 1966), pp. 197–213; an English translation is available as 'Logical Time and the Assertion of Anticipated Certainty', in *Écrits: The First Complete Edition in English*, trans. by Bruce Fink with Héloïse Fink (New York: Norton, 2006), pp. 161–75.
21. Griffin, *Object and the Cause*, p. 23.
22. Griffin, *Object and the Cause*, p. 19; For the notion of *entrelacement*, see Ferdinand Lot, *Étude sur le Lancelot en prose*, Bibliothèque de l'École des hautes études, 226 (Paris: Champion, 1918) and for the use of *entrelacement* in relation to temporal perspectives, see Katalin Halász, 'The Representation of Time and its Models in the Prose Romance', in *Text and Intertext in Medieval Arthurian Literature*, ed. by Norris J. Lacy, Garland Reference Library of the Humanities, 1997 (New York: Garland, 1996), pp. 175–86.
23. Griffin, *Object and the Cause*, p. 21.
24. Carol Chase's translation has 'household' for 'semence'. See Lacy, ed. *Lancelot-Grail*, II.
25. For this eternal present of narration, see Emmanuèle Baumgartner, 'Temps linéaire, temps circulaire et écriture romanesque (XIIe-XIIIe siècles)', in *Le Temps et la durée dans la littérature au Moyen Âge et à la Renaissance: actes du colloque organisé par le Centre de recherche sur la littérature du Moyen Âge et de la Renaissance de l'Université de Reims, novembre 1984*, ed. by Yvonne Bellenger (Paris: Nizet, 1986), pp. 7–21 (p. 13).
26. For example, Bloch, *Etymologies and Genealogies*, pp. 67–70.
27. Bloch, *Etymologies and Genealogies*, p. 69.
28. Butler, *Gender Trouble*, p. xxxi (original emphasis).
29. Barbara A. Hanawalt discusses surrogate parents and children in the lower classes in *The Ties That Bound: Peasant Families in Medieval England* (Oxford: Oxford University Press, 1986), pp. 243–56; for Christian children raised in Saracen environments, see Denis Collomp, 'L'Enfant chrétien élevé chez les Sarrasins', in *L'Épopée Romane: Actes du XVe Congrès international Rencesvals, Poitiers,*

21–27 août 2000, ed. by Gabriel Bianciotto and Claudio Galderisi, 2 vols (Poitiers: Université de Poitiers. Centre d'études supérieures de civilisation médiévale, 2002), II, pp. 655–72.
30. See Tolan, *Saracens*, pp. 10–11 and pp. 51–52 for this association.
31. Benjamin Braude, 'The Sons of Noah and the Construction of Ethnic and Geographical Identities in the Medieval and Early Modern Periods', *The William and Mary Quarterly*, 3rd ser., 54 (1997), 103–42 (pp. 107–08).
32. See Braude, 'Sons of Noah', pp. 110–15.
33. For reference to Christ's siblings, see for instance Matthew 13:55 and Mark 6:3. See also Marina Warner, *Alone of All Her Sex: the Myth and Cult of the Virgin Mary* (London: Picador, 1985; repr. with new afterthoughts 1990), pp. 20–24.
34. Griffin, *Object and the Cause*, p. 55.
35. For genealogical structure and Galahad in the *Estoire* see Griffin, *Object and the Cause*, pp. 54–58 and Chase 'Conversion des païennes', pp. 57–64.
36. Griffin, *Object and the Cause*, p. 36.
37. Zrinka Stahuljak, Virginie Greene, Sarah Kay, Sharon Kinoshita, and Peggy McCracken, *Thinking through Chrétien de Troyes*, Gallica, 19 (Cambridge: Brewer, 2011), p. 164.
38. Gautier de Coinci, *Les Miracles de Nostre Dame*, ed. by V. Frédéric Koenig, 4 vols, Textes Littéraires Français (Genève: Droz, 1955–70), I, 2nd edn (1966), Prologue, vv. 138–40.
39. Griffin, *Object and the Cause*, p. 58.
40. I take this expression from Stahuljak et. al., who discuss logical time and periods of adventure in romance in *Thinking through Chrétien de Troyes*. Quotations from p. 19.
41. See Szkilnik, *L'Archipel du Graal*, pp. 41–42 for the role of Solomon's ship more generally.
42. In contrast, Carol Chase identifies a crusading drive to convert the non-Christian and situates pagan genealogy in relation to Lancelot's sins. 'Conversion des païennes', p. 61.
43. Stahuljak, *Bloodless Genealogies*, p. 95.
44. Stahuljak, *Bloodless Genealogies*, p. 101.
45. Tolan, *Saracens*, p. 64.
46. See Tolan, *Saracens*, pp. 61–62; also Di Cesare, *Pseudo-Historical Image*, p. 250 for William of Auvergne's writings on Muhammad and prophecies from Genesis.
47. See Rodulfus Glaber, *Rodvlfi Glabri Historiarvm libri qvinqve* [The five books of the Histories], ed. and trans. by John France, published with Glaber, *Vita domni Willelmi abbatis* [The life of St William], ed. by Neithard Bulst, trans. by John France and Paul Reynolds (Oxford: Clarendon Press, 1989), pp. 18–23.
48. Akbari, *Idols in the East*, pp. 221–35.
49. Carol Chase, 'Gateway to the Lancelot-Grail', p. 73.
50. Jon Whitman, 'Transfers of Empire, Movements of Mind: Holy Sepulchre and Holy Grail', *MLN*, 123 (2008), 895–923 <http://doi.org/10.1353/mln.0.0054>, (p. 911).
51. A.J. Gurevich, *Categories of Medieval Culture*, trans. by G. L. Campbell (London: Routledge, Kegan & Paul, 1985), p. 27.
52. Stahuljak, *Bloodless Genealogies*, pp. 91–92.
53. Note that the wording used to describe Mordrain's connection to Galahad is not totally consistent: while in the *Estoire*, Mordrain prays to God that he may see 'li noevismes del lingnage Nascien' (*ESG*, p. 474) [the ninth in Nascien's line], in the *Queste* this appears as 'li noviesmes de mon lignage' (Q, p. 254) [the ninth of my line] and the editor, Bogdanow, comments that there are more manuscripts with this variant than which refer to Nascien. Those manuscripts using the version with Nascien also seem to be later (fourteenth-fifteenth century), perhaps suggesting subsequent attempts to reconcile the contradiction with the *Estoire*.
54. Stahuljak, *Bloodless Genealogies*, pp. 98–102.
55. Griffin discusses the letter of Solomon in *Object and the Cause*, p. 36.
56. Stahuljak, *Bloodless Genealogies*, p. 95.
57. Moira Gatens, *Imaginary Bodies: Ethics, Power and Corporeality* (London: Routledge 1996), p. 77.
58. *Chronica Prophetica*, trans. by Wolf.
59. Griffin, *Object and the Cause*, p. 29.
60. Whitman, 'Transfers of Empire', p. 901.

61. See Amnon Linder, '*Deus Venerunt Gentes*: Psalm: 78 (79) in the Liturgical Commemoration of the Destruction of Latin Jerusalem', in *Medieval Studies in Honor of Avrom Saltman*, ed. by Bat-Sheva Albert, Yvonne Friedman, and Simon Schwarzfuchs, Bar-Ilan Studies in History, 4 (Ramat-Gan, Israel: Bar-Ilan University Press, 1995), pp. 145–71; See also Whitman, 'Transfers of Empire', pp. 899–900 for mention of this Psalm.
62. Tolan, *Saracens*, p. 5.
63. Akbari, *Idols in the East*, pp. 29–31. For the sons of Noah associated with specific continents, see also pp. 38–47.
64. See Braude's closing comments in 'Sons of Noah', p. 142.
65. Tolan, *Saracens*, p. 10.
66. Braude, 'Sons of Noah', p. 107 and p. 116.
67. Tolan, *Saracens*, p. 10.
68. One example would be the thirteenth-century scholastic Bartholomeus Anglicus. See Akbari, *Idols in the East*, pp. 42–50 for climatic interpretations of race.
69. See for instance Mordrain's removal to the Rock of the Perilous Port (*ESG*, p. 186), Nascien's to the Turning Isle, (*ESG*, p. 249).
70. Szkilnik, *Archipel du Graal*, p. 8.
71. Szkilnik, *Archipel du Graal*, p. 9.
72. Szkilnik, *Archipel du Graal*, p. 108.
73. Szkilnik, *Archipel du Graal*, p. 54.
74. 'enseigne' is a recurring word in the *Estoire*, often having the sense of proof/sign, sometimes indicating information that others do not have access to (e.g. of divine provenance). See Ponceau's note 488.3, p. 616 in *ESG*.
75. Bloch, *Etymologies and Genealogies*, p. 211.
76. Griffin, *Object and the Cause*, p. 36.
77. See Byrne, *White Lives*, p. 16.
78. Szkilnik notes the parallels between the two ships encountered by Perceval in the *Queste* and those confronted by Mordrain in the *Estoire*, as well as the importance of the ship of Solomon. See *L'Archipel du Graal*, pp. 41–42.
79. Chase, 'Conversion des païennes', pp. 258–59.
80. Gatens, *Imaginary Bodies*, p. 76.
81. See Caspari, 'Deconstructing Race', p. 116.
82. Stahuljak, *Bloodless Genealogies*, p. 2.
83. Griffin, *Object and the Cause*, p. 58. In the *Lancelot*, we know that Galahad descends from the line of Solomon through his maternal line. Through his mother he descends from Bron, a relative of Joseph of Arimathea, and through his father Lancelot, he descends from Nascien.
84. Akbari, *Idols in the East*, p. 12.
85. Stahuljak, *Bloodless Genealogies*, p. 108.
86. Heng, *Empire of Magic*, pp. 71–73.
87. Bloch, *Etymologies and Genealogies*, p. 212.
88. Vikki Bell, 'On Speech, Race and Melancholia: An Interview with Judith Butler', *Theory, Culture & Society*, 16.2 (1999), 163–74 <https://doi.org/10.1177/02632769922050593>, (p. 169).
89. Bell, 'On Speech', p. 170.
90. Halász, 'The Representation of Time', p. 179.

CHAPTER 3

Race and Religion: Spectrality and Conversion in Gautier de Coinci's *Miracles de Nostre Dame*

Viewing identity as performative questions the role of biological, blood relations in determining racial identities, but also foregrounds the reciprocal nature of their construction. Furthermore, the central tenet of this concept — the power of repeating conventions — can involve not only intersubjective but also intrasubjective processes, reciprocal performances between the subject's own different identities that are self-reflexive, even haunting. In this sense Judith Butler's theory of performativity thus also evokes a sense of spectrality, since

> the constant reiterations of the norm required [...] are never perfect reproductions; a slippage occurs with respect to the ideal-image, resulting in a doubling or self-haunting by which the subject is constantly chasing — yet never catches — a posited "proper" self.[1]

If concepts of performativity expose the ways in which ontology is constituted rather than predetermined or fixed, spectrality shows 'the extent to which what we take to be the world of being is troubled by the not-yet or the not-now, by something "out of joint" that unsettles it'.[2] Perhaps nowhere is this potential for self-haunting and the pursuit of a 'proper self' more apparent than in exempla that emphasize the non-linear nature of religious conversions as moments 'out of joint'; above all, it is in the didactic representation of miraculous experience and its spectral dynamics that medieval Christian as well as Saracen identities emerge as performative.

Dated roughly between 1214 and 1236, the *Miracles de Nostre Dame* is a vernacular collection of 58 such exemplary and miraculous tales translated from Latin source texts that enjoyed a significant popularity, with over 100 surviving manuscripts containing at least part of the collection. The French author of the texts, Gautier de Coinci, who became grand prior of the royal Benedictine abbey of St Médard de Soissons, also added his own closing moral messages to these tales along with numerous supporting elements such as songs, prayers, and sermons.[3] Through the unique didactic layering that characterizes Gautier's texts, his tales conjoin acts of Christian and Saracen conversion and, in so doing, expose racial identity as spectral. Given the variety of the collection's transmitted forms, I do not treat a specific version in its entirety in this chapter. Rather, individual tales within the collection containing representations of Saracens will be considered in their particular manuscript contexts and their Saracen figures then situated alongside other protagonists of the *Miracles*, namely: *De l'ymage Nostre Dame* [*Of the Image of Our Lady*] (I Miracle 32), *Comment Nostre Dame desfendi la cité de Constantinnoble* [*How Our Lady Defended the City of Constantinople*] (II Miracle 12), and *De l'ymage Nostre Dame de Sardanei* [*Of the Image of Our Lady of Saydnaya*] (II Miracle 30).[4] In addition, the miracle *De Saint Basile* (II Miracle 11) also features in my discussion, as it provides a useful parallel in its narration of the conversion and punishment of non-Christians. Emperor Julian and his army are not directly labelled as Saracens in this case, but the pagan experience of an apparition directly resonates with events in the following tale.

Gautier's tales were probably intended to reach beyond the walls of a monastic community and to appeal to a broad spectrum of readers of different social spheres and vocations. The characters chosen as beneficiaries of intercessory power in the *Miracles* are drawn from a range of different social backgrounds, and there are examples of good and bad behaviour, from pregnant nuns to drunken monks, incestuous mothers and unchivalrous knights. In light of this varied audience, and mindful of the fact that this collection represents a 'tangle of performance practices and fictions, representations and ritual re-enactment',[5] the detailed linguistic devices used by Gautier on a textual level need to be set alongside the visual schemes at work in the manuscripts of his collection. Many contain lavish illumination cycles that reveal alternative engagements with the narratives and which consequently provide further insight into the use and interpretation of Saracen representations. While identity performances may occur within the events of the text, such as through disguise, or may relate to narrative, cyclical, structure, race may simultaneously play out on visual as well as linguistic levels, with Saracen representations caught between text and image. This is all the more significant in the case of the *Miracles*, firstly because the tales that concern Saracens in Gautier's collection all involve profoundly visual experiences and secondly, because the relevant illuminations often show images of images, creating moments of self-reflexivity that can be said to parallel the self-reflection encouraged in the Christian viewer.

More particularly, acknowledging the plurality of meaning produced by text-image relations places the body alongside other visual aspects of identity, such as dress, behaviour, and gesture; in turn, this repositioning of the body helps us to rethink the relationship between race and religion seen through narratives of conversion. Steven F. Kruger states that

> medieval religious difference is intimately intertwined especially with constructions of gender and sexuality, with religion, gender, and sexuality all together constituting a space of embodied otherness analogous but not identical to modern, biologized ideas of race.[6]

Contrary to this, the present chapter continues to question the idea that the body acts as the locus of identity in this manner. The religious conversion of the Saracen in the *Miracles* represents a moment of transition and integration, yet one that is also marked by identities that linger, emerge, and blur at different points of the miraculous experience being narrated. Encounters with miracles and apparitions consequently reveal the varying ways in which bodies may be involved in the process of conversion: while the recipient's own body participates in a liminal moment, he also witnesses divine bodies that may be spectral as well as spiritual, bringing different levels of sensory experience and promoting different kinds of identification within and beyond the narratives.

The myriad protagonists of the *Miracles* are, as Yasmina Foehr-Janssens has noted, 'tous affectés de défauts, manquements ou vices rédhibitoires, mais ils restent néanmoins fidèles à leurs vocations de chrétiens' [all affected by flaws, failures, or fundamentally intolerable vices, but they nonetheless remain faithful to their Christian vocations].[7] Such devotion, although seemingly insignificant compared to the crimes they have committed, is nonetheless able to redeem them in the eyes of the Virgin. Despite their non-Christian origins, Saracens are similarly treated by Gautier and whether portrayed as good or bad examples of Christian behaviour, they are very much part of Gautier's spiritual community, not simply outsiders against whom the might of Christianity may be tested. This depiction of Saracens contrasts markedly with Gautier's presentation of Jews, who were familiar residents of the Soissons region and who tend to function as persecutors of Christians in these tales. The violence of these anti-Semitic plotlines does seem to suggest that 'Gautier hait les juifs' [Gautier hates the Jews][8] — from the Jew who influences Theophile's pact with the devil (*Comment Theophilus vint a penitance*) [*How Theophilus Came to Be Penitent*], to the Jewish father who tries to roast his own son (*De l'enfant a un giu qui se crestïena*) [*Of the Jewish Child Who Became a Christian*] or the Jew who lures away then kills a Christian boy (*De l'enfant resuscité qui chantoit Gaude Maria*) [*Of the Resuscitated Child Who Sang Gaude Maria*].

The apparent disparity between representations of Saracens and Jews in Gautier's text is rendered all the more significant in light of the fact that the *Miracles* were produced shortly after the Fourth Lateran Council (1215). In Canon 68, Innocent III pronounced that there should be visible distinctions drawn between Christians and pagans living in Christian lands.[9] Both Saracens and Jews fell into this category and were to be marked out by their dress from the Christian community. As John Tolan notes, 'the two groups, Muslims and Jews, are increasingly lumped together in ecclesiastical and civil legislation' in this period and 'a polemical view of Islam informs the decisions of Lateran IV'.[10] Yet while this widespread atmosphere is apparent in Gautier's emphasis upon the victory of the Virgin over the Jews and their often violent demise, Saracens are not targeted with such animosity. Instead, the Saracen is part of a potential — if not yet realized — community based upon his privileged experience of the divine and/or the performance of shared Christian behaviours. He may even be an exemplar to emulate.

Religious conversion in these tales is not necessarily a one-directional process: faith is not simply conveyed *to* the Saracen but the performance of Christian behaviours also communicates the Saracen's faith *back* to the Christian community through his role as exemplar and sometimes also through the moral coda of the text. This process is a key difference between the relationship of Christianity to Judaism and to the Saracen faith. Such a combination of exemplarity and miraculous experience means that the Saracen convert possesses a particular kind of temporal fluidity, with the result that his transition into the Christian community exposes different kinds of haunted and haunting identities. With apparitions encountered and the Saracen's own status out-of-time, Jacques Derrida's notion of spectrality provides a conceptual framework through which to explore questions of corporeal form and presence and discuss the performativity of identity. While Slavoj Žižek and Judith Butler frame spectrality in detailed relation to political systems,[11] Derrida's original formulation allows us both to recognize the impact of apparitional and miraculous encounters on Saracen conversion in the *Miracles* and yet remain focused on the representation of bodies and performative construction of identities. With this concept of spectrality, we move beyond the familiar trope of the Saracen as flesh-bound idolater so as better to appreciate the subtle interweaving of race and religion with embodied identity in these tales.

Rethinking Saracen Idolatry

As the miracle in Gautier's collection with the most prominent Saracen protagonist, *De l'ymage Nostre Dame* relates how a Saracen directly communes with the Virgin prior to his conversion.[12] The Saracen has somehow acquired an image in tablet form of the Virgin Mary, which he prizes and honours greatly; he keeps it in excellent condition and worships it on his knees at least once a day. One day, while kneeling before the image, he begins to wonder about the possibility of God assuming a flesh and blood form in Jesus. This leads him to consider the likelihood of Jesus having been born to a virgin and to declare that if he could only know whether this were true, he would convert to Christianity. At that moment, the image before him miraculously grows breasts from which holy oil begins to flow, a phenomenon that persuades him to convert. The miracle concludes with a coda or *queue* added by Gautier about the necessity of properly cleaning altars and images.

Given the generally pervading association of Islam with idolatry in medieval literature, it is easy to see why this Saracen has mostly attracted attention for his apparent image-worshipping.[13] Such idolatry would thus be 'replaced, through the miracle, by an understanding of the spiritual presence that the Christian image represents'.[14] However, the Saracen's motivation for adoring the image is clearly not the focus of Gautier's closing moral message and we are left wondering if this is just a Saracen who kept, cleaned, or admired the picture of the Virgin, or if this is a Saracen who was in some sense *praying* to his icon? When the Saracen is introduced to the reader there are no disparaging remarks made about his origins or beliefs; we are simply told that he is 'sarrasins' (v. 4). Even if it is not entirely clear that he is motivated by anything other than the fact that the image is beautiful,[15] this is in no way criticized; in fact, he treats the image with 'mout grant reverence' (v. 13) [very great respect] and every day he 'l'aoroit une fois au mains | A genolz et a jointes mains' (vv. 17–18) [adored/worshipped it at least once on his knees with joined hands]. He also ensures that the image is kept clean, and this behaviour is emphasized by Gautier in his coda. Rather than using the Saracen as an example of a reformed idolater or highlighting his conversion from Islam to Christianity, Gautier instead advises his reader/listeners that:

> Li sarrasins ne perdi rien.
> En ce qu'il la servi si bien
> N'en ce que bien la netoia.
> La douce dame grant joie a
> Quant on la sert de bon corage
> Et quant on porte honneur s'ymage.
> Bien nos devomes deporter
> En sa samblance honeur porter
> Quant uns paiens s'i deporta. (vv. 83–91)

[The Saracen lost nothing by serving and cleaning her so well. The sweet lady takes great joy when someone serves her wholeheartedly and when he honours her image. We should greatly enjoy bringing honour to her representation since a pagan took pleasure in behaving in this way.]

The *traductio* of *deporter/porter* here both underlines the need to bring honour to the Virgin and stresses the exemplary behaviour of the Saracen.[16] The Saracen shows that the repetition of ritualized behaviour — in this case, the cleaning of altars and images — will be rewarded. By extension, the contrasting description of those who do not clean their altar areas as neither 'courtois ne sages' (v. 93) [courtly nor wise] suggests that those who do clean their homes *are* both of these things. Since these qualities are also commonly prized within secular communities, such an assessment renders the Saracen admirable in courtly, secular terms as well as in terms of his religious reverence.

At the end of the coda, just before Gautier's closing *annominatio*, he once again encourages his readers to emulate the Saracen's behaviour, reminding them that 'li bons paiens' [the good pagan] gained paradise by honouring the Virgin day and night (vv. 236–40). In this description Gautier therefore suggests that the Saracen's 'pagan' qualities are overcome by his sense of good behaviour, situating him within the Christian community by virtue of his actions rather than any underlying racial or religious affiliation. There is no precision, for instance, as to whether these actions are unwitting or deliberate in Gautier's text. The Saracen is also shown to be a model of good Christian behaviour through the repeated rhyming of 'ymage/coraige' [image/inner feelings and thoughts or soul] that begins in lines 31–32, appearing again in lines 57–58, lines 87–88, and lines 229–30.[17] This pairing emphasizes the importance of worshipping images of the Virgin heart and soul, and constitutes a common motif in Gautier's *Miracles*.[18] It does not, therefore, apply specifically to the Saracen's spiritual enlightenment but is behaviour to be emulated by any good Christian, echoing Gautier's comment that the miracle 'nous enorte toz ensamble' (vv. 718) [exhorts us all together] to love the Virgin in this wholehearted fashion. In this respect, it seems as though the Saracen's identity as

Saracen is purely marked by his lack of true understanding of the Christian faith rather than by physical features or by erroneous actions. Correct behaviour is what connects him to the Christian community rather than excludes him.

If this Saracen is presented as a figure to be emulated through the emphasis on his wholehearted dedication to the Virgin, he is also an excuse to criticize those who do not really take pleasure in dedicating themselves to the mother of God: for example, those who attend mass and take the host, but who do not actively enjoy the experience (vv. 112–16). Gautier says that it would be better for such people to sing of Ogier the Dane than to sing mass, which suggests that the lack of true dedication shown by many can be linked to the enjoyment of secular, popular material. When combined with the Saracen's representation, this comment also creates a division between the world of the epic, with its heroes like Ogier fighting against the Saracens in *La Chanson de Roland*, and the spiritual world of the *Miracles* where a Saracen may actually be a model of Christian behaviour.[19] In a sense, this miracle works precisely because the Saracen simultaneously evokes associations of non-Christian behaviour yet is capable of behaving in such a Christian manner — because Saracen identity is both absent and present and can be exploited for being such.

Far from being the preserve of the pagan, non-Christian behaviour is instead rooted within the Christian community itself through Gautier's repeated use of the image of the spider, or 'eraigne' (v. 98). The first mention of this creature occurs when Gautier praises the Saracen's commitment to keeping the image of the Virgin clean so that 'ne qu'entor li fesist mussote | erignie ne barbelote' (vv. 23–24) [neither spiders nor frogs should find a hiding place there]. This image is then maintained in Gautier's coda, where he twice rhymes *eraigne* with *daigne* to highlight the sinful reluctance of many to clean their altar areas: for instance, Gautier remonstrates that he who does not deign to clean an altar should have both of his eyes poked out by a spider (vv. 97–100).[20] The spider was associated with the Devil in medieval folklore and was often believed to be poisonous, a carrier of plague and a sign of corruption.[21] It was also associated with the temptations of the terrestrial, secular world, as can be seen in folktales such as those of fourteenth-century Geoffroi de la Tour Landry. His collection includes a tale where the Devil in the form of a spider attacks a girl who missed mass while coiffing her hair according to the latest fashion.[22] In Gautier's miracle, the Saracen not only honours the Virgin with his behaviour, but also wards off the advances of the Devil by cleaning his home, in contrast to supposedly Christian people such as 'li clers, li moignes et li prestre' (v. 174) [clerks, monks and priests] who adorn their homes but do not care for the house of God. Unlike some of his contemporaries,[23] Gautier does not seem to be attacking the Saracen for ignorant, idolatrous beliefs, but rather uses his instinctive behaviour as an indicator of good Christian practice, one that rejects worldliness and the influence of the Devil and honours the mother of God. His status as 'pagan' adds weight to Gautier's criticism of his supposedly Christian audience and the bad example that they are setting:

> Si m'aït Diex, c'est grans merveille
> Quant laiez gens püent bien faire,
> Car en nos ont povre essamplaire. (vv. 202–04)

[So help me God it's a wonder that lay people can behave well since we set such a poor example]

Potential Saracen behaviour is therefore not the target of Gautier's comments but rather his audience's own potential to be lazy and unworthy Christians; despite his lack of Christian faith, the Saracen is an exemplary Christian in his behaviour. However, it remains hard to determine the extent to which such a distinction between faith and religious action outweighs any racial aspects of Saracen identity. This is true even when acknowledging the impact of conversion on the more embodied, somatic aspects of Saracen representations.

Conversion and Spectrality

The act of religious conversion in Gautier's text, far from providing the security of assimilating an idolatrous non-Christian figure, instead challenges the very notion of a stable Christian identity; such an identity is not only revealed to be performatively produced through the repetition and recognition of conventions but is also shown to be an ideal that is constantly chased yet never caught. While Karl Morrison has noted that religious conversion in general is 'subversive of self',[24] in the exemplum of conversion, as found in the *Miracles*, both Saracen and Christian are variously shown to be (and in fact must be) subjected to a self-haunting. This process of haunting is reminiscent of Derrida's notion of spectrality, since the converting and converted self is both *revenant* and *arrivant* as per his formulation of the specter in *Specters of Marx*:

> the subject's identity is disjointed as it becomes both *revenant* and *arrivant*: it returns from the past (citing a history without being anchored in a singular origin or essence), while at the same time constituting its own futurity, arriving, as it were, from and through iterative acts yet to occur.[25]

Since the Saracen in *De l'ymage Nostre Dame* is not simply a convert but also an exemplary figure, it is not just the identity of the convert that is spectral in this sense but Christian identity more generally. The Saracen-convert-as-exemplar must both be and not be Christian, and be and not be Saracen, just as Gautier's audience is shown both to be and not be Christians in the sense of Bernard of Clairvaux's twelfth-century complaint that: 'the whole world is Christian [...] but nearly all deny Christ'.[26]

The concept of spectrality that is developed in Jacques Derrida's *Specters of Marx* is a useful theoretical lens through which to discuss Gautier's Saracen converts for two main reasons. Firstly, it highlights the effects of the temporal 'double bind' posed by the Saracen as both convert (a transient being) *and* exemplar (a timeless and enduring being); it is performative to the extent that it is 'an interpretation that transforms the very thing it interprets'.[27] According to Derrida, Western society is preoccupied by the notion of historical ends and he refers in particular to the idea that the end of Marxism seems to offer the potential for a new structuring of history. However, Derrida argues, such claims are simply performative; they are a form of wishful thinking rather than the reflection of a reality, since the present is unable to rid itself of Marxism and its ghosts. Thus 'haunted', those in the present reject the legacy of Marx but are paradoxically reliant upon it for their own self-definition. I suggest here that a similar process of rejection yet reliance features in Gautier's representations of Saracen converts. Secondly, given that spectrality also brings into question both the nature of embodied identity and bodily identity as defined by presence, it invites us to return to the idea of the Saracen as 'everywhere and nowhere' that I raised in the Introduction to this book. Questioning the supposed reliance of identity on bodily presence in this context similarly means considering the relationship between the physical and the spiritual in Saracen representations, since

> the specter is a paradoxical incorporation, the becoming-body, a certain phenomenal and carnal form of the spirit. It becomes, rather, some "thing" that remains difficult to name: neither soul nor body, and both one and the other. For it is flesh and phenomenality that give to the spirit its spectral apparition, but which disappear right away in the apparition, in the very coming of the revenant or the return of the specter.[28]

Such an indeterminable blurring of flesh and spirit is particularly relevant to the representation of conversion and its impact on Saracen identity. Nevertheless, the notion of spectrality also calls into question the nature and function of the miraculous presence that is itself perceived: the extent to which the term 'specter' might also refer to the apparitions and incarnations of the Virgin Mary in the *Miracles*. The relationship between spectrality and Christian understandings of incarnation has already been queried by Ernesto Laclau, who suggests that whereas Derrida refers to Christ as 'the most spectral of specters', spectrality supposes a somewhat different relationship between spirit and flesh to that of incarnation:

> Spectrality presupposes, as we have seen, an undecidable relation between spirit and flesh, which contaminates, in turn, these two poles. It presupposes, in that sense, a weakened form of incarnation. Weakened because a full incarnation — an incarnation in the Christian sense — transforms the flesh into a purely transparent medium through which we can see an *entirely* spiritual reality with no connection to its incarnating body. God's mediation is what establishes the link between spirit and flesh insofar as He is at an infinite distance from both. [...] in the specter the relation between spirit and flesh is much more intimate: there is no divine mediation that both sanctions and supersedes the essential heterogeneity of the two poles.[29]

If Derrida's link between spirit and flesh must therefore be further contextualized in relation to Christian understandings of 'incarnation', the same is true for the link between flesh and body in the context of medieval religious writing. In the Middle Ages, the body of Christ was not only a 'transparent medium' to access a spiritual reality, but also prompted responses that were very material and fleshly in nature: its wounds were to be kissed, its fluids and flesh touched and consumed.[30] Furthermore, while Derrida tends not to distinguish between flesh and body, for medieval writers the terms *corpus* and *caro* could convey very different meanings and associations.[31] In this respect, reading Gautier's text through the concept of spectrality also exposes particular, medieval ways of thinking about body and spirit, 'flesh and phenomenality' in the context of the miraculous more generally.

While the concept of spectrality has been related to medieval representations of Jews,[32] its relationship to Saracens and understandings of Islam has yet to be fully explored. In the Middle Ages, Judaism was often presented as belonging to the past, 'preserved as at the time of Christ, a reminder of what was past, rather than a religion capable of further development'.[33] Despite flourishing attempts to convert Jews through dialogic means during the thirteenth century, the enduring belief in the intransience of Judaism is evident in the virulence of mid-thirteenth century Christian reactions to the Talmud, which was seen as a distortion of the Jewish faith.[34] While medieval attitudes towards Jews were both varied and complex, in the work of Augustine, for example, Jews were central to Christian salvation history as essential witnesses to the truth of Christian teaching until the end of time (the doctrine of witness). Combining such notions with Derrida's formulation of spectrality, Steven F. Kruger in his study *The Spectral Jew* observes that 'the attempt to conjure Jews away also serves to conjure them up, into a certain presence: defining Jews as past involves simultaneously recognizing their (ongoing) role as Christianity's (oedipal?) competitor'. In consequence, he suggests, this 'haunting' destabilized the secured future that Christianity claimed for itself.[35]

Kruger goes on to highlight the potential of a similar 'spectral dynamic' being present in constructions of gender, sexuality, and race, referring to a well-known representation of the Prophet Muhammad in Guibert de Nogent's twelfth-century *Gesta Dei per Francos* where the supposed threat of Islam is unable to be contained despite the disparagement of the Prophet, since

> the motivation for depicting the origin of Islam is to justify the First Crusade, and at every point, even in the temporally distanced account of Muhammad, the Muslim "other" is felt somehow to touch on Christianity. Thus the history of Islam is, as Guibert emphasizes, also a history of Christian error, with Muhammad's "dogmata" discussed alongside the errors of the Eastern church and the Christian heresies.[36]

The common medieval understanding of Islam as 'heresy' built on the misinterpretations of Christianity by past Christians ultimately lends a certain circularity to the representation of Islam. Given the differing historicization of Judaism and Islam, Derrida's notion of spectrality and the idea of a double haunting might allow us to distinguish representations of Saracen and Jewish converts. If, as Kruger suggests, Jewish conversion 'calls to mind [...] the Jewish origin not just of the individual convert but of Christianity itself' and 'calls forth anxiety about the possibility of the reverse movement',[37] conversely, in the eyes of medieval Christians, the Saracen had already turned away from a once Christian self in the erroneous interpretation of the figure of Muhammad as a prophet. The Saracen in *De l'ymage Nostre Dame* could consequently be read as haunted by the heritage of a former Christian self, while the spectre of potential erroneous (at its extreme, heretical) behaviour continues to loom large over the Christian.³⁸ This double haunting emerges in the emphasis on Saracen exemplarity in this conversion narrative, an emphasis further complicated by the relationship between text and image across the three Saracen convert tales of Gautier's collection.

De l'ymage Nostre Dame (I Miracle 32)

In the visual schemes accompanying I Miracle 32, the viewer is continually invited to question the relationship between race and faith, behaviour and belief in a liminal moment between the divine and the terrestrial.³⁹ Coupled with the ambiguity of the Saracen's behaviour, what is potentially an example of inter-faith conversion seems to be translated instead into one that is intra-faith. In her doctoral thesis, Anna Russakoff notes that the scene of 'the Saracen praying in front of a Marian image' is that most commonly chosen to be illustrated in the manuscripts containing this miracle, with some also including a second image to show the Saracen's baptism.⁴⁰ In particular, she discusses the precise nature of the image of the Virgin in I Miracle 32 and examines the extent to which these images are two- or three-dimensional. Yet the illuminations of this tale are additionally significant for revealing a certain variation in the actual act performed by the Saracen: a variation which shows some flexibility, confusion, or even concern as to the status of this 'convert' and leaves Saracen identity spectral in its resulting temporal fluidity.

Sometimes, the Saracen in this miracle is depicted in a gesture of prayer, as in Paris, Bibliothèque nationale de France (BnF), MS fonds français 22928, fol. 113ᵛ or BnF, MS f. fr. 25532, fol. 68ʳ (Figures 3.1 and 3.2). This matches the description that appears in the text (on his knees with joined hands) if not necessarily the content of the rubrics.⁴¹ However, at other times he appears instead to be gesturing to the image of the Virgin, such as in Brussels, Bibliothèque royale (BR), MS 10747, fol. 67ᵛ (Figure 3.3) and in a particularly striking depiction seems to be conversing with her through a direct mirroring of their gestures (Paris, Bibliothèque de l'Arsenal (B. Ars.), MS 5204, fol. 58ᵛ, Figure 3.4). Though conspicuous in comparison with the other illustrations of this miracle, in the context of this manuscript, the poses, at least, are in no sense particular to the Saracen: fols 147ᵛ and 148ᵛ contain scenes with the Virgin in the same pose, open palmed, but facing a Christian woman and knight respectively; fol. 50ʳ shows her interlocutor in a similar stance to the Saracen; and fol. 72ᵛ has a very similar composition (although the Virgin points and holds a book). In this respect, it is not the *gesture* being enacted that conveys Saracen identity. The same holds for those cases with the Saracen kneeling in worship since, as Russakoff notes, this is only tangentially evocative of Saracen idol-worship, given that these are 'common devotional poses'.⁴² Nonetheless, while the text is clear that the Saracen is on his knees with joined hands before the image,⁴³ this does not always translate into the visual illustrations of the miracle and curiously none appear to be cleaning the image, despite this being the primary message of the coda and the focus of numerous rubrics across the manuscript corpus.⁴⁴ The poses therefore do not set the Saracen apart from Gautier's other protagonists but rather evince a

Fig. 3.1 (above). A Saracen kneeling before the Virgin and his baptism (Gautier de Coinci, *De l'ymage Nostre Dame*). Paris, BnF, MS f. fr. 22928, fol. 113ᵛ. Photo: Paris, Bibliothèque nationale de France.

Fig. 3.2 (below). A Saracen kneeling before the Virgin and his baptism (Gautier de Coinci, *De l'ymage Nostre Dame*). Paris, BnF, MS f. fr. 25532, fol. 68ʳ. Photo: Paris, Bibliothèque nationale de France.

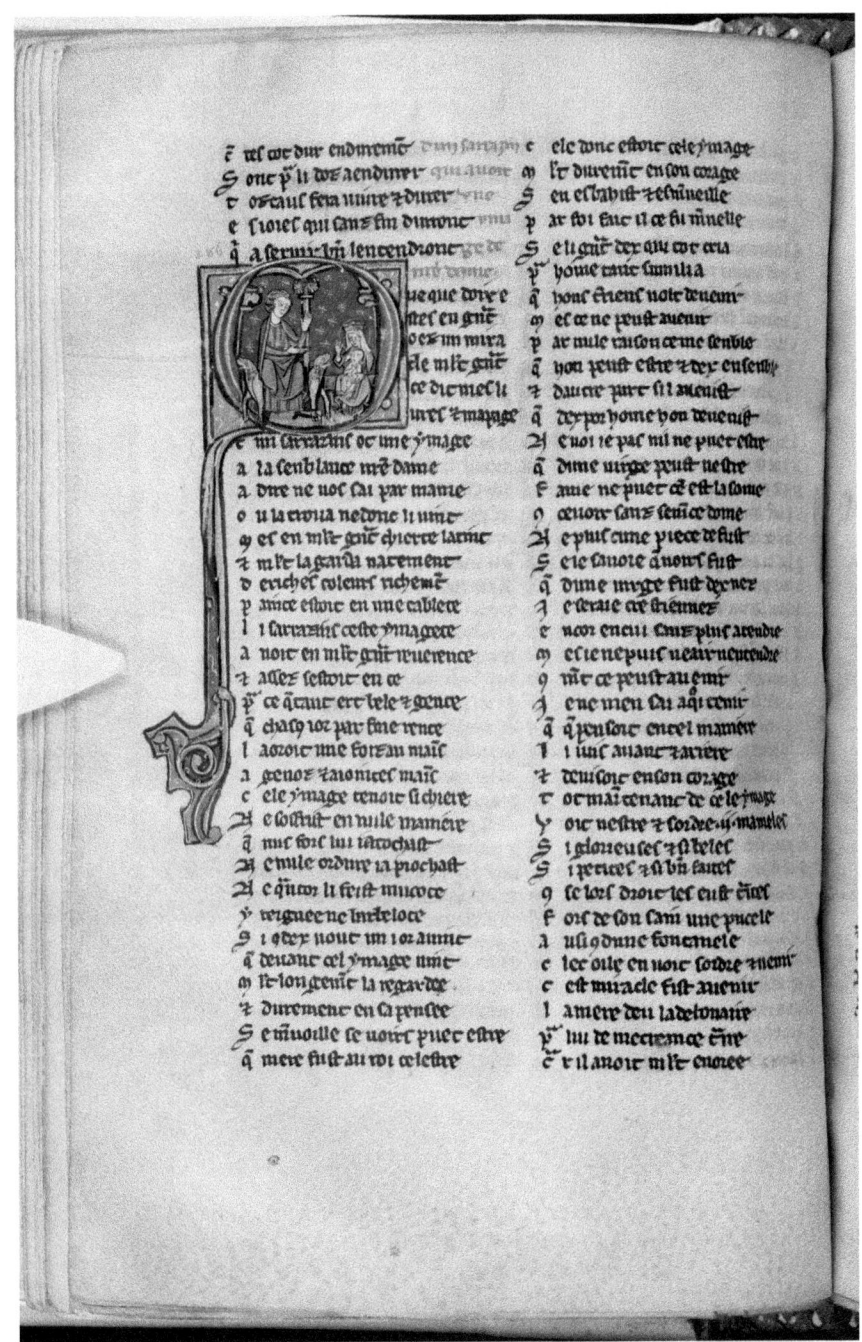

FIG. 3.3. A Saracen and the Virgin (Gautier de Coinci, *De l'ymage Nostre Dame*). Brussels, BR, MS 10747, fol. 67ᵛ. Photo: Bibliothèque Royale Albert Iᵉʳ

Fig. 3.4. Apparition scene/A Saracen and the Virgin (Gautier de Coinci, *De l'ymage Nostre Dame*). Paris, B. Ars. MS 5204, fol. 58[v].
Photo: Paris, Bibliothèque de l'Arsenal

wide variety of ways in which the particular act being performed, and by extension this Saracen's identity, may be read.

A manuscript case study: Thomas de Maubeuge

In their seminal study of the medieval Parisian book trade, Mary and Richard Rouse group three collections of Gautier's *Miracles* that stem from the workshop of the *libraire* Thomas de Maubeuge: Paris, B. Ars., MS 5204, Brussels, BR, MS 9229–30, and The Hague, Koninklijke Bibliotheek (KB), MS 71.A.24. These manuscripts were all produced within a very small timespan and all for noble or royal patrons.[45] As they note, this consequently presents an exceptional opportunity for cross-comparison, especially as these manuscripts share the same contents: 'there are no other contemporary manuscripts with this combination of texts, no earlier ones, none later'.[46] This rare opportunity therefore showcases some of the potential interpretations of Saracen identity that circulated in a defined context. Despite such similar circumstances of production,[47] Rouse and Rouse explain that

> the variations must result from a combination of the desires expressed in each patron's commission and the working habits of the artists [...] what we have here are fraternal, not identical triplets: three manuscripts containing the same texts, but made to varying specifications, and open to the impulses, even whims, of the artists.[48]

Setting the visual depictions of this miracle in these three manuscripts side by side reveals some of the potential and available representations of Saracens, if not perhaps who made such decisions and why.

Beginning with the Brussels manuscript, I Miracle 32 is accompanied by a two-column miniature (fol. 32^v, Figure 3.5) that has been associated with the sub-Fauvel Master by Alison Stones.[49] It is twenty lines high and shows the Saracen kneeling before an image of the Virgin on the left and the Saracen being baptized on the right. He is white-skinned, yet heavily bearded and wears a crown/hat that is not present in the accompanying baptism scene. The Hague manuscript 71.A.24 also contains illuminations by the sub-Fauvel Master,[50] and similarly features a two-column miniature of this miracle (fol. 31^r, Figure 3.6). Here, however, the Saracen in the left half stands holding the image of the Virgin and wears a pointed hat, while in the right half he is once again being baptized (albeit with a different assortment of onlookers and clergymen). Arsenal MS 5204 shows an entirely different scene, as noted above (Figure 3.4), and is attributed to the Maubeuge Master.[51] The black skin of this Saracen is particularly striking against the whiteness of the Virgin, a device which appears to be consistently used throughout the manuscript to depict Saracens. When briefly comparing this to other Maubeuge Master illuminations, for instance to those of the *Grandes Chroniques* manuscript BnF, MS f. fr. 10132, the same turban style does indeed appear, as it seems does black skin.[52] However, this is not universally applied, since the Battle of Roncevaux Saracens are very clearly the physical mirror image of their Christian counterparts.[53]

What we therefore have across these connected manuscripts are three versions both of Gautier's Saracen figure and of his gesture. Whether varying according to

Fig. 3.5. A Saracen kneeling before the Virgin and his baptism (Gautier de Coinci, *De l'ymage Nostre Dame*). Brussels, BR, MS 9229–30, fol. 32^v.
Photo: Bibliothèque Royale Albert Ier

taste, artistic style or interpretation, they demonstrate that representing the Saracen was not necessarily consistent in a given time, place, or similar patronage milieu — or even potentially in the work of one particular artist. While we may not, of course, know who made the relevant iconographic decisions and what motivated them,[54] such a variety of representations nonetheless tells us something about how Saracen identity was understood in a particular moment in time and how this relates to Gautier's moral message. All three show a clear tendency to 'other' the protagonist, yet the manner in which the figure is visually distinguished from the likely reader-viewer varies. The choice to include a two-column rather than single-columned miniature may well, of course, reflect pragmatic and/or financial considerations, yet the resulting presence of the Saracen's baptism scene nonetheless underscores the moment of transition, while the revealing of the Saracen's white, unclothed body creates a certain parity with that of the likely viewer.

In contrast, the Saracen of B. Ars., MS 5204 is visually separated by his skin and dress; no sense of his conversion and no hints of Christian behaviour are depicted. Instead, the image emphasizes communication between a very othered Saracen and what seems to be a full-size apparition of the Virgin rather than an obviously material object. In this sense, the image may exemplify Michael Camille's observation that when statues of the Virgin are deemed to act, they are shown as 'a separate divine manifestation' so that 'the image remains a representation on its altar while the life-size Virgin intervenes in reality'.[55] The Virgin here does not show the divine acting through or somehow from within the object; she does not possess an 'armor' or 'costume' seen in Derrida's example of the spectral blurring of *flesh* and spirit in the ghost of Hamlet's father, which 'dissimulates' and masks the body inside.[56] Instead she appears as a more unified *visio spiritualis* blurring *body*, flesh, and spirit:[57] her body provides a window onto the divine rather than highlighting the fleshliness of God. While the relationship between miracle and apparition will be discussed further below, in this case it seems that the more the body of the Virgin is rendered as spiritual and unchanging, the more visually significant and less spectral the Saracen's own flesh becomes.

To further complicate matters, there are numerous ways to interpret the term *ymage* in relation to the Virgin herself in this miracle, as studied by Russakoff, which has the additional effect of making us question which specific moment of the tale is being depicted in the illuminations. By extension, this temporal imprecision complicates our ability to read the Saracen's identity, leaving him spectral in the sense of being in a time 'out of joint',[58] betwixt and between religious communities. Some manuscripts show the Saracen's image as a tablet painting; others show it as a sculpture upon an altar. But it is the general attempt to show the transformation of the image that is most interesting for questions of conversion, spectrality, and Saracen identity. Another manuscript that is contemporary with those of Thomas de Maubeuge is BnF, MS nouvelle acquisition française 24541.[59] Russakoff observes that on fol. 67ᵛ (Figure 3.7) the illuminator (Jean Pucelle) painted the Virgin and Child with notably sculptural, three-dimensional qualities so that the holy figures seem, she says, 'on the verge of breaking through their two-dimensional setting', with fabric appearing to spill out over the frame.[60]

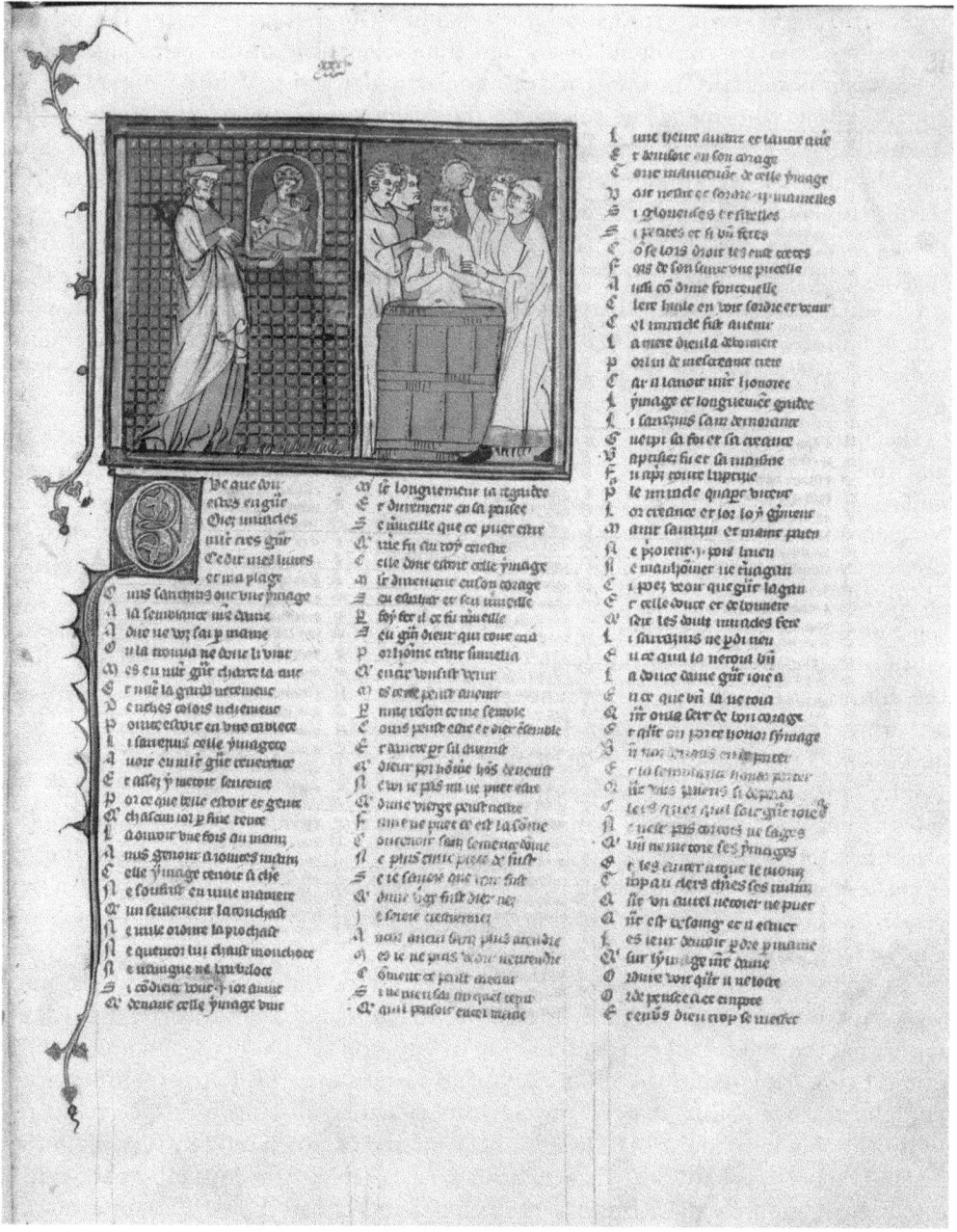

FIG. 3.6. A Saracen and the Virgin, with the Saracen's baptism (Gautier de Coinci, *De l'ymage Nostre Dame*). Den Haag, KB, National Library, MS 71.A.24, fol. 31ʳ. Photo: The Hague, KB, National Library.

Russakoff explains that the difficulty for the illuminator likely arises here in attempting to depict the miraculous moment where the three-dimensional breasts protrude from the two-dimensional picture.[61] This difficulty also impacts upon the representation of the Saracen as convert. In such images where the Saracen is 'praying', is this *before* the miraculous transformation of the icon (i.e. when he is a non-believer or potential idolater)? Or do they represent the moment of conversion itself by depicting the Virgin's response to his earlier good behaviour and questioning? Furthermore, given that it is also common for medieval illuminations to represent more than one moment within one image, the multiple, simultaneous readings of this image leave Saracen identity here spectral, since 'spectrality thus disrupts all conventional notions of time and presence'.[62] narrative and image both produce and negate the Saracen within a miraculous, anachronous moment.

This spectrality in turn reflects back on the connection between religious and racial identity, since in BnF, MS n. a. fr. 24541, for instance, the fact that the moment represented is so ambiguous also means that the racial marking of Saracen identity through features and dress becomes an unreliable indicator of religion. He potentially *looks* like a Saracen but may *act* or even perhaps *believe* like a Christian. Despite the general tendency among scholars to generalize that otherness was marked more by religion than by race, or that religious difference constituted race in this period,[63] the liminal moment of miraculous experience complicates the distinction between believer and non-believer. In particular, it is in the attempt to represent visually this absent-presence of the Virgin's body that seemingly incoherent aspects of religious and racial identities, whether of dress, behaviour, or gesture, continually play off one another without being either totally interchangeable or entirely distinct — and the same holds true for physiognomic representation.

If gesture complicates Saracen identity both in the text and images of this miracle tale, the representation of the Saracen body is also far from consistent, as Gautier's Saracens are shown with a variety of identifying attributes, such as beards, darker skin colour, or heavier facial features than their Christian counterparts. Returning to B. Ars., MS 5204, the Saracen here is specifically depicted with very black skin unlike the other illustrations of this miracle. Skin colour in this manuscript does seem to signify Saracen identity in particular (as opposed to a generic otherness or sinfulness) since those miracles involving Jews do not similarly prioritize physiognomic difference.[64] However, any reading of this use of skin colour is troubled by the curious case of I Miracle 31. The illumination of this tale, which immediately precedes that of the Saracen convert, depicts a similarly dark-skinned and apparently lecherous figure, despite illustrating the miracle of a Christian 'soucretain' [sacristan] with a supposed invitation from the Virgin to kiss her. Considering that there are no other cases where wrongdoers are portrayed with dark skin in this manuscript, we might wonder if this is a case of slippage between 'Sarrasin' and 'Soucretain'.[65] If this were true, it would suggest that skin colour was indeed used in this manuscript to mark out this particular group: to distinguish them as a different race rather than just as non-Christian in belief.

FIG. 3.7. A Saracen kneeling before the Virgin (Gautier de Coinci, *De l'ymage Nostre Dame*). Paris, BnF, MS n. a. fr. 24541, fol. 67ᵛ. Photo: Paris, Bibliothèque nationale de France.

Different again from the Maubeuge corpus is Besançon, Bibliothèque municipale (BM), MS 551, which surely offers the most interesting and textually integrated visual representation of *De l'ymage Nostre Dame*. This is the only case where three separate images are included, which is a feature of the manuscript more generally. The first and last show the Saracen on his knees before a statue on an altar, followed by his baptism (fols 58^r and 58^v, Figure 3.8 and 3.9). The middle image (fol. 58^r, Figure 3.10), however, is unusual.[66]

The Saracen is shown before a full-size, standing Virgin, her arms raised in an orans pose and whose bare breasts are displayed protruding through her gown, making this illumination a vivid illustration of the text's description that two breasts appear to grow out from the image. We could read this image as simply a manifestation of the frequently criticized fleshly preoccupations of medieval Saracens and their general inability to comprehend Christian faith. Yet it is curious that in this image the Saracen figure is the least marked as such in dress or features. Russakoff notes that the use of a beard here may function as a potential sign of Saracen otherness and observes that it remains during the scenes of his baptism.[67] However the intermediate scene depicting the apparition shows a clean-shaven Saracen; furthermore, many other non-Saracen figures in this manuscript also have beards.[68] In which case, the role of Saracen identity in this manuscript seems particularly unclear.

Despite the limitations incurred by the notorious difficulty in situating this manuscript within a precise production or reception context,[69] it is striking that the 'Saracenness' of this figure has all but disappeared. This lack of emphasis on the protagonist's status as Saracen is also apparent in the Besançon manuscript's opening rubric to this miracle, since it is one of around half a dozen among the illuminated corpus of the *Miracles* that do not refer to the Saracen. It states simply: 'De ymagine beate marie' [on the image of blessed Maria]. Uniting text and image, this manuscript's particular rendering of the miracle therefore focuses upon a generic, converting figure, who could be just as much one of the 'bad Christians' criticized by Gautier as a Saracen. The image hints at shared Christian practice and future acts of conversion yet also evokes a neglected or abandoned faith in the scene of baptism. In this respect, the protagonist's body is an entirely unreliable indicator of his 'Saracen' status; contrary to B. Ars., MS 5204, the Saracen's own body is now the 'transparent medium' through which to read the spiritual reality of conversion, while the Virgin appears before him not just in body but also in flesh, as a particularly carnal depiction of this miracle.

If this miracle narrates a spectral, atemporal moment, the Virgin here is also the most spectral in the Derridean sense: the Saracen in this version encounters a form of incarnation emphasizing the fleshliness of the body rather than its apparitional, heavenly status. Peggy McCracken notes that

> The representation of the miracle-working image and of its efficacy seems to question the difference between the image itself and what it represents, between absence and presence, and between the material and the spiritual [...] miracle stories insist on the Virgin's absence from the world of the living at the same time that they insist on her miraculous presence.[70]

Fig. 3.8 (illumination in left column). A Saracen kneeling before the Virgin.
Fig. 3.10 (illumination in right column). Apparition scene/A Saracen and the Virgin.
(Gautier de Coinci, *De l'ymage Nostre Dame*). Besançon, BM, MS 551, fol. 58ʳ.
Photo © Bibliothèque municipale de Besançon.

FIG. 3.9. The Saracen's baptism (Gautier de Coinci, *De l'ymage Nostre Dame*). Besançon, BM, MS 551, fol. 58ᵛ. Photo © Bibliothèque municipale de Besançon.

While her observation evokes a sense of spectrality, she focuses primarily on representation and the material object rather than apparitional forms of the Virgin, arguing here that 'the miraculous efficacy of the Virgin is coterminous with mimesis — miracles are enacted by a representation of the Virgin's body.' In the Besançon manuscript, however, the body of the Virgin appears as flesh and blood as much as representation, calling into question the boundary between miracle and apparition. Seen as spectral, the apparition of the Virgin highlights how medieval miracles may be the effect of a spiritual power working *through* representations rather than events enacted *by* such objects. The place of the Saracen within Gautier's Christian community can thus be nuanced: if this is an apparition rather than a miracle-working object, he is no material-bound pagan.

The result of such complex embodiments is that in Besançon, BM, MS 551 in particular, it is not entirely clear who is converting from what and to what. In this manuscript, rather than a Saracen converting to Christianity, the convert could just as easily be seen as a Christian haunted by a potential 'Saracenness', in the sense of non-Christian faith or doubt. This is furthermore suggested by the fact that the illumination of the encounter with the Virgin is placed back to back recto/verso with the scene of baptism, with one literally on top of the other. Rather appropriately, the 'ghost' of the baptism scene is even visible through the manuscript folio within the encounter scene. Moments of miraculous vision and baptism merge, just as the most 'Christian' looking Saracen is overlaid with his (technically) converting Saracen self. Moreover, the embedding of these two images within the narrative highlights the relationship between text and image in this particular manuscript, which is unique in its distribution of illuminations throughout Gautier's tales. The image depicting the Virgin occurs after the line in the text where the Saracen says that he just does not know what to believe (v. 54), so that the reader/viewer shares in the Saracen's visual experience of the Christian miraculous at the given moment. The baptism on the verso side is placed between the statement that the Virgin is joyful 'quant on porte honneur s'ymage' [when people honour her image] and, significantly, that we should 'en sa samblance honeur porter' [bring honour to her representation], meaning that the image is not framed by the actual description of the Saracen's baptism, but by the beginning of Gautier's coda emphasizing the importance of caring for images of the Virgin.

These features mean that the reader/viewer of this manuscript is being encouraged to see themselves in this converting figure, rather than to see him as 'other'. Since Gautier's interpretation of this tale in his coda is coupled with the unsettling of a linear progression of Saracen-Christian conversion and the variety of Saracen gestures seen in the illuminations, this text does not focus on the precise moment of a *Saracen*'s baptism, but on conversion in the more general sense of the continuous daily efforts made by Gautier's wider Christian community.[71] The miracle of a converting Saracen thus constitutes 'a spectral moment, a moment that no longer belongs to time, if one understands by this word the linking of modalized presents (past present, actual present: "now," future present)'.[72]

The problem is, of course, that by enacting a process of what might be termed *translatio fidei* from the tale of a convert *into* Christianity to one of converts *within*

Christianity the spectral double bind mentioned earlier emerges. In the potential repetition of apparently 'Christian' behavioural conventions through his act of worship — the performance as it were, of a Christian identity that is confirmed in his experience of the divine and subsequent baptism — the Saracen used as an exemplar exposes the facticity of such conventions more generally; confuses conventions associating race as physical appearance with religious belief; and reveals the fact that his new Christian self will continue to be haunted by the possibility of erroneous behaviour. In which case, the spectral dynamic of this miracle tale rather troublingly suggests that not only is Christian identity merely a vanishing point in an unhinged Christian eschatology but also that a Saracen's racial and/or religious identity could be described as 'the imperceptibility of that which is manifestly there'.[73]

Comment Nostre Dame desfendi la cité de Constantinnoble (II Miracle 12)

The moment of religious conversion in I Miracle 32 has three main effects: it demonstrates the difficulty of defining and distinguishing racial and religious identities; it leaves the Saracen convert a spectral presence who is neither entirely Christian nor entirely Saracen; and in a way that is related to the other effects just mentioned, it troubles Christian identity. By contrast, in II Miracle 12, the Saracen's role as a privileged visionary involves a personal, apparitional encounter in which bodily experience takes centre stage. His individual vision means that although he is an enemy to be bested, he is also a conduit to the miraculous and a potential convert.[74] On the surface, the primary narrative function of the Saracen in this miracle is to demonstrate the madness of choosing not to worship the Virgin and to emphasize the divine support given to those that do. According to this tale, the Saracen king, Muselinus, comes with an army to destroy and besiege the city of Constantinople, taking everything within. As he formulates a plan to get into the city, the inhabitants go to Saint Germain and pray to the Virgin for aid. The Virgin then appears from the heavens with an army of followers who surround the city; when the Saracens try to launch an attack with rocks, she catches the missiles in her cloak and hurls them back at the invaders. The Saracen king then comes to realize his erroneous beliefs when he sees the Virgin defending the city and, marvelling at the miracle, realizes it is a message from God. He halts the attack and goes instead to tell the citizens what he has seen before departing in peace and friendship.

Compared to the Saracen in I Miracle 32, the Saracen here is described in greater detail in terms of both his social rank and unchristian beliefs:

> Uns sarrasinz, uns rois mout plains
> De grant orguel, de grant beubance,
> Par sa tres grant outrecuidance,
> Vint Constantinnoble asseoir. (vv. 6–9)

[A Saracen, a king completely filled with great pride and conceit, came to besiege Constantinople in his very great arrogance.]

From such an opening portrait, we might expect this to be a tale based upon the folly of pride and false belief, with the anaphora in line seven above underlining the extent of Muselinus's failings. The listing of his negative motivations in yet another anaphoric structure further emphasizes this a few lines later: 'par folor, par iniquité' (v. 14) [through folly, through injustice]. The theme of pride is also introduced by Gautier's reference to the contemporary scandal of Bertrand de Rais, a commoner who claimed to be the missing former Emperor of Constantinople, Baldwin of Flanders, between 1225 and 1226. Gautier compares the audacity of this man to those who try to make 'pourpre' [rich purple cloth] out of 'viez nate' [old matting] or who compare a 'busoz' [harrier] to a 'faucon' [falcon] (vv. 34–42). By comparing the proud Saracen to the contemporary (and local) Bertrand de Rais, Gautier suggests that Muselinus's pride is not necessarily connected to his false belief (which is a frequent pairing in *chanson de geste* portrayals of Saracens); on the contrary, pride is shown to be a failing common to both Saracens and Christians and Gautier's comparisons remind us that it may manifest in material as much as spiritual ways. Although the Saracens are clearly portrayed as the military enemy in this account, Gautier nonetheless emphasizes to the reader/listener that sin may be common to both Christians and non-Christians.

More significantly, the analogy to Bertrand de Rais gives the impression that, for Gautier, identities cannot in fact be changed, since this commoner's attempt to pass as the Emperor of Constantinople was simply impossible. At first glance there thus seems to be an implied essentialism to identity present in Gautier's comparisons. Such an essentialism would potentially contradict the miracle's coda advocating a turning towards God, as epitomized in the Saracen's conversion. However, this Saracen's conversion might be seen as a return to Christian faith instead of a transformation, given attitudes towards the Saracen religion. Rather than distrust of Muselinus's conversion, the reference to Bertrand de Rais suggests that, while the Saracen should (and will) return towards posited Christian ideals of behaviour, reconfiguring his religious identity, the Christian Bertrand de Rais cannot make himself into something that he is not (and never was). Religious identity, at least, does not seem to be essentialized in Gautier's tale, echoing the tone of I Miracle 32. Yet this is not to say that the Saracen has the same experience of the divine in this text: the apparitional encounter produces slightly different interpretations of the Saracen's religious conversion to those conveyed in *De l'ymage Nostre Dame*.

The Saracen as privileged visionary

Muselinus's conversion comes about as a direct result of his attack upon the city. The transformation of his role as Saracen oppressor occurs at the moment when the Virgin appears to him in response to the pleas of the citizens and shields them from the attack. In his article on Gautier's *Miracles*, François-Jérôme Beaussart draws a distinction between the consequences of miracles and apparitions: a miracle, he suggests, 'modifie toujours de façon inexplicable a priori le déroulement logique d'un phénomène physique naturel' [on the face of things always inexplicably modifies the logical progression of a natural, physical phenomenon] and is perceived by others as well as by the beneficiary, whereas an apparition acts 'sur l'âme' [on the soul] and is personal.⁷⁵ He divides the protagonists of the miracles into those belonging to religious and lay communities and underlines that only the former are privileged enough to see the Virgin directly, which suggests a differentiation between lay and religious conditions.⁷⁶ As a result, Beaussart asserts that, for Gautier de Coinci, apparitions of the Virgin are 'l'apanage d'un seul individu' [the privilege of a single individual], stating also that Gautier 'ne rapporte pas de visions collectives' [does not recount collective visions].⁷⁷ Yet hidden in Beaussart's footnotes is a reference to II Miracle 12 under discussion here, which he dismisses as an 'histoire traditionelle' providing the only example of 'une apparition de la Vierge visible par toute une collectivité' [an apparition of the Virgin visible to a whole group].⁷⁸ In passing over the details of this miracle, Beaussart not only overlooks that this collective group of onlookers comprises a mixture of both Christians and Saracens but also that in Gautier's text the Virgin only actually appears in visible form to Muselinus, even if the miracle accompanying her apparition (the rebounding of the stones from the city walls) is visible to all.

In the society depicted in this miracle, Gautier's emphasis is initially upon the singular rather than communal experience of the divine. Unable to break through into the city, Muselinus angrily looks up to heaven and begs Muhammad not to forget him in his hour of need. However, instead of summoning Muhammad, the Saracen is witness to an altogether different spectacle:

> Quequ'il ensi le ciel esgarde,
> Mout grans merveilles a veües:
> Descendre voit devers les nues
> Une dame si mervilleuse,
> Si très bele, si glorïeuse,
> Et d'une pourpre a or batue
> Si acesmee et si vestue
> N'est nus qui le seüst retraire. (vv. 124–31)⁷⁹

[When he looked up to the sky he saw a great marvel: descending through the clouds he saw a lady so marvellous, so very beautiful and so glorious. She was clothed and adorned in a precious fabric with beaten gold such that no-one could describe it.]

The third person verbs here such as 'esgarde' and 'voit', emphasize that Muselinus alone sees the apparition of the Virgin. His individual reaction is further underlined when we are told that 'li roys paiens mout se merveille' (v. 152) [the pagan king marvels greatly]. It is also necessary for Muselinus subsequently to recount his vision to the citizens of Constantinople (v. 161), once again suggesting that they did not see it for themselves. Individual witnessing is indicated in the visual illustration of the tale in manuscript BnF, MS n. a. fr. 24541, fol. 154ᵛ (Figure 3.11): in a miniature showing the siege, the line of sight of the central Saracen figure on the left of the frame seems to lead directly to the Virgin at the top right. None of the other figures in the image appear to be looking at her, showing the singularity of Muselinus's experience within a collective environment: he alone sees an apparition, while the whole community perceives the miracle of the rebounding rocks.

The nature of the apparition here recalls us to the idea of the spectre and Derrida's theory of spectrality. For the majority of the Saracens in this tale, there is no real spectral experience of the Virgin. Whereas the spectre is a fundamental blurring of flesh and spirit, 'flesh and phenomenality' these onlookers see only inexplicable events and no hint of the body itself.[80] In contrast, the Virgin clearly appears before Muselinus's privileged gaze as 'une dame' [a lady] and is embodied enough to catch and relaunch the attackers' stones, with reference also made to her 'cler vis' (v. 134) [bright face]. She blurs the boundaries between the terrestrial and spiritual realms, reminding us of Derrida's 'paradoxical *incorporation*' where, in his discussion of Marx's 'ghost effect', ideas or spirits do not simply take on an autonomous form but there is also 'a return to the body':

> there is no ghost, there is never any becoming-specter of the spirit without at least an appearance of flesh, in a space of invisible visibility, like the disappearing of an apparition.[81]

The becoming-body of the Virgin before Muselinus's astounded gaze is central to her narrative role, since it is this, rather than the miracle produced by her intervention, that impacts upon the Saracen. We learn, for instance, that the sight of her tangible-intangible form affects him physically, since: 'son cuer li a si escité' (v. 167) [she thus stirred his heart]. Given that Muselinus is the only one of the Saracens whose conversion is explicitly described in this tale, it seems that this visual and physical interaction between the Saracen and the Virgin is vital to his religious conversion. Embodiment does not signal his religious difference but instead produces this new religious understanding. His experience reflects Suzannah Biernoff's comment that sight in the Middle Ages was a '*physical* activity', where 'vision [...] did not leave the viewer untouched or unchanged' and 'to see was to become similar to one's object'.[82] In this sense, if medieval viewing led to a certain assimilation of the object viewed, *what* Muselinus actually sees is of prime importance for the interpretation of his own bodily identity.

In contrast to Derrida's formulation of the spectre as a blurring of flesh and spirit, the apparition of the Virgin possesses a body that we might call *fleshless* rather than fleshly: she appears in a bodily form, yet lacks the sensory, desiring, or changeable qualities associated with human flesh.[83] As a result, spectrality in this context must thus be alternatively construed when medieval thinking on the relationship between flesh and body is taken into account: just as 'the fleshless body [...] is a fluent expression of the soul, both a vehicle of meaning and a subordinate member unimpaired by passion',[84] the religious apparition unites the spirit with a more heavenly understanding of the body than the carnal form suggested by Derrida. This is all the more so in the case of an apparition of the Virgin, whose body was significant in Christian thought both for its flesh and form, its sinlessness and its integrity: she was simultaneously the vessel of God and the flesh of Christ. As per the doctrine of the Assumption, her mortal body was also deemed to have ascended to heaven after death along with her soul. In this sense, whereas Derrida suggests that Christ is 'the most spectral of specters',[85] the Virgin might be regarded

FIG. 3.11. The Virgin defending Constantinople (Gautier de Coinci, *Comment Nostre Dame desfendi la cité de Constantinnoble*). Paris, BnF, MS n. a. fr. 24541, fol. 154^v.
Photo: Paris, Bibliothèque nationale de France.

as equally spectral if not more so; this is especially given the fact that, contrary to Christ, she left no corporeal traces on earth.

Apparitions of the Virgin, therefore, do not just conjoin flesh and spirit but both evoke and distinguish *body*, flesh, and spirit. She is spectral in the sense that she is *revenant* and hints at a fleshly, human phenomenality, yet she also represents the eternal life of a body that is *spiritual* and precisely not carnal. This is different to the disavowal of fleshly finitude discussed in Derrida's text and which is epitomized by the ghostly return of Hamlet's father. In the apparition of 'une dame', Muselinus sees the return of this tri-faceted, pure body that had been returned to heaven in its entirety. Fittingly, his conversion also involves three elements: sensory, fleshly experience; a more spiritual change of heart; and an offer of physical protection for the city, so that his earthly body now replaces the celestial body of the Virgin. In consequence, the Saracen's body is not superseded in the process of conversion, since it is essential that the divine acts upon it and through it in visual and thus physical ways.

The need for a personal and physical engagement with Christianity in the process of conversion is furthermore apparent in the fact that Muselinus's army does not share his change of heart, in contrast to the mass conversions often seen in epic texts.[86] A similar emphasis is also placed on the experiencing body in *De l'ymage Nostre Dame* discussed above, where the protagonist's Saracen followers only convert to Christianity 'par le myracle, qu'apert virent' (v. 75) [through the miracle that they clearly saw] rather than through force or through hearsay. Despite the fact that Muselinus enters the city with a thousand men, once again the verbs used by Gautier appear in the singular, as Muselinus alone is the one to give great gifts and pledge his faith (vv. 173–79). His army simply experience fear due to the inefficacy of their artillery attack (v. 110). Merely to witness the effect of a miracle, it seems, is not enough to produce conversion: a different kind of experience is required, one which involves a direct physical engagement with either miraculous atemporality or the apparitional, spiritual body. For the Saracen army, the miraculously impenetrable city walls show simply that 'pour cialz de la vile Diex veille' (v. 112) [God watches over those in the city], something which divides them from the community of the blessed within the city. Their leader, however, sees the invisible made visible, the divine made manifest in the apparition.

The physical effects of witnessing the apparitional are also a feature of the preceding miracle in Gautier's collection, *De Saint Basile* [*Of Saint Basil*] (I Miracle 11), firstly through the figure of Basil himself and secondly through the pagan clerk Lybanÿus. Early in the text Basil sees the Virgin in a dream where she brings an army led by Saint Mercurius to save the inhabitants of his town from the anger of Julian the Apostate. This same sight is later experienced by Lybanÿus:

> Libanÿus, uns mout haus hom,
> Ceste meïsme visïon
> En tel maniere et tout ensi
> En Perse, ou ert, revit ausi. (vv. 309–12)

Fig. 3.12. Combat between Saint Mercurius and Julian the Apostate (Gautier de Coinci, *De Saint Basile*). Paris, BnF, MS n. a. fr. 24541, fol. 149^v.
Photo: Paris, Bibliothèque nationale de France.

[Libanÿus, a very high-ranking man, then saw this same vision in exactly the same manner in Persia, where he was.]

The emphasis here upon the shared nature of this vision draws a clear parallel between the experiences of the Christian saint and the pagan clerk. Upon awakening, Basil summons the people together and 'plourant par grant devocïon, | Lors lor conte l'avisïon | que veüe a de Nostre Dame' (vv. 381–83) [crying with great devotion, he tells them about the vision that he has seen of our lady]. Proof of Julian's defeat arrives firstly in the form of Saint Mercurius's bloodied lance (which had previously gone missing from the church) and then in the form of Lybanÿus, who arrives and narrates the saint's victory. He confirms Saint Basil's vision before the townspeople, concluding that 'd'ore en avant la veritez | de vostre foy est toute aperte' (vv. 509–10) [from now on the truth of your faith is completely clear] and then contrasts this with his observation that 'apertement est aparant | que riens ne vaut loy de paiens' (vv. 514–15) [it is clearly apparent that the law of the pagans is worth nothing]. Lybanÿus's tale is also mirrored by Basil's subsequent retelling of his own vision to him, following which the pagan is baptized as a Christian.

In this example, as with that of Muselinus, the pagan sees both Christian vision and miracle first-hand and the process of conversion not only necessitates the recounting of his experience before others but similarly involves a physical effect upon his heart, as is perhaps evoked in the accompanying illumination on fol. 149^v of BnF, MS n. a. fr. 24541 (Figure 3.12). The image shows Saint Mercurius attacking a group of bearded and/or moustached pagans; he dominates the foreground and enacts a downwards motion with his lance. In particular, he spears the heart-shaped shield of the pagan before him. Such shields echo the *ardaga* often associated with Muslim fighters in this period,[87] but the image also emphasizes the effect of witnessing this blow upon Lybanÿus himself. When he comes to report the events of the battle to Saint Basil and the citizens, he claims: 'Toz li cors encor m'en fremie | et le cuer ai tout esfreé | dou felon colp dou desreé [all my body is still trembling and my heart is completely affright from the terrible blow of the formidable knight][88] (vv. 494–96). As a depiction of events happening off-stage, this miniature seems to be a representation of Lybanÿus's testimony; it portrays the more physical, literal defeat of the pagan rather than the miraculous vision of Saint Basil or the sight of the bloody lance. There is certainly no reference to the Virgin in this image, who appears to Saint Basil and summons Saint Mercurius before her in his prophetic dream-vision.[89] As a result, bodily effects are blurred with the vision itself in this manuscript, as the viewer is placed in the position of Lybanÿus rather than the saint — placed quite literally in the body of the pagan — as a privileged if flawed visionary.

Nancy Black has suggested that BnF, MS n. a. fr. 24541 was a devotional text 'individualized for the practice of royal readers',[90] so it is interesting to note that, as with the illuminations of I Miracle 32, this image appears to underline the relationship between a personal experience of the miraculous and religious conversion as much as the military protection afforded to the faithful. If seeing involves an act of assimilation, then the images in this manuscript in particular are not just about 'moving the heart to devotion',[91] but about sharing in the recipient's own transformative experience. Perhaps the greater the transformation suggested in the depiction of a dark-skinned Saracen experiencing Christian enlightenment, the greater the potential for transformation among the medieval Christian reader/viewer: if the most utterly unchristian figure can be moved to God and access the divine, the continuous, everyday acts of faith encouraged in Gautier's texts might begin to seem even more achievable.

From personal experience to communal devotion

Returning to II Miracle 12, not only does the spectral body of the Virgin encourage a bodily response in the Saracen, but the emphasis upon apparition or miracle between text and image also affects the moral agendas conveyed and Saracen identities that emerge. Marian intercession has a practical effect upon Muselinus as well as a spiritual one, since he is literally 'donté' [defeated] by the rebounding of the rocks. He does not simply see an image of the Virgin in his imagination, a *visio spiritualis*, but a form of spectre whose miraculous actions may be observed separately from her bodily apparition. While Christine Lapostolle defines three categories of *visio spiritualis* with regard to an apparition,[92] the Saracen's experience here seems less clear-cut: it merges what would be termed *visio spiritualis* (a vision involving the imagination such as in dreams) with *visio corporalis* (a vision sensorily perceived through the body). The apparition does not appear to him while asleep, and the idea of him seeing the Virgin purely in his mind is troubled by the clearly physical, tangible results of her presence. Narratives of conflict between Christians and Saracens frequently show how divine intervention allows the Christian forces to win, yet in this case, the divine intervention actually achieves the victory: it is not the Christians that have beaten Muselinus but 'la douce mere'. The combination of both miracle and apparition in this tale achieves military and spiritual defeat: while the apparition promotes a more personal, abstracted reading of events, the miracle is aligned to the physical world and communally experienced. In turn, the resulting ways in which miracle and apparition appear in the visual illustrations accompanying the narrative affect the use of the body and processes of racial/religious identity construction.

In BnF, MS n. a. fr. 24541 (Figure 3.11), the miniature shows the Virgin descending through the clouds above the city walls. She is partially obscured by these clouds, reminding us that this is a vision, not a tangible, living being, and there is no sense that the Christian knights in the fortress can see this apparition, which seems very much to float above their heads. A dark-skinned Saracen holds the gaze of the Christian knight just across the wall from him, while the Saracen at the front of the group looks up to the Virgin and her line of sight travels down towards him via the rock that has been hurled towards her. The viewer therefore sees a scene of confrontation and contrasts based upon both outward appearances and lines of sight. Such contrasts include: somatic features (the bearded and heavier-set features of the Saracen soldiers compared both with their lighter-skinned, armour-wearing counterparts and with the delicate features and fairness of the Virgin); space (the Virgin's cloak separating those within from those without); materials (the immensity and definition of the city walls versus the soft, blended borders surrounding the Virgin); and actions (the defensive and weaponless Christians versus the sword- and trebuchet-wielding Saracens). In this image, the spotlight is clearly upon the appearance of the Virgin and her role in the military conflict, with the Saracens almost hidden behind the trebuchet and fortress. The miniature does not emphasize the ensuing conversion of the Saracen leader, but does show the moment of his personal perception of the apparition. The personal nature of this experience is reminiscent of the image accompanying I Miracle 32 in this manuscript, where the Saracen's momentary, individual experience of the Virgin's transforming body is depicted rather than his subsequent baptism. Both of these depictions thus focus upon the individual's physical encounter with the spiritual, which also seems to echo the status of this particular manuscript as a talismanic object in itself. Indeed, the notion of divine military protection must have resonated with subsequent owners of this manuscript, given that it was carried to war by John II, King of France and lost at the Battle of Poitiers in 1356.[93]

FIG. 3.13. The Virgin defending Constantinople and kneeling worshippers (Gautier de Coinci, *Comment Nostre Dame desfendi la cité de Constantinnoble*). Paris, BnF, MS f. fr. 22928, fol. 200ʳ. Photo: Paris, Bibliothèque nationale de France

In contrast, the illustration of II Miracle 12 in BnF, MS f. fr. 22928 (Figure 3.13) renders the apparition of the Virgin as an integral, spiritual body experienced by a community. As discussed above, in the two-compartment image of I Miracle 32 in this manuscript, the Saracen was initially set apart, only to be integrated through the parallel image of his baptism. The miniature of II Miracle 12 similarly shows a before and after scene, in this case moving from conflict to communal worship. While the Virgin of BnF, MS n. a. fr. 24541 protects the city with her cloak and is actively engaged in hurling rocks back at its physically othered aggressors, in BnF, MS f. fr. 22928 (fol. 200^r) her whole body appears hovering between the invaders and the city. Saracens and townspeople are placed very much on the same level, with the Virgin acting as a barrier between them. There are also no obvious signs that these are in fact Saracens rather than any other enemy. The intercession of the Virgin and her function as an intermediary for the community is therefore highlighted in this tripartite image. It is almost impossible to tell that the Saracen ruler has been singled out as a privileged visionary; instead, Muselinus's integration into the Christian community is prominent.[94] In addition, in contrast to BnF, MS n. a. fr. 24541, the military miracle is downplayed in favour of the apparition, since the trebuchet and its rocks appear beyond the border of the image in the top compartment. Such an emphasis upon religious community is also visible in the bottom register, where the devotional posture of the Saracen king (left) is echoed by the praying figure of the patriarch, Saint Germain (right). Attacking and defending communities are united firstly in their experience of the apparitional body and subsequently through their expression of faith, so that the miraculous blurring of physical and spiritual worlds is far less apparent than in BnF, MS n. a. fr. 24541.

What is additionally interesting about the miniature in BnF, MS f. fr. 22928 is that there is no image of Muselinus's baptism, just his act of religious worship, so that instead of being a convert he appears instead as an integrated member of the Christian community. This is in contrast to the moments of baptism depicted in the miniature of I Miracle 32 on fol. 113^v of the same manuscript and in the historiated initial of the tale *De l'enfant a un giu qui se crestïena* (fol. 75^r). The portrayal of Muselinus therefore underscores his faith and membership of this community rather than the moment of conversion. In this respect, the illustration of this miracle echoes the text's wider emphasis on devotional constancy on the part of the community, a message emphasized when the women of the city walk together

> De grans tortis, de grans soigniez
> Devant l'ymage Nostre Dame.
> De tout son cuer, de toute s'ame
> Devant s'ymage a jointes mains. (vv. 80–83)

[With great torches and great care before the image of Our Lady. With all their heart, with all their soul before the image with joined hands.]

The alliteration and anaphora here create a rhythmic, ritualized feel for this event. Gautier's closing message, furthermore, makes emphatic use of *annominatio* to explain that by turning our hearts to the Virgin we will all be protected from attack:

> Car l'anemi ne ses estours,
> Tous ses assauz ne toz ses tours
> Douter ne puet un oef torné
> Qui son cuer a a toy torné,
> Dame, es cui flanz Diex se torna.
> Mur, forterece ne tor n'a,
> Ainz est honis au chief dou tour
> Cielz qui de toy ne fait sa tour. (vv. 247–54)

[for neither the Enemy nor his creations, all his attacks nor forms, can be feared as much as a rotten egg by he who has turned his heart towards you, Lady, in whose flanks God developed. He who does not turn towards you has no wall, fortress, nor tower and is thus condemned in the end].

His comments suggest a greater concern with circularity and with turning/returning the sinner to God than with the linear movement of a non-Christian into the Christian community. Coupled with an emphasis upon the body as spiritual rather than fleshly in this miracle, it is no wonder that the image of BnF, MS f. fr. 22928 erases the racial and even religious difference of Muselinus as 'uns sarrasinz' and offers a generic scene of communal vision and thanksgiving.

Essentially, we see a general turning towards God in this manuscript rather than the prioritization of individual experience, underlining the results of the miraculous encounter rather than focusing on the privileged visionary himself. The contrasting illustrations of II Miracle 12 in BnF, MS f. fr. 22928 and BnF, MS n. a. fr. 24541 show the very different ways in which Gautier's moral messages may be drawn out in the relationship between text and image. If the Soissons manuscript was particularly geared towards private devotion, perhaps the emphases of BnF, MS f. fr. 22928 are more suggestive of a religious community.[95] However, this comparison is also significant for revealing the roles that racial and religious aspects of Saracen identity may play in emphasizing particular elements of Gautier's moral messages to the reader/viewer. Whereas Beaussart suggests that 'l'apparition agit d'abord sur l'âme, le miracle agit sur le corps' [the apparition acts primarily on the soul, the miracle on the body], the Virgin's spectral body and Saracens' sensory experiences trouble this neat distinction. The triple evocation of body, flesh, and spirit that occurs in the apparitional encounter reveals and incites bodily responses that are as much fleshly as spiritual. Just as the visual representation of an apparitional body proves problematic, the racial representation of the Saracen's body in the manuscript images of this miracle cannot wholly transmit the transformative, religious experience narrated.

De l'ymage Nostre Dame de Sardanei (II Miracle 30)

In the final miracle detailing Saracen communication with the Virgin, Gautier presents a Saracen as the recipient of intercessory aid rather than as an explicit exemplar or as a witness to an apparition.[96] This miracle describes how a monk brings an icon from Jerusalem to a nun residing outside Damascus. The Saracen who briefly features in the story is a blind sultan from the nearby city who has heard of the power attributed to the icon of the Virgin in Sardanei (Saidnaya) and decides to visit it in the hope of regaining his lost sight. In contrast to the Saracens of I Miracle 32 or II Miracle 12, the Saracen in this miracle appears to function as a religious other who demonstrates the power and benevolence of Christianity specifically through his healed body. He is described from the outset as a sultan who is 'uns sarrazinz de grant orguel' (vv. 488–89) [a very proud Saracen] and unlike Muselinus, his pride is not placed in relation to similar sinners from within the Christian community. In spite of his pagan beliefs, the sultan's prostration before the image of the Virgin is successful and she asks her son to heed his request and give him back his sight; once this occurs, the Saracen immediately pledges himself to God and vows to send a large quantity of oil every year to the nun to replenish the lamp beside the icon, a promise that he never forgets. As with the miracle at Constantinople, *De l'ymage Nostre Dame de Sardanei* also details the witnessing and communication of miraculous events, but it is significant that this time it is the body of the sultan that transmits the power of intercession rather than his oral testimony. If, as previously noted, the spectre is 'neither soul nor body, and both one and the other'[97] then once again the miraculous presents a moment where the spiritual and material collide, disrupting and reimagining the relationship between body and identity.

On a basic level, the sultan in II Miracle 30 is physically assimilated into the Christian community through his brief experience of the miraculous by being surrounded by other pilgrims who witness his curing and who pray together to God and Mary in thanks. In this way, the Saracen acts as an example of the icon's power; he is not an exemplar for the reader/listener to emulate, contrary to the Saracen in I Miracle 32, but demonstrates the very incorporation of the miraculous. Rather than his actions, his body is used to reinforce the truth of the miracle in this tale. Questions of truth, proof, and witnessing are central to this narrative: for instance, just after the Saracen is healed, Gautier criticizes those who lack 'creance et foiz' (v. 577) [belief and faith] in such miracles, going on to claim that there is a good bourgeois man in Soissons who has seen the image himself. He even states that 'veritez est, esprouvé l'ai' (vv. 611–25) [this is the truth, I have verified it]. Belief is thus not merely a matter of hearsay but of verifiable sensory experiences. Above all, Gautier criticizes those who believe the tales of *jongleurs* more than miracles:

> Ne croient pas Sainte Escriture
> Li mescreant, li faus herite,
> Li plain de mauvais esperite,
> Des miracles le Sauveeur
> Si bien com font un jongleeur
> De Rainnoart au grant tinel. (vv. 598–603)

> [they do not believe the Holy Scripture on the miracles of the Saviour, those unbelievers and false heretics, those filled with bad souls, as much as they believe a jongleur about Renoart with the big club.]

It is perhaps no accident that Gautier refers to one of the best known literary Saracens here, the giant warrior Renoart from the Guillaume d'Orange Cycle of *chansons de geste*, who is captured by Christians and taken under the wing of the eponymous hero. By implicitly contrasting Renoart with the miraculously converted sultan of his own tale, Gautier distinguishes his depiction of the Saracen from those found in epic literature. In addition, this distinguishes the sultan, whose body is restored and brought from outsider to insider, from Renoart, whose gigantism continually sets him apart physically from those around him despite his conversion.[98] If Renoart's body is defined by its fixity, the sultan's is rather defined by its changeability; furthermore, the changing (healing) of his body signals his religious conversion. While there is evidence in medieval literature that religious conversion could effect corporeal change,[99] this is far from common, even in cases where the text draws attention to the skin colour of the protagonist. In this sense, the act of healing offers a more universally recognizable way in which a body can openly be marked by religious change in an act that both asserts and denies the place of the body within the construction of religious identity.

Spectral bodies: the Virgin and the sultan

The Saracen in II Miracle 30 is neither extremely good nor extremely bad, possessing only the quality of 'orguel' (v. 489) [pride], which can have positive and negative connotations of pride and valour. As a result, this representation differs from the exemplary or privileged Saracens in the other miracles discussed here since it seems to better suit Gautier's promise to 'raconter vraies estoyres' (II Pro 1, v. 357) [tell true stories] which, as Duys notes, offer 'spiritual, literary recreation' to his audience.[100] The miraculous healing of the sultan therefore functions here more as proof of the icon's holy status than as a demonstration of the need to baptize and integrate non-Christians.

In contrast to the polemical writings discussed by Kruger, such as those of Guibert de Nogent,[101] the Saracen body is not represented as a pollutant or threat to be shunned or denied in this miracle but something to be healed and celebrated. It does not threaten Christian integrity but confirms it. Indeed, the Christian faith of others is even improved by seeing this body:

> Il e li sien granz aleüres
> A Dammas joiant s'en ralerent.
> Dieu et sa mere mout loerent
> Et mielz l'amerent et servirent
> Cil et celes qui puis le virent. (vv. 534–38)

> [[The sultan] and his people joyfully returned with great haste to Damascus. They greatly praised God and his mother and whoever saw him loved and served Him better.]

FIG. 3.14. Scenes from Gautier de Coinci's *De l'ymage Nostre Dame de Sardanei*. Paris, BnF, MS f. fr. 22928, fol. 255ʳ. Photo: Paris, Bibliothèque nationale de France

Given the importance of the Saracen body in this tale, while there are not many illustrations of the sultan among the corpus of illuminated *Miracles* manuscripts,[102] it is nevertheless interesting to note that he is marked out by a beard but not by headwear. BnF, MS f. fr. 22928 (fol. 255ʳ, Figure 3.14) contains an illumination with six compartments where, in the third of the bottom register, a king appears kneeling at the head of a group in prayer before the image of the Virgin. He sports a crown and his only potentially Saracen identifying feature is his beard.[103] The composition of this compartment is very similar to the illumination of BnF, MS f. fr. 25532 except that in the latter the bearded sultan is next to the nun and the monk and has a lamp over his head (fol. 194ᵛ, Figure 3.15).

Fig. 3.15. Worshippers (the Saracen ?) kneeling before an image [of the Virgin]. (*De l'ymage Nostre Dame de Sardanei*). Paris, BnF, MS f. fr. 25532, fol. 194ᵛ. Photo: Paris, Bibliothèque nationale de France

This reflects how the lamp is central to his miraculous experience in the narrative and his lack of obvious demarcation as Saracen (in a manuscript where both Jews and Saracens are elsewhere marked out by headwear) prioritizes this restoration of 'clarté', both in a physical and spiritual sense. While the changing of his body from blind Saracen to seeing Christian is so central to the events of the miracle, in these illustrations the body is significant for the gestures that integrate him into the Christian community and suggest a levelling of all before God.[104]

With such an emphasis upon integration, it would be tempting to read this miracle as showing the general effacement of the Saracen body. However, the tale continues to problematize the place of the body more broadly, both as a sign of otherness and as a central element of Christian belief, echoing Kruger's observation that there are 'disturbing embodiments at the heart of the Christian mystery itself.'[105] Firstly, while the body of the sultan is healed, it remains unbaptized in both the text and its illuminations. He continues to give thanks upon his return to

Damascus, but no actual mention is made of his conversion. In a sense, the potential open-endedness to his story means that this Saracen is the epitome of the spectral double-bind mentioned earlier. To make his baptism evident in the text would be to limit the impressiveness of the miracle, as much as it would reinforce it: while the power of Marian intercession would be proved by his conversion, leaving it unstated recognizes the possibility that even an *unbaptized* Saracen can be healed by Marian intercession. He must consequently retain an identity as both Saracen *and* Christian for his role in the narrative to work.

By extension, the sultan's role as living proof of the divine means that his Saracen body can never truly be expunged in Gautier's tale, especially since the effect of and engagement with the miraculous is very much a physical affair. Both the body of the Virgin and that of the Saracen are transformed in the narrative: the icon first begins to sweat 'une liqueur' (v. 400) [a liquid] then grows breasts which exude oil (vv. 468–69) and the Saracen's lost sight is, of course, restored. In fact, the sultan seems to regain an entire eye, not just his sight, since we are originally told that 'lonc tanz n'avoit eü q'un oel' [for a long time he had only one eye] and that 'en celui li prist telz goute' (vv. 490–91) [he developed such gout in it] yet after praying for his sight 'les ieulz ouvri et vit le fu | en la lampe devant l'ymage' (vv. 516–17) [he opened his eyes and saw the flame in the lamp before the image]. In this sense, the body is not simply healed but made whole once more. Furthermore, the idea of a return to a previous state is also apparent in the vocabulary used: the Saracen has not always been blind but has 'perdi' [lost] his sight, or as the term 'clarté' might suggest, potentially also his clear-sightedness. His metaphorical spiritual blindness to Christian truth is evoked through the physical infirmity visited upon him and thus the healing received is both physical and spiritual. Just as his healing is therefore a kind of return, his conversion could also be read as a return to a faith that he has somehow lost. The Saracen body here is spectral in the sense of being an incorporation marked by its past and constituting its future simultaneously.

However, not only is the sultan's sight 'recouvree' (v. 528) [recovered] through divine intervention but he now sees more clearly than any man that ever lived (v. 522). This temporal blurring means that the Saracen's own history is in fact central to establishing both the truth of the icon in Gautier's present and, ultimately, correct Christian practice in the future. Gautier mentions that upon his return the sultan vows to send oil in thanks 'perpetüelment' (v. 530) [indefinitely], and that it continued to be given year on year, 'dusqu'au tanz a un sodan | qui Voradinz fu apelez' (vv. 542–43) [until the time of a sultan who was called Voradinz]. 'Voradinz' here is likely a variant spelling of Nur-ed-Dīn of Aleppo, predecessor of Saladin and ruler in Syria until 1174.[106] In this respect, the spectrality of the miraculous Saracen body — referencing, as it does, a past age yet also *arrivant* as Christian in this narrative — reveals Gautier's conception of recent history as a space with multiple Saracen pasts. The grateful Saracen recipient of miraculous aid and the powerful Saracen scourge of crusaders appear together, so that it is not that all Saracens are necessarily barred access to future salvation, since they are represented as possessing a kind of potential: were it not for the intervention of 'Voradinz' we are left to assume that the sultan's legacy would have continued.

Along with a temporal blurring, the spectrality of bodily identity in this miracle tale also means that there is an intimate connection between Christian and Saracen bodies. This connection is recognized through the intricate wordplay used by Gautier, which directly links the transformation of the Virgin's own body to that of the sultan. Not only is the power of her miraculous fluids to enact physical healing emphasized several times (vv. 413, 420, 480–86) but an aural link is created between the homophones 'goute' (gout), 'goute' (drop), the negative construction 'ne…goute' (not a thing) and the verb 'degouter' (to drip). Such wordplay connects illness, disability, miracle, and cure in the tale and reminds us that this is a miracle centred upon the physical effects of the miraculous, themselves instigated by the products of bodily functions produced when celestial and terrestrial worlds meet and where the limits of the human body are challenged as inanimate becomes animate.

Nonetheless, despite the linguistic mirroring of Saracen and Marian transformations, we must remember that the Saracen is healed by his own act of prostration before the image, rather than by the miraculous bodily fluids of the Virgin. The legitimacy of his act of prostration is recognized in his healing, reminding us once more that identity may be performatively produced through the repetition and recognition of gestures. Whereas the healed Saracen body becomes not just as good as new but better than new, seeming to catch this 'ideal-image' it had been pursuing,[107] the gestures of this now Christian body become the target of Gautier's coda. The result is a kind of spectral mirroring that emerges from his criticisms of the Christian body's imperfect enactment of devotional practice and exposes the performativity of embodied identity more generally.

Gesturing to faith

Alongside transformations, II Miracle 30 also focuses on bodily gestures. When Gautier addresses his readers/audience after recounting the sultan's miraculous healing, he accordingly mentions physical movement as a means of communication. He tells them to step forward if they do not believe the truth of the tale:

> S'aucun i a si affronté
> Qui le myracle qu'ai conté
> Croire ne veille, viegne avant. (vv. 605–07)

> [If there is anyone so insolent who does not wish to believe the miracle that I have recounted, let him come forward.]

While the Saracen is assimilated both physically and spiritually through his healing and change of belief, Gautier enacts a return to the afflicted body at the end of the text. In so doing, he highlights the centrality of physical actions and experiences to faith and criticizes those whose devotional gestures are lacking. Firstly, Gautier criticizes people who do not address the Virgin correctly in their prayers, saying that they should properly enunciate the word 'Maria':

> *Maria* par est si doz moz
> Que luez que la langue le touche,
> Li cuers, les levres et la bouche
> Suchier le doit, par saint Cristofle,

> Ausi com le clou de gyrofle
> Quant on le vielt bien essaier. (vv. 754–59)

[*Maria* is such a sweet word that as soon as the tongue touches it, the heart, lips, and mouth should suck it, by Saint Christopher, just like when you want to try a clove.]

The reader/listener is told to 'demorer' [remain/linger] 'por bien le mot assavourer' (v. 762) [to savour the word well]. The word is to be experienced physically, synaesthetically, not just heard but tasted and, as Gautier secondly underlines, this physical experience leads to a spiritual one:

> Qui bien le suce entre ses denz
> Si grant douceur trueve dedenz
> Que tout en est l'ame saoule. (vv. 763–65)

[whoever sucks it between his teeth finds such great sweetness in it that his soul is completely satiated.]

The boundaries between the fleshly and the spiritual here are blurred, as the sensory experience of taste impacts upon the soul, echoing how the Saracen's own restored sight materializes the divine. Gautier even tells us that the saintly nun who cared for the image 'se saouloit' [hungered] to serve the Virgin more than for 'viande terrïenne' (v. 836) [earthly meat]. Reverential gestures and sensory experience unite in this coda and are to be combined with the turning of the mind and heart towards God:

> Mais quant li cors s'abaisse jus,
> l'ame drecier se doit lassus.
> Quant li cors fait afflictïons,
> Devant Dieu soit l'ententïons.
> Quant li genoul sont en la pourre,
> Lors doit li cuers devant Dieu courre
> Et lui et sa mere aourer
> Et leur douceur asavourer. (vv. 859–66)

[But when the body is lowered, the soul should rise up, when the body is prostrate, the mind should be before God. When the knees are in the dust, then should the heart run to God and venerate Him and his mother and savour their sweetness.]

Gautier's exhortation to his audience therefore combines not just body and spirit, but *flesh*, body, and spirit by emphasizing the need for sensory experience, bodily prostration, and spiritual focus. The miracle in this tale affects the Saracen's bodily form as well as his spirit and his experiencing flesh, all of which is paralleled in the coda's message: the Saracen's newly formed Christian body continues to be haunted by the spectre of imperfect repetition — specifically of not correctly incorporating the spiritual within bodily, fleshly experience. If the Saracen body is temporally spectral in this tale, asserted and denied in its narrative of healing, the Christian body is spectral in its self-haunting performativity: it must continually be experienced, positioned, and witnessed in its repetition of conventional gestures for religious identity to be recognized.

Conclusion: Bodies of Proof

> Nor does one see in flesh and blood this Thing that is not a thing, this thing that is invisible between its apparitions, when it reappears. This Thing meanwhile looks at us and sees us not see it even when it is there. A spectral asymmetry interrupts here all specularity. It de-synchronizes, it recalls us to anachrony. We will call this the visor effect: we do not see who looks at us.[108]

In Gautier's *Miracles,* the relationship between racial and religious identity varies, influenced by the Saracen's specific function as exemplar, as visionary, and as evidential proof. It is not as simple as being able to say that religious belief determines physiognomic identity or vice versa, since the idea and representation of Saracenness may be interpreted in different ways to suit the particular moral messages to be expounded. This is even true across manuscript variants of the same tale. Above all, while for certain medieval writers and thinkers the Saracen may be profoundly 'flesh-bound',[109] and thus precluded from immortal life, in the text and manuscripts of Gautier's *Miracles* the Saracen's body does not bind him; it is often central to his conversionary experience and becomes at times spectral, highlighting how it is problematic to view the body as the primary signifier of race. All three miracle tales show the centrality of the body to a person's faith, yet this is a body with a complex spiritual and fleshly nature. In this sense, the body of the convert and his experience of the divine are closely tied to medieval thinking on the relationship between body, flesh, and spirit, a fact which impacts upon the idea that religious difference is a form of embodied otherness. As Gautier's texts have shown, the differing ways in which the Saracen experiences the body of the Virgin produce particular interpretations of what constitutes Saracen identity, so that racial and religious difference is never consistently treated between miracles and/or manuscripts.

Furthermore, the processes of identity construction in the *Miracles* are based on visual and visible interactions as much as upon internal reasoning or understanding. In *De l'ymage Nostre Dame,* the Saracen sees the very moment of miraculous transformation in which the divine becomes flesh and is incarnated through an object. In *Comment Nostre Dame desfendi la cité de Constantinnoble,* Muselinus's individual witnessing of an apparition reminds us that seeing is a physical act with physical effects. The spectral body he encounters differs from that of the miracle, since its spectrality lies more in its phenomenological status than its temporal disjunction. In *De l'ymage Nostre Dame de Sardanei,* the sultan not only looks but is looked at in return: the restoration of his sight literally allows him to see the (lamp)light, while also making him the object to be seen by others. His converted, reverted body is also proof that he has been seen by God and in turn, the spectrality of this body exposes how Christian identity itself relies upon the enactment and perception of correct devotional gestures. If Derrida suggests that the armour worn by the ghost of Hamlet's father conceals not just the body beneath but prevents us from seeing who looks at us, then the exemplary Saracen's outward surface of skin, somatic features, and dress is also a costume concealing what is really looking at Gautier's reader/viewer — namely God himself.

Text-image relations in the manuscript as object question the relationship between the (racial) body as object in Gautier's *Miracles* and the representation of race. As the case study of manuscripts containing *De l'ymage Nostre Dame* revealed, the extent to which biological features signify a kind of racial difference varies even within a very small production context and may, to a certain extent, respond to the difficulties of fixing the moment of miraculous transformation into a visual form. However, this does not mean that the more fleshly the representation of the Virgin, the more the flesh of the Saracen always matters, as the rubric, overarching moral message, and patron preferences may all play a role in the overall rendering of Saracen identity that we see and read. Furthermore, uniting image with text also highlights the inherent complexity of representing these religious experiences pictorially: the difficulty of separating *visio corporalis* from *visio spiritualis* becomes apparent, as does the difficulty of determining the relationship between the sensory body and the imagination. The physical manuscript as physical object therefore provides alternative ways of contextualizing Saracen bodies in terms of medieval religious experience as well as racial categorizations.

Marie-Geneviève Grossel observes that for Gautier, 'le siècle [...] est l'endroit de toutes les violences' [all forms of violence are located in his own age], where the author's focus is more upon his contemporaries than 'l'homme éternel' [eternal man] in a world that is 'noir et blanc' [black and white].[110] However, the Saracens clearly muddy the waters of this supposedly clear-cut and temporally specific environment. Instead of being used to show the threat to Christianity from religious others, the Saracen reveals the potential for changes of identity. These miracle tales therefore seem to be more representative of Gautier's didactic ambition than of a particular disdain for the Saracen as a racial or religious other. The *Miracles* show no genuine interest in meaningful engagement with real religious difference, but nor do they manifest the kind of hatred that Gautier directs against Jews; the various representations of the Saracen ultimately underline the importance of worshipping the Virgin earnestly and the potential benefits that such devotion may bring. Given the ritualistic qualities of both narrative and style,[111] the miracles could just be 'ways of making underlying Christian myths efficacious for assembled congregations',[112] a reflection of the purpose and performance of the text as much as the racial or religious ideals upheld within contemporary medieval society. In this respect, the moral messages expounded by Gautier are as key to understanding the processes of identity construction and integration at work as the narratives themselves.

More particularly, the Saracen protagonists in I Miracle 32 and II Miracle 30 suggest the performative nature of religious identity by highlighting the possibility that the correct repetition of conventional actions and gestures — and the recognition of this repetition through miraculous experience — might outweigh appearance, understanding, or even baptism. Yet this performativity is also at the heart of Gautier's criticisms. Repeatedly, Gautier's codas underline that it is not enough just to call yourself Christian, since you also have to act in a Christian manner. As readers, we therefore have to be equally careful not to assume that a kneeling, praying Saracen is necessarily an idolater as that a so-called Christian enacts correct Christian deeds. Indeed, Gautier's whole argument seems to be that assumed identities may belie the inner spiritual realities beneath. While it might initially seem odd to have a Saracen used for his exemplary Christian behaviour, perhaps Saracens are expedient for Gautier's messages given the catch-all nature of the very term 'Saracen'; this word can, after all, encompass racial and religious others from very broad temporal and geographical contexts, referring to non-Christians in the most general way possible and thus enabling Saracens to have a very different place within Christian eschatology from that of Jews. Kruger argues that medieval attitudes towards Judaism are marked by Christ's Incarnation, which signals a point of rupture and sets post-incarnational Jews as belonging to Christianity's past.[113] In contrast, Saracens are set within the perpetual future of Christianity, forever promising a future return to the Christian fold.

Given the temporal positioning of the Saracen through the miraculous experiences depicted in the *Miracles*, the concept of spectrality has helped to reveal the reliance upon yet denial of the Saracen body when he is both exemplar and convert. The body may play a slightly different role when required as a sensory and fleshly witness of the miraculous, as in II Miracle 30. Even if each of Gautier's tales describes a kind of becoming-body, it is nonetheless important to distinguish the processes involved, whether this is via an apparition, object made flesh, or physical restoration, as these processes involve different amounts of agency on the part of the Saracen. Whereas in *Comment Nostre Dame desfendi la cité de Constantinnoble* the apparition acts physically upon Muselinus, promoting the value of an individual reception of the divine, in the two miracles concerning material images of the Virgin the Saracen's own gestures count most: he is not converted or healed by being acted upon but by his actions being recognized in the miracle that he sees. The Saracen is not simply a figure to be converted and integrated into the Christian community of the text, but one who, by demonstrating exemplary Christian behaviour or desired experiences, is actually to be emulated and/or admired.

Conversely, the criticisms levelled at Gautier's Christian audience in the moral codas added to the narratives subject them to a kind of spectral mirroring, since while the Saracen may convert to become Christian, Gautier's Christian community is haunted by its own flaws and the need for its own conversion. His reader/listener is continually in the process of becoming a better Christian and is even explicitly encouraged to replicate the gestures enacted by these seemingly 'Saracen' figures with his own body. The Saracen, therefore, is not spectral because he is Saracen but because he is a convert, since he is not made spectral through processes of othering but through the exposure of conversion as an inherently incomplete process: he reveals the ambiguities at the very heart of Christian identity.

This is not to suggest, of course, that there is any one single message to be received from Gautier's *Miracles*: as Ardis Butterfield underlines, the *Miracles* lie 'between unity and diversity', linking 'song and narrative, sacred and secular, words and music — in unexpectedly close yet often equivocal associations'.[114] The very structure of the *Miracles* seems resistant to being considered as a homogeneous whole, with individual miracles and moral messages divided by elements of song and, as we have seen, often by images. In the *Estoire*, the importance of ordering and compiling narrative meant that deductive processes based upon retroactive genealogies and guaranteed futures could produce Saracen racial identity. Yet while these processes established a new form of spiritual race, in Gautier's *Miracles* religious conversion produces different kinds of haunted and haunting identities that both cut across and exploit racial identities. Furthermore, in the *Miracles*, the emphasis upon conversion rather than lineage means that these identities remain very much potential rather than guaranteed: while conversion is in many ways envisaged as a return, this return is far from limited to the Saracen, whether it involves a return to a physical state of being or knowing, or a return to the Christian community.

By uniting vernacular language with sacred subject matter, song with text and pagan with Christian, Gautier's work more generally encourages us to reconsider the permeability of the boundaries within the Christian community and between the human and divine. The process of looking at the spectral body in the miraculous moment, whether of Saracen or Virgin, highlights that God, in turn, always sees the reader/listener, reminding us of the visor effect described by Derrida. The Saracen does not, therefore, haunt the Christian community as per Kruger's identification of a Judaic past always rejected yet always evoked, but is a tool to show that the Christian is perpetually haunted by an underlying lack of belief, ignorance, or apathy that must be continually confronted in order to be surpassed in the desire for salvation.

Notes to Chapter 3

1. *The Spectralities Reader: Ghosts and Haunting in Contemporary Cultural Theory*, ed. by María del Pilar Blanco and Esther Peeren (London: Bloomsbury, 2013), p. 310.
2. Sarah Kay, 'Singularity and Spectrality: Desire and Death in *Girart de Roussillon*', *Olifant* 22.1–4 (Spring 1998–Fall 2003), 11–38 (p. 13).
3. Kathryn A. Duys, 'Medieval Literary Performance: Gautier de Coinci's Guide for the Perplexed', in *Acts and Texts: Performance and Ritual in the Middle Ages and the Renaissance*, ed. by Laurie Postlewaite and Wim Hüsken (Amsterdam: Rodopi, 2007), pp. 183–216 (p. 186).
4. Gautier de Coinci, *Les Miracles de Nostre Dame*, ed. by V. Frédéric Koenig, 4 vols, Textes Littéraires Français (Genève: Droz, 1955–70), I, 2nd edn (1966); II (1961); III (1966); IV (1970). All references are to Koenig's edition. Translations are my own.
5. Duys, 'Medieval Literary Performance', p. 184.
6. Steven F. Kruger, *The Spectral Jew: Conversion and Embodiment in Medieval Europe* (Minneapolis: University of Minnesota Press, 2006), p. 68.
7. Yasmina Foehr-Janssens, 'Histoire poétique du péché: de quelques figures littéraires de la faute dans les *Miracles de Nostre Dame* de Gautier de Coinci', in *Gautier de Coinci: Miracles, Music, and Manuscripts*, ed. by Kathy M. Krause and Alison Stones, Medieval Texts and Cultures of Northern Europe, 13 (Turnhout: Brepols, 2006), pp. 215–26 (p. 223).
8. Marie-Geneviève Grossel, 'Le Monde d'ici-bas, un royaume de violence: Le *Siècle* dans les *Miracles Nostre Dame* de Gautier de Conci', in *La Violence dans le monde médiéval* (Aix-en-Provence: Centre Universitaire d'Études et de Recherches Médiévales d'Aix, 1994), pp. 267–81 (p. 267). For Gautier's treatment of Jews, see also Gilbert Dahan, 'Les Juifs dans les miracles de Gautier de Coincy', *Archives juives*, 16 (1980), 41–49 and 59–68 and Barbara Haggh, 'From Auxerre to Soissons: The Earliest History of the Responsory *Gaude, Maria Virgo* in Gautier de Coinci's *Miracles de Nostre Dame*', in *Miracles, Music, and Manuscripts*, ed. by Krause and Stones, pp. 167–96. Visual representations of Jews in Gautier manuscripts are discussed by Danièle Sansy, 'Signe distinctif et judéité dans l'image', *Micrologus*, 15 (2007), 87–105.

9. For the text of Canon 68 see Jessie Sherwood, 'Notice n°30326: Le statut légal des minorités religieuses dans l'espace euro-méditerranéen (V^e–XVe siècle)', RELMIN project, Telma Web edition, IRHT, Institut de Recherche et d'Histoire des Textes–Orléans <http://www.cn-telma.fr/relmin/extrait30326/> [accessed 5 December 2018]. Such legislation was only weakly enforced, however, as highlighted by H. G. Richardson in *The English Jewry under Angevin Kings* (London: Methuen, 1960).
10. Tolan, *Saracens*, p. 198.
11. See Kay's discussion in 'Singularity and Spectrality', p. 12.
12. I Miracle 32 in *Les Miracles de Nostre Dame*, III, pp. 23–34.
13. Strickland refers to an illustration of this miracle in *Saracens, Demons, & Jews*, p. 165 (see pp. 165–72 for her broader discussion of Saracen idolatry); for Saracen idolatry, see also Peggy McCracken, 'Miracles, Mimesis and the Efficacy of Images', *Yale French Studies*, 110 (2006), 47–57 <http://www.jstor.org/stable/20060039> [accessed 22 November 2018] and Akbari, *Idols in the East*, pp. 200–16.
14. McCracken, 'Miracles', p. 47.
15. It is described as 'bele et gente' (v. 15) [beautiful and lovely].
16. For Gautier's rhetorical technique, see Tony Hunt, *Miraculous Rhymes: The Writing of Gautier de Coinci*, Gallica, 8 (Cambridge: Brewer, 2007).
17. For example:

>Mout longuement l'a regardee
>Et durement en sa pensee
>Se merveille se voirs puet estre
>Que mere fust au roi celestre
>Cele don estoit cele ymage.
>Mout durement en son coraige
>S'en esbahist et esmerveille. (vv. 27–33)

[He looked at it for a very long time and thoroughly marvelled in his thoughts as to whether it could be true that the woman in the image was the mother of the celestial king. He was deeply struck with heartfelt awe and wonder.]
18. To note but two further examples, see vv. 35–36 in *Dou cierge qui descendi au jougleour* [*Of the Candle Which Came Down to the Jongleur*] (II Miracle 21) and vv. 719–20 in *De l'ymage Nostre Dame de Sardanei* (II Miracle 30).
19. This is not to forget, of course, that Saracens are often admired for their battlefield prowess if not spiritual behaviour in such epic texts.
20. Those who do not remove spiders are criticized further in vv. 110–11 and again in vv. 117 and 120.
21. Jeffrey Burton Russell lists common associations between the devil and animals in *Lucifer: The Devil in the Middle Ages* (Ithaca, NY: Cornell University Press, 1984), p. 67. The potential soiling caused by spiders is noted by Dominique Iogna-Prat in *Order and Exclusion: Cluny and Christendom Face Heresy, Judaism, and Islam, 1000–1150*, trans. by Graham Robert Edwards (Ithaca: Cornell University Press, 2002), p. 201.
22. See Joan Young Gregg, *Devils, Women and Jews: Reflections of the Other in Medieval Sermon Stories* (Albany: State University of New York Press, 1997), p. 97; see also Roberta Krueger, '"Nouvelles choses": Social Instability and the Problem of Fashion in the *Livre du Chevalier de la Tour Landry*, the *Ménagier de Paris*, and Christine de Pizan's *Livre des Trois Vertus*', in *Medieval Conduct*, ed. by Kathleen Ashley and Robert L.A. Clark, Medieval Cultures, 29 (Minneapolis: University of Minnesota Press, 2001), pp. 49–86 (p. 58).
23. Saracen idolaters feature in the *Jeu de Saint Nicholas*, for instance, composed at the start of the thirteenth century, as well as in numerous *chansons de geste*, such as *Simon de Pouille* (also thirteenth-century).
24. Karl F. Morrison, *Understanding Conversion* (Charlottesville: University Press of Virginia, 1992), p. 7.
25. *The Spectralities Reader*, ed. by Blanco and Peeren, p. 272.
26. Morrison, *Understanding Conversion*, p. 6; For Bernard's 'Sermo ad Clericos de Conversione',

see Bernard of Clairvaux, *Sermones*, ed. by J. Leclercq and H. Rochais, *S. Bernardi opera*, 8 vols (Rome: Editiones Cistercienses, 1966), IV, 69–116.
27. Jacques Derrida, *Specters of Marx: the State of the Debt, the Work of Mourning and the New International*, trans. by Peggy Kamuf (London: Routledge, 1994 [2006]), p. 63.
28. Derrida, *Specters of Marx*, p. 5.
29. Ernesto Laclau, 'The Time is out of Joint', *Diacritics*, 25.2 (1995), 85–96.
30. For Christ's flesh as food, see Caroline Walker Bynum, *Holy Feast, Holy Fast: The Religious Significance of Food to Medieval Women* (Berkeley: University of California Press, 1987), for instance, p. 67; Suzannah Biernoff focuses on what she calls 'Ocular Communion' with Christ in *Sight and Embodiment in the Middle Ages* (Basingstoke: Macmillan, 2002), pp. 133–64.
31. For instance, in the earlier thinking of St Augustine. See Biernoff, *Sight and Embodiment*, p. 28.
32. Kruger, *The Spectral Jew*.
33. R.N. Swanson, *Religion and Devotion in Europe, c.1215–c.1515* (Cambridge: Cambridge University Press, 1995), p. 278.
34. See Kruger, *The Spectral Jew*, pp. 30–34; for Judaism as heresy, see Jeremy Cohen, *Living Letters of the Law: Ideas of the Jew in Medieval Christianity* (Berkeley: University of California Press, 1999), pp. 317–64 (for the comparison between Augustinian and Gregorian thinking regarding Jews in this period see pp. 84–85).
35. Kruger, *The Spectral Jew*, p. 11.
36. Kruger, *The Spectral Jew*, p. 53.
37. Kruger, *The Spectral Jew*, p. 19.
38. For an overview of medieval heresy, see R. I. Moore, *The Formation of a Persecuting Society: Authority and Deviance in Western Europe, 950–1250*, 2nd edn (Oxford: Blackwell, 2007), pp. 64–68.
39. For liminality in Gautier's miracle tales, see Robert L.A. Clark, 'Gautier's Wordplay as Devotional Ecstasy', in *Miracles, Music, and Manuscripts*, ed. by Krause and Stones, pp. 113–26.
40. Anna Russakoff, 'Imagining the Miraculous: *Les Miracles de Notre Dame*, Paris, BnF, n.acq. fr. 24541' (PhD Dissertation, New York University, 2006), p. 183; She adds that only one manuscript, Besançon, Bibliothèque municipale (BM), MS 551, shows the actual moment of his miraculous experience. I wish to thank the author for sharing a copy of her thesis with me at an early stage of my work.
41. BnF, MS f. fr. 22928 has 'De l'ymage nostre dame' and BnF, MS f. fr. 25532 'De l'image Nostre Dame que li sarrazins gardoit nettement' [Of the Image of Our Lady that the Saracen Kept Cleanly]. BnF, MS f. fr. 22928, fol. 114^r also has an additional rubric after the Saracen's conversion: 'Des prestres qui ne tiennent pas leur autex nes ne leur ymages' [Of Priests who Do Not Maintain their Altars or their Images].
42. Russakoff, 'Imagining the Miraculous', p. 194.
43. Such actions also feature in the potential Latin source identified by Adolfo Mussafia, *Uber die von Gautier de Coincy benützten Quellen* (Vienna: Tempsky, 1894), p. 37.
44. For example, B. Ars., MS 5204 has the rubric: 'Du sarrasin qui avoit une ymage de nostre dame quil gardoit moult nettement' [Of the Saracen who Had an Image of Our Lady that he Kept Cleanly]; BnF, MS f. fr. 25532 has 'De l'image Nostre Dame que li sarrazins gardoit nettement' [Of the Image of Our Lady that the Saracen Kept Very Cleanly].
45. They place them between 1326–28 and refer to accounts of payment. See Richard H. Rouse and Mary A. Rouse, *Manuscripts and their Makers: Commercial Book Producers in Medieval Paris, 1200–1500* (London: Miller, 2000), pp. 188–89.
46. Rouse and Rouse, *Manuscripts and their Makers*, p. 189.
47. These circumstances include, for instance, the use of the same exemplars; the same copyist's hand appearing in two manuscripts; the fact that two share an illuminator. See Rouse and Rouse, *Manuscripts and their Makers*, p. 198.
48. Rouse and Rouse, *Manuscripts and their Makers*, p. 198.
49. Alison Stones, 'Appendix IV: Illustrated *Miracles de Nostre Dame* Manuscripts Listed by Stylistic Attribution and Attributable Manuscripts Whose *MND* Selection is Unillustrated', in *Miracles, Music, and Manuscripts*, ed. by Krause and Stones, pp. 373–97 (p. 375).

50. Ibid.
51. Ibid.
52. See, for instance, the confrontation with Saracens on fol. 368^r where the lead figure may have black skin (the image is damaged, so it is difficult to be certain).
53. See fol. 180^v.
54. While B. Ars., MS 5204 contains some marginal instructions to artists, there do not seem to be any discernible on fol. 58^v.
55. Michael Camille, *The Gothic Idol: Ideology and Image-making in Medieval Art* (Cambridge: Cambridge University Press, 1989), p. 233; See also Russakoff, 'Imagining the Miraculous', p. 177.
56. Derrida, *Specters of Marx*, p. 7.
57. For the apparition as a *visio spiritualis*, see Christine Lapostolle, 'Images et apparitions: illustrations des "Miracles de Nostre Dame"', *Médiévales*, 2 (1982), 47–66 <http://dx.doi.org/10.3406/medi.1982.892>.
58. Derrida discusses the meaning and translation of the phrase 'the time is out of joint' from Shakespeare's Hamlet in *Specters of Marx*, pp. 21–34.
59. Carla Lord had previously associated this manuscript with a purchase made in 1327 by Charles IV from Thomas de Maubeuge, yet Rouse and Rouse have subsequently shown that this manuscript was in fact BnF, MS f. fr. 183 and The Hague, KB 71.A.24. See Carla Lord, 'Thomas de Maubeuge and the Miracles of the Virgin', *Source: Notes in the History of Art*, 8/9, no. 4/1 (Summer/Fall 1989), 2–4 < http://www.jstor.org/stable/23202690> [accessed 22 November 2018]; Rouse and Rouse, *Manuscripts and their Makers*, vol. I, p. 194; Russakoff also notes that Jean Pucelle and his collaborators are not known to have been associated with Thomas de Maubeuge ('Imagining the Miraculous', p. 241).
60. Russakoff, 'Imagining the Miraculous', p. 160.
61. Russakoff, 'Imagining the Miraculous', p. 183.
62. *The Derrida Reader: Writing Performances*, ed. by Julian Wolfreys (Edinburgh: Edinburgh University Press, 1998), p. 30.
63. Cf. Meriem Pages, 'Medieval Roots of the Modern Image of Islam: Fact and Fiction', in *Bridging the Medieval-Modern Divide: Medieval Themes in the World of the Reformation*, ed. by James Muldoon (Farnham: Ashgate, 2013), pp. 23–45. With reference to Ferumbras (*The Sowdone of Babylone*) and the Caliph of Baghdad (*Baudouin de Sebourc*) she notes that 'the very "Otherness" of the Saracen knight vanishes upon conversion, leading to the conclusion that conversion — and ultimately religion — informs the portrayal of the Saracen in medieval texts' (p. 41). 'Race', she says, 'held little to no significance in representing and understanding the Other in medieval Europe' (p. 41).
64. See fols 41^r and 41^v for instance.
65. Other manuscripts clearly show the sacristan as a tonsured, non-Saracen figure, e.g. BnF, MS f. fr. 22928, fol. 111^r, BnF, MS n. a. fr. 24541, fol. 66^r, or BnF, MS f. fr. 1533, fol. 99^r.
66. Russakoff notes that this is 'the only graphic example in the illustrated Gautier de Coinci manuscripts of the miraculous moment' ('Imagining the Miraculous', pp. 187–88).
67. Russakoff, 'Imagining the Miraculous', pp. 191–92.
68. See for instance the preaching Benedictine on fol. 28^v, the knight on fol. 72^v, or even Gautier de Coinci himself (fol. 82^v).
69. Alison Stones comments that it is 'the most problematic manuscript in the entire corpus' (p. 93) and that it is a 'very special case' (p. 95) in 'Notes on the Artistic Context of Some Gautier de Coinci Manuscripts', in *Miracles, Music, and Manuscripts*, ed. by Krause and Stones, pp. 65–98 (see also 'Appendix IV', p. 392).
70. McCracken, 'Miracles', p. 48.
71. Morrison, *Understanding Conversion* (p. xii) notes the idea of conversion as a long-term process.
72. Derrida, *Specters of Marx*, p. xix.
73. *The Spectralities Reader*, ed. by Blanco and Peeren, p. 310.
74. II Miracle 12 in *Les Miracles de Nostre Dame*, II, pp. 31–41.
75. François-Jérôme Beaussart, 'Visionnaires et apparitions dans les "Miracles de Nostre Dame" de Gautier de Coinci', *Romance Philology*, 43 (1989), 241–57, (p. 242).

76. Beaussart, 'Visionnaires', pp. 242–43.
77. Beaussart, 'Visionnaires', p. 245.
78. Beaussart, 'Visionnaires', fn. 7, p. 245.
79. Muselinus's description of the Virgin here as 'une dame' is not specifically because he is Saracen: in *Dou soucretain que Nostre Dame visita* [Of the Sacristan that Our Lady Visited], the sacristan also refers to her as 'une dame' (v. 82). However, since he does then recognize that she is 'Nostre Dame sainte Marie' (v. 110) [Our Lady Saint Mary], the fact that Muselinus does not identify this could be said to display his non-Christian faith.
80. Derrida, *Specters of Marx*, p. 6.
81. Derrida, *Specters of Marx*, p. 157.
82. Biernoff, *Sight and Embodiment*, p. 137 (original emphasis).
83. This notion of the fleshless body is mentioned by Roger Bacon in his thirteenth-century treatise on 'Moral Philosophy'. See Biernoff, *Sight and Embodiment*, p. 21 and pp. 37–39.
84. Biernoff, *Sight and Embodiment*, p. 38.
85. Derrida, *Specters of Marx*, p. 180.
86. In epic literature, it is more common that when the Saracen ruler/hero converts, his entire people must either follow him or die. See for instance *Fierabras*, vv. 6220–21. For the hero's own conversion, see Marianne Ailes, 'Faith in *Fierabras*', in *Charlemagne in the North: Proceedings of the Twelfth International Conference of the Société Rencesvals, Edinburgh 4th to 11th August 1991*, ed. by Philip E. Bennett, Anne Elizabeth Cobby, and Graham A. Runnalls (Edinburgh: Société Rencesvals British Branch, 1993), pp. 125–33.
87. Strickland, *Saracens, Demons, & Jews*, p. 227.
88. 'desreer' conveys the idea of someone who has stepped out of the ranks/out of order or who is 'démesuré'.
89. In contrast, the multi-compartment image of BnF, MS f. fr. 22928, fol. 194^v shows both the lance-blows of the opponents *and* what appears to be a miraculous moment of interaction with the Virgin.
90. Nancy Black, 'Images of the Virgin Mary in the Soissons Manuscript (Paris, BNF, nouv. acq. fr. 24541)', in *Miracles, Music, and Manuscripts*, ed. by Krause and Stones, pp. 253–77 (p. 270).
91. Black, 'Images of the Virgin, p. 274.
92. Lapostolle, 'Images et apparitions', pp. 54–55.
93. See Black, 'Images of the Virgin', p. 256.
94. Note that an individual vision is also made communal in this manuscript's illustration of *Juitel*. See Lapostolle, 'Images et apparitions', p. 61. It seems there is more work to be done to nuance ideas of individual and community in relation to apparitions.
95. Keith Busby, *Codex and Context: Reading Old French Verse Narrative in Manuscript*, 2 vols (Amsterdam: Rodopi, 2002), p. 209, mentions this manuscript alongside three others in Soissonais dialect in conjunction with religious communities. However, Levente Seláf has recently suggested a lay audience for this manuscript in *Chanter plus haut: La chanson religieuse vernaculaire au Moyen Age (essai de contextualisation)* (Paris: Champion, 2008), p. 504.
96. II Miracle 30 in *Les Miracles de Nostre Dame*, IV, pp. 378–411.
97. Derrida, *Specters of Marx*, p. 5.
98. His sheer size renders his attempts to learn chivalrous behaviour comical — for instance, instead of knocking a knight from his horse, Renoart crushes both horse and rider in one swoop of his club. See *Aliscans*, ed. by Claude Régnier, 2 vols (Paris: Champion, 1990) II, vv. 5700–807, pp. 216–17. Similarly, in *La Bataille Loquifer*, he fathers a child so 'gros et quarrés' (v. 785) [big and large-limbed] that his wife is unable to deliver it (vv. 782–90). See *La Bataille Loquifer*, ed. by Monica Barnett (Oxford: Blackwell, 1975).
99. For instance, the transformation of the lump child in the Middle English *King of Tars* romance. See Siobhain Bly Calkin, 'Marking Religion on the Body: Saracens, Categorization, and "The King of Tars"', *The Journal of English and Germanic Philology*, 104 (2005), 219–38 < https://www.jstor.org/stable/27712494> [accessed 22 November 2018].
100. Kathryn A. Duys, 'Performing Vernacular Song in Monastic Culture: The *lectio divina* in Gautier de Coinci's *Miracles de Nostre Dame*', in *Cultural Performances in Medieval France: Essays in Honor*

of Nancy Freeman Regalado, ed. by Eglal Doss-Quinby, Roberta L. Krueger, and E. Jane Burns, Gallica, 5 (Cambridge: Brewer, 2007), pp. 123–34 (p. 123).
101. See Kruger, *The Spectral Jew*, pp. 39–49.
102. There are five illuminations of the miracle across the corpus, only two of which show the Saracen. See Russakoff, Appendix 7 and 8 in 'Imagining the Miraculous', pp. 328–37.
103. This is not a definitive indicator of Saracen identity in this manuscript, since the illumination of II Miracle 12 shows a clean-shaven Saracen.
104. Lapostolle discusses illness and bodies in the illuminations of this manuscript in 'Images et apparitions', p. 53.
105. Kruger, *The Spectral Jew*, p. 59.
106. See D. A. Trotter, *Medieval French Literature and the Crusades (1100–1300)* (Geneva: Droz, 1987), fn. 105, p. 164.
107. *The Spectralities Reader*, ed. by Blanco and Peeren, p. 310.
108. Derrida, *Specters of Marx*, p. 6.
109. Tolan, *Saracens*, p. 283.
110. Grossel, 'Le Monde d'ici-bas', p. 267.
111. For the ritualistic nature of Gautier's texts, see Robert L.A. Clark, 'Gautier's Wordplay'.
112. Nils Holger Petersen, 'Introduction', in *The Cultural Heritage of Medieval Rituals: Genre and Ritual*, ed. by Eyolf Østrem, Mette Birkedal Bruun, Nils Holger Petersen, and Jens Fleischer, Special Issue, *Transfiguration* (Copenhagen: Museum Tusculanum Press, University of Copenhagen, 2005), p. 16.
113. Kruger, *The Spectral Jew*, pp. 1–8.
114. Ardis Butterfield, 'Introduction. Gautier de Coinci, *Miracles de Nostre Dame*: Texts and Manuscripts', in *Miracles, Music, and Manuscripts*, ed. by Krause and Stones, pp. 1–20 (p. 8).

CHAPTER 4

Race and Community: Knowledge, Faith, and the Prophet in the *Roman de Mahomet*

No study of the Saracen in medieval literature would be complete without reference to the figure of the Prophet Muhammad, who was not only depicted as the genealogical root of the Saracen people but was also both arch heretic and Antichrist, with many presenting him as 'a monster who begot a monstrous race'.[1] Examples of extreme anti-Islamic propaganda appear in the works of writers such as Guibert de Nogent or Embrico of Mainz while idolatrous figures abound in the *chansons de geste*.[2] Nonetheless, these depraved and heretical representations of Muhammad are not the only portrayals to be found. Indeed, the variety of emphases that characterize medieval portrayals of Muhammad lead us to question whether he is representative of Saracens more generally. Rethinking the nature of his representativeness in this way also exposes the extent to which religious identity can be said to determine or even stand in for racial identity — here, this means the extent to which Saracen religious affiliation is racialized through and by Muhammad. Central to his representativeness is therefore the idea of exemplarity and its performative power to construct, yet also paradoxically undermine, identities and claims to rhetorical authority.

One of the more unusual medieval works involving a representation of the Prophet is the thirteenth-century *Roman de Mahomet* by Alexandre du Pont: a translation and adaptation of Gautier de Compiègne's *Otia de Machomete*.[3] This work is the only Old French translation of the life of Muhammad and is striking above all for its lack of overt anti-Islamic authorial commentary. More particularly, through its focus upon exempla and its quasi-hagiographic feel, it reveals the role of the Prophet in the construction of Saracen (communal) identity.[4] The text narrates a fictional account of Muhammad's life, from birth to death, in a mere 1997 lines. It begins with his qualities, education, and service to his rich master, before relating his visit to a hermit, who reveals his destiny to establish a new faith. It then describes Muhammad's courtship and marriage to his master's widow, presenting it as a cunning ploy to gain wealth and influence and situating his rise to power as the result of trickery, bribery, and generally objectionable behaviours. After suffering an epileptic seizure at his wedding feast, the Muhammad of the *Roman* disguises this to his wife as the result of divine visions before presenting himself as a prophet to the people via two false miracles. Sparked by Muhammad's apparently fraudulent possession of territory, a war erupts with the neighbouring Persians during which Muhammad stages a third miracle and once more convinces his people of his wisdom and leadership. The narrative closes with Muhammad's death at an old age and erroneous descriptions of his burial in Mecca and elaborate levitating tomb.

Monstrous versions of the life and death of the Prophet were commonly known by the thirteenth century, yet even from this short summary, it is clear that the *Roman* adopts a slightly different tack. While certain motifs from previous traditions are maintained, the poet's free adaptation of such materials arguably reaches for an objectivity it never quite achieves.[5] Both an alternative contextualization of the work's production and compositional environment and a close reading of Muhammad's role as orator and rhetorical seducer reveal its more general preoccupation with the boundary between knowledge and faith. In turn, the slippery nature of this boundary brings into question the performative power of words, since Muhammad's identity as prophet is shown to be dependent upon the reaction of the community around him, yet his exemplarity renders him capable of producing a new Saracen race to accompany his new religion. Alongside his questioning of the relationship between knowledge and faith, Alexandre du Pont therefore shows how the failure to recognize the performative power of eloquence might create misplaced belief; how this belief might in turn create a community; and how community produces race.

Despite the uniqueness of this work, its intellectual context remains very much understudied, explained perhaps by the paucity of concrete details regarding its composition. Unfortunately, next to nothing is known about the poet, Alexandre du Pont, except that he composed the *Roman* at Laon in 1258 (vv. 1994–97) and that the Latin text of a certain 'Gautier' was his source. A sole manuscript copy survives in the miscellany Paris, Bibliothèque nationale de France (BnF), MS fonds français 1553. The *Roman* consequently presents the modern scholar with questions that prove particularly difficult to answer: for instance, what was its purpose and who was the intended audience? Why do we not have more Old French examples of such a text, given the apparent literary interest in the Middle East and its residents evinced in numerous genres, from epic to romance? While this chapter cannot hope to provide definite responses to these conundrums, it nonetheless examines questions of reception and purpose by focusing upon the interaction of faith and reason through exempla and narratorial interventions in this work. By extension this also involves reassessing the bias towards a propagandistic purpose (whether crusading or antiheretical) that has dominated scholarship. Far from being a clumsy translation of a concise and innovating Latin original,[6] the *Roman de Mahomet* prioritizes secular and communal behaviour rather than the heretical practices of individuals and targets ignorance and credulity as much as idolatry. As was the case with Gautier de Coinci's *Miracles*, the *Roman* does not simply entertain a lay audience but aims to be instructive; this is not to say that it engages directly with Islam as a religion, but that it provides its readers with the skills to recognize the supposed falsity of Islam and to critique the Muslim religion through a process of reasoning and intellectual proof. In this respect, like Gautier's use of the Saracen's exemplary cleanliness in I Miracle 32, Alexandre does not offer an unambiguous representation of a non-Christian but instead provides a complex portrait of Muhammad that encourages his audience to reflect upon their own qualities, behaviours, and faith.

As its most recent editor Yvan Lepage has underscored, the *Roman* is an adaptation of its Latin predecessor in the spirit of Alexandre du Pont's contemporary Jean de Meun, who was known for his addition of enumerations, commentaries, and explanations.[7] Placing close readings of the text alongside the manuscript and context of the work's production can, however, situate the *Roman* within a literary milieu beyond that of Latin anti-Islamic polemic. This recontextualization makes it seem less unique and more in keeping with contemporary intellectual pursuits and concerns. The fact that much secondary criticism has not taken its manuscript context into account means that this text has remained pigeon-holed as a perplexing and unpopular off-shoot of Latin propaganda, whether for missionary or crusading purposes.[8]

Arguing strongly in favour of the propagandistic drive of the *Roman*, Reginald Hyatte has suggested that it aims to denigrate the basis of Islam, and he specifically notes that the romance 'contributes to a program on the French home front of discrediting Muhammad's teachings' and thus dissuading potential converts.[9] Similarly, Sini Kangas follows John Tolan in seeing such twelfth- and thirteenth-century works as 'a defensive reaction to the strengthening power of the Muslim world'.[10] Suzanne Akbari details the parodic nature of the episode of Muhammad's coffin, as depicted in the romance, and discusses this in relation to notions of idolatry and retrogressive religious belief.[11] While these are in themselves very worthy interpretations, it does seem that the wider literary context of the *Roman* has been rather overlooked in the emphasis on anti-Islamic sentiment and that the poet's interaction with his reader/audience might help to nuance the picture. Kangas has argued that 'the quest for love and wealth' is the main focus of Gautier de Compiègne's *Otia de Machomete*, the Latin source text of the *Roman*, suggesting that it was the product of a secular rather than an ecclesiastical milieu.[12] Secular or not, my own view is that the *Roman* does provide its readers with knowledge that may be applied beyond the specific context of conflict between Christianity and Islam; it can be set within a tradition of translating wisdom literature into the vernacular that was blossoming from the mid-twelfth century,[13] rather than isolated as the unique example of an Old French life of Muhammad.

Two interconnected axes reveal other potential messages transmitted by this romance. Firstly, rather than simply evincing a desire to dissuade potential converts on the home front, the portrayal of Muhammad in the *Roman* speaks to fundamental upheavals in intellectual culture occurring in the course of the thirteenth century, while nonetheless remaining rooted within a latent tradition of anti-Islamic criticism. In this light, Muhammad's supposed threat and power as a heretic may be viewed within a context of conflict between the disciplines of reason and faith. Alongside the motifs of false miracles and epileptic seizures that are common to the

Latin tradition, Alexandre du Pont has expanded the figure of Muhammad into a would-be scholastic who attempts not only to bribe those around him but more importantly to reason with them. As a result, the text rationalizes Islamic faith by rendering its mysteries and miracles explicable; this is not to say that we find a more realistic or more positive representation of either the Prophet or of Islam, but that this process of rationalization is in fact what makes him heretical for Alexandre.

Secondly, the *Roman* examines the broader issue of how one is to trust others and to think for oneself. The work not only targets those who would follow the heretical teachings of learned figures such as Muhammad or who could even be seduced into conversion, but more importantly provides them with the knowledge necessary to recognize the sacrilegious nature and human origins of such rhetoric. It is not just the case that Islam is figured as materialistic and its followers as unable to comprehend the spiritual, as occurs in so many medieval works; the *Roman* additionally suggests that Islam must rely upon proof to create faith and that the mistaken recognition of this proof is what produces the Saracens as a community. While the false reasoning of the Saracens therefore leads them further from God, Alexandre du Pont's exegetical interventions attempt to counter such erroneous practices, teaching rather than preaching and using reason as defence rather than as proof. The intellectual context of north-eastern France in the thirteenth century is thus a crucial backdrop to my interpretation, along with the reception of vernacular translation and traditions of representing Muhammad.

Chapters One to Three of this book have shown Saracen identities to be performative to the extent that the repetition of social and literary conventions exposes them as malleable, and the *Roman de Mahomet* is no exception. In this text, however, what is at stake is whether or not faith can similarly be presented and even acknowledged as conventional or repeatable, and, more particularly, how this plays out in the relationship between rhetoric, reason, and faith rather than through gesture and bodily experience of the spiritual, which was the case in the *Miracles*. In the *Roman*, speech may have the power to interpellate Muhammad as Prophet and interrogate the very performativity of faith itself.

Education by Example

While the representation of Muhammad in the *Roman* may echo the Saracens of Gautier de Coinci's *Miracles* in its surprising ambiguity, this does not mean that exemplarity functions in exactly the same way. In contrast to Gautier's exempla, the Saracen here is not a figure to be emulated, but one whose exemplarity exposes threats to Christianity. The receiving community is not addressed for its lack of faith or apathy, but rather for too much, and even misplaced, faith. Albeit as part of a different overarching focus, it is nonetheless true that exempla once again play a crucial role in the construction of identity, in this case owing to the performativity of spoken rather than behavioural or gestural conventions. The productive power of exempla has been observed by Larry Scanlon, who notes that the exemplum is not a passive form, but involves active, narrative processes:

> The exemplum illustrates a moral because what it recounts is the enactment of that moral. The moral does not simply gloss the narrative. It establishes a form of authority, enjoining its audience to heed its lesson, and to govern their actions accordingly. It is more than an abstract principle.[14]

Expressing similar sentiments, Miri Rubin describes exempla as 'the performative tokens of medieval culture, the persuasive enactments of cultural tropes'.[15] Given the potential power of exemplary materials, Alexandre's most significant innovation with regard to his Latin source is therefore his incorporation or expansion of exempla rather than his representation of the Prophet in and of itself.[16]

One such exemplum, related just after Muhammad's meeting with the prophetic hermit, concerns the tale of the knight and the squire. It preserves yet expands upon the moral message of the Latin *Otia*, doing so through a narrative centred upon the interconnectivity of society and which involves a microcosm of secular social hierarchy. In this tale, a knight and a squire are riding through a wood when the squire drops the knight's purse, which is then discovered by a woodcutter. When the knight realizes this, he cuts off the foot of his squire as punishment. A hermit then happens upon the scene and, confused by the squire's narrative, is enlightened by an angel, who explains that the knight had wronged the woodcutter and the squire had shamefully kicked his mother and so each had received his necessary punishment or reward. The tale not only emphasizes the relationship between acts and consequences but also demonstrates God's omnipotence within a divine scheme that may sometimes seem obscure to human beings. In his gloss the poet even speculates accordingly, explaining that God may sometimes reward the wicked man for his deeds while on earth in order to make him suffer more after death 'quant cheüs ert de haut en bas' (v. 298) [after falling low from the heights].

Immediately following this gloss, Alexandre briefly mentions Muhammad, whom he likens to Nero, and then narrates the parable of the rich man and Lazarus. This second, biblical tale concerns a rich man who refuses to give food to a starving leper and who, despite eating well on earth, will consequently go to hell: 'Orendroit a chou que il vaut | cil ki soloit estre pourris; | en infier est li bien nourris' (vv. 318–20) [Henceforth he who used to be leprous | has what he deserves; | The well-fed man is in hell]. The theme of earthly pain for celestial gain is then maintained through a further reference, this time to the saints and Christ who all suffered on earth before they 'conquisent paradys' (v. 332) [won paradise]. In a sense, not only is this exemplum used to draw a contrast between earthly and heavenly experience, but it also underscores that it is impossible to know God's purpose, evident above all in the rhetorical question posed by the poet in this regard (v. 221). While it is true that the overall moral message here may have been applicable to Muslim successes in the Holy Land, the exemplum carries no such clear associations: the exemplum does not engage with potential Christian crusaders or possible apostates but instead with the notion of knowledge and faith in God.

Emphasis is further placed upon the acceptance rather than questioning of God's purpose when the poet uses his exemplum to address the reader/listener directly:

> Or dois dont estre establement
> Fors et prendre en gré povreté
> Et le malvais avoir plenté,
> Par l'example que je t'ai dit
> Dou Ladre et dou Riche mendit. (vv. 346–50)
>
> [Therefore you should be unfalteringly
> Firm and accept poverty,
> As well as the wicked man's prosperity,
> In accordance with the exemplum that I related to you
> About the leper and the destitute rich man.]

In this light, the meaning of the tale of the rich man and Lazarus is not at all aimed at countering Islam or combating heresy but rather underlines that those on earth do not know what awaits them in the afterlife. The poet does, however, try to justify its inclusion (as occurs in the *Otia*) by noting that the tale is 'bien couvignable' (v. 353) [very fitting] for his subject matter. Similarly, it is significant that he introduces this sermonizing section following an account of Muhammad's economic prosperity, commenting that God's judgment is hard to fathom (vv. 219–21). This observation does occur in the *Otia*, but it is here that Alexandre du Pont introduces the first exemplum. His response to the Latin text is therefore to add detail: detail which explains Muhammad's behaviour in the context of Christian parable and rationalizes his terrestrial successes. Such additions may of course reflect the fact that this text was written shortly after Louis IX's largely unsuccessful Seventh Crusade and the accompanying Saracen successes.[17] Yet the mechanisms of these exempla are also important because they make Muhammad's success negative by comparison, rather than leaving it inexplicable or known only to God, providing knowledge that, while seemingly incompatible with Christian faith, is nonetheless crucial to the deconstruction of the Saracen heresy. Alexandre's use of exempla that carry general, Christian moral meanings could be seen as a means not of making Muhammad into a counter-exemplar but rather of explaining his actions according to a Christian eschatology — an explanation that mitigates the more disturbing qualities of his behaviour. As a result, Muhammad is not used as an anti-saint or arch-heretic and thus singled out as being important, but is subtly belittled as part of a Christian master plan. The representation of Muhammad's success would echo Tolan's assessment that: 'reason can be used to destroy rival creeds and defend one's own doctrines from the charge of irrationality but not to prove the truth of Christianity.'[18]

This prioritization of reason and knowledge runs somewhat contrary to Kangas's assessment of the *Otia* and its engagement with secular power structures:

> The author refers frequently to Machomet's licentiousness and error, but equally to the consequences of deliberate sinning. The text emphasizes the search for power and social mobility. Gautier's text is a travesty but [...] it is a travesty of a heretical knight and, more precisely, a crusader knight.[19]

While the question of 'deliberate sinning' remains one of the clear priorities of the *Roman*, I would argue that the 'travesty' does not concern a crusader knight, but rather the travesty of communal credulity or false reasoning and in turn the power that this has to produce a communal racial identity. The incorporation of exempla into a romance work is not unusual, as 'there was evidently a two-way traffic' between these two traditions;[20] nevertheless, this means that alongside the entertainment provided by such tales, there was an important educational side to this material. As Jocelyn Wogan-Browne reminds us, the socialization that could be achieved through romance texts applies to those needing to adapt to religious as well as secular lives: 'the process seems to have been carried out not only by Latin school instruction, but by story-telling, by "romans" in its primary sense of vernacularization'.[21] Although the generalized exemplum used by Alexandre moves away from the polemical, anti-Islamic treatises of the period, it is far from inconsistent with the drives of romance and may in fact reflect the broader educative trend in vernacular translation from Latin occurring in the twelfth and thirteenth centuries, especially in light of the manuscript context of this work.

This questioning of fact and fiction, appearance and reality suggests a quest for knowledge and interest in the world that can also be observed in other works of the manuscript containing the *Roman*, BnF, MS f. fr. 1553, from a version of *Barlaam et Josephat* (a medieval version of the life of the Buddha) to the *Roman de Troie* [*Romance of Troy*], and scientific treatises on dreams (*Des songes et des esperimens des songes*) and the formation of the world (*L'Ymage du monde en romans*). The last work mentioned here (*L'Ymage du monde en romans*) provides further evidence of the intellectual context of the *Roman*. This is a popular encyclopaedic work composed by Gossuin de Metz in the mid-thirteenth century, which problematizes the relationship between knowledge and faith. As Chantal Connochie-Bourgne notes in relation to the chapter *De nature, comment ele oevre et que ce est* [Of nature, how it operates and what it is]:

> connaître la nature, c'est accéder à l'art de Dieu. L'accès est dangereux, on le sait, mais les voies de la perdition semblent devenir celles du salut [...] La relation de l'homme à Dieu passe par la nature, celle de l'homme à la nature passe par Dieu, et la relation de Dieu à la nature s'inscrit dans l'homme.[22]

> [to know nature is to gain access to God's art. We know that this access is dangerous, but the roads to perdition seem to become those of salvation [...] man is connected to God via nature, man and nature connected via God, and the connection between God and nature is incorporated within man.]

This work is thus very much an acknowledgement that the relationship between nature, man, and God is potentially difficult. Yet it is curiosity for the world that also brings man closer to God and, for Connochie-Bourgne, this interest is above all mediated by the clergy, hence her reference to this work as the 'laïcisation du savoir' [laicization of knowledge]. If, during this period, man has to 'prendre religieusement conscience de sa rationalité' [become religiously aware of his rationality],[23] a similar framework or thought process also seems to be at work in the *Roman de Mahomet*, given that this text questions the interaction of proof, knowledge, and faith.

The pattern of interaction between the poet and his audience in the *Roman* sheds further light on the status of reason and the exegetical additions of the poet. Moments where the poet sermonizes reveal some of the moralistic drives of the work. The first example of this occurs when the narrator comments upon the hermit's prayers, advising that prayers should be said both for oneself and for others (vv. 100–02). Further examples appear when Muhammad bribes the barons to support his cause with his master's widow, where Alexandre du Pont reminds us that 'avarisce est de tous pechiés | commenchemens' (vv. 605–06) [the root of all sins is | greed]; when Muhammad's bribes have overturned social hierarchies (vv. 611–12); when the Prophet's fit disrupts the wedding feast ('molt souvent voit on avenir | grant joie a dolour revertir' (vv. 787–88) [very often one sees it happen | that great joy turns into grief]); and when the narrative voice comments on the fickleness of women: 'femme est de molt legier corage: | tost a dit parole volage | quant pensé l'a, ou fole ou sage' (vv. 1253–55) [woman has a most frivolous spirit: | right away she says a flighty word, | be it foolish or wise, as soon as it enters her head]. Excepting the initial comment about prayer, it is clear that Muhammad's underhand actions are frequently used as a means of introducing a generalized Christian moral precept, rather than of dispelling specific, heretical assertions. Equally, as with many other cases in this romance, these comments either presage or follow episodes where Muhammad is erroneously taken as a prophet by the community thanks to their flawed acceptance of evidence of his power. The priority is to ensure that the reader/listener relates to the narrator during moments where the credulity, acceptance, or ignorance of the community is highlighted, rather than during the poet's exposure of Islam's supposedly fraudulent religious practices.

Beyond direct engagement with his audience, the poet also troubles the association of reason, faith, and evidence through his expanded etymological section at the end of the text. This section evokes the idea of Saracen identity as both physical and spiritual lineage, setting Muhammad's construction as Prophet alongside the construction of the Saracens as a race. Here, Alexandre claims that the name Mecca means adulteress and is so named because Muhammad both instigated and partook of this adultery:

> De Meke gist en la cité:
> Cest non a par s'iniquité,
> Car cil nons Meke velt tant dire
> Com cele ki fait avoutire
> Car avoutire controuva
> Mahons en la loy k'il trouva,
> Ensi com il le demoustra:
> Avoec les autres avoutra. (vv. 1956–63)

> [He lies in the city of Mecca.
> This name shares in his wickedness
> Because the word 'Mecca' means
> A woman who commits adultery,
> For Muhammad dreamed up adultery
> In the religion that he fabricated,
> Just as he exemplified it:
> He committed adultery along with the others.][24]

The close connection between Muhammad and the city is clear in the assonance which joins 'avoutire' with 'controuva' and 'demoustra' and this intimate linguistic connection echoes the concept of the exemplum that has continued throughout the work: Muhammad becomes the exemplum, since he both creates the moral message here and is created by it. In this respect, the message of this anecdote is as if to say, if you commit these sins then you are one of his followers too. This message is further underlined by the fact that Alexandre du Pont goes on to explain that the process of naming in general occurs due to something that happened (vv. 1967–68) or because of a prediction that came true, which repeats the argument that the occurrence of adultery is what led to the naming of the city. The etymological argument set out here consequently displays the preference for logical rather than chronological explanations identified by Bloch, where words have 'not essential meanings, but diverse essential modes of meaning'.[25] Such a logical approach inevitably also reminds us of the way in which Saracens were retrospectively produced as a race in the *Estoire del saint graal*, as discussed above, albeit via processes of spiritual enlightenment and engendering rather than reasoning.

Seen as part of the logical construction of the Saracens as a race, the expansion of the more general example of Babel/Babylon in this section also takes on a new meaning, and is not just poor translation technique on the part of Alexandre du Pont, as was suggested by Lepage.[26] It places greater emphasis on the Christian parallel than on the specific debauchery attributed to Muhammad, since it underlines that the act of naming is based upon actions rather than just Muhammad's introduction of adultery. Compared to eleven lines dealing with Muhammad and Mecca, there are over twenty concentrated upon Babylon. Given the obvious emphasis on disorder and confusion transmitted by the reference to the tower of Babel, yet the seeming paradox of using this disorder as a way to rationalize the city's etymology, the poet focuses attention here upon the limits rather than the possibilities of reasoning. The chaos of the tower of Babel was above all the result of competition between mankind and God and, in this respect, such a reference used to close the *Roman* reminds the reader of the sinful pride of humanity's aspiration for the heavens. By extension, the *Roman* could be seen as part of an attempt not to portray the religious doctrine of Islam accurately or rationally, but to show that Islam is trapped within a system depending on reason and logical proof and that its followers are too devoted to knowledge instead of faith, just as Muhammad is paradoxically both highly rational and irrational.

Representing Muhammad in the *Roman* and Beyond

Like those of any other Saracen, medieval representations of Muhammad in no way conform to a single set of conventions. Art historian Debra Higgs Strickland provides numerous examples where the Prophet is associated with the Antichrist, arch-heretics, monstrous beasts, and inverted saints, though she notes that 'it is puzzling that Western medieval images of Muhammad produced during the period of the crusades are not more abundant' given that there is 'plenty of literary fodder for pejorative visual representation'.[27] One of the most commonly referenced representations of the Prophet appears in a twelfth-century Toledan manuscript (Paris, Bibliothèque de l'Arsenal, MS 1162, fol. 11^r), where Muhammad is shown as a hybrid fish-like figure in a scribal ornament.[28] Walter B. Cahn sees this as a reflection of Peter the Venerable's criticism that Islam is 'eclectic and incoherent',[29] where in the *Summa totius haeresis Saracenorum* Peter cites the start of Horace's *Ars Poetica*: 'et sic undique monstruosus ut ille ait (Horat,. *De art. poet.*), humano capiti, cervicem equinam et plumas avium copulat' [And thus as he says (Horace, *De art. poet.*) it is utterly monstrous that he joins to a human head a horse's neck and birds' feathers].[30] Muhammad's physical monstrosity is in this case determined by the deformity of his religious teachings, so that the overriding message conveyed is one of nonsense. In contrast, Strickland provides the example of Muhammad from Matthew Paris's *Chronica Majora* (Cambridge, Corpus Christi College, MS 26, p. 87) where the Prophet holds a banner that promotes a life of luxury.[31] As a kind of perverted saint, this figure does not rely upon common visual signs of evil but instead frames nonsense teachings (from the Christian perspective) within a rational physical form. Different again are the images of Muhammad from apocalyptic works where he appears as a beast or dog-like figure, echoing Innocent III's association of Muhammad and Antichrist in his fifth-crusade propaganda (1213).[32] Compared to many medieval representations of the Prophet then, the single illumination that prefaces the *Roman* depicts Muhammad in a subtle (if no less ideologically significant) manner, since he is presented as light-skinned and light-haired and lacks distinguishing Saracen artistic tropes such as a hat or heavy beard (Figure 4.1).

This image is more in keeping with the white-skinned Saracens so frequently found both described and visually portrayed in medieval manuscripts. The image in the *Roman* differs too from many later images where Muhammad appears as preacher and prophet before the people. Such later illuminations often include the false miracle common to various versions of his legend where a dove transmits knowledge to Muhammad. Examples of this motif appear, for instance, in manuscripts of Boccaccio's *De Casibus Virorum Illustrium* (Paris, Bibliothèque nationale, MS fonds français 226, fol. 243^r or Paris, Bibliothèque nationale, MS fonds français 234, fol. 171^v) and in an image showing Muhammad's preaching and his marriage to Khadija found in a fifteenth-century manuscript of Giovanni Colonna's universal history, *Mare Historiarum*, Paris, Bibliothèque nationale, MS Latin 4915, fol. 301^v. In contrast, the illumination in the *Roman* depicts Muhammad standing before two kneeling witnesses, his hand resting upon his tamed white bull (a reference to another of his false miracles). Although the presence of the dove would suggest an obvious inversion of the representation of the Christian Holy Spirit,[34] the bull is instead associated with Muhammad's own ingenuity: it is not the explicit inversion of a Christian symbol but rather his means of explaining and exploiting faith. The potential didactic process evoked by this illumination is supported by the fact that the preceding illumination in the manuscript — which introduces a version of the *Sept Sages de Rome* — follows a very similar compositional layout. The *Sept Sages* is a frame tale of eastern origin which recounts how a group of learned clerics and their royal pupil are pitted against the boy's evil stepmother in a battle of wits and

FIG. 4.1. Opening initial of *Le Roman de Mahomet*. Paris, BnF, MS f. fr. 1553, fol. 367ᵛ. Photo: Paris, Bibliothèque nationale de France.

eloquence. The young prince's father has remarried, and his new bride quickly accuses her stepson of attempted rape and treason. To exonerate him, the clerics spend seven days relating tales about the wickedness of women, parrying the queen's own tales of treacherous sons, before the prince finally speaks to defend himself and prove his own innocence on the eighth day. In Paris, BnF, MS f. fr. 1553, this tale is illustrated by a single image (fol. 338^v) where a crowned and seated figure on the left of the image appears to be engaging with the arguments of three facing figures whose hands are here raised in instruction rather than prayer. This representational echo between the images accompanying the *Roman* and the *Sept Sages* could suggest that the emphasis, in this case, is upon Muhammad's skills as orator: upon his ability to convince others through argumentation rather than the more material 'carnal enticements and pleasures' characterizing the alleged seductions of Muhammad criticized by Innocent III.[35]

As regards the literary tradition of representing Muhammad, Akbari neatly summarizes this as loosely divided into two 'modes', the 'realistic' and the 'fanciful', although she underlines that scholars have by and large underestimated the interdependence of these traditions. She also prioritizes the concept of idolatry in the *Roman*, saying that what is often ignored is 'the extent to which in both traditions idolatry is presented as the focus of Saracen worship'.[36] Despite such recognition that the boundaries between literary traditions are often very blurred, scholarship on this work tends to draw divisions between a Latin polemical tradition stemming from the Iberian Peninsula and Byzantium on the one hand, and the production of other genres of contemporary literature on the other. The workings of exemplarity challenge this division and reveal how emphasis is placed on the reason rather than faith of the Saracens. Exempla have similarly been subject to a traditional division between sermon exempla and public or classical exempla, despite the many commonalities of form and function between the two.[37] However, the exempla found in the *Roman* trouble this classification, since often the messages being conveyed are not what we expect from a text depicting the life of a religious leader: while the sermonizing elements serve to advise and to caution the community, it is perhaps surprising that the exemplum provided by the figure of Muhammad himself is less explicit.

To determine the impact of this exemplum and appreciate the establishment of the Prophet through his rhetorical abilities, we can instead return to Scanlon's performative reading of exempla, where 'an exemplary action is already a saying because it transmits its authority to the community. An exemplary saying is already a doing because it produces a moral obligation which must be enacted'.[38] The idea of speech as 'a doing' harks back to J. L. Austin's early, and very much linguistic, conceptualization of performativity as meaning the power of language to enact rather than simply reflect realities, yet it also evokes later formulations of this concept in the context of interpellation. Interpellation, as developed by the French philosopher Louis Althusser and discussed by Judith Butler in connection with performativity, concerns the production of subjectivities in response to lived, human interactions. It is where a person responds to the call of ideology, often through social discourse, and is produced as a subject in the process. Since the speech under consideration in this case is that of depicted characters or the voice of the narrator, the use of the term 'interpellation' within a narrative context diverges somewhat from these theorists. Muhammad does not gain 'subjectivity' as a result of being interpellated, as occurs in Althusser's original example of a person hailed by a policeman.[39] Rather, this term highlights how verbal interactions in the *Roman* are determined by ideological conventions and profoundly affect the production of identities, even if this is in a negative sense: the idea of interpellation in this context helps to expose the confirmation or rejection of Muhammad's authority as speaker and the processes that are involved. As a literary representation, Muhammad is shown to develop a certain level of self-awareness through being 'hailed' during spoken exchanges, and the depiction of this linguistic, reciprocal process displays the role of literary conventions in the formation of Saracen identity. Self-awareness may, furthermore, be encouraged at the level of reception through the positioning of the reader/listener as the addressee of the text itself.

Butler's comments on the performativity of speech (specifically of injurious speech) and reformulation of Althusser's notion of interpellation shed light on the relationship between speech and performativity in the *Roman*, since she emphasizes that a speaker does not wield a sovereign power; language always exceeds his or her control, meaning that the addressee can respond in a way that reformulates conventions. However, Butler's critique of sovereignty does not amount to a total removal of agency from the speaking subject. Instead, Butler notes that 'agency begins where sovereignty wanes',[40] which suggests that the power of a specific speaker only comes into play at the point where his supposed absolute power over his words is unsettled. In short, it is only once the conventional elements of a speaker's words are recognized that the speaker's own responsibility and control over his words becomes apparent and that conventions can be challenged.

The more generally performative potential of Muhammad as an exemplar combines with the potential of his speech (and that of others) to interpellate: he both interpellates and is interpellated throughout the text. Such processes also have the potential to produce moral obligations among the audience, even if the nature of these obligations is not necessarily connected to the rejection of apostasy and idolatry as we might expect, but rather to the nature of deception. While Ganor's successful deception in *Aye d'Avignon* — his disguise — could visually prove his non-Saracen identity features, in Muhammad's case, the success of his false miracles, the 'proof' of his words is not only used to underscore the failings of the community but is also what *deconstructs* his very status as a prophet. Muhammad's words are his own undoing in this work, as the more he tries to prove his assertions with rhetorical reasoning, the more his faith is disproved. Butler suggests that in order for identities to be produced, the reliance upon conventional formulations must be concealed, and a speaker established instead as the ultimate origin of his words.[41] In the *Roman*, common contemporary concerns (such as those surrounding the validity of miracles and the relationship of reason to faith) are exposed by the emphasis upon the community around Muhammad and, in particular, by the poet's open use of exemplary materials. The subject matter of Muhammad's life is therefore something of a red herring, as his identity as Prophet is only produced in the course of the narrative in order to be unravelled: his Saracen religious identity is formed by a process in which it exposes itself as fake, since the reliance upon conventional formulations is exposed not concealed for the reader/listener. By extension the Saracen identity of the community around Muhammad appears as the result of a certain blindness to such conventions; recognizing the performativity of Muhammad's words — his attempts to rationalize and explain what should be accepted through faith alone — would in turn undo the formation of the Saracens as a race.

Nonetheless, in the formation of a Saracen community, it is tricky to see the wood for the trees where the relationship between faith and race is concerned: how much does Alexandre du Pont really attempt to discourage apostasy or directly denigrate Islam and how much does he simply imbue a convenient scapegoat (Muhammad) with misdemeanours that are as much socially commonplace as heretically threatening? Notwithstanding the impact of literary devices and rhetoric, the idea that fear of conversion to Islam would be the motivating factor for the production of the *Roman* seems too sweeping a generalization, based broadly upon medieval attitudes to Islam rather than upon the contextual detail of the work at hand. Had this text appeared several hundred years previously, this reasoning would seem more plausible, particularly with regard to the polemical Latin tradition: John Tolan notes that early Christian responses to contact with Islam in the ninth century, particularly in Mediterranean regions, denigrated the new religion 'in an attempt to stem the tide of conversions'.[42] This is unsurprising given that, as Richard Bulliet has shown, for the Iberian Peninsula alone, the proportion of the population that was Muslim went from around twenty-five percent in 900, to seventy-five percent by the first half of the eleventh century.[43] Conversions to Islam continue to have caused confusion and consternation in thirteenth-century Valencia, and Robert Burns notes numerous examples and their resulting (usually financial) consequences.[44]

However, while cases of conversion to Islam during the crusading period are not unknown in lands under Muslim rule, the same cannot be said for examples from the Old French speaking world. In her study of the short prose tale *La Fille du Comte de Pontieu*, Peggy McCracken observes, for instance, that 'conversions to Islam are rarely represented in medieval French literature'.[45] Indeed, the heroine of this work is perhaps the only explicit example of conversion to Islam that does not also involve an act of treachery,[46] and even here, her willing embrace of a new faith is not unproblematic, as I discuss below. In this respect, the idea that the translation of Gautier de Compiègne's Latin *Otia* into French at Laon was to placate anxieties over conversion to Islam appears a little far-fetched.

Muhammad as Rhetorician

The Muhammad of the *Roman* engineers his own destiny, since, as scholars have suggested, he is as much as 'a pseudo-prophet who represents himself as what he is not',[47] as a 'Machiavellian' social upstart.[48] When he is initially described by the narrator, the Prophet's learned rather than divinely bestowed abilities come to the fore:

> Bons clers ert de geometrie,
> De musike et d'astrenomie,
> De grammaire et d'artimetike,
> De logike et de retorike. (vv. 39–42)
>
> [He was very learned in geometry,
> Music and astronomy,
> Grammar and arithmetic,
> Logic and rhetoric.]

Though he is a bondsman of humble birth, Muhammad fulfils his role aptly: as well as being responsible for all his master's needs (v. 86), he serves his lord 'loiaument' [loyally] and 'saghement' [wisely]. In displaying skills that amount to a list of the seven liberal arts,[49] Muhammad's intellectual abilities can be seen as classical rather than courtly in their emphasis on rhetoric and logic rather than upon knightly prowess or courtly pastimes. He begins life as a well-trained clerk and is additionally educated in the Christian faith: 'toute la loy de Jhesucrist | savoit par letre et par escrist' (vv. 37–38) [he was fully acquainted with the religion of Jesus Christ | through instruction and written works]. This emphasis conforms to the notion of the public exemplum, which is described by Scanlon as drawing its material from antiquity more than from folklore or hagiography.[50] Public exempla were often negative examples which were able to 'demonstrate the efficacy of their *sententiae* by enacting violations of them' and, for the most part, were concerned with the concept of secular or lay authority.[51] This would seem an oddly appropriate way to characterize the exemplarity of Muhammad in the *Roman*, as his machinations on the whole are concentrated upon his hierarchical relations to the rest of the court and his manipulation of his position of servitude. This is not to say that he does not also become, at the end of the text, a heresiarch by falsifying miracles, but simply to indicate that there is an overarching concern for the subversion of social norms and the credulity of the community here, rather than for his fraudulent revelations.

Perhaps the main way in which Muhammad's own words prove themselves false occurs as a result of paradox, rendering him a form of rhetorical rather than ecclesiastical exemplar. Alongside the community depicted around Muhammad in the text, the community receiving the work also plays a part in the negative construction of Muhammad during these episodes. For instance, the vocabulary used by Muhammad when he attempts to explain away his epilepsy relies upon the fact that the reader/listener knows him to be lying, creating a moment of complicity between poet and audience. In a single speech to his lady, Muhammad calls Khadija 'sage et prisie' (v. 838) [wise and esteemed] but then tries to claim, regarding his attempt to explain away his epilepsy, that 'ne ja de mot n'en mentirai'

(v. 842) [every word of it will be true]. This is then immediately followed by his wife's request that he does not deceive her with his words (v. 845). Muhammad's claim is thus an ironic paradox: the mere fact that he says he will not lie is then contradicted by his subsequent lie about his illness, as well as by the fact that we have previously been told that he deliberately wishes to deceive Khadija: 'il parole par grant savoir, | car sa dame velt dechevoir' (vv. 413–14) [he speaks with great skill | for he wants to deceive his lady]. Ultimately, his original statement that he will not lie is, in fact, a lie!

Muhammad continues this exchange by suggesting that his wife should cut out his tongue if she hears him lie (vv. 847–50), when of course, he knows that he is just about to do so. The readers or audience, presumably, are also expecting this, given his past performance. His speech consequently establishes him as a walking contradiction. Furthermore, the reasoning of the audience is used here to expose his inconsistency and thus demonstrate his false identity as prophet based upon their hearing of the narrative. In this respect, the hermeneutic processes involved in reading the literary work (in this case paradox) trigger a process of reasoning that deconstructs Muhammad's self-image. In a similar vein, we see irony later used by Muhammad when he tells his wife that the hermit will confirm the story of his visions and cannot be made to lie 'par peür | ne par don' (vv. 1043–44) [through intimidation | or gifts], the irony being that Muhammad has already bribed his wife's retainers to support his cause in this exact manner. Where Muhammad is concerned, it is thus his own rhetoric more so than his actions that establishes his untrustworthiness by allowing the reader/listener to see the disparity between his words and the truth of events.

Even when Muhammad speaks extensively during a religious discussion, his reference to the angel Gabriel and his supposed visions comes in the wake of his epileptic seizures, as a means to conceal his illness.[52] Furthermore, he phrases his explanation in terms of Christian tradition, likening his own 'visions' to the annunciation of the Virgin. This long speech is at first sight the simple replication of Christian beliefs, including reference to the crucifixion, for example, and contains so many lines that it is easy to forget that it is actually Muhammad who is speaking. This is especially true when he says 'que vous iroie jou disant?' (v. 993) [what more might I tell you?]: a rhetorical question that could just as easily have stemmed from the narrator as from Muhammad.

Another similar instance of this doubling between the narrator and the Prophet occurs when Muhammad tells the hermit that 'bons est li maus ki le pis garde' (v. 1105) [a bad thing that wards off something worse is good] in his attempt to garner support. While the use of the rhetorical question above highlights the seductiveness of Muhammad's words, the moralizing maxim here conceals the violence of his threat, which although dripping with piety, nonetheless expresses outright heresy (vv. 1000–17) and reinforces the notion of imposture surrounding Muhammad by temporarily merging his voice with that of the narrator. It is this motif of false speech and naïve belief that enables us to situate the *Roman* in a literary and intellectual context beyond that of Latin anti-Islamic polemic with reference to its manuscript tradition and contemporary environment. By extension, this leads both to the problematization of faith and reason and to the particular coupling of Saracen racial and religious identities that occurs in the text.

Production Contexts: Knowledge and Deception

The position of the *Roman de Mahomet* within the codex as a whole and its associated production contexts help to place it within a wider literary environment and provide alternative ways of reading its message and meaning. Materialist philologists underline that: 'far from being a transparent or neutral vehicle, the codex can have a typological identity that affects the way we read and understand the texts it presents'.[53] As previously noted, the only surviving copy of the *Roman de Mahomet* appears in BnF, MS f. fr. 1553, which is a late thirteenth-century miscellany of verse and prose materials.[54] Although this codex contains a large range of works (fifty-two to be precise), its dimensions are relatively small (265 x 185mm). This collection is not only one of the major fabliaux manuscripts, but as Keith Busby observes, it possesses 'very distinct northeastern characteristics' and contains 'many texts of local interest', such as *Courtois d'Arras* and *De Engerran, vesque de Cambrai* to name but two.[55] In this context, Hyatte's suggestion that the *Roman* was 'far removed from the geographical location and, presumably, regional or even European concerns of his domestic audience' is potentially problematic.[56] Acknowledging the fact that this is the sole copy of the *Roman*, I suggest that such regional concerns are not only present but that, along with contemporary social changes, they may even provide part of the impetus for the interest in the life of the Prophet.

For example, perhaps the most obvious point to mention is that the prominence of the Champagne trade fairs in the thirteenth century attracted merchants from far-flung regions. The poet even states in the *Roman* that the work was completed at Laon (v. 1994), which was one of several Champagne towns 'well placed at the focal points of the transcontinental traffic' offering 'convenient meeting places for the merchants of Italy and Provence on the one hand and those of Germany and the Low Countries on the other'.[57] Given that the manuscript has also been located to a probable Picard scriptorium,[58] the localization of the work to this region evokes Le Goff's assessment of the incorporation of Arabic thought into the contemporary intellectual climate beyond Spain and Italy:

> The centers where Oriental thought was incorporated into Western Christian culture were located elsewhere. The most important were in Chartres and Paris, surrounded by the more traditional ones in Laon, Reims, and Orleans. All were located in that other zone, one of exchange and the perfection of finished products, where the worlds of the North and the South met. Between the Loire and the Rhine, in the very region where great commerce and the bank settled in the markets of Champagne, there developed that culture which was to turn France into the primary heir of Greece and Rome, just as Alcuin had predicted, and as Chrétien de Troyes was proclaiming.[59]

Far from being unconcerned with the subject matter of the *Roman*, it is tempting at least to speculate that the community receiving the work had some degree of contact with those who had been to Islamic lands and it is also possible that these were people who may have worked with the intellectual output of these regions or at the very least, lived alongside those who did. In this respect, the *Roman* responds to both the polemical literary traditions of previous centuries and the scholarly context of north-eastern France in the mid-thirteenth century.

Although based on an earlier work, Alexandre du Pont's *Roman* remains a very loose translation and those significant alterations, such as exempla, may hint at the reception of an anti-Islamic work within a later context (Gautier's *Otia* is dated to between 1137 and 1155) and different literary milieu.[60] However, the possible function of the *Roman* beyond anti-Islamic Latin polemic is also suggested by the extant manuscript. In his overview of BnF, MS f. fr. 1553, Lepage divides the codex into A, B, C, and D to reflect the identifiable hands and composition rate. While D is somewhat less ordered and was probably compiled over a longer period, A, B, and C respectively reflect the hands of three copyists.[61] The *Roman* appears on folios 367^v–379^r within section C (which spans fols. 288–383) and is preceded in the section by the *Roman de la Violette* (fols. 288^r–325^v); the *Roman de Witasse le moine* (fols. 325^v–338^v); and a copy of the *Sept Sages* (fols. 338^v–367^v). It is followed by a version of *De Vaspasien <ou Vengeance Nostre Seigneur>* (fols. 379^r–393^v) though this was finished by a different scribe. Without delving here into the practice of dividing labour among scribes, there does seem to be a thematic coherence to the placing of these works together in the codex, which would be in accordance with Keith Busby's notion of a 'coherence of fragmentation': 'the generation of sequences of texts as determined by theme and/or genre'. Busby notes that this grouping of materials 'seems to be a fundamental structuring device of the longer anthology manuscript';[62] however, scholars of the *Roman* do not seem to have taken this grouping into account.

The final text of section C offers a fairly obvious link to the *Roman* given that it narrates the destruction of Jerusalem in 70 AD by the Roman emperor Vespasian and the 'vengeance' enacted upon the Jewish population for the death of Christ. It seems almost to offer a corrective to Muhammad's seemingly successful creation of a Saracen community, uniting Christian readers by depicting the defeat and undoing of Christianity's enemies and thus showcasing God's power. Setting aside this text, however, the three preceding works along with the *Roman* are also linked, as all convey narratives of trickery, whether through disguise or disputation. In further support of this theme, the Muhammad of the *Roman* bears more than a passing resemblance to a fabliau trickster; he uses his eloquence for his own gain, disrupting social hierarchies in the process. Alison Williams notes that tricksters 'are themselves defined by the boundaries which they supposedly transgress', suggesting that they inhabit 'the threshold between the licit and the illicit'. She defines a trickster as 'a character whose deliberate aim is to achieve material gain or psychological victory using wit and deception', commenting also that 'ambivalence is at the heart of the trickster's nature and function'.[63] A life of Muhammad that lacks the extreme denigration so often characterizing references to the Prophet by Christian writers, but which underscores the response to his words and the impact of his deception would seem to share a similar spirit. In the *Roman*, as fast as the character of Muhammad attempts to dupe others, his own fraudulence is exposed to the reader/audience. Alongside the potential geographical connections outlined above, there is therefore an overarching thematic emphasis upon language use and deception in this section of the codex that provides an alternative analytical context. Numerous fabliaux are contained within BnF, MS f. fr. 1553; these include, for instance, *Dou Maunier de Aleus*, in which a master helps his servant to sleep with a pretty girl (only to discover that his wife has in fact switched places with her) and *La Riote du monde*, a version of *Le Roi d'Angleterre et le jongleur d'Ely* which involves linguistic duplicity and double-entendres. What these texts share with the *Roman* is thus a preoccupation with the problems of trusting the words of others, a theme that attracts much of Alexandre's critical commentary.

Collective Responsibility and the Gullibility of the Masses

While it is common in Latin versions of the life of Muhammad to attribute his initial break with Christianity to a corrupt or heretical priest figure, in the *Roman* it is not only the case that Muhammad is not the driving force behind his instauration as a prophet, but that the responses of the community around him clearly determine his success and are criticized for such. This is in keeping with the idea that the text questions the extent to which one can trust the words of others. Even before Muhammad's supposed ability to see the future through God is revealed, he is praised by the knights at court for his qualities: 'De bonté est plus renommés; | que nus hom qui i soit nommés' (vv. 1288–89) [he is extolled more for goodness | than any other man named there]. Although sceptical, the community reason that he must be favoured by God: 'car bien le voient entechié | de chou que au deseur se met | de toute rien dont s'entremet' (vv. 1313–15) [for they see well that he is graced | by success | in everything he undertakes]. It is not simply a case that Muhammad presents himself as a prophet, since those at court are also responsible for constructing him as such: the erroneous, rational explanation of his success is what leads them to believe in Muhammad's divine support. Despite being the central character of this text, Muhammad's identity is presented as a communal effort. The tale portrays a broad spectrum of secular society and their collective power to create a false leader through their mistaken reasoning and misplaced credulity. As a result, religious affiliation in this sense becomes racialized in the sense that a community — a collective identity — is also constructed around Muhammad in turn, as the people are referred to as the 'gens Mahom' (v. 1947) [Muhammadans].

An emphasis upon the broader community and particularly upon the courtly masses is further apparent in the episode of Muhammad's wedding feast. While Hyatte has noted the anachronism of some of the items described at the gathering,[64] there is actually almost as much detail provided about those who attend as about the opulence of the venue. All unimportant men are said to be replaced by 'mains haus prinches' (v. 765) [many high princes], as well as 'tante dame avenans et biele | et tante noble damoisiele | tant borjois et tant eskuier' (vv. 767–69) [numerous beautiful and graceful ladies | and many noble maids | and several burghers and squires] all accompanied by the obligatory minstrels. In this respect, the wedding is as much a parade of the courtly community as of material finery, so that alongside the luxurious nature of Muhammad's life, the tale underscores a sense of the diversity of the society around the Prophet: a society that is also noticeably secular and European in its organization. This is also later reflected in the coming together of the court, where once again all levels of society appear to be present, from knights, barons, and squires to ladies, maidens, and damsels. Here, the correct arrangement of the court according to status is also highlighted, since 'barons, chevalier, chastelain | furent paraus, et li vilain | de l'autre part lor liu avoient' (vv. 1248–50) [the barons, knights, and castellans | are grouped by themselves, and the peasants | have their place on the other side].[65] This marks a slight departure from the Latin of Gautier de Compiègne, which only mentions the separation of the women from the men: a detail necessary for the subsequent discussion between Khadija and her maids to unfold (*Otia*, vv. 673–74). As a result, Alexandre du Pont's roll call of secular society shows a focus on people as well as objects, on reactions as well as descriptions.

Those around Muhammad are not only shown to misrecognize his character, but are also directly responsible for Muhammad's initial break with the Christian faith. Muhammad is blissfully unaware of his role as the enemy of Christianity until he visits a hermit for guidance. While the recluse is a devout Christian in the *Roman* rather than the Christian heretic of other contemporary portrayals,[66] his comments nonetheless make Muhammad susceptible to the lure of the devil. He tells him:

> Mahom, chou dist li sains hermites,
> Tu ies au dÿable toz quites
> Et si ies sa possessïons.
> Par tes grans tribulatïons
> Sera la loys Jhesu destruite
> Et la malvaise lois estruite. (vv. 151–56)
>
> ["Muhammad," said the saintly hermit,
> "You belong to the devil body and soul,
> And so you are his property.
> Because of your grievous oppression,
> Jesus' religion will be subverted
> And the wicked rule instituted".]

The trust that Muhammad places in the hermit's prophetic words seems to be criticized by the poet, who notes that he has become mad, since 'plus croit a l'omme saintisme | que il ne fait a lui meïsme' (vv. 185–86) [he trusts more in the very holy man | than he does in himself]. At this moment, Muhammad also loses control of his own actions: 'n'est pas ja en sa poësté: | Li dÿables l'a conquesté, | ki en faisoit chou k'il voloit' (vv. 189–91) [he is no longer in control of himself: | the devil has conquered him, | and he does with him what he wants] and so it seems that the moment he relinquishes self-belief is the moment that the words of the hermit interpellate him as a heretic, as Muhammad accepts his destiny as a prophet. In this sense, this text does not appear to caution those who would follow false prophets and fall under their influence but rather to warn the community about their collective power to create such a figure, even if inadvertently. The words and reactions of the broader community, in particular their performative powers, are therefore held up as problematic in the *Roman*, demonstrating as they do poor reasoning skills and an evident naivety.

Such a meaning would also tally with the episode when the same hermit later agrees to corroborate Muhammad's lies to Khadija about his epilepsy in this version of the tale, in exchange for protection for a small group of Christians. Although Alexandre claims that his source praises the hermit for this (vv. 1158–67) he also suggests that the source must be mistaken. This has been variously interpreted by Hyatte as the result of the poet's knowledge of other Latin writings, and by Lepage as a misunderstanding of the justifiable nature of the hermit's decision.[67] However, Alexandre's comment also brings the episode from the poet's source text in line with his own agenda, namely a desire to criticize those who accept the influence of others or to caution against the creation of heretical leaders. What is at stake in this work is therefore the credulity of the masses: the lack of, if not intelligence in an academic sense, then sense or rational thought, particularly evident in the poet's frequent use of forms of the word *fol* (for example, 'la gent fole' in v. 1578 referring to the people who believe one of his false miracles). In this case the threat does not come from lies told by Muhammad but from lies propagated by the text itself to be exposed by the vernacular poet.

The actions of those around Muhammad are also criticized by the narrative voice when Muhammad is able to bribe Khadija's followers to support his suit with the lady (vv. 588–604). If these barons had not been so easily bribed, then Muhammad would not have been able to marry his former overlord's wife and thereby increase his social status and power. As with the hermit, the words and promises of Muhammad persuade the barons here: 'tant a par sa promesse fait | qu'a s'aide a chascun atrait (vv. 591–92) [he accomplishes so much through his promises | that he wins everyone over to aiding him]. The behaviour of these greedy lords seems very much connected to social hierarchy, as the narrator notes that: 'par devant si signour estoient, | par dons a lui se sousmetoient' (vv. 611–12) [those who earlier were his superiors | submit to him for the sake of gifts]. It is not just the fact that these men have been persuaded to act in exchange for material goods that poses a problem but, more importantly, that in doing so they have upset the social order of the court.

Another instance of subtle criticism directed at those who would be easily persuaded occurs when Muhammad's followers have been convinced by their wives of his divinely inspired visions, leading them to comment that they will worship him as a God in human form (vv. 1355–59). While there is no comment made by the narrator and no sermonizing tone regarding the question of idolatry here, the credulity of the men comes in the wake of the narrator's assertion that women say meaningless things (v. 1254, 'volage' [flighty word]) as soon as they think of them, whether they are 'fole ou sage' (v. 1255) [foolish or wise]. Not only is the behaviour of the men therefore suspect, but the women are also criticized for their lack of forethought. Once again, the message of the poem is not really about idolatrous

Saracen behaviour at all; instead it seems to use Muhammad as a touchstone: a respondent presented as the most untrustworthy figure imaginable who interacts with a range of people to outline commentaries on truth, lies, and wisdom. While the text may well narrate a return to the Old Law of idolatry and pre-Christian beliefs, as suggested by Akbari,[68] this does not seem to be the overriding moral message.

The untrustworthy nature of speech in this work is perhaps most clearly shown in the figure of the old knight, who is an advisor to Muhammad's wife, Khadija.[69] The tale of Noah is related to the court by '.I. chevalier, viel homme et sage | et bon clerc et de haut parage' (vv. 677–78) [a knight, an old man of noble birth, | wise and well-read], whereas in Latin the dominant word used to describe him is 'senex' ('old' or 'old man', *Otia*, v. 339), thus lacking the same courtly tone. Given that the tale told by the old knight occurs while the lady's barons are trying to promote Muhammad as a potential husband, one might expect the wise man to convey a moral message that draws upon this. However, he mentions the universal principle that all men were originally free of sin before the Fall and uses the courtly terms 'franc et gentil' (v. 700) [free and noble][70] to describe prelapsarian man in contrast to the Latin emphasis on freedom: 'omnis tunc homo liber erat' (*Otia*, v. 344) [every man was free then]. This combination of the Christian universal with the courtly is continued through his advice to the lady not to trust in mutable things (v. 719), meditating upon the concept of *servage*. While the idea of mutability may seem to be a comment upon materiality, what then follows is an explanation of 'servages' (v. 721) or servitude to God:

> Quant a Diu servir se sousmet,
> Ses fils devient et il ses peres;
> S'est rois des rois et empereres:
> Dont ne le puet on pas serf dire. (vv. 724–27)
>
> [When he submits to serving God,
> He becomes His son, and He his Father;
> Thus he is king of kings and emperor.
> Then no one can say that he is a slave.]

Albeit indirectly, the old man's comments contrast the earthly service that Muhammad has provided to his lady with the spiritual service that a Christian should give to God. His words could almost have been addressed to Muhammad himself, given that, as Kangas suggests, 'he knows very well that he is not a prophet but wants to be rich and famous, and works hard to attain this end'.[71] In this respect, what we have here is a subtle reference to Muhammad's claim to fame and power, hidden within a generalized exhortation to serve God and accept one's place in life that echoes the exemplum of the knight and the squire which appears in lines 219–98.

Yet confusingly, the wise man then goes on to press Muhammad's suit with Khadija, describing him in accordance with standard courtly conventions, both in terms of his character and his appearance: he is 'fiers et estous' (v. 740) [valiant and brave] as well as 'bien tailliés, de menbres adrois' (v. 743) [well-formed, with straight limbs]. In contrast to the commonplace remark made of Saracens that they would be the best knights if only they were Christian, here the old knight also comments that Muhammad would be worthy of being king 'se ses linages ne fust sers' (v. 746) [if his lineage were not servile]. Recognizing Muhammad as a prophet and leader therefore also involves overcoming or casting aside his apparently base lineage, so that although once servile, he would become a ruler. His construction as a religious leader has an effect upon how his bloodline is to be viewed, and his elevation forges a new people that also involves the racialization of religious affiliation: the court/ chivalric collectivity morphs at times into a homogenized people sharing faith in Muhammad, as seen in the episode of conflict between the Saracens and Persians.

When the Persian army arrives and the Saracens are threatened by an enemy from without, the community is described as 'les gens Mahom' (v. 1595) [Muhammad's people] who follow 'la loy Mahom' (v. 1785) [Muhammad's religion] and occupy 'la terre Mahom' (v. 1598) [Muhammad's lands]. This collective identity is perhaps most clearly asserted in their subsequent opposition to the invading Persians: 'li persant la gent Mahom tüent' (v. 1947) [the Persians slay Muhammad's troops]. At the very end of the text, this ostensible formation of a race of people reaches its peak, where 'la gens Mahom, fors du sens' (v. 1947) [the crazed Muhammadans] have now turned away from God and are said to worship Muhammad. Although Hyatte's translation of 'Muhammadans' is jarring to the modern reader, it helpfully underlines this construction of a now racial as much as religious identity. Echoing somewhat the idea of a spiritual lineage that emerged in the Vulgate Cycle, the production of Muhammad as Prophet also produces the Saracens as a race in this text, and this notion of lineage is further evoked in the closing etymological description of Mecca discussed above.

Ultimately, the process of constructing the Prophet's own identity in this text becomes a means to highlight the formation of an entire community around misplaced faith. We read a truly mutable portrait of the Prophet that draws upon courtly conventions of beauty and values, making him the embodiment of the old man's warning. Yet while the old knight says one thing, he paradoxically means something very different and the circularity of his argument is indeed framed by the repetition of the syllable 'ser-' seven times within twenty-six lines (vv. 720–46): a certain irony appears in the placement of a line replete with sibilance just after a narrative of the Fall (v. 746), as if the very idea of raising Muhammad from his servile heritage had come from Eden's snake itself. The episode consequently problematizes the question of reason and proof once again, as although the old man's words seem to fit within a Christian context, his message is rather hypocritical in its focus on the physical, material qualities of Muhammad. The unreliable nature of his words is even signalled by the fact that the old man tries to call upon God as proof for his argument:

> A tesmoing en trai Nostre Sire
> Et saint Jehan l'Ewangeliste,
> De la parole Diu manistre;
> A cest tesmoing doit on bien croire:
> Tos jors est sa parole voire. (vv. 728–32)

> [As proof of this I cite Our Lord
> And Saint John the Evangelist
> Regarding the term 'servant of God.'
> Certainly one should believe this evidence —
> Its word is always true.]

In contrast to the acceptable, metaphorical use of proof that occurs, for instance, in the well-known religious debate of Saint Catherine and the pagan philosophers, the old man does not use metaphor or allegory for his process of reasoning but claims to show direct proof from God, arguably rationalizing faith in an unreliable manner.[72]

Of course, the ultimate example and criticism of proof being used in the context of faith appears during the false miracles enacted by Muhammad before the community. He first conceals a channel of milk and honey atop a mountain, then leads the people to the spot but claims that it has been sent by God.[73] The revelation of the channel occurs after Muhammad has prayed to God for 'aucun signe certain' (v. 1430) [some sure sign] and the word 'signe' is also repeated in line 1458. Given the text's overarching emphasis on credulity, this suggests that the problem here is the desire (and need) for proof from God in the hope that the burden of the world can be lessened by this (vv. 1455–62). The theme of acceptance is also central to Alexandre's use of exemplary material, as seen above, and so the need for evidence of God seems almost as much of a temptation as Muhammad's fearsome eloquence (vv. 1380–82). Following the revelation of the channel, Muhammad even provides a kind of false exegesis of the event:

> Car par le miel est figuree
> La loys ki nous sera donnee,
> Et par le lait k'i est, nos Peres
> Ki nous oste les loys amere. (vv. 1485–88)
>
> [For the honey signifies
> The law that will be given unto us,
> And the milk here,
> Our Father Who revokes the harsh laws for us.]

The power of his words to convince 'la gent fole' [the foolish people] is then confirmed by Alexandre, who notes how their beliefs are thus determined (vv. 1577–82). Religious identity is figured as collective, as produced by the formation of a community, and as subsequently becoming the basis for a race of people. In such a context, the *Roman* prioritizes the theme of proof and belief among the masses rather than that of anti-conversion propaganda or indeed engagement with Islam.

In fact, returning briefly to the manuscript of the *Roman*, the immediately preceding work, the *Sept Sages de Rome*, provides a still stronger rationale for situating the *Roman* within this intellectual framework, given that it concerns the verbal confrontation of a queen and a group of learned advisors. As Mary B. Speer notes, the *Sept Sages* is fundamentally a tale where 'a learned masculine community of clerics and their pupil just barely outwits an unscrupulous woman',[74] which makes it less surprising that the *Roman de Mahomet* should be a version of the life of the Prophet that underscores the power of rhetoric and the nature of evidence.

Emphasis on rhetoric and processes of reasoning also appears in the intellectual debates raging throughout the thirteenth century regarding the applicability of reason to faith. The thirteenth century saw dramatic developments and violent conflicts within scholarly environments. It was not only a time of localized clashes between monastic and secular members of the University of Paris, whether in terms of administrative control or Averroist heresy, but was also a period when the more general relationship between scientific rationality and faith was being put to the test. The influx of Aristotelian thought through works translated from Arabic brought with it 'a return to reasoning',[75] that was nonetheless problematic, although strangely, this was not because of its Arabic (and thus Islamic) origins.[76] Rather, problems arose since faith was considered to be beyond reason. Thomas Aquinas, for instance, stated that: 'any arguments made against the doctrines of faith are incorrectly derived from the self-evident first principles of nature'.[77] Similar sentiments had also been summarized by Guibert de Nogent over a century earlier:

> If, I say, these things and others also can be proposed as either true or false, then what will they say about the Holy Spirit, those who impiously argue, in accordance with the vestiges of the Arian heresy, that He is less than the Father and the Son.[78]

John Tolan explains that in the context of thirteenth-century missionary activity, concerns were raised by various theologians regarding how to combat the Muslim faith on the frontline, as it were, of the Holy Land.[79] He cites the example of Thomas Aquinas's *Reasons for the Faith against the Muslims*, produced for the Cantor of Antioch, in which Aquinas states that one 'should not try to prove the Faith by necessary reasons' as this would 'belittle the sublimity of the Faith'. Instead, 'any Christian disputing about the articles of the Faith should not try to prove the Faith, but defend the Faith'.[80] While the defensive stance of apologetic works may well characterize twelfth-century anti-Islamic tracts such as the *Risâlat al-Kindî* (Apology of Al-Kindi) and the *Dialogues against the Jews* of Petrus Alfonsi, the *Roman de Mahomet* does not engage with Islamic practices through gloss or explanatory passages. Instead, it relies upon subtler processes of reasoning characterized by rather less obvious authorial interventions and exempla that function more tangentially to the central narrative than we might first expect.

Conclusion

In the *Roman de Mahomet* the Saracen is not used to expound upon the threat of Islam to all but functions within a specific environment of educating the masses, of showing processes of reasoning, and exposing the risks of relying upon the words of others. In this sense, Muhammad is portrayed as a threat to the ignorant, to those who do not use their reason to defend their faith, but is also a threat to those who need proof in order to have faith. Of course, the relationship between proof and faith was also recognized by Gautier de Coinci in his *Miracles*, as previously discussed. Yet in the miraculous experiences of Gautier's Saracens, faith (or at least the semblance of faith produced through devotional gesture) often seemed to precede the bodily experiences of the spiritual. Such an emphasis upon the nature and use of proof is also evident in the sole manuscript illumination to the *Roman*, in which a bull that Muhammad has trained appears next to him before two followers. Physical proof is therefore an unreliable indicator of spiritual legitimacy according to the *Roman*, since the very evidence that convinces the people of the truth of Muhammad's words (the bull) is depicted as the result of his own conniving rather than a divine manifestation.

However, when situated in the context of faith rather than evidential proof, reason, as suggested by the numerous authorial comments, helps us to see the world as determined by God and not to be unsatisfied with our lot. In essence, it reminds the reader to beware of those who would try to prove faith: the concealed epilepsy, the tamed bull, the channels of milk and honey, the disappearing treasure, and the levitating coffin are all supposedly miraculous events in the *Roman* that are designed as proofs of the divine, yet they in fact turn out to be no more than terrestrial objects falsely peddled and erroneously received. In this light, Muhammad is a version of the trickster figure found in the fabliaux rather than the heretic and potential Antichrist of anti-Islamic polemic. This vernacular text thus underscores the need for wisdom among the non-clerically trained to help them recognize the false words of others, in this case of someone who is also portrayed as highly learned, if of humble origins.

While this work might not reflect any one specific change in intellectual culture or academic practice of the mid- to late-thirteenth century, it does seem to engage more generally with the movement from the traditional education of the past, as based upon the trivium/quadrivium, to a 'redefinition of Christian belief in relation to philosophy' in its questioning of the role of reason in relation to faith.[81] The text epitomizes the coming together of theology and the arts, uniting as it does interest in secular/popular folk motifs, doctrinal perversion, and elements of Latin polemic with an emphasis on rhetorical ability, knowledge, and reason. In this respect, the main danger of taking this text as simply a reformulation of Latin anti-Islamic propaganda, whether in response to fears of apostasy on the home front, or as a means of encouraging missionary activity, is that the extent of the work's engagement with broader social currents becomes lost. Despite the fact that critics of this work have noted the predominance of secular references in the text,[82] none have gone beyond this to think in greater detail about the role fulfilled by Muhammad and, ultimately, about the purpose and audience of this unusual literary oeuvre. Although Muhammad is clearly represented as a heretical and deceitful figure in the *Roman*, the work speaks more generally to the dangers of using rationality to justify credulity; the principle of faith over reason is thus applicable beyond the frontline of face-to-face Christian-Saracen interaction in the medieval period and even beyond the 'home front' of heresy suggested by Hyatte.

The preoccupation with reason and faith is visible above all through the moral lessons in the text, whether those provided by exempla or by the poet's direct engagement with his public. These episodes are more about the audience being able to accept their status and the unknowable nature of God gracefully in the knowledge that there is a better life in heaven than they are about discouraging the specific seduction of Islam. In this light, Muhammad acts as an example of such a one who does not accept what he is given in life but tries to change it. Given the wider critique of reason achieved in the *Roman*, it seems that, rather than placing Muhammad into a Christian frame, Alexandre du Pont has used a reductive caricature of Islam as a framing device for such a treatise, especially in light of his digressions and extensions to his source material.

By presenting Islam as easily understandable and rationalized, Alexandre's engagement with this religion remains only superficial; this is particularly evident in moments where Muslim belief is present but distorted, which all have some basis in previous literary works on the Prophet. However, even the representation of Muhammad is not quite as distorted as it appears in other contemporary texts, as although he tricks the community around him, they also trick each other, as can be seen in the poor advice given by the barons to Khadija. Consequently, this work is not just concerned with presenting Muhammad as a false prophet or heresiarch but actually with stressing his similarity to a secular audience and this is achieved, above all, by the exposure of his false rhetoric and the credulous characters around him. As further evidence of the text's misunderstanding of Islam and secular focus, the representation of Muhammad shows that he fails to live up to the expectations of romance as much as it underlines his status as a heretical Christian. His wish to deliberately deceive Khadija, for instance, is highly uncourtly and some of his false miracles are specifically cast within secular contexts, such as when he pretends that God has returned the wealth of those killed in a war with the Persians (vv. 1843–67). Tangentially, it is interesting that in making Muhammad the opposite of a bona fide prophet, the poet seems in the process to have made him poor and intellectual, since, as Le Goff notes, there were conflicts that arose in the thirteenth century regarding the question of poverty and begging among intellectuals and scholars.[83]

To a certain extent, this is a story that uses exempla to deny exemplarity; in contrast to the Saracens of Gautier de Coinci's *Miracles*, in the *Roman*, the very fact that those around Muhammad believe and honour him is what proves that he is not an exemplar, as their belief is based upon proofs and rationalizing speeches rather than faith. What this text ultimately shows therefore is that Muhammad has been created as a prophet by other people, not by God, so that in performative terms it is the Prophet's own words that, in being (mistakenly) recognized by the community, construct him as a religious leader. In turn, this mistaken construction of a religious leader also produces an identifiable community — a Saracen race — united not by physiognomy or blood but through faith. This spiritualization of genealogy is also somewhat reminiscent of the 'Grail race' seen in the *Estoire*, as discussed in Chapter Two. Yet whereas in the *Estoire* the logical time of the narrative cycle led to such genealogies being (supposedly) uncovered through the discovery of faith, in the *Roman* a religiously determined lineage system is not uncovered but created. Paradoxically, Muhammad's body is central to the Saracens' racial identity not for its flesh and blood appearance or even bloodline but for its power to create a religious community: it is as an object of worship and veneration. While the community are said to be aware of the scientific explanation for his levitating sarcophagus, they do not wish to admit this (v. 1913). It is therefore the very misrecognition of his religious identity by the community rather than shared biology that produces the concept of a united Saracen people or race. In fact, bloodlines are very much surpassed in the process of Muhammad's elevation in the course of this particular narrative.

The *Roman* also evinces a different relationship between geography and race to that seen above. In the *Estoire*, geography produced race, with the Saracens taking their name from the city of Sarras, and it was even central to the creation of a spiritual race through their predestined place in Britain. In contrast, geography in the *Roman* is produced by the act of adultery, which performatively constructs the adulterer as both sinner and member of the Saracen community, as seen in the etymological description of Mecca. Although the work is thus about Muhammad, it is also about the process through which the community makes him a prophet; it shows how religious affiliation to the new law proposed by Muhammad constructs community and in turn produces the Saracens as a people. While the general idea of faith as performative — as the mere repetition of conventional behaviours and gestures — might seem problematic for a Christian context, the notion of Islam as a faith is troubled in this text through the separation of rationality and faith. If faith may consequently produce race in this text, it is nonetheless a misplaced faith based in the terrestrial not spiritual world. It is not a case that religion is synonymous with race but that the performativity of Saracen faith may produce a form of racial identity in turn.

By exploiting the general catch-all symbolism of Muhammad, the *Roman* creates a figure that bridges the divide between terrestrial and spiritual, religious and secular. Rather than domesticating the Prophet, despite the poet's claim to be providing a tale for those who wish to know about Muhammad, Muhammad's tale is instead used as the exemplum par excellence which can be transformed into whatever Christian moral message needs to be advocated. What we have here is a discussion of reason and faith and the validity of proofs along with a critique of false reasoning or unquestioning credulity. In this respect, the *Roman* can be viewed as part of a broader tradition of instructional literature: a fact that is also evinced by the compilation of the miscellany as a whole. Although the *Roman* is an isolated vernacular example, scholars should not necessarily generalize about the emphasis placed upon Islam in such a work. Whereas some texts on the Prophet strive to create a mirror image of Christianity, an inversion, some convey quite different Christian messages, as is the case here with the question of proof and the acceptance of God's omniscience.

John Tolan notes in relation to Robert I. Moore's *The Formation of a Persecuting Society* that: '"Reason" for Moore, became in the twelfth and thirteenth centuries the "flag" of this clerical elite, justifying its power over Christian society. Those who opposed that power, from inside or out, were branded as irrational'.[84] In this context, it would be unsurprising for Islam to be painted as senseless in the *Roman*. However, this text actually provides the opposite: a representation of the Prophet that is so rational as to be non-religious. It is an excess of reason that seems to condemn Muhammad in his claims of divine explanation for mundane events, a concept critiqued by the closing remarks of the poet in relation to Babel.

In a sense, the Muhammad of the *Roman* echoes the sentiments of scholastics of the period, such as those of twelfth-century Englishman Daniel Morley, who exhorted his fellow scholars to plunder the 'sapientiam et eloquentiam' [wisdom and eloquence] of pagan philosophers and enrich themselves with the 'spoiliis' [spoils].[85] The exegesis and reasoning of the Prophet have quite literally robbed him of his eloquence, so that his false words are exposed and faith shown to be performative. Highly influential for the thirteenth-century development of Aristotelian thought and for the link between reason and faith, Arabic wisdom, it seems, is far from absent from the *Roman*, a text which subtly uses reason both to promote blind Christian faith and criticize the doubtful. In such a scenario, Muhammad plays the philosopher who must be robbed of his oratorical bells and whistles to leave faith wordless rather than senseless.

Notes to Chapter 4

1. See Arjana, *Muslims in the Western Imagination*, p. 33.
2. For an overview of the Latin tradition dealing with the Prophet, see Di Cesare, *Pseudo-Historical Image*; note that there remains speculation surrounding Embrico's authorship of this work. See Guy Cambier, 'Embricon de Mayence (1010?–1077) est-il l'auteur de la Vita Mahumeti?', *Latomus*, 16 (1957), 468–79.
3. The edition I use is: Alexandre du Pont, *Le Roman de Mahomet de Alexandre du Pont (1258) avec le texte des "Otia de Machomete" de Gautier de Compiègne (XIIe siècle)*, établi par R. B. C. Huygens, ed. by Yvan G. Lepage, Bibliothèque française et romane, Series B, 16 (Paris: Klincksieck, 1977). Translations are from *The Prophet of Islam in Old French: The Romance of Muhammad (1258) and The Book of Muhammad's Ladder (1264)*, trans. by Reginald Hyatte, Brill's Studies in Intellectual History, 75 (Leiden: Brill, 1997).
4. John Tolan characterizes an earlier Latin biography of the Prophet by Embrico of Mainz as a form of (counter) saint's life. See 'Anti-Hagiography'.
5. Lepage comments on the 'originalité' of the *Roman* in his Introduction to *Le Roman de Mahomet*, pp. 84–85.
6. See Lepage's discussion of Alexandre du Pont's translation, 'Introduction', in *Roman*, pp. 80–91.
7. Lepage, 'Introduction', in *Roman*, p. 86; for the exegetical approaches of vernacular translators, see for instance, Rita Copeland, *Rhetoric, Hermeneutics, and Translation in the Middle Ages: Academic Traditions and Vernacular Texts* (Cambridge: Cambridge University Press, 1991), pp. 103–07.
8. Akbari, in contrast, focuses on critiques of Islam in the context of idolatry and conventions of Saracen materiality. See *Idols in the East*, pp. 224–28.
9. See Hyatte's 'Introduction', in *The Prophet of Islam*, pp. 1–3 (quotation from p. 3). See also his 'Muhammad's Prophethood in Two Old French Narratives: Divergent Traditions and Converging Ends', *Allegorica*, 18 (1997), 3–19.
10. Kangas, 'Saracens and their Prophet', p. 132.
11. See Akbari, *Idols in the East*, pp. 224–47.
12. Kangas, 'Saracens and their Prophet', p. 144.
13. I use the term 'wisdom literature' here following the recent discussion of Marie de France's *Ysopë* provided by Sharon Kinoshita and Peggy McCracken, who connect Marie's work to texts such as the *Sept Sages de Rome* and *Barlaam et Josephat*, noting, for instance, that the *Sept Sages* appears in the miscellany BnF, MS f. fr. 1553 discussed in the present chapter. See Sharon Kinoshita and Peggy McCracken, *Marie de France: A Critical Companion*, Gallica, 24 (Cambridge: Brewer, 2012), pp. 37–38.

14. Larry Scanlon, *Narrative, Authority, and Power: The Medieval Exemplum and the Chaucerian Tradition* (Cambridge: Cambridge University Press, 1994), pp. 33–34.
15. Miri Rubin, *Gentile Tales: The Narrative Assault on Late Medieval Jews* (Philadelphia: University of Pennsylvania Press, 2004. First published New Haven, CT: Yale University Press, 1999), p. 12.
16. Lepage, 'Introduction', in *Roman*, pp. 85–87.
17. See Hyatte, 'Introduction', in *The Prophet of Islam*, p. 2.
18. Tolan, *Saracens*, pp. 244–45. Interestingly Laon was not Dominican, and this text does not seem to have been intended as part of conversion efforts towards Muslims, although Tolan's reference here to Dominican missionary strategies seems nonetheless appropriate.
19. Kangas, 'Saracens and their Prophet', p. 145.
20. Dianne Speed, 'Middle English Romance and the *Gesta Romanorum*', in *Tradition and Transformation in Medieval Romance*, ed. by Rosalind Field (Woodbridge: Brewer, 1999), pp. 45–70 (p. 55).
21. Jocelyn Wogan-Browne, 'Bet...to...rede on holy seyntes lyves...': Romance and Hagiography Again', in *Readings in Medieval English Romance*, ed. by Carol M. Meale (Cambridge: Brewer, 1994), pp. 83–98 (p. 86).
22. Chantal Connochie-Bourgne, ' "Nature" et "clergie" dans l'oeuvre de vulgarisation scientifique de Gossuin de Metz (Image du Monde, 1245)', in *Comprendre et maîtriser la nature au moyen âge: Mélanges d'histoire des sciences offerts à Guy Beaujouan*, ed. by Danielle Jacquart (Geneva: Droz, 1994), pp. 9–29 (p. 26). She uses manuscript: Florence, Biblioteca Laurenziana, Ashburnham 114.
23. Connochie-Bourgne, ' "Nature" et "clergie" ', pp. 26–27.
24. As Hyatte notes, this etymology appears both in Gautier's *Otia* and in Mark of Toledo's preface to the translation of the Koran; in medieval Latin the word 'mecha' also means 'adulteress'. See *The Prophet of Islam*, fn. 42, p. 94.
25. Bloch, *Etymologies and Genealogies*, p. 157.
26. Lepage argues that the disparity between the texts is due to differences in versification (*Roman*, p. 88).
27. Strickland, *Saracens, Demons, & Jews*, pp. 189–90.
28. See references in Strickland, *Saracens, Demons, & Jews*, p. 190; Marie-Thérèse d'Alverny, *La Connaissance de l'Islam dans l'Occident médiéval*, ed. by Charles Burnett, with an appreciation by Margaret Gibson (Aldershot: Variorum, 1994), p. 58.
29. Walter B. Cahn, 'The "Portrait" of Muhammad in the Toledan Collection', in *Reading Medieval Images: the Art Historian and the Object*, ed. by Elizabeth Sears and Thelma K. Thomas (Ann Arbor: University of Michigan Press, 2002), pp. 51–60.
30. *Patrologiae cursus completus*, ed. by J.-P. Migne, Series Latina, 221 vols (Paris: [n.pub.], 1841–1905), CLXXXIX (1854), p. 655. My own translation.
31. Strickland, *Saracens, Demons, & Jews*, p. 191.
32. Strickland, *Saracens, Demons, & Jews*, pp. 222–26.
33. I use the ink numbering of folios here (following Lepage) rather than the pencil or thirteenth-century roman numerals, for the sake of continuity. See Yvan G. Lepage, 'Un recueil français de la fin du XIIe siècle (Paris, Bibliothèque Nationale, fr. 1553)', *Scriptorium*, 29 (1975), 23–46 (p. 25).
34. Anna Czarnowus, for instance, discusses this motif in Langland's work in 'Muhammad in Hell, or Dante and William Langland on the Prophet's Afterlife', in *Thise Stories Beren Witnesse: The Landscape of the Afterlife in Medieval and Post-medieval Imagination*, ed. by Liliana Sikorska, Medieval English Mirror, 7 (Frankfurt: Peter Lang, 2010), pp. 31–42 (pp. 36–37).
35. See his *Quia Major* (April 1213) translated in *Crusade and Christendom: Annotated Documents in Translation from Innocent III to the Fall of Acre, 1187–1291*, ed. by Jessalynn Bird, Edward Peters, and James M. Powell (Philadelphia: University of Pennsylvania Press, 2013), pp. 107–12 (p. 108).
36. Akbari, *Idols in the East*, p. 225 and p. 226.
37. Scanlon, *Narrative, Authority, and Power*, pp. 57–58.
38. Scanlon, *Narrative, Authority, and Power*, p. 34.
39. See Louis Althusser, 'Ideology and Ideological State Apparatus (Notes Towards an Investigation)',

in *Lenin and Philosophy, and Other Essays*, trans. by Ben Brewster (New York: Monthly Review Press, 2001), pp. 85–127 (pp. 117–20).
40. Judith Butler, *Excitable Speech: A Politics of the Performative* (New York: Routledge, 1997), pp. 15–17 (quotation from p. 16).
41. See Butler, *Excitable Speech*, p. 50.
42. Tolan, *Saracens*, p. 41.
43. Richard W. Bulliet, *Conversion to Islam in the Medieval Period: An Essay in Quantitative Reasoning* (Cambridge MA: Harvard University Press, 1979), p. 124.
44. Robert I. Burns, 'Renegades, Adventurers, and Sharp Businessmen: The Thirteenth-Century Spaniard in the Cause of Islam', *The Catholic Historical Review*, 58 (1972), 341–66.
45. Peggy McCracken, *The Romance of Adultery: Queenship and Sexual Transgression in Old French Literature* (Philadelphia: University of Pennsylvania Press, 1998), p. 128.
46. Note the negative portrayal of Eleanor of Aquitaine, who offers to convert to Islam and elope with Saladin in the thirteenth-century minstrel's chronicle, *Ménestrel de Reims*, as highlighted in E. Jane Burns, *Sea of Silk: A Textile Geography of Women's Work in Medieval French Literature* (Philadelphia: University of Pennsylvania Press, 2009), p. 153. A further example of a treacherous convert to Islam would be Dudon, the eponymous hero's uncle in the *chanson de geste* of *Huon de Bordeaux*.
47. Akbari, *Idols in the East*, p. 224.
48. Kangas, 'Saracens and their Prophet', p. 145.
49. These are the trivium (grammar, rhetoric and logic) and the quadrivium (arithmetic, geometry, astronomy and music). See Hilde de Ridder-Symoens, ed., *Universities in the Middle Ages*, vol. 1 of *A History of the University in Europe*, ed. by Walter Rüegg (Cambridge: Cambridge University Press, 1992), p. 308.
50. Scanlon, *Narrative, Authority, and Power*, p. 57.
51. Scanlon, *Narrative, Authority, and Power*, p. 81.
52. While the term epileptic is not directly used here, we are told that he falls to the floor, his eyes roll, his mouth foams, and he thrashes about (vv. 789–93). The attribution of epilepsy to the Prophet is a common motif in anti-Islamic polemic. See Owsei Temkin, *The Falling Sickness: A History of Epilepsy from the Greeks to the Beginnings of Modern Neurology*, 2nd edn, rev. (Baltimore: Johns Hopkins Press, 1971), pp. 150–59.
53. *The Whole Book: Cultural Perspectives on the Medieval Miscellany*, ed. by Stephen G. Nichols and Siegfried Wenzel (Ann Arbor: University of Michigan Press, 1996), p. 2.
54. For an overview of this manuscript, see Lepage, 'Un recueil français'.
55. Keith Busby, *Codex and Context*, p. 533.
56. Hyatte, 'Introduction', in *The Prophet of Islam*, p. 17.
57. Michael Postan, 'The Trade of Medieval Europe: the North', in *Trade and Industry in the Middle Ages*, ed. by M.M. Postan and Edward Miller, vol. 2 of *The Cambridge Economic History of Europe*, 2nd edn (Cambridge: Cambridge University Press, 1987), pp. 168–306 (p. 230).
58. Lepage, 'Un recueil français', p. 25.
59. Jacques Le Goff, *Intellectuals in the Middle Ages*, trans. by Teresa Lavender Fagan (Cambridge, MA: Blackwell, 1993), pp. 19–20.
60. See Lepage, 'Introduction', in *Roman*, p. 15.
61. Lepage, 'Un recueil français', pp. 25–26.
62. Busby, *Codex and Context*, p. 480.
63. Alison Williams, *Tricksters and Pranksters: Roguery in French and German Literature of the Middle Ages and the Renaissance*, Internationale Forschungen zur allgemeinen und vergleichenden Literaturwissenschaft, 49 (Amsterdam: Rodopi, 2000), pp. 1–3.
64. Hyatte, 'Introduction', in *The Prophet of Islam*, p. 4.
65. Note that Hyatte translates 'paraus' as meaning 'by themselves', whereas Lepage suggests that this might carry a sense of hierarchy. See Hyatte, *The Prophet of Islam*, fn. 26, pp. 72–73.
66. See Hyatte, 'Introduction', in *The Prophet of Islam*, p. 10.
67. Hyatte, 'Introduction', in *The Prophet of Islam*, p. 17; Lepage, *Roman*, note to vv. 1158–61, p. 221.

68. Akbari, *Idols in the East*, p. 227.
69. Note that she is not named as such in the text.
70. 'Franc' of course conveys the sense of noble qualities as well as non-servility.
71. Kangas, 'Saracens and their Prophet', p. 145.
72. See Maud Burnett McInerney, *Eloquent Virgins from Thecla to Joan of Arc* (New York: Palgrave Macmillan, 2003), pp. 185–86.
73. Christian views of the Saracen heaven, such as those detailed by Theophanes in the eighth-ninth century, often included descriptions of flowing milk and honey. See Arjana, *Muslims in the Western Imagination*, pp. 33–34.
74. Mary B. Speer, 'Seven Sages of Rome', in *Medieval France: An Encyclopedia*, ed. by William W. Kibler and Grover A. Zinn, Garland Reference Library of the Humanities, 932 (New York: Garland, 1995), pp. 878–79 (p. 878).
75. Le Goff (trans. Fagan) *Intellectuals in the Middle Ages*, p. 20.
76. See Charles Burnett, 'Arabic into Latin: The Reception of Arabic Philosophy into Western Europe', in *The Cambridge Companion to Arabic Philosophy*, ed. by Peter Adamson and Richard C. Taylor (Cambridge: Cambridge University Press, 2005), pp. 370–405 (p. 375).
77. 'The Summa Against the Gentiles (Summa Contra Gentiles), Book 1, Chapter 7', in *St Thomas Aquinas on Politics and Ethics: A New Translation, Backgrounds, Interpretation*, ed. and trans. by Paul E. Sigmund (New York: Norton, 1988), pp. 4–5.
78. *The Deeds of God through the Franks: A Translation of Guibert de Nogent's Gesta Dei per Francos*, ed. and trans. by Robert Levine (Woodbridge: Boydell, 1997), p. 31.
79. See Tolan, *Saracens*, pp. 242–45.
80. Thomas Aquinas, *De rationibus fidei contra Saracenos, Graecos et Armenos ad Cantorem Antiochenum: Reasons for the Faith against the Muslims (and one Objection of the Greeks and Armenians) to the Cantor of Antioch*, trans. by Joseph Kenney, *Islamochristiana*, 22 (1996), 31–52 (p. 33).
81. Ridder-Symoens, *Universities in the Middle Ages*, p. 311.
82. Hyatte, 'Introduction', in *The Prophet of Islam*, p. 2; Kangas, 'Saracens and their Prophet', pp. 145–46.
83. See *Intellectuals in the Middle Ages*, p. 97.
84. Tolan, *Saracens*, p. 279.
85. Gregor Maurach, 'Daniel von Morley, "Philosophia"', *Mittellateinishes Jahrbuch*, 14 (1979), 204–55 (p. 213); See also Charles Burnett, *The Introduction of Arabic Learning into England* (London: British Library, 1997).

CONCLUSION

Indeterminacy Made Readable: Rethinking the Body and Medieval Race

> "Race" is thus thinkable as a kind of speech act. As such, "race" is not an effect of biological truths, but is one of the ways that hegemonic social fictions are produced and maintained as "natural" facts about the world and its inhabitants.
>
> Ann Pellegrini, *Performance Anxieties*[1]

Rhetoric and the misrecognition of speech acts played a key role in the construction of the Saracens as a race in the *Roman de Mahomet*. This brings us back to how the concept of performativity was originally rooted within linguistics and the power of discourse. In her study of race and gender, Ann Pellegrini considers the role of language use in forming racial boundaries and refers, in the process, to Frantz Fanon's *Peau noire, masques blancs* (1952). She notes that 'Fanon's mastery of French was one way for France to master Fanon', highlighting the potential relationship of language to cultural assimilation and appropriation.[2] While there may be other potential parallels between colonial self-other and medieval Christian-Saracen relationships, language, in both cases, shares a power to constitute racial identity — to produce rather than simply to describe. However, performativity is not limited to speech, and racial identities are not only produced through explicit speech acts.[3] A wider interpretation of performativity has better revealed the workings of race in literary representations of the medieval Saracen: Chapter One above suggested that behaviour and dress may produce identity as much as racial labels or forms of address; Chapter Two addressed the impact of retrospective causality upon genealogical identities; and Chapters Three and Four examined how the rhetorical transmission of religious experiences and faith may produce identities that integrate or exclude the Saracen, whether via the blurring of body, flesh, and spirit or the formation of community.

It is therefore speech act theory in its broadest sense that has offered a paradigm for examining the representation of the Saracen, one grounded in notions of fixity versus potentiality and ultimately in concepts of performativity. Though treating four very different sets of primary materials, the chapters of this book have married key features constituting medieval identity with the central preoccupations of several interconnected theories of performativity. Butlerian theory highlighted that speech, behaviour, and social conventions, as well as bodily form, are all able both to construct identity and be constructed. Intersectional studies brought race into dialogue with gender, genealogy, geography, and faith; future avenues of research might involve uniting the performativity of race with questions of class and nation, as well as engaging further with other, growing theoretical frameworks such as those of Critical White Studies to think more explicitly about ways in which whiteness might also operate within the performative processes that construct racial identities in this period.[4] By seeing race as performative — as the repetition of rhetoric, discourses, behaviours, and perceptual practices — we are able to return to the body and its relationship to medieval racial identity with fresh eyes.

Rethinking the role of the body in medieval conceptualizations and representations of race is necessary in order to explore how Saracen identities may be constructed and to appreciate the different forms of agency that may be involved. This is especially true where questions of genealogy and the role of the visual are concerned. In Gautier's *Miracles*, for instance, the experience of the miraculous produces bodies that are spectral and behaviours that are left perpetually in a state of being recognized; while procreative acts in the Nanteuil Cycle define successful cross-dressing by reappropriating genealogical conventions, in *Le Roman de Mahomet* a Saracen race is produced by ties of community that are based upon mistaken reasoning disguised as faith. Performative processes consequently show that medieval racial identity, as far as the Saracen was concerned, was not perceived to be fixed as a result of its being innate, or founded primarily in biology.

In my Introduction, I noted how the nebulousness and invisibility of Saracen identity mean that their literary representations epitomize the problematic nature of concepts of race in the Middle Ages. This concluding section returns to the question of visibility and in particular to the gap between 'being visible and being seen' from the angle of racial passing.[5] Tensions between being visible and being readable in both literal and metaphorical senses are very much at stake in acts of passing, which often stage the body and narrate the construction and appropriation of identities in ways that challenge our recognition and reading of the hierarchies and power structures at work in a given society. Combining notions of causality, genealogy, conversion, and crossdressing, passing draws upon the theories of performativity so far explored because it fundamentally concerns the readability of identities — by which I mean how they are interpreted and understood via non-visual as well as visual processes — and exposes how the perception of racial difference is never prediscursive, even when seeming to rely upon supposed biological truths and ideals of inheritance. As Bridget Byrne notes

> The visualization of 'race' needs to be understood as discursively constructed. Perceptual practices, particularly those centred on visible difference, performatively construct 'race' [...] Visibility and invisibility are both dependent on the acts of seeing and looking as well as the experience of being seen, unseen or ignored.[6]

Passing therefore leads us to question the very meaning of visibility and the values of flesh and blood bodies in the context of medieval racial identity. This can be seen in the way that indeterminacy is constructed and exploited in the genealogically charged tales of the Count of Ponthieu's daughter.

'Je sui Sarrasine': Passing and Visibility

In a sense, the outline of *La Fille du Comte de Pontieu* responds to a range of latent social, political, and theological concerns that ebbed and flowed within medieval France, such as the need to claim Saracen military successes as Christian, the possibility (if perhaps not likelihood) of apostasy, and the need for nobles to ensure legitimate succession.[7] At its heart, however, also lies the difficulty of distinguishing and recognizing just what might constitute Christian and Saracen identities. Its earliest witnesses are from the late thirteenth-early fourteenth century: a short, seemingly independent, prose work (contained in Paris, Bibliothèque nationale de France (BnF), MS fonds français 25462) and a section of the *Estoires d'Outremer et de la naissance Salehadin*, an historical narrative that is part of one branch of the Old French continuations of William of Tyre known as the Ernoul-Bernard Abrégé and which incorporates episodes on the life and deeds of Saladin (BnF, MS f. fr. 770 and BnF, MS f. fr. 12203). The narrative is also incorporated into a fifteenth-century prose romance trilogy (*Jehan d'Avennes, La Fille du Comte de Pontieu, Saladin*) and texts of the Second Crusade Cycle, namely *Baudouin de Sebourc* and *Le Chevalier au Cygne et Godefroi de Bouillon*.[8] These various narratives of *La Fille*, as well as the final text of the prose trilogy, *Saladin*, represent racial crossings that differ from those of the Nanteuil Cycle discussed in Chapter One above in their motivation, manner, and navigation of social structures. The basics of the thirteenth-century tale are as follows: the story begins with details of the Count of Ponthieu's heirs, followed by the marriage of his sole child, a daughter, to his nephew and heir Thibaut de Dommart (in the fifteenth-century tale, the young couple's love comes to the fore, and Thibaut is presented as a kind of protégé of the Count). Unfortunately, however, this marriage remains sterile after five years, prompting the lady and Thibaut to undertake a pilgrimage to Santiago de Compostela. On the way, the couple are attacked by bandits in the forest, Thibaut is tied up, and the lady is raped before her husband's eyes. When she eventually manages to free herself, she (seemingly inexplicably) attempts to kill him. Upon their return from the pilgrimage, Thibaut relates the events to his father-in-law, and the lady is cast adrift in a barrel — in the earlier texts, for her violent behaviour, in the fifteenth-century prose romance, because of the shame she has brought upon the family. She is rescued from the sea by merchants and given to the Saracen Sultan of Almeria, who falls in love with her and with whom she has two children.[9] During her absence, her father, first husband, and half-brother are afflicted by the memory of their guilt and undertake a crusade/pilgrimage to the Holy Land. While returning, they are captured by Saracens and brought before the Sultan. The lady recognizes them and, after hearing them regret their behaviour towards her, she engineers their escape. She leaves with them, taking her Saracen-born son and they return via Brindisi then Rome, where the lady is rebaptized and remarried to Thibaut before bearing two fine sons. The daughter who remains in Almeria, known as the 'Belle Chétive' goes on to become the grandmother of Saladin (in some versions the *fille* herself is the mother of Saladin).

This text frequently features in discussions of medieval Christian-Saracen unions and the children that are produced. Lynn Ramey, for instance, sets questions of inheritance in relation to medieval theories of reproduction, while Sharon Kinoshita explores how the tale addresses European genealogical failures.[10] In this respect, as Donald Maddox notes, 'genealogy thus provides the fundamental infrastructure of textuality'.[11] Nevertheless, both the variations in the narratives of *La Fille* and its genealogical focus have yet to be read in the context of racial passing. Theories of performativity have allowed me thus far to highlight that racial identity is always an effect of performance; any idea of an innate identity is an illusion of origins that is retroactively produced by behaviours, dress, and gestures, among other things. With regard to gender performativity, crossings — whether of gender, sex, or sexuality — are often deemed to show how all gender identities are constructed rather than innate, since these acts in particular have the potential to make the gap between sex and gender (in that case) so 'readable'.[12] As a related form of boundary crossing, racial passing extends this question of readability to discussions of race and draws attention to those figures who cross, but also challenge, categorized racial identities. This final study therefore traces the lady's strategies of passing across the narrative and manuscript tradition of *La Fille*, and sets them in relation to the comparable journey of her famous descendant, Saladin, to the West.

Somewhat in opposition to the drag act, which involves spectacle and displays the apparent contradictions between inner and outer identity, reality and illusion, acts of passing tend to focus more on the concealment, if also instrumentalization and exploitation, of such contradictions. 'Passing' is a term frequently associated with nineteenth- and twentieth-century America and is most commonly used to refer to those who possessed African ancestry (and so were therefore legally and culturally deemed to be black) but who could live as white, thereby gaining access to better rights and attempting to escape the racist and violent oppression of the Jim Crow Laws and 'one-drop rule' (a legal principle where anyone said to possess a single drop of 'black African blood' was to be regarded as black). More recently, notions of passing have been greatly extended beyond this historical, social, and geographic context and used, for instance, to refer to those who choose to live as a particular race, gender, sexuality, class, religion, or ethnicity that might be seen as different to their legally and/or socially defined race, gender, sexuality, class, religion, or ethnicity.[13]

While there have been very few studies to date that focus explicitly on this concept in the context of medieval race, the term 'passing' does appear in scholarship on cross-dressing. With reference to tale 10.9 from Boccaccio's *Decameron*, which narrates the meetings and travels of Saladin and a Pavian gentleman called Messire Torello, Ana Grinberg, for instance, treats 'ethnic, cultural, or religious cross-dressing' where 'a character is able to effectively represent the religious or cultural Other, at least intradiegetically'. Focusing on sartorial performances, Grinberg very much engages with Barbara Fuchs's definition of 'ethnic passing' as a 'form of transvestism'.[14] While her study importantly interrogates the relationship between textiles and identity, in the context of racial thinking it is nonetheless true that the power relations and hierarchies involved in acts of passing do not always work in the same ways as those involving cross-dressing. If 'crossdressing is one manifestation of gender passing',[15] then perhaps the same should be said of racial cross-dressing as a form of racial passing — while connected, they are not simply interchangeable acts or terms. At the risk of stating the obvious, even if cross-dressing, as Jonathan Dollimore notes, may, like passing, concern 'both inversion and displacement' of binaries,[16] it is also fundamentally tied to the particular value and function of dress within a given socio-historical and literary context.

Before turning to narratives of *La Fille*, the contextual framing and mechanisms of passing, both historical and social, need to be taken into account, along with its relationship to cross-dressing. Elaine Ginsberg, for example, highlights how the 'status and privilege' accompanying both whiteness and being male in the context of American history and the American cultural imaginary is central to the desire to pass. In such an environment, she notes that 'cultural logic presupposes a biological foundation of race visibly evident in physical features such as facial structure, hair colour and texture, and skin colour', where the body is 'the site of identic intelligibility'.[17] In this sense, passing functions because the society around the individual believes in assumed identities that are, significantly, visible *and* biologized *and* encoded into legal systems. While troubling binary systems of racial identity, passing nonetheless also relies upon them to an extent: 'presumably one cannot pass for something one *is not* unless there is some other, pre-passing, identity that one *is*'.[18] Hierarchical relationships are therefore central to racial passing, since, Ginsberg adds, 'an individual crossed or passed through a racial line or boundary — indeed *trespassed* — to assume a new identity, escaping the subordination and oppression accompanying one identity and accessing the privileges and status of the other'. In short, he or she was 'usually motivated by a desire to shed the identity of an oppressed group',[19] in this case, those regarded as non-white. Passing can therefore be seen as a form of 'passive resistance' to political and social invisibility, even if it often remains conservative as regards wider social hierarchies;[20] yet it is also most often coerced, requiring significant personal trauma, sacrifice, and loss. Given that passing is not one-directional, recognizing this coerciveness is key to appreciating the power structures involved: for example, those who choose to pass from a privileged identity to one accompanied by oppression may expose hierarchical systems in reverse, raising questions of appropriation, mimicry, and denigration. In essence, while exploiting the performativity and contingency of identity, racial passing is a political act in a society where racial identities are constructed upon visible differences, regarded as biologically determined, and specifically used to structure, categorize, and oppress.

The difficulty, then, with studying racial crossings in a medieval context is that, as I have argued, medieval racial thinking — and thus the potential status and privilege associated with particular racial identities — was pluralistic rather than binary and did not privilege a biologized, primary locus of racial identity. Medieval legal writings, for example, do not focus on differences of skin colour or notions of biological difference, even if forms of racial and racist categorization are continually enacted in other ways, such as via laws relating to clothing:[21] by extension, it is perhaps worth remembering that 'skin, in the Middle Ages, was commonly understood to be a kind of clothing'.[22] Similarly, blood in a biological sense was not generally used to refer to genealogical continuity until the fifteenth century, with familial relationships instead often articulated through vocabularies of flesh and corporeal metaphors.[23] Against this contextual backdrop, the dynamics of visibility and readability that underpin acts of racial passing undoubtedly change in a medieval context where racial identities are, in many ways, alternatively construed and societies alternatively structured. Figures may still pass even if the ways in which differences are used to categorize and oppress are non-binary. For instance, genealogical systems, linear or otherwise, were central not only to the organization of aristocratic society in the Middle Ages but also to racial thinking.[24] To return to the narratives of *La Fille du Comte de Pontieu* with this in mind, although the lady does not possess Saracen ancestry in any biological sense, she does live as a Saracen and her potential passing revolves around her dynastic identity. Furthermore, this passing is key to her status, privilege, and social visibility: her 'identic intelligibility', we might say, is based upon a different kind of visibility, one grounded in genealogical narrative rather than physical appearance, and this in turn has an effect upon the ways in which racial identity is made readable.

In the course of her exile in Almeria, the *fille* passes as Saracen in the sense that she lives as a different identity to her legally and socially defined one. In so doing she constructs a racial identity for herself that is neither (yet also both) Christian and Saracen by replicating a variety of cultural norms and behaviours: alongside her native French, she learns to speak the Saracen language very well; she tells her captured Christian family that she knows the Saracen (magic) arts; she also does nothing to help a poor, unknown Christian sent to be martyred, despite the comment by the narrator of the *Estoires* version that 'ne li plaisoit pas li martyres ke li Sarrazin faisoient des crestiiens' (p. 32) [she did not like the Saracen martyrdom of Christians]. While the earlier texts provide no details about her dress or appearance, in the fifteenth-century prose version her adoption of foreign attire is particularly emphasized; she appears before her family 'en habit incongneu' [in unfamiliar clothing] and is 'estrangement [...] advestue' (p. 104) [dressed as a foreigner]. This is perhaps not surprising, given the late-medieval interest in, and fashion for, such eastern costumes.[25]

What is somewhat surprising, however, is that when it comes to the manuscripts of the *Fille* tradition and their visual representations of the narrative, very few actually include images of the lady herself. The manuscript of the independent version, Paris, BnF, MS f. fr. 25462, has no illustrations; both manuscripts of the *Estoires* show the male protagonists only (Thibaut and the Count in Paris, BnF, MS f. fr. 770). Of the two fifteenth-century Burgundian prose romance manuscripts, Paris, Bibliothèque de l'Arsenal (B. Ars.), MS 5208 only contains one miniature in

Fig. C.1. The lady persuades the Sultan to accept Thibaut's military aid (*La Fille du Comte de Pontieu*). Paris, BnF, MS f. fr. 12572, fol. 155^v.
Photo: Paris, Bibliothèque nationale de France

this tale (on fol. 92ᵛ) and shows a scene split between military activity (potentially preparations for war) and the birth of a child — possibly the *fille* herself. While, as Rosalind Brown-Grant notes, this image echoes the importance of 'la vaillance chevaleresque des hommes, et la capacité reproductive des épouses de la maison de Ponthieu, quelle que soit la génération à laquelle ils appartiennent' [the chivalric bravery of men, and the reproductive capacity of wives in the House of Ponthieu, no matter the generation to which they belong], it also makes no mention of the significant rape scene, or of the lady's time in Almeria.²⁶ In stark contrast, the other Burgundian manuscript, Paris, BnF, MS f. fr. 12572, includes nine visual representations of this tale attributed to the artist known as the Wavrin Master and, furthermore, depicts the lady in several of these.

The image on fol. 155ᵛ (Figure C.1) offers a particularly significant representation of passing, as it shows the lady trying to persuade the Sultan to take Thibaut with him in his war against the ruler of Granada as part of her plot to engineer their eventual freedom. Her portrayal is notably different to the earlier scene depicting her engagement to Thibaut (fol. 131ᵛ).²⁷ Here, her turban-like hat along with that of the Sultan clearly contrast with the golden armour of Thibaut; the latter not only fills nearly half the image, but adopts a commanding pose, with feet splayed and hands upon his sword hilt — a sword placed in a phallic position between his legs. As if to echo Thibaut's sexualized stance, the lady's fitted dress highlights the curves of her breasts and waist. As Brown-Grant has argued, the unusual focus on the lady in this manuscript reflects how she is a pivotal and exemplary figure in this version and is not eclipsed by its broader chivalric emphasis.²⁸ Yet the Wavrin master's representation of the female body is also significant for a reading of passing and racial identity in this narrative. If reproduction is central to the Arsenal manuscript, and indeed to the *Fille* tradition more generally, it is strikingly absent from the Wavrin production. Given that the Wavrin Master frequently seems to interpret the textual content of the romances he illustrates,²⁹ the Almerian scene of BnF, MS f. fr. 12572 instead offers an ironic staging of the lady's body as readable in a text where her body is unreliable: the physical violence she suffers does not diminish her moral worth any more than her exotic garments reflect an innate Saracen essence. The unreliability of physical appearance also features in the Wavrin Master's final image in this narrative, which shows the lady's cunning return to France with her family and subtly signals her disguise to the viewer via a glimpse of her veil under her hat (fol. 163ᵛ). Rather than emphasizing dynasty and reproduction, this manuscript therefore not only frames and compares the father-daughter and husband-wife relationships in the text, as Brown-Grant has shown,³⁰ but, in so doing, encourages the reader/viewer to question the readability of visible identity. Furthermore, we might also observe that the Sultan's garments on fol. 155ᵛ are very similar to those worn by the lady's father on fol. 141ʳ (a blue tunic trimmed with fur), seeming to nod towards her simultaneous identities as daughter of the (Christian) Count and wife of the (Saracen) Sultan.

In fact, in all versions of the narrative the lady's Christian family and the Sultan have trouble deducing her identity from appearances alone: in the early versions, when she is first brought before the Sultan, she refuses to give details of her lineage, and while he is able to *see* that she is 'haute femme' [an eminent lady] (the word 'voit' is used) he has to *ask* (via an interpreter) if she is Christian, suggesting the unreadability of religious as well as racial identity (p. 23). Her Christian family also show no sign of recognition when they are reunited, which is most marked when her father addresses her as 'O femme sarrasine' in the fifteenth-century text (p. 104). His comment echoes the earlier laments of Thibaut when the lady is raped, who exclaims: 'O fenme esplouree' (p. 83) [O weeping lady] and 'O femme desesperee' (p. 84) [O desolate lady]. By setting the Count's attempt to equate appearance with essence against Thibaut's sympathetic response to his wife's suffering, the exclamations cast another light on the different behaviour of Thibaut and the Count of Ponthieu and their respective roles as husband/father: while the Count responds to what is visible, Thibaut *reads* the situation. As a result, this version of the narrative therefore magnifies the gap between being visible and being seen — a gap that is revealed by the lady's act of passing. Furthermore, this gap is perhaps most apparent in BnF, MS f. fr. 12572, reflecting as it does the Wavrin Master's apparent penchant for reading and interpreting his materials.[31]

In this respect, the representation of the lady consistently produces an indeterminacy that plays on the fact that Saracen identity is not always, and never entirely, visually perceptible: even as she reveals her origins to her Christian relatives by stating her familial ties to her father, (first) husband, and brother, she also states 'je sui Sarrasine' (pp. 38–39) [I am a Saracen woman]. In contrast to the characters of the Nanteuil Cycle discussed above, the lady in all texts of *La Fille du comte de Ponthieu* is not disguised as a Saracen while in Almeria but seems to live a plural, if coerced, identity. Sharon Kinoshita (citing Olivia Remie Constable) discusses a twelfth-century tale from Iberia where a Cordovan buyer purchased a girl believed to be a Christian slave because she spoke a 'northern language', who turned out to be a free, Arabic-speaking Muslim woman. Bilingualism, Kinoshita reminds us, troubles the 'either/or binary' of conversion and 'introduces the more unsettling logic of the both/and';[32] this is a logic also seen, I would suggest, not just in the lady's linguistic proficiency in *La Fille* but in other aspects of her racial identity.

It is clear that the lady performs identity traits of both the Christian noblewoman and Saracen sultana; however it is also clear that the relationship between this indeterminacy and her genealogical position varies across the text corpus: on the day that her father is brought before her as a prisoner, the narrator of the independent thirteenth-century text describes the lady as 'la dame qui femme estoit au soudant' [the lady who was the wife of the Sultan], whereas the *Estoires* calls her 'fille le conte et feme a cel soudan' [daughter of the Count and wife of the Sultan] (p. 28). Such an emphasis on both her filial relationship and marital status also appears in the rubric introducing this episode in the fifteenth-century text: 'Comment le conte de Pontieu fut amené en la place pour lapider, quy dist son nom a sa fille, femme du soudan' (p. 104) [How the Count of Ponthieu was brought into the room to be stoned and told his name to his daughter, wife of the Sultan]. Significantly, the lady's motivations in this encounter also shift between texts: while she is moved to speak to her father 'en compassion du païs de France' [out of compassion for the land of France] in this later version, such nationalistic motives contrast with a general compassion induced by 'Nature' in the *Estoires* text (p. 29) and no explanation is given in the independent version, where her heart is simply 'atenri' (p. 28) [moved]. Given that both the *Estoires* and fifteenth-century versions form part of larger works focusing on the life of Saladin — indeed, one manuscript of the *Estoires*, BnF, MS f. fr. 12203, opens the tale with the phrase 'comment li rois Salehadins fu estrais de la terre de France de par sa mere' [how King Saladin originated from the land of France through his mother] — it is understandable that these texts attempt to provide greater clarity in relation to the representation of genealogical ties, such as: where do the lady's loyalties lie? And what moves her to speak with her (unrecognized) father? While Kinoshita suggests that the *fille* becomes 'a genuine Saracen queen', 'a prize whose defection would openly signify Latin Christendom's superiority over Islam',[33] the constant play of visible/invisible and origin/destiny within the act of passing instead seems to challenge any idea of 'genuine' identity. The *fille*'s racial identity emerges instead in an indeterminate space predicated upon dynastic roles: her past origins as a Christian noblewoman are evoked only to be dismissed, paired with her Saracen marriage or, as we shall see next, displaced by a future-looking Saracen maternity. After all, while the Saracen queen is frequently childless in medieval narratives, the *fille* is miraculously fertile; her act of passing and newfound status as mother are therefore mutually constituting, with both revealing the construction and conventions of an identity as Saracen queen. While her racial passing shows how this identity can be adopted, her motherhood shows that it can also be appropriated and repeated differently.

Geraldine Heng has recently demonstrated how the indeterminacy associated with acts of passing in the context of religious conversion might endure across generations. Noting the similarities between attitudes towards medieval religious conversion from Judaism to Christianity and the idea of racial passing, she observes that converts in the Middle Ages were often seen as 'permanently once-Jews' and could provoke feelings of uncertainty for Christians, since their status as convert endured: 'not Jews any more, but unable to disappear into the mass of Christian subjects either, these new Christians troubled the category of "Jew" and that of "Christian" by embodying an indeterminacy of status and identity'.[34] In other words, the religious convert possessed a hybrid identity that could potentially enable him or her to 'pass' as both Christian and non-Christian. The *fille*'s religious conversion during her time in Almeria is marked by a similar indeterminacy to that identified by Heng, since the various versions of the narrative attempt to offer different interpretations of her desire to convert; while the thirteenth-century independent version suggests that she accepts conversion, albeit inevitably under duress, in the Second Crusade Cycle text *Baudouin de Sebourc* she willingly abandons her faith after being spurned in love, and in the fifteenth-century romance she renounces her faith, but after clear resistance.[35] Peggy McCracken observes that these interpretations are always related to her marriage, so that the narratives of her conversion 'point to an anxiety about motherhood and the corruption of lineage'.[36]

Yet we might also say that the lady's passing does not corrupt but rather exploits the historical and social visibility provided by genealogical narrative to make racial indeterminacy readable. Indeterminacy becomes heritable, so that her descendant, Saladin, is situated as 'permanently once-Christian', allowing him to be forever both Christian and Saracen, yet also neither.

In the narratives of *La Fille du Comte de Pontieu*, the acknowledgement that the close connection between genealogical identity and race is problematic reveals the importance of making indeterminacy readable. In order to return to France with the Count and Thibaut, the *fille* of both thirteenth-century texts claims to the Sultan that she is pregnant and that the resulting sickness means that she needs to be on 'terre de droite nature' (pp. 41–42) [rightful, natural land] or she will die.[37] This is a claim which not only constructs her Christian origins as necessary to fulfilling her Saracen dynastic role but is also reminiscent of medieval climatic theories associating bodies and identities with geographical climes.[38] A similar rhetoric is later adopted by the Pope, who subsequently reintegrates the lady into 'droite crestienté' [rightful Christianity] and 'droit mariage' [rightful marriage] (p. 45). The repeated references to 'droit' here convey ideas of conformity, legitimacy, and directness and evoke the idea of a 'true' identity to be recovered. Yet the echoes also remind us that any identity is in fact performative and open to exploitation, since the anxious assertion of 'droit' identity attempts to construct a genuine, or essential identity that the text itself has consistently undermined. Even the very notion of a 'genuine' Christian identity, it seems, not only relies upon the replication of conventional acts and their appropriate recognition but must explicitly be (re) constructed, so that the *fille*'s act of passing as Saracen serves to make this process retrospectively (and linguistically) visible.

The *fille* can therefore be regarded as a hybrid figure, a dual convert whose pluralistic identity enables her to switch between racial communities. The extent of her conversion to the Saracen religion and the extent to which she is perceived as a 'sarrasine' remain ambiguous, a fact that one paratextual intervention in manuscript BnF MS f. fr. 12572 attempts to remedy by adding the comment that her conversion is a ploy or 'par fainte' (p. 98; fol. 146^v). Nonetheless, even at the end of the tale, her own historical visibility endures via her illustrious Saracen descendant, despite the fact that she is newly positioned as the mother of two Christian sons. Within the power dynamics of passing in this narrative, the lady does not gain or lose status and privilege in an obvious legal sense in the way we might associate with acts of racial passing in later periods. While she moves from being Christian to Saracen, it is not as straightforward as saying that she moves from a privileged, white to an oppressed, non-white racial group, firstly because status and privilege are associated with race along more varied social and legal lines than those based predominantly upon skin colour, and secondly because she undoubtedly occupies a better hierarchical position as a *sarrasine* than as a Christian noblewoman: if her marriage to Thibaut was clearly politically expedient (he is her father's heir/protégé), the marriage remained sterile, and in the thirteenth-century versions no mention is made of any love between them. In contrast, the Sultan provides her with children and thus with maternal influence, also, in the earlier texts, showing her 'molt grant amour' (p. 23).[39]

However, in contrast to another memorable medieval tale involving a mixed-race union, the Middle English romance *The King of Tars*, children in themselves do not function as material flesh through which to inscribe racial and religious identity in the *Fille* narratives. In *The King of Tars*, a Christian noblewoman is married to a Saracen ruler and the child that is born from their union remains a lump of unformed flesh until his father is convinced to convert to Christianity, at which point the Saracen ruler's own skin also turns from black to white. Baptism, in this fourteenth-century text, forms flesh into child so that, as Katie L. Walter notes, 'in narrative terms, then, the flesh becomes legible — it takes on human form — only at the point that the story can begin to make sense of interracial, interreligious marriage'. In addition, she says, 'the change in color of the Saracen's own skin substitutes, or makes legible, the text of Christian faith', within a binary fantasy where skin acts as the 'marker of unassimilable difference' yet flesh remains illegible.[40] In the *Fille*, it is not flesh that is made legible or skin colour used to read Christian belief but the readability of racial identity comes instead from genealogical narrative. If this tale is 'a vast genealogical analepsis in the biography of Saladin',[41] it is also proleptic in the sense that Saladin's status and biography determine the representation of his ancestors. By extension, this unsettling of causality also has a profound impact upon the construction of the *fille*'s own racial identity.

Within the context of modern American history, 'racial readability' has been interpreted as going hand in hand with a metaphorical 'invisibility', since being visibly identified as black meant being invisible as a social subject.[42] In contrast, making the *fille*'s racial identity readable (albeit readable in its indeterminacy) makes her genealogically — and thus socially and historically — visible. As a result, the readability of these crossings reveals the constructedness of all identity, not just the racial identity of either Christian or Saracen. For instance, while her conversion to the Saracen faith has been interpreted as a rebellion against masculine power and the feudal patriarchy,[43] this resistance stems not just from her willingness to change religion but from her willingness to adopt the indeterminacy of racial passing: if racial passing troubles social invisibility and enacts passive resistance, in the *Fille* tales it does not trouble an invisibility caused by her racial but her dynastic identity, and does so by enabling her to adopt a maternal role. This is significant because, as Natasha Hodgson reminds us in relation to mothers in crusading texts,

> To medieval authors, it was to a certain extent the capacity for motherhood that justified women having any authority. In medieval society, and particularly in a frontier society like the Latin kingdom of Jerusalem, the status of a noble woman hinged upon her lineage, what birthright she inherited and was thus able to pass on to her children through motherhood.[44]

Motherhood is therefore not simply about biological replication but about transmission. When the *Fille* narratives are considered together, it becomes apparent that the lady participates in legitimized genealogical structures that are set in relation to the broader march of Christian time, not just in relation to biological inheritance. If, as in the *Estoire del Saint Graal*, narrative progression and religious conversion could construct genealogy through alternative systems of causality, in the *Fille* narratives it is also genealogy, or more particularly genealogy as the writing of history, that determines conversion and racial identity. Gabrielle Spiegel has shown not only how genealogy in the thirteenth century 'governs the very shape and significance of the past' but that history is 'a perceptual field, to be seen and represented instead of constructed and analyzed'.[45] This notion of history as 'to be seen' is central to the way in which genealogy, and by extension race, is made readable. While Maddox, in his study of the thirteenth-century independent version of the *Fille*, highlighted how the relationship between genealogy and pilgrimage narratives is evidence of a 'providential design',[46] this still does not quite account for the lady's apparent period of assimilation — or for the subsequent addition of Saladin's own act of passing to this tradition. The answer, I think, lies in the conceptual and temporal distinctions between blood as matter and bloodline in the sense of genealogy that circulated in the medieval period; while both are discursively produced, the one related to material flesh and form that could be seen, the other to psychological and metaphorical fictions to be read. In the words of Zrinka Stahuljak, 'blood [...] was first and foremost viewed as matter, before it also became a genealogical term at the end of the Middle Ages'.[47] In which case, we might say that history, rather than biological matter and form, is the 'perceptual field' through which race in this text is articulated and made readable: passing as a Saracen relies upon, yet also constructs, the *fille*'s historical visibility as the mother/grandmother of Saladin.

The historical visibility afforded both the lady and Saladin and its relationship to acts of passing is also reflected in the later formulations of the *Fille* narratives, especially in the predictions or *annonces* that appear in the texts of the Second Crusade Cycle. For instance, in the fourteenth-century verse version of Le Chevalier au Cygne et Godefroi de Bouillon (*CCGB*), a text which narrates Christian triumphs and disasters in the Holy Land along with the glorification of the lineage of Godfrey of Bouillon, the mother to the Turkish ruler Kerbogha during the First Crusade (known here as Calabre) prophesizes the impending Frankish victory, before adding:

> Et apriès celuy temps, je vous say bien nommer,
> Que de France venra princesse deçà mer,
> Qui serra Sarrasine, je le say bien nommer,
> Fille de crestyenne qui le volra porter;
> Et ceste crestyenne se venra marier
> A ung rice soudant, qui le volra amer;
> Cieus qui en istera fera tant à douter,
> Que trestous les royalmes c'on pora conquester.
> Fera chus Sarrasins desous luy retourner;
> Et n'ara crestiien qui s'y puist revéler,
> N'encontre ce soudant sa banière moustrer;
> Et enssy avenra, je le say tout au cler.
> (*CCGB*, vv. 27112–24)[48]

[And after this time, I confidently proclaim that a princess from France will come across the sea who will be Saracen, I am sure of it, and daughter of a Christian woman who is destined to bear her/will bear her willingly; and this Christian woman will come to marry a rich sultan who will desire to love her; he who will descend from them will be more greatly feared than all the kingdoms to be conquered. He will bring down all those Saracens who oppose him; and there will be no Christian who could rise up or show his banner against him; it will thus come to pass, I know it for certain.]

While there is no explicit reference to Ponthieu here, the underlying elements of the *fille*'s narrative remain.[49] The fluidity of the French princess's status as both Saracen and Christian comes to the fore in this prophecy and is tied to her foretold role as mother (in this version) to the renowned Saladin, who will himself, seemingly indiscriminately, defeat both Christians and Saracens, albeit for very different reasons. In addition, the use of the expression 'qui le volra porter' here simultaneously evokes both the Christian woman's willingness and destiny, reminding us that the *fille* and her descendants result from legitimate, consensual unions. Despite the fact that Calabre's prophesizing occurs in many earlier, historical accounts and chronicles of the First Crusade,[50] including the twelfth-century *Gesta Francorum*, she does not refer to the *fille* until this version of the *Chevalier au Cygne et Godefroi de Bouillon*.[51] Here, therefore, she does not just prophesize Kerbogha's defeat by the first crusaders but now frames it in relation to another ruler who seems to lie between Christians and Saracens and in relation to familial structures.

In this sense, Calabre's prophecy is not about claiming the historical Saladin as Christian but about making his racial identity indeterminate. It is also about inserting the *fille*'s narrative into an historical episode that was recognizable from chronicles (if no less fictional), linking events of the First and Third Crusade via a genealogical narrative authenticated by Calabre's own status as a good mother to her son. In the *Gesta Francorum*, her words emphasize the military skill of Kerbogha yet the protective strength of the Christian God, and she underscores that the Christians are the 'filii adoptionis et promissionis' [sons of adoption and promise], 'heredes Christi' [heirs of Christ] given a promised inheritance.[52] In *Le Chevalier au Cygne et Godefroi de Bouillon*, Calabre's prophecy emphasizes instead the treachery of men and the effect of Kerbogha's defeat upon his family: his daughter will be married to Baldwin of Bouillon, his sister, Florie, to Godfrey of Bouillon, and his nephew, Abilans, baptized (vv. 27105–11). Here, Calabre's words place the *fille* and Saladin within a terrestrial, genealogical context, not just spiritual heredity, which seems to reflect the fact that 'the genealogical strands that run through this world represent the visible patterns of divine order'.[53] The Christians will not just succeed in the Holy Land because they are spiritually destined but because they are genealogically destined. If, as Hans Hummer suggests, to have a genealogy indicated a place within 'the eschatological march of time',[54] Saladin's destiny to defeat all similarly means that he requires a genealogy, and this is a genealogy that exploits the heritability of passing and of indeterminate identity, a narrative of genealogical rather than biological determinism.

In *Baudouin de Sebourc*, another fourteenth-century text of the Second Crusade Cycle, the lady's displacement is again framed genealogically, heralding not only the future narrative (if also historical) successes of Saladin,⁵⁵ but also introducing his own act of passing. This act forms the central focus of the closely affiliated romance *Saladin*, and involves the Saracen leader travelling to the West incognito, as presaged here:

> Par dedens Babilone fu elle mariee
> au fort riche soudan, qu'en li fist en[ge]nree
> d'un hoir par cui no loy fu forment declinee:
> che fu Salehadins, qui passa mer salee.
> A tournoy a Cambray vint monstrer sa posnee. (vv. 2027–31)

[She was married in Babylon to the very rich sultan, who in her engendered an heir through whom our religion was greatly debased: this was Saladin, who crossed the sea. He came to demonstrate his pride at a tournament in Cambray.]

The tale of the Dame de Ponthieu (as she is called in this text) has been distilled so that the pilgrimage narratives that constructed a divine order in the thirteenth-century texts are eclipsed by her maternal role in establishing Saladin's genealogical ties to France, underscored when the narrator notes: 'de par se mere fu de Franche l'onneree' (v. 2038) [through his mother he was from renowned France]. Passing is therefore a way to establish genealogical determinism: Saladin will pass because his mother passed, and can do so because passing, in this context, is not about biology and blood, but is nevertheless heritable.

'Duquel lignage mes peres anchiens sont yssus': Passing and Genealogy

Indeterminacy and genealogical readability are also central to Saladin's own passing in *Le Roman de Saladin*, the last text of the fifteenth-century prose trilogy, which is, moreover, linked to the texts of the Second Crusade Cycle.⁵⁶ The romance narrates Saladin's encounter with his supposed French relative, Jehan de Ponthieu, during the battle for Jerusalem, followed by his knighting and journey to the West, where he rescues a cousin, participates in a tournament, and wins the love of the Queen of France. He then returns to the East and launches an invasion of France (which is fortuitously redirected by Jehan and another knight, Huon de Tabarie, to England instead). After he is defeated at the *Pas Saladin* by the very same tournament knights he had previously encountered in France, he returns to the East and the Christians launch a crusade against him. He is wounded at Damascus while attempting to flee and dies after seeming to convert to Christianity.

Upon their first meeting, Saladin's connection to his relative, Jehan de Ponthieu is not established by any shared physical resemblance, but somewhat more indirectly by the narrative that Jehan relates of his origins and lineage: as he talks, Saladin realizes that Jehan's aunt is the same 'Belle Chétive' who was his own grandmother (VIII, 12–15).⁵⁷ Although Saladin's French ancestry seems to justify, or at least explain, his chivalrous nature and subsequent knighting in this early encounter, when he later attempts to conquer France he tries to legitimize his claim by evoking his descent from Alexander the Great, not the nobles of Ponthieu. During the episode of the *Pas Saladin* and his invasion of England, he claims:

> que ce pays et tout le demourant du monde est a moy appartenant a cause du bon roy Alixandre le Grand, duquel lignage mes peres anchiens sont yssus et descendus, et par ce me compette par vraye et directe sucession. Et en suis cy venus pour en avoir la possession, laquelle vous m'enpesciés, non pas deuement mais a grand tort. (XXII, 2–4)
>
> [that this land and all the rest of the world belongs to me because of the good king Alexander the Great, of whose lineage my forefathers descended and through this it belongs to me by true and direct succession. And I have come here to take possession of it, which you are illegally and wrongly preventing.]

Saladin also adds that he is the 'heritier vray et legitisme de celluy que je vous ay nommé, lequel tinst toute la terre du monde soubz sa main' (XXII, 5–6) [true and legitimate heir of he who I have named, who held all the world in his hands]. In this respect, Saladin does not use his biological connection to Ponthieu to claim material inheritance, but evokes a form of mythic heritage, perhaps echoing, as Catherine Gaullier-Bougassas has argued, the *Roman de Perceforest* and its narrative of Alexander's conquest of Britain.[58] The romance trilogy that includes the *Roman de Saladin* was likely composed at the court of Charles the Bold, the future Duke of Burgundy,[59] and Alexander the Great was a particularly significant figure for these dukes, since his eastern travels and conquests allowed them to identify with him in their own projects against an emerging Ottoman power. Numerous literary and visual productions of the period therefore draw comparisons between them and this ancient ruler. Vasco de Lucena, for instance, in 1468, describes Philip the Bold, John the Fearless, John of Portugal, and Philip the Good as 'Alexandre de leurs temps' [Alexanders of their time].[60] By claiming such a lineage, the Saladin of this Burgundian romance consequently cites a recognizable spiritual and political ancestor with a vast literary tradition. In this respect, while his descent from the families of Avennes and Ponthieu provides him with an ancestral connection shared by the Dukes of Burgundy, the particular link to Alexander adds another layer of genealogical representation: it is as if his passing has authorized his access to a much larger legitimizing system of genealogical thinking than simply terrestrial and ephemeral blood ties, merging mythic and biological thinking.

Alongside Saladin's genealogical inscription, the indeterminacy of visible identity is frequently emphasized as the tale progresses: when Saladin travels to France with Jehan and another Christian knight, Huon de Tabarie, the latter are described as being dressed 'en abit de chevaliers estranges' (XI, 26) [in the clothes of unfamiliar/foreign knights], yet no reference is made to Saladin's own outward appearance and it seems that neither clothing nor physical disguise is necessary for him to go undetected. This is no moment of ethnic or racial drag, since as Gaullier-Bougassas notes, 'jamais il ne se présente dans sa double identité d'Oriental musulman et de parent de la famille de Ponthieu' [he never shows his double identity as Muslim easterner and relative of the Ponthieu family].[61] Instead, Saladin passes as a Christian knight. This is echoed in the images of the Wavrin Master manuscript, BnF, MS f. fr. 12572: despite the exotic hat that Saladin wears in the first image of the tale, which is set in the East and depicts the King of Persia's act of homage (fol. 171^r), his armour when in France does not seem to distinguish him from the knights around him (e.g. fol. 207^v).[62] Similarly, while Saladin is known as 'l'estrange chevalier' (XVI, 7) when participating in the tournament at Cambray, there are many such 'estrange' knights present (XIV, 8–9). The term 'estrange' can refer to someone from another country at this time, yet can also simply mean someone who is not local, or even someone who is not part of a person's close family — an outsider, as it were — so is not specific to Saladin's Saracen status.[63] Indeed, the impossibility of equating appearance with racial identity is explicitly addressed in this text when Saladin reveals his identity to the Queen of France, who has fallen in love with him. While she is surprised when she learns that he is 'payen' [pagan], she continues to love him even 'quant elle aperçut que Salhadin estoit estrangier' (XVI, 53–55) [when she realized that Saladin was foreign]. In this reference, 'estrangier' seems to be more particularly racial and religious than elsewhere in the text, since the Queen was already aware that he was an outsider of some kind before this revelation. However, just which elements of identity play a role in this attribution remains unclear.

Despite the fact that the story of Saladin's knighting and even his potential Christian origins appears in other medieval works, his detailed integration into a Christian genealogy only features in conjunction with narratives of passing, and passing challenges any assumed relationship between blood or biological inheritance and racial identity, binary or otherwise. While Heng suggests that the narrative of Saladin's origins is one of genetic determinism where 'Saladin's essential European-ness in the *Roman de Saladin* [...] becomes instantly intelligible because we know that he is really part-French *dans le sang*', medieval genealogy, as Hummer has recently shown is 'a manifestation of carnality, not blood' and placed individuals in relation to eschatological temporal order.[64] As a result, the cultural fantasy of Saladin's Christian, French family is perhaps one where racial identity is constructed by genealogical and temporal determinism rather than blood or genetics.

The focus on the genealogical construction of racial identities in this narrative tradition becomes still more apparent when set in relation to other medieval accounts of Saladin's supposed Christian mother, such as those of Jean Le Long and Matthew Paris. In both cases, the Christian woman concerned is not explicitly integrated into a dynastic framework. Around 1370, Jean Le Long says in his *Chronicon Sancti Bertini* that 'Salahadinus Turchus, sed de matre Gallica Pontiva' [Saladin was a Turk, but had a French mother from Ponthieu] yet makes no mention of marriage or family,[65] while Matthew Paris in the *Historia Anglorum* (mid thirteenth-century) notes that he was born 'ex quadam muliere nobili Christiana et Anglica, sclava, et a viro suo rapta' [from a certain noble Christian, English woman, a slave kidnapped from her husband].[66] Likewise, although Margaret Jubb notes early precedents for attributing Christian origins to other Saracen rulers, these similarly focus on captive women forced into sexual unions. For instance, the Turkish Atabeg Zengi is rumoured in one chronicle to have descended from Ida, Markgräfin of Austria, after she was captured at the Battle of Heraclium in 1101:

> Itam comitissam, matrem Leopaldi marchionis orientalis, que similiter in

eodem comitatu fuit, unus de principibus Sarracenorum rapuit, et inpurissimo sibi matrimonio copulavit ex eaque sanguinem illum sceleratissimum, ut aiunt, progenuit.⁶⁷

[Thus the countess [Ida of Austria], mother of Leopold, marquis of the East, who was also in that same retinue, was snatched by one of the Saracen princes and he joined her to him in a most impure marriage, and from her he begat, so they say, that most wicked blood.]

This is clearly no legitimate marriage but 'inpurissimo' and the emphasis lies on the wicked *blood* that results. Consequently, the representation of such relationships may evoke aspects of historical practice among many Muslim rulers of the Middle Ages, who frequently took Christian slaves as concubines and treated their shared offspring as heirs.⁶⁸ The political impetus behind these unions was actually to avoid the trappings of any genealogical ties brought by the mother, who also had to be non-Muslim, since Islamic law does not permit the enslavement of Muslims. As D. Fairchild Ruggles observes in relation to Ottoman society: 'the concubine, by virtue of her slave status, had no known bloodline to compete with that of the Ottomans'.⁶⁹ Given such common practice and early textual precedents, it is important that in the case of the *Fille* narratives Saladin is not just given Christian blood but a Christian genealogy: having blood from a Christian mother was one thing — having a Christian *family* quite another. With the lady's conversion to the Saracen faith and acceptance of the Sultan's offer (even if reluctant), a legitimate form of marriage is produced, as is also recognized by the Pope's later need to re-establish her 'droit' Christian marriage to Thibaut.⁷⁰ The addition of marriage to narratives of Saladin's ancestry means that motherhood in these tales is thus not a corruption of lineage but a means to legitimize indeterminacy and to present it as both transmissible and enduring.

In the various narratives of *La Fille du Comte de Pontieu*, it seems that racial passing exploits the performativity of identity to provide alternative kinds of visibility in systems based on genealogical and dynastic connections rather than the racialization of blood and biology. Passing not only makes the indeterminacy of racial identity readable by facilitating different genealogical narratives but also reminds us that even perception is discursive, especially in a context where history itself is a 'perceptual field'. In this light, I return briefly to the text of the *Estoires* and to one particular manuscript: Paris, BnF, MS f. fr. 770. In contrast to the other two manuscripts of the *Estoires d'Outremer*, which are bound with historical texts connected to the Béthune family, the *Estoires* here follows three Arthurian romances: the *Estoire del Saint Graal, Li Roman de Merlin,* and the *Suite Vulgate du Merlin*. While Jubb notes that the generic identity of the *Estoires d'Outremer* is difficult to classify, she sees this manuscript as evidence that 'in the eyes of some contemporaries at least, the *Estoires* was regarded as more akin to the fiction of romances than to historiography'.⁷¹ Yet given the construction of racial identities via passing narratives and genealogical systems, a different kind of coherence is discernible. The tales that bookend this manuscript trouble conventional concepts of west-east travel and Christian triumph vs defeat, while also presenting indeterminate racial identities that problematize the linear reading of ancestry and history, as well as ideas of biological determinism: the *Estoire del Saint Graal*, as discussed above, is concerned with retroactive genealogies and presents the Saracen origins of Christian heroes, while also troubling the very notion of 'origins'; the *Estoires d'Outremer*, as I have argued here, mirrors this process, uniting a tale of passing with genealogical exposition to make the indeterminacy of racial identity readable and performatively construct Christian origins for the most famous of Saracen leaders.

★ ★ ★ ★ ★

Epilogue: Non-Essentially Speaking

In December 2016, a mosque in Cumbernauld, Scotland, was spray-painted with the words: 'Saracens go home' and 'Deus vult'. More and more, it seems, the Middle Ages are metonymically evoked as a supposed era of widespread intolerance, racial 'purity', and an intransigent religious binarism between Christians and Muslims. In concluding a book where I have discussed a range of non-essentialist representations of race in the Middle Ages, I am therefore struck anew by how important it is to counter racist and ignorant appropriations of medieval history and continue to debate the ways in which medieval identities may be constructed. At a time when extreme political groups would claim the Middle Ages as a repository of essentialist and racist attitudes, as witnessed in the presence of shields marked 'Deus vult' in Charlottesville, USA, during the 2017 Unite-the-Right rally, it has become crucial not just to show the need to think critically about medieval race but also to highlight the shades of grey, subjectivity, and malleability of medieval representations of racial difference, literary or otherwise.

This book was a study neither of present-day medievalism, nor of the wider appropriation of history for contemporary political ends. Its theoretical slant will possibly appeal more to those within academia than without. Nonetheless, my focus on the performativity of racial identity challenges the kinds of essentialist rhetoric seen in slogans like 'Saracens go home', which attempted to construct racial and religious identities and incite intolerance by cherry picking one particular strand of a discourse linking crusade and religious zeal from among many circulating in this period. Not all Saracens were the enemies of crusaders, just as crusader motivations were complex and based on more than just a desire to engage in religious warfare. Performativity has helped to show that many different elements of identity worked (and still work) to construct ideas of the Saracens as a race.

Alongside the productive potential of language and rhetoric, several of my chosen texts share moments of liminal experience, whether produced by temporary cross-dressing, logical processes (in a Lacanian sense), religious conversion, or dialogue. Haunting and haunted, producing yet defined by lineage, and exposing the reappropriation of literary convention, the figure of the Saracen clearly fulfilled a variety of needs within the narratives themselves and for the reader/viewer; these literary representations cannot be reduced to a binary relationship of self to other within a fixed paradigm of religious or racial difference. While Ramey previously noted that Saracens 'could play multiple roles', the roles she considers are primarily set in relation to Christian 'counterparts' and so remain based upon implicit dualisms, whether mirroring, adversarial, or amorous.[72] The examples studied here could instead lead us to believe that Saracen identity in cultural representations was not only multiple but also ambiguous and, more importantly, changeable. By treating these texts as literary productions and examining their devices and conventions, the true extent of this changeability becomes visible, even within single works, so that genre-based categories such as 'the Saracens of epic' or 'the Saracens of romance' seem rather reductive.

As textual study reveals, racial identity is performative and is produced by the various narrative processes at work as much as by the replication of social, behavioural, or cultural conventions — processes which may be in the service of spiritual didacticism, gender troubling, the criticism of reason, or the establishment of the text's relation to its cyclical or narrative siblings. Whatever attributes are collected under the term 'Saracen' at any one time, the fact remains that this identity is actively produced rather than statically reflected in the medieval French literary works discussed. However, the performativity of racial identity is not always revealed or exploited in the same manner, regardless of genre or other elements of identity. For instance, while recognizing the non-essential nature of both concepts in medieval texts, conventions of gendered and racial identity are not produced and reproduced identically. Key differences have emerged from my examples regarding the ways in which gender identity and racial identity are performative; although similar processes and acts may be involved in their construction, these identities are dissimilarly maintained. For instance, in the Nanteuil Cycle, while disguise can exploit conventions of physical appearance, leaving racial identity malleable, gender identity seems rooted in the physical body and the production of heirs, so that in the last text, *Tristan de Nanteuil*, divine intervention is needed to transform it and thus maintain the associated identity crossing. Of course, medieval gender identity is not always tied to biology in this way, but this does seem to be a feature of such intersectional encounters; perhaps in the face of such changeable racial identities, gender is constructed as somehow more narrowly determined and recognizable (if no less performative), almost as a way to off-set the fact the fact that racial categorizations are acknowledged to be problematic. Nonetheless, it is also true that even the production of heirs does not always assume a biological or linear construction of racial identity when narrative processes lead us to question causality and to take into account complex medieval understandings of genealogy.

If gender and racial identity differ in their performativity due to the respective roles of appearances and/or the body, racial and religious identities differ greatly in terms of their performative possibilities. The simultaneous performance of race and religion undoes the notion of a fixed Saracenness and means that the Saracen can shift identity, such as in cases where conventions of physical appearance, worship, or discourse are exploited. However, the performativity of *faith* in particular is rather more controversial, as the *Roman de Mahomet* revealed, since the notion that all faith is citational also troubles the idea that a Saracen's faith might be false. While the performativity of practical acts of worship may blur Christian and Saracen bodies, faith itself cannot be acknowledged to be confected but must be seen to result from direct experience of the divine. Furthermore, as this experience of faith is often physical in nature, it calls into question the relationship between body, flesh and spirit, in turn problematizing the ways in which these relate to the idea of Saracenness and indeed to racial identity more generally.

Given that notions of performativity emphasize the potential for identity to be produced rather than just described, they have additionally revealed the impact of narrative and stylistic processes upon Saracen identity beyond the communities depicted within texts. Many of the texts discussed in this book engage with the reader/audience in a way that both determines and relies upon the nature of the depicted Saracen. For instance, the exemplary behaviour of the Saracen in *De l'ymage Nostre Dame* is crucial to Gautier de Coinci's didactic project, so that the Saracen is produced not just by literary convention but by the aesthetic experience of the text, both aural and visual: an experience which may even involve encouraging the audience to emulate the Saracen's behaviour. In this respect, when used as exempla, Saracen representations often extend far beyond Christian-Saracen religious conflicts and touch upon matters affecting a general Christian audience, such as processes of conversion, reasoning, and community construction.

Since, as noted by Seshadri-Crooks, 'exploring the structure of race requires a toleration of paradox, an appreciation of the fact that it is an inherently contradictory discourse',[73] theories of race help us to consider the nuances of the medieval Saracen, even if the modern and medieval identity traits that fall within this concept are not necessarily comparable. The fact is that although the term 'race' and its underlying concepts mean very different things in very different times and contexts, where the Saracen is concerned there nonetheless seems to have been a form of identity that one might call 'racial' and representations we might label as 'raced' and/or 'racist' due to the similarities in, if not consistency of, determining factors. However, racial and religious identities are both created and undone by the performative nature of their production, a fact that is influenced by the stylistic and generic attributes of the literary work at hand. As a result, racial and/or religious identity in literary texts would seem to be relative in the manner of other character identity traits. When so much variation in the representations of Saracens appears in texts and manuscripts produced in such close proximity (whether geographical or temporal) attempts to identify a consistent chronological trajectory must prove difficult.[74]

In addition, it seems that the term *Sarrasin* does not alternately refer to the race or the religion of figures in medieval works, and does not demonstrate that race and religion are simply one and the same thing, since the nuances of this word are highly contextual. It is not the case that post-Darwinian, biological concepts of race were already present in this period, simply labelled as religion. Rather, religious difference could often convey many of the same associations and meanings that we might today ascribe to the term 'race', and vice versa. Indeed, religion often transmits or even creates, yet does not simply equate to, race in these narratives. Thinking back to the *Estoire del Saint Graal*, for instance, knowledge of bloodlines and lineage is produced by religious enlightenment and in Gautier de Coinci's *De l'ymage Nostre Dame*, the Christian behaviour of the Saracen is what occludes other racial differences. In future, it may be more useful to think about the significance of internal divisions within an expansive notion of medieval religion, such as those encompassing birth, faith, appearances, and nation, than to seek to draw lines between concepts of race and/or religion, which also continue to be conflated in the modern world.[75]

Despite the fact that the Saracens considered here are constructed by writers who do not share in the culture they depict and are of course representations within a literary work, race may still be presented as a matter of perception rather than objective fact. For example, in the *Estoire del Saint Graal*, it is the very structure of the narrative that enables race to be subjectively construed by both characters and audience through logical processes, rather than simply bestowed through description. Similarly, in the *Fille* narratives, race is made readable in all its indeterminacy via narratives of passing that both construct yet undermine genealogical thinking and historical visibility. In this sense, Byrne's comment that 'race is in the eye of the beholder' continues to be relevant in a medieval context, as it epitomizes the fact that race is a subjective process rather than objective attribute where the Saracen is concerned. Moreover, the fact that the Saracen body can be reconsidered as the primary site of identity in these works suggests that approaches to medieval race can take inspiration from modern theorists of race and their calls to think beyond biological essentialisms. The relationship between bodily form and medieval race should thus be contextualized rather than altogether ignored: so often appearances are able to be manipulated, and although the body is important to the way that the Saracen is depicted, the frequent failings of visual recognition and the invisibility of identities also go acknowledged.

This paradoxical reliance upon, yet distrust of appearances is far from alien to modern discussions of race, as highlighted in the work of both Seshadri-Crooks and Davids, which suggests that similar approaches to race that prioritize intellectual and psychological processes may also be fruitful in a medieval context. As many scholars commenting upon Saracens have observed, skin colour may be dictated by morality and skill as much as by an inherited and/or biological identity,[76] with numerous well-known Saracens shown to be white skinned (such as the eponymous chivalric hero of the *chanson de geste Fierabras*).[77] It is therefore understandable that other elements of identity can just as easily be used to determine and even alter racial identity. Given that the literary works studied in this book were largely (or likely) authored by Christian men, I do not deny, or wish to downplay in any way, the fact that their treatment of Saracen figures is prejudicial, often profoundly so. Instead I would challenge the assumption, in the case of the Saracen at least, that race is always a question of the body first and foremost: unlike some modern racist discourses, medieval literature does not necessarily focus on physical difference in the same way (though it is deeply objectionable and racist in copious other ways). Medieval race, as seen through the Saracen, is instead characterized by flexibility. Akbari suggests that 'bodily diversity' in both the medieval past and present world creates a kind of us-and-them division,[78] yet when other potential components constituting Saracen identity come to the forefront (such as lineage, behaviour, dress, speech, and worship) it seems that this racial identity is not definitive enough to produce and/or maintain stable binary divisions.

If it has been suggested that the continued recourse to concepts of race in the modern world is rooted in the desire for an 'absolute wholeness',[79] then scholars seem to have been guilty of a similar drive in relation to the medieval society that we are inevitably (re)constructing. Perhaps part of the problem in many approaches to medieval race follows the analogy of a square peg in a round hole, in that nebulous figures such as the Saracen simply do not map onto what we *think* this term should mean: namely, that it should primarily differentiate those who are visibly different in the way that modern racial and racist labels so frequently do. Even if the Old French term *Sarrasin* often appears to be used indiscriminately, the literary figures examined in this book suggest that the Saracen should be viewed neither in purely oppositional terms, nor as a repository for totally vague notions of otherness; theories of performativity have provided a means of recognizing the flexibility of this identity, yet also of acknowledging the need for contextualization above the assumption of a fixed set of cultural oppositions. While there is an often practical emphasis upon genre in studies of the Saracen,[80] the range of representations found in just a handful of medieval French literary works has shown that strict models of Saracen identity may be untenable. There is a need not only to return to literary technique and function in the construction of these figures but also to take into account their material presentation and, perhaps most importantly, reassess our own potentially retroactive essentialisms.

In a sense, this study has come full circle, to end as it began with an acknowledgement of absent presence. Although we might like to find a clear-cut perception of race in medieval literature, the writers of literary texts may have been as deliberately imprecise as they were unsure about what a Saracen was and often seem just as perplexed as we are in the modern world when it comes to what may have constituted a racial identity. As a result, I conclude that the act of representing the medieval Saracen was never concluded: as modern society continues to struggle to define and/or distinguish race and ethnicity, so the medieval world recognized and exploited the ambiguity of its own definitions of Saracen identity more than has previously been assumed. As Cohen and Steel so succinctly state, 'race *is* real, even if more process than thing'.[81]

Notes to the Conclusion

1. Pellegrini, *Performance Anxieties*, p. 98.
2. Ibid.
3. See Butler's comments in Bell, 'On Speech', p. 168.
4. Heng discusses the art historical work of Madeline Caviness in relation to whiteness in *The Invention of Race*, pp. 182–84 and focuses on questions of skin colour more generally throughout Chapter 4.
5. This tension is discussed in Linda Schlossberg's work on racial passing. See her 'Introduction: Rites of Passing', in *Passing: Identity and Interpretation in Sexuality, Race, and Religion*, ed. by María Carla Sánchez and Linda Schlossberg (New York: New York University Press, 2001), p. 5.
6. Byrne, *White Lives*, p. 74.

7. Capitalized italics here refer to the tradition in general. Particular versions will be specified as necessary throughout my discussion.
8. Both manuscripts of *Baudouin de Sebourc* are unillustrated (Paris, BnF, MS f. fr. 12552 and 12553). For more on this textual tradition and Saladin, see Margaret Jubb, *The Legend of Saladin in Western Literature and Historiography* (Lewiston: Edwin Mellen Press, 2000), especially pp. 53–65.
9. *La Fille du comte de Pontieu, conte en prose, versions du XIIIe et du XVe siècle*, ed. by Clovis Brunel (Paris: Champion, 1923).
10. Lynn Ramey, 'Medieval Miscegenation: Hybridity and the Anxiety of Inheritance', in *Contextualizing the Muslim Other in Medieval Christian Discourse*, ed. by Jerold C. Frakes (New York: Palgrave Macmillan, 2011), pp. 1–19; Sharon Kinoshita, 'The Romance of Miscegenation: Negotiating Identities in *La Fille du Comte de Pontieu*', in *Medieval Boundaries*, pp. 176–200.
11. Donald Maddox, 'Domesticating Diversity: Female Founders in Medieval Genealogical Literature and *La Fille du comte de Pontieu*', in *The Court and Cultural Diversity: Selected Papers from the Eighth Triennial Congress of the International Courtly Literature Society, the Queen's University of Belfast, 26 July–1 August 1995*, ed. by Evelyn Mullally and John Thompson (Woodbridge: Brewer, 1997), pp. 97–107 (p. 100).
12. See Judith Halberstam, 'Telling Tales: Brandon Teena, Billy Tipton, and Transgender Biography', in *Passing: Identity and Interpretation*, ed. by Sánchez and Schlossberg, pp. 13–37 (p. 16); and Jay Prosser, *Second Skins: The Body Narratives of Transsexuality* (New York: Columbia University Press, 1998), pp. 21–22.
13. Elaine K. Ginsberg, 'Introduction: The Politics of Passing', in *Passing and the Fictions of Identity*, ed. by Elaine K. Ginsberg (Durham, NC: Duke University Press, 1996), p. 3.
14. Grinberg, 'Robes, Turbans, and Beards'. Note that Grinberg is currently the only entry in the recent 'Race and Medieval Studies: A Partial Bibliography' by Jonathan Hsy and Julie Orlemanski that explicitly addresses passing in its title. See *postmedieval*, 8 (2017), 500–31 <https://doi.org/10.1057/s41280-017-0072-0>; see Barbara Fuchs, *Passing for Spain: Cervantes and the Fictions of Identity* (Chicago: University of Illinois Press, 2003).
15. See Jessica Rabin, *Surviving the Crossing: (Im)migration, Ethnicity, and Gender in Willa Cather, Gertrude Stein, and Nella Larsen* (New York: Routledge, 2004), pp. 13–15 (p. 15).
16. Jonathan Dollimore, *Sexual Dissidence: Augustine to Wilde, Freud to Foucault* (Oxford: Oxford University Press, 1991), p. 288.
17. Ginsberg, 'Introduction', in *Passing and the Fictions of Identity*, pp. 4–5.
18. Ginsberg, 'Introduction', in *Passing and the Fictions of Identity*, p. 4.
19. Ginsberg, 'Introduction', in *Passing and the Fictions of Identity*, p. 3.
20. Schlossberg, 'Introduction', in *Passing: Identity and Interpretation*, ed. by Sánchez and Schlossberg, p. 3.
21. See the excellent database resource, RELMIN: 'Le statut légal des minorités religieuses dans l'espace euro-méditerranéen (V^e–XVe siècle)', Édition électronique Telma, IRHT, Institut de Recherche et d'Histoire des Textes — Orléans <http://www.cn-telma.fr/relmin/index/> [accessed 4 December 2018]
22. Isabel Davis, 'Cutaneous Time in the Late Medieval Literary Imagination', in *Reading Skin in Medieval Literature and Culture*, ed. by Katie L. Walter (New York: Palgrave Macmillan, 2013), pp. 99–119 (p. 113).
23. See Zrinka Stahuljak, *Pornographic Archaeology: Medicine, Medievalism, and the Invention of the French Nation* (Philadelphia: University of Pennsylvania Press, 2013), pp. 60–62.
24. Ideas of medieval kinship and genealogy have recently been revisited by Hans Hummer, *Visions of Kinship in Medieval Europe* (Oxford: Oxford University Press, 2018).
25. See Joyce Kubiski, 'Orientalizing Costume in Early Fifteenth-Century French Manuscript Painting (Cité des Dames Master, Limbourg Brothers, Boucicault Master, and Bedford Master)', *Gesta*, 40 (2001), 161–81.
26. Rosalind Brown-Grant, 'Le Rapt et le rapport texte/image dans les manuscrits du remaniement bourguignon de *La Fille du Comte de Pontieu*', in *Rapts: Réalités et imaginaire du Moyen âge aux Lumières*, ed. by Gabriele Vickermann-Ribémont and Myriam White-Le Goff (Paris: Classiques Garnier, 2014), pp. 49–70 (p. 55).

27. I am grateful to Rosalind Brown-Grant for drawing my attention to this contrast.
28. Brown-Grant, 'Rapt'.
29. See, for instance, the recent work of Rosalind Brown-Grant on this artist: 'Prologues and Frontispieces in Prose Romance Manuscripts', in *Inscribing Knowledge in the Medieval Book: Power and the Paratext*, ed. by Rosalind Brown-Grant, Patrizia Carmassi, Gisela Drossbach, Anne D. Hedeman, Victoria Turner, and Iolanda Ventura (Kalamazoo: Medieval Institute Publications, forthcoming 2019), and Rosalind Brown-Grant, 'Laughing At or With the Text? The Wavrin Master as Illuminator of Burgundian Prose Romances', *Cahiers de recherches médiévales et humanistes*, 30 (2015), 407–19, 455–59 (colour plates).
30. Brown-Grant, 'Rapt', p. 52.
31. Brown-Grant, 'Prologues and Frontispieces'.
32. Kinoshita, *Medieval Boundaries*, pp. 185–86; see Olivia Remie Constable, *Trade and Traders in Muslim Spain: The Commercial Realignment of the Iberian Peninsula, 900–1500* (Cambridge: Cambridge University Press, 1994).
33. Kinoshita, *Medieval Boundaries*, pp. 188–89.
34. Heng, *The Invention of Race*, pp. 77–79.
35. See the discussion by McCracken, *The Romance of Adultery*, pp. 128–31.
36. McCracken, *Romance of Adultery*, p. 131.
37. In the fifteenth-century text, she claims to the Sultan that: 'l'ayr m'infect et me corrompt' (p. 125) [the air is infecting and polluting me]. In this version, the term 'droit' is only used to refer to her conversion: 'droite crestienté' (p. 127). I have translated 'droit' with 'rightful' here to try to reflect the polyvalence of this word, which carries associations of legal authority, correctness, justness, appropriateness etc.
38. See Strickland, *Saracens, Demons, & Jews*, pp. 33–34.
39. The fifteenth-century manuscripts do not mention the Sultan's love for the lady, in keeping with their emphasis on the love between her and Thibaut.
40. Katie L. Walter, 'The Form of the Formless: Medieval Taxonomies of Skin, Flesh, and the Human', in *Reading Skin*, ed. by Katie L. Walter, pp. 119–39 (p. 131).
41. Maddox, 'Domesticating Diversity', p. 103.
42. Schlossberg, 'Introduction', in *Passing: Identity and Interpretation*, ed. by Sánchez and Schlossberg, pp. 4–5.
43. Kinoshita, *Medieval Boundaries*, p. 184.
44. Natasha R. Hodgson, 'The Role of Kerbogha's Mother in the *Gesta Francorum* and Selected Chronicles of the First Crusade', in *Gendering the Crusades*, ed. by Susan B. Edgington and Sarah Lambert (Cardiff: University of Wales Press, 2001), pp. 163–76 (p. 165).
45. Spiegel, 'Genealogy', p. 44.
46. Maddox, 'Domesticating Diversity', p. 105.
47. Stahuljak, *Pornographic Archaeology*, p. 61.
48. *Le Chevalier au Cygne et Godefroi de Bouillon*, ed. by M. le Baron de Reiffenberg and M.A. Borgnet, 3 vols (Brussels: Hayez, 1846–54), III.
49. See Robert F. Cook and Larry S. Crist, *Le Deuxième Cycle de la Croisade: Deux études sur son développement: Les textes en vers* (Geneva: Droz, 1972), pp. 120–24.
50. See Hodgson, 'The Role of Kerbogha's Mother', fn. 2, p. 173 for details. Note that she is usually unnamed, though is known as 'Calabre' in the *Chanson d'Antioche*.
51. See the table created by Cook and Crist, pp. 100–19 (Table 4, pp. 116–17).
52. *Gesta Francorum et aliorum Hierosolimitanorum. The Deeds of the Franks and the other Pilgrims to Jerusalem*, ed. and trans. by Rosalind Hill (London: Nelson, 1962), pp. 53–54.
53. Hummer, *Visions of Kinship*, p. 273.
54. Hummer, *Visions of Kinship*, p. 280.
55. See lines 2375–79 where Saladin's birth is announced alongside his future victories against Godfrey and Baldwin of Bouillon. *Baudouin de Sebourc*, ed. by Larry S. Crist [and Robert F. Cook], 2 vols (Paris: Société des anciens textes français, 2002).
56. See Cook and Crist, *Deuxième Cycle* for the relationships between these texts.
57. *Saladin: Suite et fin du deuxième cycle de croisade*, ed. by Larry S. Crist (Geneva: Droz, 1972).

58. See Catherine Gaullier-Bougassas, *La Tentation de l'Orient dans le roman médiéval: Sur l'imaginaire médiéval de l'Autre* (Paris: Champion, 2003), p. 363; for Alexander as ancestor of French/Burgundian rulers, see also her 'Alexandre le Grand et la conquête de l'Ouest dans les *romans d'Alexandre* du XIIe siècle, leurs mises en prose au XVe siècle et le *Perceforest* (1ère partie)', *Romania*, 118 (2000), 83–104 <https://doi.org/10.3406/roma.2000.1521>.
59. See Crist's 'Introduction', in *Saladin*, p. 10; see also Gaullier-Bougassas, *Tentation*, p. 386.
60. See Vasco de Lucena, trans. *Quinte Curce, Histoire d'Alexandre*, BnF, MS f. fr. 6440, <https://gallica.bnf.fr/ark:/12148/btv1b90604270> [accessed 6 December 2018], fol. 1^v; Catherine Gaullier-Bougassas, 'Jean Wauquelin et Vasque de Lucène: le "roman familial" d'Alexandre et l'écriture de l'histoire au XVe siècle', *Cahiers de recherches médiévales et humanistes*, 5 (1998), <http://dx.doi.org/10.4000/crm.1442>.
61. Gaullier-Bougassas, *Tentation*, p. 391.
62. The Arsenal manuscript (B. Ars., 5208) does not show Saladin's time in France, but the sole image shows a combat scene before Jerusalem, with some figures wearing turbans where Saladin is distinguished only by a crown.
63. See the entry in the *DMF: Dictionnaire du Moyen Français*, version 2015 (DMF 2015), ATILF–CNRS & Université de Lorraine, <http://www.atilf.fr/dmf/> [accessed 4 December 2018].
64. Heng, *The Invention of Race*, pp. 139–40; Hummer, *Visions of Kinship*, pp. 271–73.
65. Jean Le Long, *Chronica monasterii Sancti Bertini auctore Iohanne Longo*, ed. by O. Holder-Egger, Monumenta Germaniae Historica Scriptores, 25 (Hannover: Hahn,1880), pp. 736–866 (p. 818) <http://www.mgh.de/> [accessed 4 December 2018]; See the discussion by Jubb, *Legend of Saladin*, pp. 53–57.
66. Matthew Paris, *Historia Anglorum sive, ut vulgo dicitur, Historia Minor*, ed. by Frederic Madden (1866–69), 3 vols (London: Longman, Green, Reader, and Dyer, 1866; repr. Cambridge: Cambridge University Press, 2012), I, p. 430.
67. *Historia Welforum Weingartensis*, ed. by L. Weiland, Monumenta Germaniae Historica Scriptores, 21 (Hannover: Hahn, 1869), pp. 454–72 (p. 462) <http://www.mgh.de/> [accessed 4 December 2018].
68. Kinoshita, *Medieval Boundaries*, pp. 140–42; D. Fairchild Ruggles, 'Mothers of a Hybrid Dynasty: Race, Genealogy, and Acculturation in al-Andalus', *Journal of Medieval and Early Modern Studies*, 34 (2004), 65–94 (p. 74).
69. Ruggles, 'Mothers of a Hybrid Dynasty', p. 74.
70. For documents pertaining to the legality of interfaith marriages, see RELMIN.
71. Jubb, *Legend of Saladin*, p. 170.
72. Ramey, *Christian, Saracen, and Genre*, p. 101.
73. Seshadri-Crooks, *Desiring Whiteness*, p. 9.
74. While providing a much-needed focus on gender and the exotic in Franco-Byzantine exchanges, Megan Moore, for instance, hints at such a chronological approach in *Exchanges in Exoticism: Cross-Cultural Marriage and the Making of the Mediterranean in Old French Romance* (Toronto: University of Toronto Press, 2014).
75. See for instance Jasbir K. Puar's discussion of the term 'Muslim' as a racial category in *Terrorist Assemblages: Homonationalism in Queer Times* (Durham NC: Duke University Press, 2007).
76. See Strickland, *Saracens, Demons, & Jews*, p. 174; Ramey, *Christians, Saracens and Genre*, p. 45.
77. See the discussion of the Saracen knight Fierabras's chivalrous qualities and Christian conversion in Marianne Ailes, 'Chivalry and Conversion'.
78. Akbari, *Idols in the East*, p. 282.
79. Seshadri-Crooks, *Desiring Whiteness*, p. 5.
80. For instance, de Weever's, *Sheba's Daughters* focuses on *chansons de geste* as does Bancourt in *Les Musulmans*.
81. Cohen and Steel, 'Race, Travel, Time, Heritage', p. 108.

BIBLIOGRAPHY

Primary Sources

Manuscripts

Besançon, BM, MS 551
 <http://memoirevive.besancon.fr/ark:/48565/a011323184960P9CLLr/1/29>
Brussels, BR, MS 9229–30
Brussels, BR, MS 10747
The Hague, KB, MS 71.A.24
Paris, B. Ars., MS 5204 <http://gallica.bnf.fr/ark:/12148/btv1b55008557j>
Paris, B. Ars., MS 5208 <https://gallica.bnf.fr/ark:/12148/btv1b52501151k>
Paris, BnF, MS f. fr. 770 <https://gallica.bnf.fr/ark:/12148/btv1b52503818d>
Paris, BnF, MS f. fr. 1533 <https://gallica.bnf.fr/ark:/12148/btv1b9009683f>
Paris, BnF, MS f. fr. 1553 <http://gallica.bnf.fr/ark:/12148/btv1b9007508h>
Paris, BnF, MS f. fr. 6440 <https://gallica.bnf.fr/ark:/12148/btv1b90604270>
Paris, BnF, MS f. fr. 10132 <https://gallica.bnf.fr/ark:/12148/btv1b90632136>
Paris, BnF, MS f. fr. 12572 <https://gallica.bnf.fr/ark:/12148/btv1b90609462>
Paris, BnF, MS f. fr. 22928 <https://gallica.bnf.fr/ark:/12148/btv1b84546831>
Paris, BnF, MS f. fr. 25462 <https://gallica.bnf.fr/ark:/12148/btv1b90633532>
Paris, BnF, MS f. fr. 25532 <https://gallica.bnf.fr/ark:/12148/btv1b90631786>
Paris, BnF, MS n. a. fr. 24541 <https://gallica.bnf.fr/ark:/12148/btv1b6000451c>

(The above links were all accessed 4 December 2018.)

Printed materials

ALEXANDRE DU PONT, *Le Roman de Mahomet de Alexandre du Pont (1258) avec le texte des "Otia de Machomete" de Gautier de Compiègne (XIIe siècle), établi par R. B. C. Huygens*, ed. by Yvan G. Lepage, Bibliothèque française et romane, Series B, 16 (Paris: Klincksieck, 1977)
Aliscans, ed. by Claude Régnier, 2 vols (Paris: Champion, 1990)
Aye d'Avignon: Chanson de geste anonyme, ed. by S. J. Borg (Geneva: Droz, 1967)
La Bataille Loquifer, ed. by Monica Barnett (Oxford: Blackwell for the Society for the Study of Mediaeval Languages and Literature, 1975)
Baudouin de Sebourc, ed. by Larry S. Crist [and Robert F. Cook], 2 vols (Paris: Société des anciens textes français, 2002)
BERNARD OF CLAIRVAUX, *Sermones*, ed. by J. Leclercq and H. Rochais, *S. Bernardi opera*, 8 vols (Rome: Editiones Cistercienses, 1966), IV
La Chanson de Roland, ed. and trans. by Ian Short, Lettres gothiques, 2nd edn (Paris: Livre de Poche, 1990)
Le Chevalier au Cygne et Godefroi de Bouillon, ed. by M. le Baron de Reiffenberg and M.A. Borgnet, 3 vols (Brussels: Hayez, 1846–54)
Chronica Prophetica, trans. from the Latin by Kenneth Baxter Wolf,
 <https://sites.google.com/site/canilup/chronica_prophetica> [accessed 28 November 2018]

The Deeds of God through the Franks: A Translation of Guibert de Nogent's Gesta Dei per Francos, ed. and trans. by Robert Levine (Woodbridge: Boydell, 1997)

L'Estoire del Saint Graal, ed. by Jean-Paul Ponceau, Les Classiques français du Moyen Âge, 120–21, 2 vols (Paris: Champion, 1997)

Fierabras: Chanson de geste du XIIe siècle, ed. by Marc Le Person, Les Classiques français du Moyen Âge, 142 (Paris: Champion, 2003)

La Fille du comte de Pontieu, conte en prose, versions du XIIIe et du XVe siècle, ed. by Clovis Brunel (Paris: Champion, 1923)

GAUTIER DE COINCI, *Les Miracles de Nostre Dame*, ed. by V. Frédéric Koenig, 4 vols, Textes Littéraires Français (Genève: Droz, 1955–70), I, 2nd edn (1966); II (1961); III (1966); IV (1970)

Gesta Francorum et aliorum Hierosolimitanorum. The Deeds of the Franks and the other Pilgrims to Jerusalem, ed. and trans. by Rosalind Hill (London: Nelson, 1962)

GLABER, RODULFUS, *Rodvlfi Glabri Historiarvm libri qvinqve* [The five books of the Histories], ed. and trans. by John France; published with Glaber, *Vita domni Willelmi abbatis* [The life of St William], ed. by Neithard Bulst, trans. by John France and Paul Reynolds (Oxford: Clarendon Press, 1989)

Gui de Nanteuil: Chanson de geste, ed. by James R. McCormack, Textes Littéraires Français, 161 (Geneva: Droz, 1970)

Historia Welforum Weingartensis, ed. by L. Weiland, Monumenta Germaniae Historica Scriptores, 21 (Hannover: Hahn, 1869), pp. 454–72 (p. 462) <http://www.mgh.de/> [accessed 4 December 2018]

JEAN D'ARRAS, *Le Roman de Mélusine ou La Noble Histoire de Lusignan*, ed. by Jean-Jacques Vincensini (Paris: Livre de Poche, 2003)

JEAN LE LONG, *Chronica monasterii Sancti Bertini auctore Iohanne Longo*, ed. by O. Holder-Egger, Monumenta Germaniae Historica Scriptores, 25 (Hannover: Hahn, 1880), pp. 736–866 <http://www.mgh.de/> [accessed 4 December 2018]

Lancelot-Grail: The Old French Arthurian Vulgate and Post-Vulgate in Translation, Norris J. Lacy, General Editor, 5 vols (New York: Garland, 1993–96)

MATTHEW PARIS, *Historia Anglorum sive, ut vulgo dicitur, Historia Minor*, ed. by Frederic Madden (1866–69), 3 vols (London: Longman, Green, Reader, and Dyer, 1866; repr. Cambridge: Cambridge University Press, 2012), I

Patrologiae cursus completus, ed. by J.-P. Migne, Series Latina, 221 vols (Paris: [n.pub.], 1841–1905), CLXXXIX (1854)

La Prise d'Orange: Chanson de geste de la fin du XIIe siècle, ed. by Claude Régnier, Bibliothèque française et romane, Series B, 5, 2nd edn (Paris: Klincksiek, 1969)

The Prophet of Islam in Old French: The Romance of Muhammad (1258) and The Book of Muhammad's Ladder (1264), trans. by Reginald Hyatte, Brill's Studies in Intellectual History, 75 (Leiden: Brill, 1997)

La Quête du Saint-Graal: Roman en prose du XIIIe siècle, ed. by Fanni Bogdanow, trans. by. Anne Berrie, Lettres gothiques, 4571 (Paris: Librairie Générale Française, 2006)

RELMIN: 'Le statut légal des minorités religieuses dans l'espace euro-méditerranéen (V^e–XVe siècle)', Édition électronique Telma, IRHT, Institut de Recherche et d'Histoire des Textes — Orléans <http://www.cn-telma.fr/relmin/index/> [accessed 4 December 2018]

Saladin: Suite et fin du deuxième cycle de croisade, ed. by Larry S. Crist (Geneva: Droz, 1972)

THOMAS AQUINAS, *De rationibus fidei contra Saracenos, Graecos et Armenos ad Cantorem Antiochenum: Reasons for the Faith against the Muslims (and one Objection of the Greeks and Armenians) to the Cantor of Antioch*, trans. by Joseph Kenney, *Islamochristiana*, 22 (1996), 31–52

—— *St Thomas Aquinas on Politics and Ethics: A New Translation, Backgrounds, Interpretation*, ed. and trans. by Paul E. Sigmund (New York: Norton, 1988)

Tristan de Nanteuil: Chanson de geste inédite, ed. by K. V. Sinclair (Assen: Van Gorcum, 1971)
VASCO DE LUCENA, TRANS. *Quinte Curce, Histoire d'Alexandre*, BnF, MS f. fr. 6440 <https://gallica.bnf.fr/ark:/12148/btv1b90604270> [accessed 6 December 2018]

Secondary Sources

ADAMS, MICHAEL VANNOY, *The Multicultural Imagination: "Race", Color, and the Unconscious* (London: Routledge, 1996)
AHMED, SARA, 'Race as Sedimented History', *postmedieval*, 6 (2015), 94–97 <https://doi.org/10.1057/pmed.2015.5>
AILES, MARIANNE, 'Chivalry and Conversion: The Chivalrous Saracen in the Old French Epics *Fierabras* and *Otinel*', *Al-Masāq*, 9 (1996–97), 1–21
—— 'Faith in *Fierabras*', in *Charlemagne in the North: Proceedings of the Twelfth International Conference of the Société Rencesvals, Edinburgh 4th to 11th August 1991*, ed. by Philip E. Bennett, Anne Elizabeth Cobby, and Graham A. Runnalls (Edinburgh: Société Rencesvals British Branch, 1993), pp. 125–33
AKBARI, SUZANNE CONKLIN, *Idols in the East: European Representations of Islam and the Orient, 1100–1450* (Ithaca, NY: Cornell University Press, 2009)
—— 'The Rhetoric of Antichrist in Western Lives of Muhammad', *Islam and Christian-Muslim Relations*, 8 (1997), 297–307
ALTHUSSER, LOUIS, 'Ideology and Ideological State Apparatus (Notes Towards an Investigation)', in *Lenin and Philosophy, and Other Essays*, trans. by Ben Brewster (New York: Monthly Review Press, 2001), pp. 85–127
ALVERNY, MARIE-THÉRÈSE D', *La Connaissance de l'Islam dans l'Occident médiéval*, ed. by Charles Burnett, with an appreciation by Margaret Gibson (Aldershot: Variorum, 1994)
[ANON.], 'History of Saracens', *Saracens Amateur Rugby Football Club Ltd*, Information section, <http://www.saracensamateurrugby.com/a/history-of-saracens-9702.html> [accessed 2 December 2018]
ARJANA, SOPHIA ROSE, *Muslims in the Western Imagination* (Oxford: Oxford University Press, 2015)
AUSTIN, J.L., *How to Do Things with Words: The William James Lectures delivered in Harvard University in 1955* (Oxford: Oxford Scholarship Online, 2011) <http://dx.doi.org/10.1093/acprof:oso/9780198245537.001.0001>
BANCOURT, PAUL, *Les Musulmans dans les chansons de geste du Cycle du roi*, 2 vols in 1 (Aix en Provence: Université de Provence, 1982)
BARTLETT, ROBERT, 'Medieval and Modern Concepts of Race and Ethnicity', in 'Race and Ethnicity in the Middle Ages', ed. by Thomas Hahn, Special Issue, *JMEMS*, 31 (2001), 39–56
BAUMGARTNER, EMMANUÈLE, 'Temps linéaire, temps circulaire et écriture romanesque (XIIe-XIIIe siècles)', in *Le Temps et la durée dans la littérature au Moyen Age et à la Renaissance: actes du colloque organisé par le Centre de recherche sur la littérature du Moyen Age et de la Renaissance de l'Université de Reims, novembre 1984*, ed. by Yvonne Bellenger (Paris: Nizet, 1986), pp. 7–21
BEAUSSART, FRANÇOIS-JÉRÔME, 'Visionnaires et apparitions dans les "Miracles de Nostre Dame" de Gautier de Coinci', *Romance Philology*, 43 (1989), 241–57
BELL, VIKKI, 'On Speech, Race and Melancholia: An Interview with Judith Butler', *Theory, Culture & Society*, 16.2 (1999), 163–74 <https://doi.org/10.1177/02632769922050593>
BENNETT, PHILIP E. and LESLIE ZARKER MORGAN, 'The Avatars of Orable-Guibourc from French *chanson de geste* to Italian *romanzo cavalleresco*. A Persistent Multiple Alterity', *Francigena*, 1 (2015), 165–215

BIERNOFF, SUZANNAH, *Sight and Embodiment in the Middle Ages* (Basingstoke: Macmillan, 2002)

BIRD, JESSALYNN, EDWARD PETERS, and JAMES M. POWELL, eds, *Crusade and Christendom: Annotated Documents in Translation from Innocent III to the Fall of Acre, 1187–1291* (Philadelphia: University of Pennsylvania Press, 2013)

BLACK, NANCY, 'Images of the Virgin Mary in the Soissons Manuscript (Paris, BNF, nouv. acq. fr. 24541)', in *Gautier de Coinci: Miracles, Music, and Manuscripts*, ed. by Kathy M. Krause and Alison Stones, Medieval Texts and Cultures of Northern Europe, 13 (Turnhout: Brepols, 2006), pp. 253–77

BLANCO, MARÍA DEL PILAR, and ESTHER PEEREN, eds, *The Spectralities Reader: Ghosts and Haunting in Contemporary Cultural Theory* (London: Bloomsbury, 2013)

BLOCH, R. HOWARD, *Etymologies and Genealogies: A Literary Anthropology of the French Middle Ages* (Chicago, IL: University of Chicago Press, 1983)

BLY CALKIN, SIOBHAIN, 'Marking Religion on the Body: Saracens, Categorization, and "The King of Tars"', *The Journal of English and Germanic Philology*, 104 (2005), 219–38 <https://www.jstor.org/stable/27712494> [accessed 22 November 2018]

BONNAZ, YVES, *Chroniques asturiennes: fin IXe siècle* (Paris: Éditions du Centre national de la recherche scientifique, 1987)

BRAUDE, BENJAMIN, 'The Sons of Noah and the Construction of Ethnic and Geographical Identities in the Medieval and Early Modern Periods', *The William and Mary Quarterly*, 3rd ser., 54 (1997), 103–42

BROWN-GRANT, ROSALIND, 'Laughing At or With the Text? The Wavrin Master as Illuminator of Burgundian Prose Romances', *Cahiers de recherches médiévales et humanistes*, 30 (2015), 407–19, 455–59 (colour plates)

—— 'Prologues and Frontispieces in Prose Romance Manuscripts', in *Inscribing Knowledge in the Medieval Book: The Power of Paratexts*, ed. by Rosalind Brown-Grant, Patrizia Carmassi, Gisela Drossbach, Anne D. Hedeman, Victoria Turner, and Iolanda Ventura (Kalamazoo: Medieval Institute Publications, forthcoming 2019)

—— 'Le Rapt et le rapport texte/image dans les manuscrits du remaniement bourguignon de *La Fille du Comte de Pontieu*', in *Rapts: Réalités et imaginaire du Moyen âge aux Lumières*, ed. by Gabriele Vickermann-Ribémont and Myriam White-Le Goff (Paris: Classiques Garnier, 2014), pp. 49–70

BULLIET, RICHARD W., *Conversion to Islam in the Medieval Period: An Essay in Quantitative Reasoning* (Cambridge, MA: Harvard University Press, 1979)

BULLOUGH, VERN L., and BONNIE BULLOUGH, 'Cross Dressing and Social Status in the Middle Ages', in *Cross Dressing, Sex, and Gender* (Philadelphia: University of Pennsylvania Press, 1993), pp. 45–73

BURNETT, CHARLES, *Arabic into Latin in the Middle Ages: The Translators and their Intellectual and Social Context* (Farnham: Ashgate, 2009)

—— 'Arabic into Latin: The Reception of Arabic Philosophy into Western Europe', in *The Cambridge Companion to Arabic Philosophy*, ed. by Peter Adamson and Richard C. Taylor (Cambridge: Cambridge University Press, 2005), pp. 370–405

—— *The Introduction of Arabic Learning into England* (London: British Library, 1997)

BURNS, E. JANE, *Sea of Silk: A Textile Geography of Women's Work in Medieval French Literature* (Philadelphia: University of Pennsylvania Press, 2009)

BURNS, ROBERT I., 'Renegades, Adventurers, and Sharp Businessmen: The Thirteenth-Century Spaniard in the Cause of Islam', *The Catholic Historical Review*, 58 (1972), 341–66

BUSBY, KEITH, *Codex and Context: Reading Old French Verse Narrative in Manuscript*, 2 vols (Amsterdam: Rodopi, 2002)

BUTLER, JUDITH, *Bodies That Matter: On the Discursive Limits of "Sex"* (London: Routledge, 2011. First published New York: 1993)
—— *Excitable Speech: A Politics of the Performative* (New York: Routledge, 1997)
—— *Gender Trouble: Feminism and the Subversion of Identity*, 2nd edn (New York: Routledge, 1990; repr.2008; Preface 1999)
—— 'Performative Acts and Gender Constitution: An Essay in Phenomenology and Feminist Theory', in *Performing Feminisms: Feminist Critical Theory and Theatre*, ed. by Sue-Ellen Case (Baltimore: Johns Hopkins University Press, 1990), pp. 270–82
—— *The Psychic Life of Power: Theories in Subjection* (Stanford, CA: Stanford University Press, 1997)
BUTTERFIELD, ARDIS, 'Introduction. Gautier de Coinci, *Miracles de Nostre Dame*: Texts and Manuscripts', in *Gautier de Coinci: Miracles, Music, and Manuscripts*, ed. by Kathy M. Krause and Alison Stones, Medieval Texts and Cultures of Northern Europe, 13 (Turnhout: Brepols, 2006), pp. 1–20
BYNUM, CAROLINE WALKER, *Holy Feast, Holy Fast: The Religious Significance of Food to Medieval Women* (Berkeley: University of California Press, 1987)
BYRNE, BRIDGET, *White Lives: The Interplay of "Race", Class and Gender in Everyday Life* (London: Routledge, 2006)
CAHN, WALTER B., 'The "Portrait" of Muhammad in the Toledan Collection', in *Reading Medieval Images: the Art Historian and the Object*, ed. by Elizabeth Sears and Thelma K. Thomas (Ann Arbor: University of Michigan Press, 2002), pp. 51–60
CAMBIER, GUY, 'Embricon de Mayence (1010? –1077) est-il l'auteur de la *Vita Mahumeti*?', *Latomus*, 16 (1957), 468–79
CAMILLE, MICHAEL, *The Gothic Idol: Ideology and Image-making in Medieval Art* (Cambridge: Cambridge University Press, 1989)
CASPARI, RACHEL, 'Deconstructing Race: Racial Thinking, Geographic Variation, and Implications for Biological Anthropology', in *A Companion to Biological Anthropology*, ed. by Clark Spencer Larsen (Oxford: Blackwell, 2010), pp. 104–23
CHASE, CAROL, 'La Conversion des païennes dans l'*Estoire del Saint Graal*', in *Arthurian Romance and Gender: Selected Proceedings of the XVIIth International Arthurian Congress* [Masculin/Féminin dans le roman arthurien médiéval; Geschlechterrollen im mittelalterlichen Artusroman], ed. by Friedrich Wolfzettel, Internationale Forschungen zur allgemeinen und vergleichenden Literaturwissenschaft, 10 (Amsterdam: Rodopi, 1995), pp. 251–64
—— 'The Gateway to the Lancelot-Grail Cycle: *L'Estoire del Saint Graal*', in *A Companion to the Lancelot-Grail Cycle*, ed. by Carol Dover, Arthurian Studies, 54 (Cambridge: Brewer, 2003), pp. 65–74
—— 'Des Sarrasins à Camaalot', *Cahiers de recherches médiévales et humanistes*, 5 (1998) <http://dx.doi.org/10.4000/crm.1372>
CLARK, ROBERT L.A., 'Gautier's Wordplay as Devotional Ecstasy', in *Gautier de Coinci: Miracles, Music, and Manuscripts*, ed. by Kathy M. Krause and Alison Stones, Medieval Texts and Cultures of Northern Europe, 13 (Turnhout: Brepols, 2006), pp. 113–26
—— AND CLAIRE SPONSLER, 'Othered Bodies: Racial Cross-Dressing in the *Mistere de la Sainte Hostie* and the Croxton *Play of the Sacrament*', *JMEMS*, 29 (1999), 61–87
—— AND —— 'Queer Play: The Cultural Work of Crossdressing in Medieval Drama', *New Literary History*, 28 (1997), 319–44 <http://www.jstor.org/stable/20057418> [accessed 16 November 2018]
COHEN, JEFFREY J., *Medieval Identity Machines*, Medieval Cultures, 35 (Minneapolis: University of Minnesota Press, 2003)
—— 'On Saracen Enjoyment', in *Medieval Identity Machines*, Medieval Cultures, 35 (Minneapolis: University of Minnesota Press, 2003), pp. 188–222

——— and KARL STEEL, 'Race, Travel, Time, Heritage', *postmedieval*, 6 (2015), 98–110 <https://doi.org/10.1057/pmed.2014.39>

COHEN, JEREMY, *Living Letters of the Law: Ideas of the Jew in Medieval Christianity* (Berkeley: University of California Press, 1999)

COHEN, MEREDITH, and JUSTINE FIRNHABER-BAKER, eds, *Difference and Identity in Francia and Medieval Europe* (Farnham: Ashgate, 2010)

COLLOMP, DENIS, 'L'Enfant chrétien élevé chez les Sarrasins', in *L'Epopée Romane: Actes du XVe Congrès international Rencesvals, Poitiers, 21–27 août 2000*, ed. by Gabriel Bianciotto and Claudio Galderisi, 2 vols (Poitiers: Université de Poitiers. Centre d'Études supérieures de civilisation médiévale, 2002), II, pp. 655–72

COMFORT, WILLIAM WISTAR, 'The Literary Rôle of the Saracens in the French Epic', *PMLA*, 55 (1940), 628–59 <http://www.jstor.org/stable/458731> [accessed 6 December 2018]

CONNOCHIE-BOURGNE, CHANTAL, '"Nature" et "clergie" dans l'œuvre de vulgarisation scientifique de Gossuin de Metz (Image du Monde, 1245)', in *Comprendre et maîtriser la nature au moyen âge: Mélanges d'histoire des sciences offerts à Guy Beaujouan*, ed. by Danielle Jacquart (Geneva: Droz, 1994), pp. 9–29

CONSTABLE, OLIVIA REMIE, *Trade and Traders in Muslim Spain: The Commercial Realignment of the Iberian Peninsula, 900–1500* (Cambridge: Cambridge University Press, 1994)

COOK, ROBERT F., and LARRY S. CRIST, *Le Deuxième Cycle de la Croisade: Deux études sur son développement: Les textes en vers* (Geneva: Droz, 1972)

COPELAND, RITA, *Rhetoric, Hermeneutics, and Translation in the Middle Ages: Academic Traditions and Vernacular Texts* (Cambridge: Cambridge University Press, 1991)

CUTLER, ANTHONY, 'Everywhere and Nowhere: The Invisible Muslim and Christian Self-Fashioning in the Culture of Outremer', in *France and the Holy Land: Frankish Culture at the End of the Crusades*, ed. by Daniel H. Weiss and Lisa Mahoney (Baltimore: Johns Hopkins Press, 2004), pp. 253–82

CZARNOWUS, ANNA, 'Muhammad in Hell, or Dante and William Langland on the Prophet's Afterlife', in *Thise Stories Beren Witnesse: The Landscape of the Afterlife in Medieval and Post-medieval Imagination*, ed. by Liliana Sikorska, Medieval English Mirror, 7 (Frankfurt: Peter Lang, 2010), pp. 31–42

DAHAN, GILBERT, 'Les Juifs dans les miracles de Gautier de Coincy', *Archives juives*, 16 (1980), 41–49 and 59–68

DANIEL, NORMAN, *Heroes and Saracens: An Interpretation of the Chansons de Geste* (Edinburgh: Edinburgh University Press, 1984)

DAVIDS, M. FAKHRY, *Internal Racism: A Psychoanalytic Approach to Race and Difference* (London: Palgrave Macmillan, 2011)

DAVIS, ISABEL, 'Cutaneous Time in the Late Medieval Literary Imagination', in *Reading Skin in Medieval Literature and Culture*, ed. by Katie L. Walter (New York: Palgrave, 2013), pp. 99–119

DERRIDA, JACQUES, *Specters of Marx: the State of the Debt, the Work of Mourning and the New International*, trans. by Peggy Kamuf (London: Routledge, 1994; repr. 2006)

DE WEEVER, JACQUELINE, 'Nicolette's *Blackness*: Lost in Translation', *Romance Notes*, 34 (1994), 317–25

——— *Sheba's Daughters: Whitening and Demonizing the Saracen Woman in Medieval French Epic* (New York: Garland, 1998)

DI CESARE, MICHELINA, *The Pseudo-Historical Image of the Prophet Muhammad in Medieval Latin Literature: A Repertory*, Studien zur Geschichte und Kultur des islamischen Orients, 26 (Berlin: De Gruyter, 2012)

DMF: Dictionnaire du Moyen Français, version 2015 (DMF 2015), ATILF–CNRS & Université de Lorraine, <http://www.atilf.fr/dmf/> [accessed 4 December 2018]

DOLLIMORE, JONATHAN, *Sexual Dissidence: Augustine to Wilde, Freud to Foucault* (Oxford: Oxford University Press, 1991)
DUCROT-GRANDERYE, ARLETTE P., *Études sur les Miracles Nostre Dame de Gautier de Coinci: Description et classement sommaire des manuscrits, notice biographique, édition des miracles*, Annales academiae scientiarum fennicae, Series B, 25 (Helsinki: Impr. de la Société de Littérature Finnoise, 1932)
DUYS, KATHRYN A., 'Medieval Literary Performance: Gautier de Coinci's Guide for the Perplexed', in *Acts and Texts: Performance and Ritual in the Middle Ages and the Renaissance*, ed. by Laurie Postlewaite and Wim Hüsken (Amsterdam: Rodopi, 2007), pp. 183–216
—— 'Performing Vernacular Song in Monastic Culture: The *lectio divina* in Gautier de Coinci's *Miracles de Nostre Dame*', in *Cultural Performances in Medieval France: Essays in Honor of Nancy Freeman Regalado*, ed. by Eglal Doss-Quinby, Roberta L. Krueger, and E. Jane Burns, Gallica, 5 (Cambridge: Brewer, 2007), pp. 123–34
FALK, AVNER, *Franks and Saracens: Reality and Fantasy in the Crusades* (London: Karnac, 2010)
FANON, FRANTZ, *Peau noire, masques blancs* (Paris: Seuil, 1995. First published 1952)
FENSTER, THELMA S., 'The Family Romance of Aye d'Avignon', *Romance Quarterly*, 33 (1986), 11–22
FOEHR-JANSSENS, YASMINA, 'Histoire poétique du péché: de quelques figures littéraires de la faute dans les *Miracles de Nostre Dame* de Gautier de Coinci', in *Gautier de Coinci: Miracles, Music, and Manuscripts*, ed. by Kathy M. Krause and Alison Stones, Medieval Texts and Cultures of Northern Europe, 13 (Turnhout: Brepols, 2006), pp. 215–26
FUCHS, BARBARA, *Passing for Spain: Cervantes and the Fictions of Identity* (Chicago: University of Illinois Press, 2003)
GATENS, MOIRA, *Imaginary Bodies: Ethics, Power and Corporeality* (London: Routledge, 1996)
GAULLIER-BOUGASSAS, CATHERINE, 'Alexandre le Grand et la conquête de l'Ouest dans les *romans d'Alexandre* du XIIe siècle, leurs mises en prose au XVe siècle et le *Perceforest* (1ère partie)', *Romania*, 118 (2000), 83–104 <https://doi.org/10.3406/roma.2000.1521>
—— 'Jean Wauquelin et Vasque de Lucène: le "roman familial" d'Alexandre et l'écriture de l'histoire au XVe siècle', *Cahiers de recherches médiévales et humanistes*, 5 (1998), <http://dx.doi.org/10.4000/crm.1442>
—— *La Tentation de l'Orient dans le roman médiéval: Sur l'imaginaire médiéval de l'Autre* (Paris: Champion, 2003)
GILBERT, JANE, 'The Practice of Gender in *Aucassin et Nicolette*', *Forum for Modern Language Studies*, 33 (1997), 217–28
GINSBERG, ELAINE K., ed., *Passing and the Fictions of Identity* (Durham, NC: Duke University Press, 1996)
GREGG, JOAN YOUNG, *Devils, Women and Jews: Reflections of the Other in Medieval Sermon Stories* (Albany: State University of New York Press, 1997)
GREIMAS, ALGIRDAS JULIEN, *Dictionnaire de l'ancien français*, 3rd edn (Paris: Larousse, 2004)
GRIFFIN, MIRANDA, *The Object and the Cause in the Vulgate Cycle* (London: Legenda/Modern Humanities Research Association; Leeds: Maney Publishing, 2005)
GRINBERG, ANA, 'Robes, Turbans, and Beards: "Ethnic Passing" in *Decameron* 10.9', in *Medieval Clothing and Textiles*, 13, ed. by Robin Netherton and Gale R. Owen-Crocker (Woodbridge: Boydell, 2017), pp. 67–81
GROSSEL, MARIE-GENEVIÈVE, 'Le Monde d'ici-bas, un royaume de violence: Le *Siècle* dans les *Miracles Nostre Dame* de Gautier de Conci', in *La Violence dans le monde médiéval* (Aix-en-Provence: Centre Universitaire d'Études et de Recherches Médiévales d'Aix, 1994), pp. 267–81
GUREVICH, A. J., *Categories of Medieval Culture*, trans. by G.L. Campbell (London: Routledge, Kegan & Paul, 1985)

HAGGH, BARBARA, 'From Auxerre to Soissons: The Earliest History of the Responsory *Gaude, Maria Virgo* in Gautier de Coinci's *Miracles de Nostre Dame*', in *Gautier de Coinci: Miracles, Music, and Manuscripts*, ed. by Kathy M. Krause and Alison Stones, Medieval Texts and Cultures of Northern Europe, 13 (Turnhout: Brepols, 2006), pp. 167–96

HAHN, THOMAS, 'The Difference the Middle Ages Makes: Color and Race before the Modern World', in 'Race and Ethnicity in the Middle Ages', ed. by Thomas Hahn, Special Issue, *JMEMS*, 31 (2001), 1–38

——ed., 'Race and Ethnicity in the Middle Ages', Special Issue, *JMEMS*, 31 (2001)

HALÁSZ, KATALIN, 'The Representation of Time and its Models in the Prose Romance', in *Text and Intertext in Medieval Arthurian Literature*, ed. by Norris J. Lacy, Garland Reference Library of the Humanities, 1997 (New York: Garland, 1996), pp. 175–86

HALBERSTAM, JUDITH, 'Telling Tales: Brandon Teena, Billy Tipton, and Transgender Biography', in *Passing: Identity and Interpretation in Sexuality, Race, and Religion*, ed. by María Carla Sánchez and Linda Schlossberg (New York: New York University Press, 2001), pp. 13–37

HANAWALT, BARBARA A., *The Ties That Bound: Peasant Families in Medieval England* (Oxford: Oxford University Press, 1986)

HEINTZE, MICHAEL, *König, Held und Sippe: Untersuchungen zur Chanson de geste des 13. und 14. Jahrhunderts und ihrer Zyklenbildung*, Studia Romanica, 76 (Heidelberg: Winter, 1991)

HENG, GERALDINE, *Empire of Magic: Medieval Romance and the Politics of Cultural Fantasy* (New York: Columbia University Press, 2003)

—— *The Invention of Race in the European Middle Ages* (Cambridge: Cambridge University Press, 2018)

—— 'The Invention of Race in the European Middle Ages I: Race Studies, Modernity, and the Middle Ages', *Literature Compass*, 8(5) (2011), 315–31 <https://doi.org/10.1111/j.1741-4113.2011.00790.x>

—— 'The Invention of Race in the European Middle Ages II: Locations of Medieval Race', *Literature Compass*, 8(5) (2011), 332–50 <https://doi.org/10.1111/j.1741-4113.2011.00795.x>

HODGSON, NATASHA R., 'The Role of Kerbogha's Mother in the *Gesta Francorum* and Selected Chronicles of the First Crusade', in *Gendering the Crusades*, ed. by Susan B. Edgington and Sarah Lambert (Cardiff: University of Wales Press, 2001), pp. 163–76

HOTCHKISS, VALERIE R., *Clothes Make the Man: Female Cross Dressing in Medieval Europe*, Garland Reference Library of the Humanities, 1991 (New York: Garland, 2000. First published 1996)

HSY, JONATHAN, and JULIE ORLEMANSKI, 'Race and Medieval Studies: A Partial Bibliography', *postmedieval*, 8 (2017), 500–31 <https://doi.org/10.1057/s41280-017-0072-0>

HUMMER, HANS, *Visions of Kinship in Medieval Europe* (Oxford: Oxford University Press, 2018)

HUNT, TONY, *Miraculous Rhymes: The Writing of Gautier de Coinci*, Gallica, 8 (Cambridge: Brewer, 2007)

HUNTLEY, ROBERT, *Saracens: 125 Years of Rugby* (London: Saracens Ltd, 2001)

HYATTE, REGINALD, 'Muhammad's Prophethood in Two Old French Narratives: Divergent Traditions and Converging Ends', *Allegorica*, 18 (1997), 3–19

INGRAM, PENELOPE, *The Signifying Body: Toward an Ethics of Sexual and Racial Difference* (Albany: State University of New York Press, 2008)

IOGNA-PRAT, DOMINIQUE, *Order and Exclusion: Cluny and Christendom Face Heresy, Judaism, and Islam, 1000–1150*, trans. by Graham Robert Edwards (Ithaca, NY: Cornell University Press, 2002)

JORDAN, WILLIAM CHESTER, 'Why "Race"?', in 'Race and Ethnicity in the Middle Ages', ed. by Thomas Hahn, Special Issue, *JMEMS*, 31 (2001), 165–74

JUBB, MARGARET, *The Legend of Saladin in Western Literature and Historiography* (Lewiston: Edwin Mellen Press, 2000)
KANGAS, SINI, 'Inimicus Dei et sanctae Christianitatis? Saracens and their Prophet in Twelfth-Century Crusade Propaganda and Western Travesties of Muhammad's Life', in *The Crusades and the Near East*, ed. by Conor Kostick (London: Routledge, 2011), pp. 131–60. Kindle edition
KAY, SARAH, *Chansons de Geste in the Age of Romance: Political Fictions* (Oxford: Clarendon Press, 1995)
—— 'Singularity and Spectrality: Desire and Death in *Girart de Roussillon*', *Olifant* 22.1–4 (Spring 1998–Fall 2003), 11–38
KELL, LEANA, 'History of Saracens', *Centurion Rugby/Primo Play Ltd*, <https://www.centurion-rugby.com/blogs/rugby/93310785-history-of-saracens> [accessed 2 December 2018]
KIBLER, WILLIAM W., and GROVER A. ZINN, eds, *Medieval France: An Encyclopedia*, Garland Reference Library of the Humanities, 932 (New York: Garland, 1995)
KINOSHITA, SHARON, 'Beyond Philology: Cross-Cultural Engagement in Literary History and Beyond', in *A Sea of Languages: Rethinking the Arabic Role in Medieval Literary History*, ed. by Suzanne Conklin Akbari and Karla Mallette (Toronto: University of Toronto Press, 2013), pp. 25–42
—— *Medieval Boundaries: Rethinking Difference in Old French Literature* (Philadelphia: University of Pennsylvania Press, 2006)
—— and PEGGY MCCRACKEN, *Marie de France: A Critical Companion*, Gallica, 24 (Cambridge: Brewer, 2012)
KRAUSE, KATHY M., and ALISON STONES, eds, *Gautier de Coinci: Miracles, Music, and Manuscripts*, Medieval Texts and Cultures of Northern Europe, 13 (Turnhout: Brepols, 2006)
KRUEGER, ROBERTA '"Nouvelles choses": Social Instability and the Problem of Fashion in the *Livre du Chevalier de la Tour Landry*, the *Ménagier de Paris*, and Christine de Pizan's *Livre des Trois Vertus*', in *Medieval Conduct*, ed. by Kathleen Ashley and Robert L. A. Clark, Medieval Cultures, 29 (Minneapolis: University of Minnesota Press, 2001)
KRUGER, STEVEN F., 'Conversion and Medieval Sexual, Religious and Racial Categories', in *Constructing Medieval Sexuality*, ed. by Karma Lochrie, Peggy McCracken, and James A. Schultz, Medieval Cultures, 11 (Minneapolis: University of Minnesota Press, 1997), pp. 158–79
—— *The Spectral Jew: Conversion and Embodiment in Medieval Europe* (Minneapolis: University of Minnesota Press, 2006)
KUBISKI, JOYCE, 'Orientalizing Costume in Early Fifteenth-Century French Manuscript Painting (Cité des Dames Master, Limbourg Brothers, Boucicault Master, and Bedford Master', *Gesta*, 40 (2001), 161–81
LACAN, JACQUES, 'Logical Time and the Assertion of Anticipated Certainty', in *Écrits: The First Complete Edition in English*, trans. by Bruce Fink with Héloïse Fink (New York: Norton, 2006), pp. 161–75
—— 'Le Temps logique et l'assertion de certitude anticipée. Un nouveau sophisme', in *Écrits* (Paris: Seuil, 1966), pp. 197–213
LACLAU, ERNESTO, 'The Time is out of Joint', *Diacritics*, 25.2 (1995), 85–96
LAGACHERIE, BERTRAND, 'Finale de la Coupe d'Europe: Huit choses à savoir sur les Saracens', *L'Équipe*, 12 May 2017 <https://www.lequipe.fr/Rugby/Actualites/Sept-choses-a-savoir-sur-les-saracens/551375> [accessed 2 December 2018]
LANDRY, BART, ed., *Race, Gender, and Class: Theory and Methods of Analysis* (Abingdon: Routledge, 2016 [Pearson, 2007])

Lapostolle, Christine, 'Images et apparitions: illustrations des "Miracles de Nostre Dame"', *Médiévales*, 2 (1982), 47–66 <http://dx.doi.org/10.3406/medi.1982.892>

Le Goff, Jacques, *Intellectuals in the Middle Ages*, trans. by Teresa Lavender Fagan (Cambridge, MA: Blackwell, 1993)

Lepage, Yvan G., 'Un recueil français de la fin du XIIe siècle (Paris, Bibliothèque Nationale, fr.1553)', *Scriptorium*, 29 (1975), 23–46

L'Estrange, Elizabeth, and Alison More, eds, *Representing Medieval Genders and Sexualities in Europe: Construction, Transformation, and Subversion, 600–1530* (Farnham: Ashgate, 2011)

Linder, Amnon, '*Deus Venerunt Gentes*: Psalm: 78 (79) in the Liturgical Commemoration of the Destruction of Latin Jerusalem', in *Medieval Studies in Honor of Avrom Saltman*, ed. by Bat-Sheva Albert, Yvonne Friedman, and Simon Schwarzfuchs, Bar-Ilan Studies in History, 4 (Ramat-Gan, Israel: Bar-Ilan University Press, 1995), pp. 145–71

Lochrie, Karma, Peggy McCracken, and James A. Schultz, eds, *Constructing Medieval Sexuality* (Minneapolis: University of Minnesota Press, 1997)

Lord, Carla, 'Thomas de Maubeuge and the Miracles of the Virgin', *Source: Notes in the History of Art*, 8/9, no. 4/1 (Summer/Fall 1989), 2–4 <http://www.jstor.org/stable/23202690> [accessed 22 November 2018]

Lot, Ferdinand, *Étude sur le Lancelot en prose*, Bibliothèque de l'École des hautes études, 226 (Paris: Champion, 1918)

Low, Gail Ching-Liang, *White Skins/Black Masks: Representation and Colonialism* (London: Routledge, 1996)

Loxley, James, *Performativity* (London: Routledge, 2007)

Maddox, Donald, 'Domesticating Diversity: Female Founders in Medieval Genealogical Literature and *La Fille du comte de Pontieu*', in *The Court and Cultural Diversity: Selected Papers from the Eighth Triennial Congress of the International Courtly Literature Society, the Queen's University of Belfast, 26 July–1 August 1995*, ed. by Evelyn Mullally and John Thompson (Woodbridge: Brewer, 1997), pp. 97–107

Maurach, Gregor, 'Daniel von Morley, "Philosophia"', *Mittellateinishes Jahrbuch*, 14 (1979), 204–55

McCracken, Peggy, 'The Boy Who Was A Girl: Reading Gender in the *Roman de Silence*', *Romanic Review*, 85 (1994), 517–36

—— *In the Skin of a Beast: Sovereignty and Animality in Medieval France* (Chicago: University of Chicago Press, 2017)

—— 'Miracles, Mimesis and the Efficacy of Images', *Yale French Studies*, 110 (2006), 47–57 <http://www.jstor.org/stable/20060039> [accessed 22 November 2018]

—— *The Romance of Adultery: Queenship and Sexual Transgression in Old French Literature* (Philadelphia: University of Pennsylvania Press, 1998)

McInerney, Maud Burnett, *Eloquent Virgins from Thecla to Joan of Arc* (New York: Palgrave Macmillan, 2003)

Menocal, Maria Rosa, 'Signs of the Times: Self, Other, and History in *Aucassin et Nicolette*', *Romanic Review*, 80 (1989), 497–511

Mills, Robert, 'Invisible Translation, Language Difference and the Scandal of Becket's Mother', in *Rethinking Medieval Translation: Ethics, Politics, Theory*, ed. by Emma Campbell and Robert Mills (Cambridge: Brewer, 2012), pp. 125–46

Moore, Megan, *Exchanges in Exoticism: Cross-Cultural Marriage and the Making of the Mediterranean in Old French Romance* (Toronto: University of Toronto Press, 2014)

Moore, R. I., *The Formation of a Persecuting Society: Authority and Deviance in Western Europe, 950–1250*, 2nd edn (Oxford: Blackwell, 2007)

Morrison, Karl F., *Understanding Conversion* (Charlottesville: University Press of Virginia, 1992)

MUIR, LYNETTE R., *Literature and Society in Medieval France: The Mirror and the Image 1100–1500* (London: Macmillan, 1985)
MUSSAFIA, ADOLFO, *Uber die von Gautier de Coincy benützten Quellen* (Vienna: Tempsky, 1894)
NEWTON, ESTHER, *Mother Camp: Female Impersonators in America* (Chicago: University of Chicago Press, 1979)
NICHOLS, STEPHEN G., and SIEGFRIED WENZEL, eds, *The Whole Book: Cultural Perspectives on the Medieval Miscellany* (Ann Arbor: University of Michigan Press, 1996)
PAGES, MERIEM, 'Medieval Roots of the Modern Image of Islam: Fact and Fiction', in *Bridging the Medieval-Modern Divide: Medieval Themes in the World of the Reformation*, ed. by James Muldoon (Farnham: Ashgate, 2013), pp. 23–45
PELLEGRINI, ANN, *Performance Anxieties: Staging Psychoanalysis, Staging Race* (New York: Routledge, 1997)
PERRET, MICHÈLE, 'Travesties et transsexuelles: Yde, Silence, Grisandole, Blanchandine', *Romance Notes*, 25 (1985), 328–40
PETERSEN, NILS HOLGER, 'Introduction', in *The Cultural Heritage of Medieval Rituals: Genre and Ritual*, ed. by Eyolf Østrem, Mette Birkedal Bruun, Nils Holger Petersen, and Jens Fleischer, Special Issue, *Transfiguration* (Copenhagen: Museum Tusculanum Press, University of Copenhagen, 2005)
PICHERIT, JEAN-LOUIS, 'Les Sarrasins dans Tristan de Nanteuil', in *Au carrefour des routes d'Europe: la chanson de geste: Xe Congrès international de la Société Rencesvals pour l'étude des épopées romanes, Strasbourg, 1985*, Sénéfiance, 20–21 (Aix-en-Provence: Publications du CUERMA, Université de Provence, 1987), pp. 941–57
POSTAN, MICHAEL, 'The Trade of Medieval Europe: the North', in *Trade and Industry in the Middle Ages*, ed. by M. M. Postan and Edward Miller, *The Cambridge Economic History of Europe*, 2nd edn, 8 vols (Cambridge: Cambridge University Press, 1987), II, pp. 168–306
PROSSER, JAY, *Second Skins: The Body Narratives of Transsexuality* (New York: Columbia University Press, 1998)
PUAR, JASBIR K., *Terrorist Assemblages: Homonationalism in Queer Times* (Durham, NC: Duke University Press, 2007)
RABIN, JESSICA, *Surviving the Crossing: (Im)migration, Ethnicity, and Gender in Willa Cather, Gertrude Stein, and Nella Larsen* (New York: Routledge, 2004)
RAMEY, LYNN TARTE, *Black Legacies: Race and the European Middle Ages* (Gainesville, FL: University Press of Florida, 2014)
——— *Christian, Saracen, and Genre in Medieval French Literature*, Studies in Medieval History and Culture, 3 (New York: Routledge, 2001)
——— 'Medieval Miscegenation: Hybridity and the Anxiety of Inheritance', in *Contextualizing the Muslim Other in Medieval Christian Discourse*, ed. by Jerold C. Frakes (New York: Palgrave Macmillan, 2011), pp. 1–19
RICHARDSON, H. G., *The English Jewry under Angevin Kings* (London: Methuen, 1960)
RIDDER-SYMOENS, HILDE DE, ed., *Universities in the Middle Ages*, vol. 1 of *A History of the University in Europe*, ed. by Walter Rüegg (Cambridge: Cambridge University Press, 1992)
ROTTENBERG, CATHERINE, ' "Passing": Race, Identification, and Desire', *Criticism*, 45 (2003), 435–52
——— *Performing Americanness: Race, Class and Gender in Modern African-American and Jewish-American Literature* (Hanover, NH: Dartmouth College; University Press of New England, 2008)
ROUSE, RICHARD H., and MARY A. ROUSE, *Manuscripts and their Makers: Commercial Book Producers in Medieval Paris, 1200–1500*, 2 vols (London: Miller, 2000)
RUBIN, MIRI, *Gentile Tales: The Narrative Assault on Late Medieval Jews* (Philadelphia: University of Pennsylvania Press, 2004. First published New Haven, CT: Yale University Press, 1999)

RUGGLES, D. FAIRCHILD, 'Mothers of a Hybrid Dynasty: Race, Genealogy, and Acculturation in al-Andalus', *Journal of Medieval and Early Modern Studies*, 34 (2004), 65–94

RUSSAKOFF, ANNA, 'Imagining the Miraculous: *Les Miracles de Notre Dame*, Paris, BnF, n.acq.fr. 24541' (PhD Dissertation, New York University, 2006)

RUSSELL, JEFFREY BURTON, *Lucifer: The Devil in the Middle Ages* (Ithaca, NY: Cornell University Press, 1984)

SÁNCHEZ, MARÍA CARLA, and LINDA SCHLOSSBERG, eds, *Passing: Identity and Interpretation in Sexuality, Race, and Religion* (New York: New York University Press, 2001)

SANSY, DANIÈLE, 'Signe distinctif et judéité dans l'image', *Micrologus*, 15 (2007), 87–105

SCANLON, LARRY, *Narrative, Authority, and Power: The Medieval Exemplum and the Chaucerian Tradition* (Cambridge: Cambridge University Press, 1994)

SCHEIN, SYLVIA, 'Women in Medieval Colonial Society: The Latin Kingdom of Jerusalem in the Twelfth Century', in *Gendering the Crusades*, ed. by Susan B. Edgington and Sarah Lambert (Cardiff: University of Wales Press, 2001), pp. 140–53

SELÁF, LEVENTE, *Chanter plus haut: La chanson religieuse vernaculaire au Moyen Âge (essai de contextualisation)* (Paris: Champion, 2008)

SESHADRI-CROOKS, KALPANA, *Desiring Whiteness: A Lacanian Analysis of Race* (London: Routledge, 2000)

SHERWOOD, JESSIE, 'Notice n°30326: Le statut légal des minorités religieuses dans l'espace euro-méditerranéen (V^e–XVe siècle)', RELMIN project, Telma Web édition, IRHT, Institut de Recherche et d'Histoire des Textes–Orléans <http://www.cn-telma.fr/relmin/extrait30326/> [accessed 5 December 2018]

SHUTTERS, LYNN, 'Christian Love or Pagan Transgression? Marriage and Conversion in Floire et Blancheflor', in *Discourses on Love, Marriage and Transgression in Medieval and Early Modern Literature*, ed. by Albrecht Classen (Tempe: Arizona Centre for Medieval and Renaissance Studies, 2004), pp. 85–108

SIEG, KATRIN, *Ethnic Drag: Performing Race Nation, Sexuality in West Germany* (Ann Arbor: University of Michigan Press, 2002)

SINCLAIR, FINN E., *Milk & Blood: Gender and Genealogy in the 'Chanson de Geste'* (Oxford: Peter Lang, 2003)

SPEED, DIANNE, 'Middle English Romance and the *Gesta Romanorum*', in *Tradition and Transformation in Medieval Romance*, ed. by Rosalind Field (Woodbridge: Brewer, 1999), pp. 45–70

SPEER, MARY B., 'Seven Sages of Rome', in *Medieval France: An Encyclopedia*, ed. by William W. Kibler and Grover A. Zinn, Garland Reference Library of the Humanities, 932 (New York: Garland, 1995), pp. 878–79

SPIEGEL, GABRIELLE M., 'Genealogy: Form and Function in Medieval Historical Narrative', *History and Theory*, 22 (1983), 43–53 <http://www.jstor.org/stable/2505235> [accessed 28 November 2018]

STAHULJAK, ZRINKA, *Bloodless Genealogies of the French Middle Ages: Translatio, Kinship, and Metaphor* (Gainesville, FL: University Press of Florida, 2005)

—— *Pornographic Archaeology: Medicine, Medievalism, and the Invention of the French Nation* (Philadelphia: University of Pennsylvania Press, 2013)

—— VIRGINIE GREENE, SARAH KAY, SHARON KINOSHITA, and PEGGY MCCRACKEN, *Thinking through Chrétien de Troyes*, Gallica, 19 (Cambridge: Brewer, 2011)

STONES, ALISON, 'Appendix IV: Illustrated *Miracles de Nostre Dame* Manuscripts Listed by Stylistic Attribution and Attributable Manuscripts Whose *MND* Selection is Unillustrated', in *Gautier de Coinci: Miracles, Music, and Manuscripts*, ed. by Kathy M. Krause and Alison Stones, Medieval Texts and Cultures of Northern Europe, 13 (Turnhout: Brepols, 2006), pp. 373–97

―― 'Notes on the Artistic Context of Some Gautier de Coinci Manuscripts', in *Gautier de Coinci: Miracles, Music, and Manuscripts*, ed. by Kathy M. Krause and Alison Stones, Medieval Texts and Cultures of Northern Europe, 13 (Turnhout: Brepols, 2006), pp. 65–98
STRICKLAND, DEBRA HIGGS, *Saracens, Demons, & Jews: Making Monsters in Medieval Art* (Princeton: Princeton University Press, 2003)
SWANSON, R.N., *Religion and Devotion in Europe, c.1215–c.1515* (Cambridge: Cambridge University Press, 1995)
SZKILNIK, MICHELLE, *L'Archipel du Graal: Étude de 'l'Estoire del Saint Graal'*, Publications romanes et françaises, 196 (Geneva: Droz, 1991)
TEMKIN, OWSEI, *The Falling Sickness: A History of Epilepsy from the Greeks to the Beginnings of Modern Neurology*, 2nd edn, rev. (Baltimore: Johns Hopkins Press, 1971)
TOLAN, JOHN VICTOR, 'Anti-Hagiography: Embrico of Mainz's *Vita Mahumeti*', *Journal of Medieval History*, 22 (1996), 25–41
―― *Saracens: Islam in the European Imagination* (New York: Columbia University Press, 2002)
TROTTER, D. A., *Medieval French Literature and the Crusades (1100–1300)* (Geneva: Droz, 1987)
TURNER, VICTOR, *The Anthropology of Performance*, Performance Studies, 4 (New York: PAJ Publications, 1987)
UEBEL, MICHAEL, *Ecstatic Transformation: On the Uses of Alterity in the Middle Ages* (New York: Palgrave Macmillan, 2005)
WALTER, KATIE L., 'The Form of the Formless: Medieval Taxonomies of Skin, Flesh, and the Human', in *Reading Skin in Medieval Literature and Culture*, ed. by Katie L. Walter (New York: Palgrave Macmillan, 2013), pp. 119–39
WARNER, MARINA, *Alone of All Her Sex: the Myth and Cult of the Virgin Mary* (London: Picador, 1985; repr. with new afterthoughts 1990)
WHITAKER, CORD J., ed., 'Making Race Matter in the Middle Ages', Special Issue, *postmedieval*, 6(1) (2015)
WHITMAN, JON, 'Transfers of Empire, Movements of Mind: Holy Sepulchre and Holy Grail', *MLN*, 123 (2008), 895–923 <http://doi.org/10.1353/mln.0.0054>
WILLIAMS, ALISON, *Tricksters and Pranksters: Roguery in French and German Literature of the Middle Ages and the Renaissance*, Internationale Forschungen zur allgemeinen und vergleichenden Literaturwissenschaft, 49 (Amsterdam: Rodopi, 2000)
WOGAN-BROWNE, JOCELYN, 'Bet...to...rede on holy seyntes lyves...': Romance and Hagiography Again', in *Readings in Medieval English Romance*, ed. by Carol M. Meale (Cambridge: Brewer, 1994), pp. 83–98
WOLFREYS, JULIAN, ed., *The Derrida Reader: Writing Performances* (Edinburgh: Edinburgh University Press, 1998)
WOODS, ELLEN ROSE, *Aye d'Avignon: A Study of Genre and Society*, Histoire des idées et critique littéraire, 172 (Geneva: Droz, 1978)

INDEX

Adam 38, 63
adultery 142–43, 162, 164 n. 24
Akbari, Suzanne Conklin 5, 7, 9–10, 57, 71, 77, 137, 146, 156, 188–89
Alexander the Great 3, 182
Alexandre du Pont 136–43, 148, 152–55, 161
Almeria 170, 172, 174–76
    Sultan of 169, 173–75, 177, 184, 191 n. 37 and n. 39
Althusser, Louis 15, 146–47
ancestry 2, 53–54, 57, 60, 62–63, 67, 70, 77–78, 170, 172, 181, 184–85
    see also genealogy
anti-Semitism 86
apostasy, apostates 112–13, 139, 147–48, 160, 169, 184
    see also conversion
apparitions 85–87, 91–92, 99, 103, 106–10, 112, 115, 117–19, 126, 128, 132 n. 57, 133 n. 94
    see also visions
appearance 5, 7, 10, 14, 16–18, 29–36, 42, 48, 50, 53, 65, 74, 107, 110, 115, 127, 156–57, 161, 172, 174–75, 182–83, 186, 188
appropriation 28, 34, 167–68, 171
    and drag 17
    of the Middle Ages 2, 11, 185
Arabic 4, 151, 159, 176
armour 114–15, 126, 174, 183
Arthur 55
Arthurian romance 56, 68
    time in 54–62, 68, 70, 77–80, 184–85
assimilation 40, 46, 167, 179
    and seeing 110, 114
Assumption, doctrine of the 110–11
Aucassin et Nicolette 3, 6, 51 n. 28
Austin, J.L. 14, 146
Aye d'Avignon, *see* Nanteuil Cycle

Babel, tower of 41, 143, 163
Babylon 35, 41, 72, 143, 181
    Sultan of 38–39
Baldwin of Bouillon 180, 191 n. 55
Baldwin of Flanders, Emperor of Constantinople 108
baptism 39, 49, 68, 75–76, 93–94, 97–100, 103–07, 117, 123, 127, 178
Bartlett, Robert 12–13
Basil, Saint 112–14
beards 33, 36, 38, 97, 101, 103, 114–15, 121, 144
Beaussart, François-Jérôme 108–09, 118

behaviour:
    behavioural conventions 17, 18, 20, 27, 29, 34–36, 41–42, 47–49, 54, 60, 90, 93, 107, 138, 162, 168, 172, 186, 189
    and emulation 38, 86, 88–89, 119, 128, 138, 187
    as erroneous 89, 92–93, 107, 138, 142, 153, 155
    see also devotion (acts of) *and* exemplarity
Belle Chétive 170, 181
Bernard of Clairvaux 90
Bertrand de Rais, pretendant Emperor of Constantinople 108
Bible, the 61, 70
Biernoff, Suzannah 110
bilingualism 41–42, 175
binaries 4, 16, 18–20, 27, 38, 72, 171–72, 175, 178, 183, 185, 189
biology:
    biological determinism 28, 38–39, 57–58, 171, 180, 183, 185
    and genealogy 2, 36–37, 42–44, 46, 47, 48, 49, 50, 53, 56, 64, 65, 68, 69, 78, 84, 178–82
    and identity 15, 16, 28, 29, 39, 46
    and race 2, 10, 12, 13, 77, 84–85, 90, 115, 126–27, 162, 167, 168, 171, 172, 184, 185–88
    see also bloodlines, the body, determinism, *and* identity
biopolitics 41
Black, Nancy 114
blackness 5, 16, 48
blindness 55, 119, 122–23, 148
Bloch, R. Howard 43, 59, 74, 79, 143
blood 2, 21–22, 42, 44, 50, 55–61, 63–66, 68–70, 77–78, 84, 87, 106, 113–14, 126, 161, 168, 170, 172, 179–84
    see also biology
bloodlines 2, 40–44, 46–47, 50, 54, 58, 60–61, 66, 68, 74, 76–77, 80, 157, 161–62, 179, 184, 188
Boccaccio, Giovanni:
    De Casibus Virorum Illustrium 144
    Decameron 10.9: 170
Bodel, Jean:
    Le Jeu de Saint Nicolas 3, 130 n. 23
body, the:
    and biological form, *see* biology
    as carnal/and carnality 69, 74, 91, 103, 110, 112, 183
    of Christ 91–92, 112, 128
    and the divine 39, 47, 56, 86, 91, 99, 112, 123, 125–26, 128, 135–36

and flesh 9, 30, 39, 44, 58, 66, 70, 80, 87, 91–92, 99, 103, 106, 110, 112, 118, 125, 126–28, 161, 167, 168, 172, 178, 179, 187
  as 'fleshless' 110, 133 n. 83
  and gender 14–17, 29–30, 36–41, 48–49, 54, 85–86, 186
  and gesture, *see* behaviour
  and healing 55, 120, 123–25
  instability of 9–10, 18
  maternal body 36–37
  as object 15–16, 106, 126, 127, 128, 161
  as 'transparent medium' 91, 103
  of the Virgin Mary, *see* Virgin Mary
  see also incarnation, skin, *and* transformation
Bramimonde 51 n. 45
Braude, Benjamin 61, 71
Britain 55, 57, 59, 65, 67, 70, 72, 78–80, 162, 182
  as a new Jerusalem 54, 57, 70
Brown-Grant, Rosalind 174
Bulliet, Richard W. 148
Bullough, Vern and Bonnie 40
Burns, Robert I. 148
Busby, Keith 151–52
Butler, Judith 14–20, 28–32, 35, 47–49, 60, 79, 84, 87, 146–47, 167–68
  and race 15–19, 35, 79
Byrne, Bridget 16, 18, 48–49, 168, 188

Cahn, Walter B. 144
Calabre, mother of the Turkish ruler Kerbogha 179–80, 191 n. 50
Camille, Michael 99
Caspari, Rachel 53
Catherine, Saint 158
Causality 22, 53, 54, 56–58, 60, 63, 67, 71, 80, 167–68, 178–79, 186
  see also time
Champagne 151
La Chanson de Roland 5, 23 n. 22, 34, 51 n. 45, 89
Charlemagne 4, 6, 33, 39, 48
Charles the Bold, Duke of Burgundy 182
Chase, Carol 67, 76
chivalry 3, 5–6, 46–47, 64, 85, 133 n. 98, 181
Chronica Prophetica 2, 67, 69–70
chronology, *see* time
citationality 16, 22, 32, 47, 54, 60, 187
Clark, Robert L. A. (and Claire Sponsler) 27–28, 34–35
class 3, 13, 28, 40, 49, 51 n. 22, 168, 170
cleanliness 73, 87–89, 93, 137
climatic theory (of race) 20, 53, 57, 71, 177
clothing 29–30, 36, 38, 39, 44, 45, 99, 109, 172, 182, 192 n. 62
  headwear 1, 97, 121–22, 144, 174, 183
  see also cross-dressing, disguise, drag, *and* passing
Cohen, Jeffrey Jerome 8–9, 11–12, 32, 42, 48, 189

community 30, 34, 45–48, 55, 57, 109, 112, 117, 136, 142, 146–47, 149, 151–52, 154–55
  formation of 138, 148, 153, 157–58, 161–63, 167, 168, 187
  religious or spiritual community 13, 21, 28, 74, 85–89, 106, 117, 118, 119, 122, 128–29, 161–63
  see also credulity, faith, *and* witnessing
concubinage 184
Connochie-Bourgne, Chantal 141
Constable, Olivia Remie 175
Constantinople 70, 85, 107–11, 116, 119
conversion 8, 20–21, 28, 31, 34, 44, 46, 47–49, 75, 83–86, 99, 120, 123, 138, 148, 158, 164 n. 18
  fantasies of 53, 78
  and genealogy 54, 59, 63, 67, 69, 73–74, 77
  to Islam, *see* apostasy
  as process 86, 90–92, 103, 106, 112, 114, 128, 129
  see also faith
corporeality, *see* the body
courtly love 17–18, 37, 48
credulity 136, 141–42, 149, 153, 155, 158, 160, 162
Critical Race Studies 10
cross-dressing 20, 22, 27–32, 34–35, 38–42, 46–49, 168, 170–71
  see also clothing, disguise, drag, *and* passing
crusade:
  Fifth Crusade 144
  First Crusade 92, 179–80
  Fourth Crusade 70
  Seventh Crusade 140
  Third Crusade 180
crusaders, crusading 1, 4, 37–38, 54, 67, 72, 136–37, 140, 143–44, 148, 178, 185
cultural fantasy 183
Cutler, Anthony 1

Damascus 119–20, 123, 181
Daniel Morley 163
Daurel et Beton 50 n. 14
Davids, M. Fakhry 10, 188
deception 32, 34, 44, 48, 147, 151–53, 160
Derrida, Jacques, *see* spectrality
desire 3, 15, 28, 34, 37, 38, 53, 70, 71, 97, 128–29, 137, 155, 158, 171, 176, 180, 185, 189
destiny 53, 58, 59, 67–70, 79, 135, 149, 154, 176, 180
devil(s) 39, 72, 86, 89, 118, 154
devotion, acts of 11, 21, 93, 113, 117–18, 124, 126, 159
de Weever, Jacqueline 5, 48
disguise 6, 7, 9, 20, 27–50, 51 n. 22, 85, 135, 147, 152, 168, 174–75, 182, 186
  see also clothing, cross-dressing, drag *and* passing
Dollimore, Jonathan 171
drag 17, 27–32, 35, 49, 79, 170, 182
dress, *see* clothing
dynasty 22, 27, 41, 45, 59, 172, 174, 176–78, 183–84

Eleanor of Aquitaine 165 n. 46
eloquence 22, 136, 146, 152, 158, 163
embodiment 9, 39, 106, 110, 122, 157
    see also the body
Embrico of Mainz:
    Vita Mahumeti 21, 135
engendering 7, 39, 41, 45–47, 50, 56, 68–69, 74, 77, 80, 143, 181
    see also paternity
entrelacement 58, 63, 78, 80
Estoires d'Outremer et de la naissance Salehadin 169, 184–85
etymology 3, 142–43, 157, 162, 164 n. 24
Eve 38, 63–64
exemplarity 21, 59, 64, 84, 86–88, 90, 93, 107, 119–20, 126, 128, 135–40, 141, 143, 146, 149, 156, 158, 161–62, 174, 187
exotic, -ism 6, 7, 9, 12, 17, 183

fabliaux 151, 152–53, 160
faith:
    Christian faith 46, 55, 56, 61, 66, 72, 77, 78, 89–90, 103, 106, 108, 113–17, 119, 120, 123, 126, 137, 149, 154, 176, 178
    and knowledge 136, 139–41, 143
    as misplaced 136, 138, 153, 157, 162
    performativity of 162–63, 186–87
    and reason 21–22, 138, 142, 146–48, 151, 158–63, 168
    Saracen faith 60, 87, 108, 162, 177–78, 184 see also Islam
    tests of 62–64, 73–76
    see also baptism, community, Judaism, and genealogy (spiritual genealogy)
Fall, the 65, 156, 157
Fanon, Frantz 10, 16–17, 167
Fierabras 3, 7, 25 n. 61, 133 n. 86, 188
La Fille du Comte de Pontieu 22, 148, 169, 172–85
    manuscripts of:
        Paris, B. Ars., MS 5208: 172, 192 n. 62
        Paris, BnF, MS f. fr. 770: 169, 172, 184
        Paris, BnF, MS f. fr. 12572: 173–75, 177, 183
        Paris, BnF, MS f. fr. 25462: 169, 172
Floire et Blancheflor 6
Foehr-Janssens, Yasmina 86
foreignness 3, 6, 31, 43, 172, 182, 183
Fourth Lateran Council 4, 86
Francis, Saint 4
Fuchs, Barbara 171

Gabriel, angel 150
Ganelon 6, 7, 46
Gatens, Moira 69, 77
Gaullier-Bougassas, Catherine 182
Gautier de Coinci 84, 109, 129
    and wordplay 124
    see also Miracles de Nostre Dame

Gautier de Compiègne:
    Otia de Machomete 135, 137, 148, 154
gender:
    and crossdressing 27–42, 47, 170, 171
    and performativity 14–19
    and race, relationship between 2, 4, 5, 8, 10–13, 15–20, 49–50, 53, 54, 85, 92, 167–68
    see also the body, identity. and performativity
genealogy 2, 7, 9, 11, 19–22, 28, 31, 36, 43–47, 53–61, 170, 178–86
    as deduced 54, 60–61, 70–71, 80, 129
    and gender 40–42, 181–85
    and passing 181–84
    as spiritual 54, 61, 64–69, 74–80, 129, 142, 161
    see also ancestry, biology, bloodlines, geography, inheritance, and time (genealogical time)
genre 5, 6, 152, 186, 189
Geoffroi de la Tour Landry 89
geography 4, 5, 53, 57, 61, 62, 70, 71, 74–80, 162, 168
    as deduced and/or subjective 54, 68, 72, 80
    and inheritance 67–68, 76–77, 180
    islands 6, 53, 63–65, 72–73
    as logical 67
    maps 57, 59, 61, 74
Germain, Saint 107, 117
Gesta Francorum 180
Ginsberg, Elaine 171
Giovanni Colonna 144
Glaber, Rodulfus 66
Godfrey of Bouillon 179–80, 191 n. 55
Gossuin de Metz 141
Grail 54, 55, 59, 62, 63, 65, 67, 78, 79, 80
    Grail quest 54, 55, 56, 57, 59, 64, 65, 67, 79
    'Grail race' 65, 66, 71, 78, 80, 161
Granada 174
Griffin, Miranda 54, 58, 62, 63, 75, 77
Grinberg, Ana 170, 190 n. 14
Grossel, Marie-Geneviève 127
Guibert de Nogent 120, 135, 159
    Gesta Dei per Francos 21, 92
Guillaume d'Orange Cycle 25 n. 61, 46, 50 n. 14, 120

Hahn, Thomas 9, 12
Hattin, Battle of 4, 70
Heng, Geraldine 12, 13, 29, 78, 176, 183
Heraclium, Battle of 183
heresy 21, 92, 131 n. 34, 135–36, 138, 140, 142, 148, 150, 153, 155, 159, 160–61
heteronormativity 38
hierarchy 139, 155
history 45, 54, 55, 59, 63, 67, 69, 70, 71, 77, 90–92, 123, 144, 171, 178–79, 184–85
    and linearity 58, 62–63, 77, 185
    as 'perceptual field' 179, 184
    see also genealogy and time
Hodgson, Natasha 178

Holy Land 38, 57, 70, 78, 139, 169, 179, 180
Hummer, Hans 180, 183
Hyatte, Reginald 137, 151, 153, 155, 157, 160
hybridity 9, 42, 144, 176, 177

Ida, Markgräfin of Austria 183
identity:
  as biologized 13, 85, 171–72
  as collective 109, 153–59
  contingency of 2, 19, 28, 29, 32, 58–59, 171
  and fixity 3, 9, 13–14, 57, 58, 62, 76, 168, 186, 189
  and Frankishness 17–18, 28, 30, 31–36, 42, 46, 48–49
  as haunted/haunting 21, 87, 91–92, 106–07, 128–29, 185
  and imitation 32, 39, 40
  as inherited 13, 17, 31, 33, 39, 45–47, 49, 63, 73, 74, 77–78, 178, 188
  and language use 4, 8, 9, 14, 16–18, 146–47, 153, 167, 185
  malleability of 11, 138, 186
  religious 2, 4, 8, 13, 20–22, 29, 64, 76, 79, 107–08, 115, 120, 125–28, 135, 148, 157–58, 162, 178, 187–88
  see also indeterminacy, gender, performativity, *and* race
idolatry, idolaters 3, 87–89, 101, 127, 130 n. 23, 135–37, 146–47, 155–56
idyllic romance 6
impotence 55
incarnation 91, 103, 128
indeterminacy 22, 91, 167, 169, 175–78, 180–82, 184–85, 188
inheritance 11, 43, 50, 66–68, 70, 75, 76–80, 168, 170, 179, 180, 182, 183
Innocent III 4, 86, 144, 146
intercession 115, 117, 119, 123
interpellation 15–16, 76, 138, 146–47, 154
intersectionality 10, 20, 35, 40, 168, 186
intolerance 185
irrationality 140, 143, 162
Isidore of Seville:
  Etymologies 71
Islam 2, 4, 5, 13, 21, 86–88, 135–38, 140, 141, 143, 144, 148, 150, 152, 158–62, 176, 184
  comparative historicization of 92
  and falsity 136, 142
  see also heresy

Jean de Meun 137
Jean Le Long:
  Chronicon Sancti Bertini 183
Jehan d'Avennes 169
Jerusalem 54, 57, 70, 72, 80, 119, 152, 178, 181
Jesus Christ 37, 46, 55, 61, 68, 72–75, 87, 90–92, 110–12, 128, 139, 149, 152, 154, 180
Jews 9, 60, 61, 86, 92, 101, 122, 128, 131 n. 34, 159, 176

John I, King of Portugal 182
John II, King of France 117
John the Fearless, Duke of Burgundy 182
Jordan, William Chester 12
Jubb, Margaret 183, 184
Judaism 87, 92, 128, 176
  doctrine of witness 92
Julian the Apostate, Roman Emperor 85, 112–13

al-Kâmil, Sultan of Egypt 4
Kangas, Sini 137, 140, 156
Kay, Sarah 43
Kerbogha 179–80
Khadija, wife of Muhammad, *see* Roman de Mahomet
The King of Tars 133 n. 99, 178
Kinoshita, Sharon 170, 175–76
Kruger, Steven F. 15, 46, 85, 92, 120, 122, 128, 129

Lacan, Jacques:
  'logical time' 19–20, 54, 57, 58–60, 64, 79–80, 161
Laclau, Ernesto 91
language, *see* bilingualism, identity (and language), Saracens (language of)
Laon 30, 136, 148, 151, 164 n. 18
Larsen, Nella:
  Passing 15
Lazarus, beggar and leper 139–40
legitimacy 32, 43, 62, 68, 78, 79, 124, 160, 169, 177, 178, 180–84
Lepage, Yvan 137, 143, 152, 155
liminality 76, 86, 93, 101, 131 n. 39, 185
lineage, *see* ancestry, bloodlines, genealogy, *and* legitimacy
'logical time', *see* Lacan, Jacques
Louis IX, King of France 140

magic 17, 172
Mandeville, Sir John 71
marriage 6, 20, 23, 34, 40–41, 42, 44, 45–49, 64, 68, 135, 144, 146, 169, 176–78, 180, 181, 183–84
materialism 10, 60, 138, 151
maternity, mothers 2, 22, 36, 45, 51 n. 48, 64, 83 n. 83, 85, 89, 120, 125, 139, 144, 170, 176–81, 183–84
Matthew Paris:
  Chronica Majora 144
  Historia Anglorum 183
McCracken, Peggy 36, 41, 103, 148, 176
Mecca 7, 30, 136, 142–43, 157, 162
melancholia 70, 79
memory 56, 66, 69, 75, 79, 124, 169, 172
Les Miracles de Nostre Dame:
  Comment Nostre Dame desfendi la cité de Constantinnoble (II Miracle 12) 85, 107–18, 126–28
    Muselinus, Saracen King 107–12, 114–19, 126, 128, 133 n. 79
  as didactic 84, 127, 144, 187

manuscripts of:
  Besançon, BM, MS 551: 103–06, 131 n. 40
  Brussels, BR, MS 9229–30: 97–98
  Brussels, BR, MS 10747: 93, 95
  The Hague, KB, MS 71.A.24: 97, 100
  Paris, B. Ars., MS 5204: 93, 96, 97, 99, 101, 103, 131 n. 44, 132 n. 54
  Paris, BnF, MS f. fr. 22928: 93, 94, 116–18, 121, 131 n. 41, 132 n. 65, 133 n. 89
  Paris, BnF, MS f. fr. 25532: 93, 94, 121–22, 131 n. 41
  Paris, BnF, MS n. a. fr. 24541: 99, 101–02, 109, 111, 113, 114–18, 132 n. 65
De Saint Basile (II Miracle 11) 85, 112–14
  Lybanÿus, pagan clerk 112–14
  Mercurius, Saint 112–14
De l'ymage Nostre Dame (I Miracle 32) 85, 87–107, 112, 126–27
De l'ymage Nostre Dame de Sardanei (II Miracle 30) 85, 119–26
see also Gautier de Coinci
Moore, Robert I. 162
morality 9, 15, 37, 42, 45, 84, 87, 99, 115, 118, 126–28, 139–40, 142, 143, 146–47, 150, 156, 160, 162, 174, 188
Morrison, Karl 90
Muhammad (Mahomet, Machomet) 5, 8, 21–22, 46, 109
  and Antichrist 135, 143, 144, 160
  denigration of 137–38, 140, 142–46, 148, 152
  and fraudulence 136–37, 142, 144, 147, 149, 153, 155, 158–60, 161
  and lineage 2, 60, 69, 153, 157
  as prophet 66–67, 92, 136, 142, 149, 153, 154, 157, 161
  supposed epilepsy of 135, 137, 149–50, 155, 160, 165 n. 52
  tomb of 136–37, 160
  see also heresy
myth 41, 78, 127, 182

names, naming 1, 15, 38, 43, 44, 61, 62, 68, 73–76, 79, 91, 142–43, 162, 175
Nanteuil Cycle
  Aiglentine, wife of Gui de Nanteuil 35, 36, 38, 40, 41, 43–45, 49
  Antoine, son of Ganor and Aye d'Avignon 7, 35, 36, 45–46, 51 n. 34
  Aufalerne, town/tower in Ganor's realm 35, 37
  Aye d'Avignon 6–8, 17–18, 27, 30–48, 57
  Aye d'Avignon 5–8, 17, 20, 27, 30–48, 60, 63, 69, 147
    Berenger, Frankish traitor 6, 17, 30, 33–34, 42
    Garnier de Nanteuil, first husband of Aye 6, 7, 30, 33, 42–45, 51 n. 22
    Milon, Frankish traitor 32, 45
    Ganor, Saracen ruler of Majorca, second husband to Aye 6–8, 17–18, 20, 24 n. 37, 26 n. 97, 27–28, 30–36, 39, 40, 42–50, 69, 147

  Gui de Nanteuil, son of Aye and Garnier de Nanteuil 7, 27, 35, 31–39, 41–46
  Gui de Nanteuil 8, 17, 27, 45, 47, 48
    Grandoine, Emir de Coine 17–18, 47
  Tristan de Nanteuil 20, 27, 28, 35, 36–38, 39, 41–49
    Blanchandin/e, wife of Tristan, later transformed into a man 20, 35, 38–41, 44, 47, 49
    Clarinde, daughter of the Sultan of Babylon 39–40, 44
    Doon, illegitimate son of Gui and the Saracen princess Honorée 39, 43, 46
    Garcion, illegitimate son of Tristan and the Saracen princess Clarisse 39, 44, 46, 47
    Gaudion, Saracen knight (Aye's alter-ego) 35, 38, 40
    Gilles, son of Blanchandin and Clarinde 39
    Guintelin de Trémogne, Saracen ruler and adoptive father of Garcion 41–47
    Tristan de Nanteuil, son of Gui and Aiglentine 35, 36, 38, 39, 41, 43, 44–47
nation 4, 23 n. 22, 42, 50 n. 15, 168, 176, 188
Nero, Roman Emperor 139
Noah 61, 71, 156
Nur-ed-Dīn 123

Ogier the Dane 89
Oliver 3
oppression 108, 154, 170, 171, 172, 177
Orable 46
origin(s) 1–3, 8, 13, 18, 20, 28, 31, 53, 55, 58, 60–61, 65, 70, 71, 73–80, 86–87, 90, 92, 138, 147, 159, 160, 170, 175–77, 181, 183, 185
Ottomans 1, 182, 184

Paris, University of 159
Pas Saladin, the 181–82
passing 15, 22, 25 n. 86, 27, 168–88
  see also cross-dressing, disguise, *and* drag
Passion of Christ, the 55
paternity 42–48, 56, 62, 64, 66, 68–69, 73–74, 77, 83 n. 83, 99, 112, 126, 133 n. 98, 146, 156, 159, 169, 174, 175–80, 182
  see also engendering, genealogy, *and* surrogacy
Pellegrini, Ann 16–17, 19, 29, 167
performativity 4, 21–22, 32, 42, 59, 65, 124, 127, 135–36, 138, 146–47, 155, 161–63, 177
  definition of 14–20, 27–30
  and interpellation 76, 146–48
  and logical time 54, 58–60, 80
  and passing 168–71, 184
  and race 18–20, 34–35, 38, 48–50, 53, 74, 77–79, 167–68, 185–89
  and spectrality 84, 87, 90–91, 124–25, 127
  see also Butler, Judith, faith, *and* gender
Perret, Michèle 36, 38, 40, 41

Persians 13, 136, 157, 161
Peter Comestor 61
Peter the Venerable 144
Petrus Alfonsi 159
Philip the Bold, Duke of Burgundy 182
physiognomy 2, 9, 12, 13, 20, 38, 48, 101, 126, 161
   see also biology *and* determinism
Pierre Dubois 41
pilgrimage 7, 29–33, 42, 48, 119, 169, 179, 181
Poitiers, Battle of 117
procreation 34, 39, 40, 46, 48, 53, 56, 66, 68, 69, 75, 77, 168
prolepsis 53, 59, 178
propaganda 4, 135, 137, 144, 158, 160
prophecy 55, 66–67, 69, 79, 114, 139, 154, 180
   see also Muhammad (as prophet)
Pucelle, Jean 99, 132 n. 59
punishment 55, 56, 66, 85, 139

race:
   and ambiguity 4–5, 15, 17, 41, 101, 186, 189
   concept of 2, 3–14, 185–89
   and essentialism 13, 20–21, 57, 77, 108, 185, 188, 189
   as 'faithline' 61
   and gender (*see* gender)
   and perception 22, 30, 34, 60, 168, 184, 188, 189
   race theory (*see* Critical Race Theory)
   readability of 22, 45, 167, 168, 170, 172, 174–75, 177–79, 181, 184–85, 188
   as retrospectively produced 53–54, 57–59, 64, 66–67, 69, 80, 143, 167, 177
   and self-other (*see* binaries)
   and somatic features (*see* biology)
   as subjective 19, 59–60, 62, 79, 80, 185, 188
   and terminology 10–13
   and visibility 17–18, 22, 31–32, 34, 43, 45, 48–49, 78, 86, 110, 126, 160, 168–69, 171–72, 175, 177–79, 182, 184, 188
   visuality of 5, 9–11, 16, 18, 41, 60, 85, 99, 115, 118, 126, 144, 147, 168, 175, 188
   see also biology, body, the, genealogy, performativity, *and* recognition
racism 10–12, 38, 170, 172, 185, 187, 188, 189
Ramey, Lynn Tarte 12, 13, 19, 170, 186
rape 146, 169, 174, 175
rationality 21–22, 70, 71, 138, 140–41, 143, 144, 148, 153, 155, 158, 159, 160–62
readability (*see* race)
reason, reasoning 21, 54, 61, 71, 75, 126, 136–38, 140–43, 147, 150, 151, 153, 155, 157–63
recognition 16–18, 30, 33, 34, 36, 39, 41, 56, 62, 65, 68–69, 73, 79, 92, 123–25, 128, 133 n. 79, 136, 138, 157, 160, 168, 175–76, 182, 188
   of conventions 3, 14, 47, 49, 54, 90, 127, 147–48, 177

   and identities 16–18, 21, 34, 38, 44, 64, 68, 76, 168–69, 189
   misrecognition 16, 21, 31, 42, 74, 79, 138, 154, 161–62, 167
Renoart 7, 25 n. 61, 120, 133 n. 98
repetition 13–18, 21, 30, 31, 32, 37, 40, 43, 45, 47, 53–55, 58, 64, 65, 69, 76, 78, 79, 80, 84, 88–89, 90, 107, 124, 125, 127, 138, 143, 157, 158, 162, 168, 176, 177
reproduction 43, 47, 170, 174
   see also paternity, maternity, *and* procreation
resemblance 43, 181
return 72, 110, 112, 124, 156, 159
   to faith 21, 90–91, 108, 118, 122–23, 128, 129
   to land 6–7, 30–31, 33, 45, 55, 65, 78–80, 169, 174, 177, 181
Risâlat al-Kindî 159
Robert de Boron 55
Roger Bacon 133 n. 83
Le Roman de Mahomet:
   and anti-Islamic polemic 21, 135, 137, 141, 150, 152, 159, 160, 165 n. 52
   hermit in 135, 139, 142, 150, 154–55
   Khadija, wife of Muhammad in 144, 149, 150, 154, 155, 156, 161
   manuscript of:
      Paris, BnF, MS f. fr. 1553: 136, 141, 145, 146, 151–53
   and/as propaganda 135, 137, 144, 158, 160
Le Roman de Mélusine 51 n. 48
Le Roman de Perceforest 182
Le Roman de Saladin (*see* Second Crusade Cycle)
Roncevaux, Battle of 97
Rottenberg, Catherine 38
Rouse, Richard and Mary 97
Rubin, Miri 139
rubrics 93, 103, 127, 131 n. 41 & 44, 175
Ruggles, D. Fairchild 184
Russakoff, Anna 93, 99, 101, 103

Saladin 1, 4, 70, 123, 165 n. 46, 169
   genealogy of 22, 47, 170, 176–78, 180–81
   knighting of 181, 183
   and passing 179, 181–84
Santiago de Compostela 169
Saracens:
   as 'always-already Christian' 59, 70, 78
   definitions of 2–8, 185–89
   language of 34, 41, 42, 48, 172, 175
   as pagans 13, 41, 49, 85–90, 106, 109, 112–14, 119, 129, 183
   Saracen women 38–48, 169–81
Sarah 2, 60–61
Saydnaya (Sardanei) 85, 119, 121–22, 126
Scanlon, Larry 138, 146, 149

Second Crusade Cycle 22, 169, 176, 179, 180–81
  Baudouin de Sebourc 132 n. 63, 169, 176, 180–81, 190 n. 8
  Le Chevalier au Cygne et Godefroi de Bouillon 169, 179, 180
  Huon de Tabarie 181, 182
  Le Roman de Saladin 181–83
Sedgwick, Eve Kosofsky 14
self/other, *see* binaries
sensory experience 86, 110, 112, 118, 119, 125, 127, 128
Sept Sages de Rome 144, 146, 152, 158, 163 n. 13
Seshadri-Crooks, Kalpana 10–11, 187–88
sexuality 13, 15, 38, 79, 85, 92, 170
Sieg, Katrin 30
sight 39, 46, 63, 68, 72, 107, 109, 110, 112, 114, 115, 119, 123, 125–26, 128–29
  see also apparitions, sensory experience, *and* visions
Simon de Pouille 3, 130 n. 23
sin 108, 156
  greed 142, 155
  lechery, lust 17, 20, 34, 101
  pride 107–08, 119, 120, 143, 181
skin:
  and/as clothing 172
  colour of 2, 3, 7, 9–13, 16, 20, 27, 29, 38, 97, 99, 101, 114–15, 120, 126, 144, 171–72, 177–78, 188
  see also biology, blackness, *and* the body
slaves, slavery 3, 69, 79, 156, 175, 183–84
Soissons 84, 86, 118, 119
spectrality 19, 21, 84, 87, 90–93, 99, 101, 106, 110, 123–24, 126, 128
  'double bind' of 90, 107
  Hamlet's father, ghost of 99, 112, 126
  and haunting/self-haunting 19, 21, 84, 87, 90, 92–93, 125, 129, 185
  spectre, the 15, 90–92, 110, 115, 125
  'visor effect' 126, 129
Speer, Mary B. 158
Spiegel, Gabrielle 58, 179
Sponsler, Claire, *see* Clark, Robert L. A.
Stahuljak, Zrinka 56, 66, 68, 77, 78, 179
status 3, 6, 8, 9, 15, 40, 59, 62, 64, 66–68, 70, 76, 78, 79, 87, 89, 93, 103, 120, 126, 142, 147, 154, 155, 160, 161, 171, 172, 175–78, 180, 183, 184
Steel, Karl 9, 12, 189
sterility 46, 169, 177
Strickland, Debra Higgs 7, 143–44
Suite Vulgate du Merlin 184
supernatural, the 35, 36, 39, 47, 52 n. 48
surrogate (father) 27, 42–46, 48, 60
Szkilnik, Michelle 72–73

temporality, *see* time
Thomas Aquinas 159
Thomas Becket, Saint 4
Thomas de Maubeuge 97, 99, 103

time:
  and Christianity 63–64, 66, 71, 74, 92, 178
  and chronology 53–55, 58, 62–63, 65, 66, 69, 71, 76–77, 80, 143, 187
  as disrupted 60, 62, 87, 101, 106, 112, 129, 131 n. 58
  genealogical time 57–58, 62, 63, 78–79, 80, 180
  guaranteed futures 58, 79, 80, 129
  and narration 59, 65, 67, 68, 70–71, 81 n. 25, 76–80, 101, 128–29, 161, 177–81
  as non-linear 57–58, 76, 80
  and space 64, 70, 72, 79–80, 123
  as subjective 58–60, 68
  see Lacan, Jacques ('logical time') *and* prolepsis
Tolan, John V. 2, 9, 13, 66, 71, 86, 137, 140, 148, 159, 162
traitors, treachery 6, 7, 17, 32–33, 43, 45, 148, 180
transformation 9, 34, 35, 39, 42, 47, 78, 90, 91, 99, 101, 108, 114, 117–18, 123, 124, 126, 127, 133 n. 99, 162, 186
truth 30, 32, 41, 54, 69, 92, 113, 119, 123–24, 140, 150, 156, 160, 167, 168
Turks 2–3

Vasco de Lucena 182
Vespasian, Roman Emperor 55, 152
Virgin Mary, the 59, 61, 63–64, 86, 87–89, 91, 97–109, 111, 114–22, 128, 150
  body of 99, 103, 106, 110, 112, 115, 123–29
  and Immaculate Conception 74, 87
visibility, *see* race (and visibility)
vision, *see* sight
visions 55, 56, 58, 62–64, 67–69, 106, 107, 109, 112–15, 118, 136, 150, 155
  visio spiritualis 99, 115, 127
  see also apparitions, sight
Vulgate Cycle:
  Celidoine 55, 58, 64–65, 67–68, 76, 78
  L'Estoire del Saint Graal:
    Tholomer, King of Babylon. Adversary of Evalach 73, 75
    Tout en Tout 76
  L'Estoire Merlin 55
  Evalach/Mordrain 53, 55–58, 63, 67–69, 72–76, 78–79, 81 n. 10, 82 n. 53, 83 n. 69
  Galahad 4, 54–57, 59, 62–65, 67–69, 74–78, 83 n. 83
  Joseph of Arimathea 55, 57, 74, 83 n. 83
  Josephus 55–57, 59, 67, 69, 73–75
  Lancelot 68, 82 n. 42, 83 n. 83
  Lancelot 55, 83 n. 83
  Le Mort Artu 55
  Perceval 62, 83 n. 83
  La Queste del Saint Graal 55, 56, 68, 76, 82 n. 53
  Le Roman de Merlin 55, 184
  Sarras, Saracen city, 55, 61, 72, 73, 76, 79, 162

Seraphe/Nascien 53–55, 58, 59, 62–69, 73–76, 78, 82 n. 53
Solomon 59, 62–65, 68, 73–76, 78
Turning Isle, the 62–65, 71, 72

Walter, Katie L. 178
Wavrin Master, the 174–75, 182
whiteness 15, 16, 38, 97, 168, 171, 189 n. 4
Whitman, Jon 67, 70
William of Tyre 169
Williams, Alison 152
wisdom 21, 136, 137, 156, 160, 163

witnessing 75, 86, 92, 109, 112, 114, 119, 125–26, 128, 144
see also sensory experience
Wogan-Browne, Jocelyn 141
worship 3, 18, 20, 87–88, 93, 107, 116–17, 122, 127, 146, 155, 157, 161, 186–87, 189
see also devotion, acts of

Yde et Olive 35, 52 n. 59

Zengi, Turkish Atabeg 183
Žižek, Slavoj 87

www.ingramcontent.com/pod-product-compliance
Lightning Source LLC
LaVergne TN
LVHW061250060426
835507LV00017B/2002